D1468797

The Family Handbook

SERIES EDITORS

DON S. BROWNING AND IAN S. EVISON

BOOKS IN THE SERIES

THE FAMILY HANDBOOK

Herbert Anderson, Don Browning, Ian S. Evison, and Mary Stewart Van Leeuwen, editors

FROM CULTURE WARS TO COMMON GROUND: RELIGION AND THE AMERICAN FAMILY DEBATE

Don S. Browning, Bonnie J. Miller-McLemore,
Pamela D. Couture, K. Brynolf Lyon, Robert M. Franklin

FROM SACRAMENT TO CONTRACT: MARRIAGE, RELIGION AND LAW IN THE WESTERN TRADITION

John Witte, Jr.

COVENANT AND COMMITMENTS: FAITH, FAMILY, AND ECONOMIC LIFE

Max L. Stackhouse

FOR THE LOVE OF CHILDREN: GENETIC TECHNOLOGY AND THE FUTURE OF THE FAMILY

Ted Peters

FAITH TRADITIONS AND THE FAMILY

Phyllis D. Airhart and Margaret Lamberts Bendroth, editors

RELIGION, FEMINISM, AND THE FAMILY

Anne Carr and Mary Stewart Van Leeuwen, editors

FAMILIES IN ANCIENT ISRAEL

Leo G. Perdue, Joseph Blenkinsopp, John J. Collins, Carol Meyers

FAMILIES IN THE NEW TESTAMENT WORLD: HOUSEHOLD AND HOUSE CHURCHES

Carolyn Osiek and David L. Balch

The Family Handbook

Herbert Anderson
Don Browning
Ian S. Evison
Mary Stewart Van Leeuwen
editors

Westminster John Knox Press
Louisville, Kentucky

Book and cover design by Jennifer K. Cox

First Edition

Published by Westminster John Knox Press
Louisville, Kentucky

This book is printed on acid-free paper that meets the American National Standards Institute Z39.48 standard. ♾

Library of Congress Cataloging-in-Publication Data

The family handbook / Herbert Anderson . . . [et al.], editors. — 1st ed.
      p.   cm. — (The family, religion, and culture)
   Includes bibliographical references and index.
   1. Family—Religious aspects—Comparative studies.   2. Church work with families—United States.   3. Family—United States.   4. United States—Religion—date.   I. Anderson, Herbert, 1936.   II. Series.
   BL2525.R455   1998
   261.8'3585—DC21   97-50227

Contents

Contributors   ix

Series Foreword

    Don S. Browning and *Ian S. Evison*   xv

Acknowledgments   xvii

Introduction   xix

PART 1
FAMILIES AND MARRIAGE:
CONTEMPORARY PERSPECTIVES

1. Marriage   3

    A Jewish Perspective   3
    A Catholic Perspective   10
    A Protestant Perspective   13
    A Secular Perspective   17

2. Family   21

    A Protestant Perspective   21
    A Catholic Perspective   24
    A Jewish Perspective   28
    A Secular Legal Perspective   31

3. Divorce and Remarriage   34

    A Legal Perspective   34
    A Catholic Perspective   39
    A Protestant Perspective   43
    A Jewish Perspective   47

4. Advances in Reproductive Technology   51
    A Protestant Perspective   51
    A Catholic Perspective   54
    A Jewish Perspective   57

5. Work of Families: Roles of Families   63
    The Nature of Parenting   63
    The Tasks of Men in Families   71
    The Tasks of Women in Families   76
    The Tasks of Grandparents in Families   83
    Families, Work, and Economic Pressures   89

    The Role of Churches in Relationship to Government
       on Behalf of Families   96
    A Theoretical Perspective   96
    A Practical Perspective   101

PART 2
APPROACHES TO SPECIAL SITUATIONS
OF FAMILY MINISTRY

6. Marital Preparation   107
    A Catholic Perspective   107
    A Jewish Perspective   111
    A Protestant Perspective   114
    Some Secular Approaches   118

7. Ministry with Couples   122
    A Jewish Perspective   122
    A Catholic Perspective   125
    A Protestant Perspective   129

8. Ministry with Children and Youth   132

9. Ministry with Single Parents   138

10. Ministry with Stepfamilies   142

11. Ministry with Families with Homosexual
    Sons or Daughters   146
    A Jewish Perspective   146
    A Catholic Perspective   151
    An Evangelical Protestant Perspective   153
    A Mainline Protestant Perspective   156

12. Ministry with the Elderly   159

13. Ministry with Families Troubled by Abuse   164

14. Ministry with Families Experiencing Loss   172

15. Families and Popular Culture   176

16. Families and Violence   181

17. Families and Substance Abuse   187

PART 3
RESOURCES FOR CONGREGATIONAL MINISTRY
WITH FAMILIES

18. Hebrew Scriptures and the Family   195
    The Family Stories in Genesis (Genesis 12–50)   195
    The Creation Story (Genesis 1:26–28)   198
    The Grounding of Marriage in the Order of Creation
       (Genesis 2:18–24)   201
    The Ten Commandments
       (Exodus 20:2–17; Deuteronomy 5:6–21)   204
    The Family in Community (Leviticus 25)   207
    A Prophetic Critique of Divorce (Malachi 2:10–16)   210
    Naboth's Vineyard: A Clash of Family Values
       (1 Kings 21:1–16)   214
    Family Relationships as Metaphor (Hosea 1–3)   218
    A Good Man's Code of Ethics (Job 31)   221

19. New Testament Scriptures and the Family   224
    An Alternative Household Structure
       (Matthew 19–20)   224

Ascetic Widows in the Early Church
(Luke-Acts and 1 Timothy) 229
Jesus' Relationship to His Own Family 233
Lost: Two Rebellious Sons—Who Will Find?
(Luke 15:11–32) 238
Family in a Time of Social
and Eschatological Crisis 242
Family Conflict Generated by Jesus' Proclamation
of the Kingdom of God 246
Marital Relations (1 Corinthians 7:1–11) 249
Healed Women as Models of Servant Leadership
(Luke 4:38–39; 8:1–3) 254

20. Families and Worship 258

PART 4
FAMILIES IN HISTORY

21. Families in Ancient Israel 277

22. Families in the Greco-Roman World 282

23. Families in Early Christianity 287

24. Families in Medieval Christianity
and the Reformation 291

25. Families in the Nineteenth and Twentieth Centuries 295

PART 5
GENERAL RESOURCES
FOR FAMILY MINISTRY

A Directory of Resources for Families 303

Contributors

ROBERT H. ALBERS, PH.D., Professor of Pastoral Theology at Luther Seminary, St. Paul: editor of *Journal of Ministry in Addiction and Recovery;* author of *Shame: A Faith Perspective* (Haworth Press, 1995).

HERBERT ANDERSON, PH.D., Professor of Pastoral Theology, Catholic Theological Union, Chicago; author of *Living Alone* (Westminster John Knox Press, 1997), *Promising Again* (Westminster John Knox Press, 1995), and *Regarding Children: New Respect for Children and Families* (Westminster John Knox Press, 1994).

RAY S. ANDERSON, PH.D., Professor of Theology and Ministry, Fuller Theological Seminary, Pasadena, Calif.; author of *The Soul of Ministry: Forming Leaders for God's People* (Westminster John Knox Press, 1997) and *Self Care: A Theology of Personal Wholeness and Spiritual Healing* (Victor Books, 1995).

WILLIAM V. ARNOLD, PH.D., Professor of Pastoral Counseling at Union Theological Seminary, Richmond; author of *Pastoral Responses to Sexual Issues* (Westminster/John Knox Press, 1993) and *When You Are Alone* (Westminster/John Knox Press, 1990).

BRADLEY SHAVIT ARTSON, Rabbi of Congregation Eilat, Mission Viejo, Calif.; author of *It's a Mitzvah! Step by Step to Jewish Living* (Behrman House, 1995).

HOMER U. ASHBY, JR., PH.D., Professor of Pastoral Care, Dean of Faculty, McCormick Theological Seminary, Chicago.

S. SCOTT BARTCHY, PH.D., Director, Center for the Study of Religion, and Adjunct Professor of Christian Origins and History of Religions at University of California at Los Angeles; author of *Undermining Ancient Patriarchy: Paul of Tarsus, Gender Roles, Slave Ownership, and Elite Privilege* (Hendrickson, forthcoming) and *First-Century Slavery and the Interpretation of 1 Corinthians 7:21* (Scholars Press, 1985).

STEPHEN C. BARTON, PH.D., Lecturer of New Testament in the Department of Theology at the University of Durham, England; author of *Discipleship and Family Ties in Mark and Matthew* (Cambridge University Press, 1995) and *Spirituality of the Gospels* (Hendrickson, 1994).

STEVEN BAYME, National Director for Jewish Community Affairs, American Jewish Committee; coeditor of *Jewish Family and Jewish Continuity* (KTAV Publishing House, 1994) and *Rebuilding the Nest: A New Commitment to the American Family* (Families International, 1990).

ALICE OGDEN BELLIS, PH.D., Associate Professor of Old Testament Language and Literature, Howard University School of Divinity, Washington, D.C.; author of *Doing the Twist to Amazing Grace* (Pilgrim Press, forthcoming) and *Helpmates, Harlots, and Heroes: Women's Stories in the Hebrew Bible* (Westminster John Knox Press, 1994).

DON BROWNING, PH.D., Professor of Ethics and Social Science at the University of Chicago Divinity School; Senior Scholar and Director of Research at the Center of Theological Inquiry, Princeton, N.J.; coauthor of *From Culture Wars to Common Ground: Religion and the American Family Debate* (Westminster John Knox Press, 1998).

ROBERT L. BROWNING, PH.D., Emeritus Professor of Religious Education at the Methodist Theological School of Ohio, Delaware, Ohio; coauthor of *Models of Confirmation and Baptismal Affirmation: Liturgical and Educational Issues and Designs* (Religious Education Press, 1995).

RICHARD P. CARLSON, PH.D., Union Theological Seminary, Richmond; Associate Professor of Biblical Studies at Luther Theological Seminary at Gettysburg, Gettysburg, Va.

WARREN CARTER, PH.D., Associate Professor of New Testament at St. Paul School of Theology, Kansas City, Mo.; author of *Matthew: Storyteller, Interpreter, Evangelist* (Hendrickson, 1996) and *What Are They Saying about Matthew's Sermon on the Mount* (Paulist Press, 1994).

GERALD P. COLEMAN, S.S., PH.D., President/Rector and Professor of Moral Theology at St. Patrick's Seminary, Menlo Park, Calif.; author of *Homosexuality: Catholic Teaching and Pastoral Practice* (Paulist Press, 1996) and *Human Sexuality: An All-Embracing Gift* (Alba House, 1992).

JOHN J. COLLINS, Professor, Hebrew Bible and Post-Biblical Judaism, The University of Chicago Divinity School, Chicago; author of *Jewish Wisdom in the Hellenistic Age* (Westminster John Knox Press, 1997); coauthor of *Families in Ancient Israel* (Westminster John Knox Press, 1997).

JAMES L. CRENSHAW, PH.D., Professor of Old Testament at Duke University Divinity School, Durham, N.C.; author of *Across the Deadening Silence: Education in Ancient Israel* (Doubleday, 1998) and *Urgent Advice and Probing Question: Collected Writings on Old Testament Wisdom* (Mercer University Press, 1995).

RALPH A. DALIN, Rabbi of White Meadow Temple, Rockaway, N.J.; initiator and cofacilitator of "Getting Marriage Going," a group premarital counseling program in northern New Jersey.

BOB DAVIES, North American director of Exodus International, a worldwide network of Christian ministries to men and women overcoming homosexuality; coauthor of *Coming Out of Homosexuality* (InterVarsity Press, 1993) and *Someone I Love Is Gay* (InterVarsity Press, 1996).

JAMES G. EMERSON, JR., Chair of editorial board of *Pastoral Psychology* and member of the editorial board of *Pastoral Care;* Consultant to the Division of World Ministries, Presbyterian Church, (U.S.A.); author of *Suffering: Its Meaning and Ministry* (Abingdon Press, 1986).

WILLIAM J. EVERETT, PH.D., Professor of Christian Social Ethics, Andover Newton Theological School, Newton Centre, Mass.; author of *Blessed Be the Bond: Christian Perspectives on Marriage and Family* (University Press of America, 1990).

IAN EVISON, PH.D., Director of Research, Alban Institute; series editor of Westminster John Knox Press book series on The Family, Culture, and Religion.

TERENCE E. FRETHEIM, PH.D., Professor of Old Testament, Luther Seminary, St. Paul; author of *Genesis* (New Interpreter's Bible, 1994) and *Exodus* (Westminster John Knox Press, 1994).

TIKVA FRYMER-KENSKY, PH.D., Professor of Hebrew Bible, The University of Chicago Divinity School; author of *In the Wake of the Goddesses* (Free Press, 1992).

ELLIOT B. GERTEL, Rabbi of Congregation Rodfei Zedek, Chicago; contributing editor for *Conservative Judaism* and the *Jewish Spectator;* film and television critic for *National Jewish Post and Opinion;* author of *Jewish Views on Divorce* (American Jewish Committee, 1984).

PAUL R. GIBLIN, PH.D., Associate Professor of Pastoral Counseling and Pastoral Studies in the Institute for Pastoral Studies and Former Director of M.A. Program in Pastoral Counseling at Loyola University, Chicago.

FRANK H. GORMAN, JR., PH.D., Professor of Religion Studies and Head of Department, Bethany College, Bethany, W.Va.; author of *Leviticus: Divine Presence and Community* (Wm. B. Eerdmans Publishing Co., 1997) and *The Ideology of Ritual* (Sheffield Academic Press, 1990).

M. CHRISTIAN GREEN, J.D./M.T.S., Emory University School of Law, Atlanta; student in the Ph.D. program in Ethics at the University of Chicago Divinity School.

BLU GREENBERG, author of *How to Run a Traditional Jewish Household* (Jason Aronson, 1997) and *On Women and Judaism: A View from Tradition* (Jewish Publication Society, 1981).

JOANN HEANEY-HUNTER, PH.D., Associate Professor of Theology, St. John's University, New York; author of *Unitas: A Process of Sacramental Marriage Formation* (Crossroad, 1998).

CARLYN LAKEY HESS, PH.D., Assistant Professor of Christian Education at Princeton Theological Seminary, Princeton, N.J.; author of *Caretaking of Our Common House: Women's Development in Communities of Faith* (Abingdon Press, 1997).

CHRISTINE FIRER HINZE, PH.D., University of Chicago Divinity School; Associate Professor of Christian Ethics, Marquette University, Milwaukee; author of *Comprehending Power in Christian Social Ethics* (Scholars Press, 1995).

RICHARD A. HUNT, M.DIV., PH.D., Senior Professor of Psychology, School of Psychology, Fuller Seminary, Pasadena, Calif.; author, with wife, Joan, of "Growing Love in Christian Marriage," "Caring Couples Network" manual and video, other United Methodist and ecumenical resources.

HARRIET M. KING, LL.M., Associate Professor of Law and Vice Provost for Academic Affairs, Emory University, Atlanta; teaches courses on family law at Emory University School of Law.

JAMES N. LAPSLEY, PH.D., Emeritus Professor of Pastoral Theology, Princeton Theological Seminary, Princeton, N.J.; author of *Renewal in Late Life Through Pastoral Counseling* (Paulist Press, 1992).

PAUL LAURITZEN, PH.D., Professor of Religious Studies at John Carroll University, University Heights, Ohio; author of *Religious Belief and Emotional Transformation* (Bucknell, 1998) and *Pursuing Parenthood: Ethical Issues in Assisted Reproduction* (Indiana University, 1993).

MICHAEL G. LAWLER, PH.D., Professor of Catholic Theological Studies and Director of the Center for Marriage and Family at Creighton University, Omaha; author of *Family: American and Christian* (Loyola Press, 1997).

BARBARA MARKEY, PH.D., Director of Family Life Office, Archdiocese of Omaha; Associate Director of the Center for Marriage and Family at Creighton University, Omaha; author of marriage preparation inventory, FOCCUS, and marriage enrichment instrument, REFOCCUS.

ROLAND D. MARTINSON, S.T.D, Professor of Pastoral Care, Luther Seminary; member of National Council on Family Relations; author of video series: "Families, Quality Relationships in Changing Times" (Cokesbury, 1990) and *Effective Youth Ministry* (Augsburg, 1988).

SHARON A. MARTINSON, B.S. in Home Economics; wife, mother, and grandmother; community volunteer; artist in textiles; weaver.

DIANE MEDVED, PH.D., clinical psychologist in private practice; coauthor with Dan Quayle of *The American Family: Discovering Values that Make us Strong* (Zondervan, 1996) and author of *The Case Against Divorce* (Ivy Books, 1990).

MICHAEL MEDVED, chief film critic for the *New York Post;* radio talk-show host on a daily call-in show originating at KVI-AM in Seattle to be syndicated nationally in 1998 through Salem Radio Network. Member of the Board of Contributors of *USA Today;* author of *Hollywood vs. America; Popular Culture and the War on Traditional Values* (HarperCollins, 1992).

MARGARET M. MITCHELL, PH.D., Associate Professor of New Testament, McCormick Theological Seminary, Chicago; author of *Paul and the Rhetoric of Reconciliation: An Exegetical Investigation of the Language and Composition of 1 Corinthians* (Westminster John Knox Press, 1993).

DENNIS T. OLSON, PH.D., Associate Professor of Old Testament at Princeton Theological Seminary, Princeton, N.J.; author of *Numbers* (Westminster John Knox Press, 1996) and *Deuteronomy and the Death of Moses* (Augsburg, 1994).

CAROLYN A. OSIEK, R.S.C.J., PH.D, Professor of New Testament Studies, Catholic Theological Union, Chicago; coauthor of *Families in the New Testament World* (Westminster John Knox Press, 1997).

SHARON PACE, PH.D., Associate Professor of Biblical Studies at Marquette University, Milwaukee; author of *The Women of Genesis: From Sara to*

Potiphar's Wife (Fortress Press, 1990) and *The Greek Translation of Daniel 7:12* (Catholic Biblical Quarterly Monograph Series, 1987).

MAYER PERELMUTER, D.MIN, Hebrew Union College and Post-Graduate Center for Mental Health, New York; Rabbi of the Reform Temple of Forest Hills, Forest Hills, N.Y.

TED PETERS, PH.D., Professor of Systematic Theology, Pacific Lutheran Theological Seminary, Berkeley, Calif.; author of *For the Love of Children: Genetic Technology and the Future of the Family* (Westminster John Knox Press, 1996).

DAVID POPENOE, PH.D., Professor of Sociology and Associate Dean of the Division of the Social Sciences, Rutgers University, New Brunswick, N.J.; author of *Life Without Father* (Free Press, 1996).

STEPHEN G. POST, PH.D., Chicago; Professor of Biomedical Ethics at the School of Medicine, Case Western Reserve University, Cleveland; author of *Spheres of Love: Toward a New Ethics of the Family* (Southern Methodist University, 1994).

ROY A. REED, Emeritus Professor of Worship and Music at the Methodist Theological School in Ohio, Delaware, Ohio; coauthor of *Models of Confirmation and Baptismal Affirmation: Liturgical and Educational Issues and Designs* (Religious Education Press, 1995).

BARBARA E. REID, O.P., PH.D., Catholic University of America, Washington, D.C.; Associate Professor of New Testament Studies, Catholic Theological Union, Chicago; author of *Choosing the Better Part?: Women in the Gospel of Luke* (Liturgical Press, 1996).

MARIE-ELOISE ROSENBLATT, PH.D., Associate Dean of the Faculty at the Graduate Theological Union in Berkeley, Calif.; author of *Paul the Accused: His Portrayal in the Acts of the Apostles. Zacchaeus Series* (Michael Glazier/Liturgical Press, 1995).

TURID KARLSEN SEIM, DR. THEOL., University of Oslo, Oslo, Norway; Professor of New Testament at The Divinity School, University of Oslo; author of *The Double Message: Patterns of Gender in Luke-Acts* (Abingdon Press, 1995); coeditor of *Mighty Minorities: Minorities in Early Christianity—Positions and Strategies* (Oslo/Boston, 1995).

WALLACE CHARLES SMITH, D.MIN., Senior Pastor of Shiloh Baptist Church, Washington, D.C.; author of *The Church in the Life of the Black Family* (Judson Press, 1985).

ROBERT F. STAHMANN, PH.D., Professor of Family Sciences at Brigham Young University, Provo, Utah; coauthor of *Premarital and Remarital Counseling* (Jossey-Bass, 1997), *Dynamic Assessment in Couples Therapy* (Lexington Books, 1993), and *Counseling in Marital and Sexual Problems* (Free Press, 1991).

NAOMI STEINBERG, PH.D., Associate Professor of Religious Studies at DePaul University, Chicago; author of *Kinship and Marriage in Genesis: A Household Economics Perspective* (Augsburg, 1993).

MARY STEWART VAN LEEUWEN, PH.D., Professor of Psychology and Philosophy, Eastern College, St. David's, Pa.; coeditor of *After Eden: Facing the Challenge of Gender Reconciliation* (Wm. B. Eerdmans Publishing Co., 1993); author of *Gender and Grace* (InterVarsity Press, 1990).

THEODORE A. STONEBERG, PH.D., Northwestern University, Evanston, Ill.; Professor of Pastoral Care and Counseling at Anderson School of Theology, Anderson, Ind.

PAUL J. WADELL, C.P., PH.D., Professor of Ethics, Catholic Theological Union, Chicago; author of *The Primacy of Love: An Introduction to the Ethics of Thomas Aquinas* (Paulist Press, 1992) and *Friendship and Moral Life* (University of Notre Dame, 1991).

JOHN WALL, Ph.D. candidate at the Divinity School of the University of Chicago and Coordinator of Research of the Family Culture and Religion Project at the University of Chicago Divinity School.

TODD DAVID WHITMORE, PH.D, Associate Professor of Social Ethics, University of Notre Dame; recipient of a Henry Luce III Fellowship in Theology; author of *The Common Good and the Care of Children: Catholicism, American Public Life and the Challenge of Abortion* (University of Notre Dame, forthcoming).

MARK P. WIBERG, D.MIN., Des Plains, Ill; retired pastor, Evangelical Lutheran Church in America.

JOHN WITTE, JR., PH.D., Professor of Law and Ethics and Director, Law and Religion Program, Emory University School of Law, Atlanta; author of *From Sacrament to Contract: Marriage, Religion, and Law in the Western Tradition* (Westminster John Knox Press, 1997).

CLAIRE WOLFTEICH, PH.D., Assistant Professor of Practical Theology and Spiritual Formation, Boston University School of Theology, Boston.

ANITA WORTHEN, Administrator of New Hope Ministry, San Rafael, Calif., and North American board member of Exodus International, a worldwide outreach to men and women seeking freedom from homosexuality; coauthor of *Someone I Love Is Gay* (InterVarsity Press, 1996).

TODD YONKMANN, M.DIV., University of Chicago Divinity School; minister at Pilgrim Faith Church, UCC, Oak Lawn, Ill.

LAURIE ZOLOTH-DORFMAN, PH.D., Associate Professor of Social Ethics and Jewish Philosophy, and Director, Program in Jewish Studies, San Francisco State University; author of *The Ethics of Encounter: A Jewish Conversation on Health Care and Justice* (University of North Carolina Press, 1998); coauthor of *Notes from a Narrow Ridge: Faith and Reason in Bioethics* (University Press Publishing Group, 1998).

Series Foreword

There is an important debate going on today over the present health and future well-being of families in American society. Although some people on the political right and left use concern about the state of the family primarily to further their respective partisan causes, the debate is real, and it is over genuine issues. The discussion, however, is not well informed and is riddled with historical, theological, and social-scientific ignorance.

This is not unusual as political debates go. The American family debate, however, is especially uninformed and dogmatic. This is understandable, for all people have experienced a family in some way, feel themselves to be experts, and believe that they are entitled to their strong opinions.

The books in this series, The Family, Religion, and Culture, discuss these issues in ways that will place the American debate about the family on more solid ground. The series is the result of the Religion, Culture, and Family Project, which was funded by a generous grant from the Division of Religion of the Lilly Endowment, Inc., and took place in the Institute for Advanced Study in The University of Chicago Divinity School. Part of the project proceeded while Don Browning, the project director, was in residence at the Center of Theological Inquiry in Princeton, New Jersey.

The series advances no single point of view on the American family debate and gives no one solution to the problems concerning families today. The authors and editors contributing to the volumes represent both genders as well as a variety of religious and ethnic perspectives and denominational backgrounds—liberal and conservative; Protestant, Catholic, and Jewish; evangelical and mainline; and black, white, and Asian. A number of the authors and editors met annually for a seminar and discussed—often with considerable intensity—their outlines, papers, and chapters pertaining to the various books. The careful reader will notice that many of the seminar members did influence one another; but it is safe to say that each of them in the end took his or her own counsel and spoke out of his or her own convictions.

The series is comprehensive, with studies on the family in ancient Israel and early Christianity; economics and the family; law, feminism, and reproductive technology and the family; the family and American faith traditions; and congregations and families; as well as two overview books—one a critical overview of the American family debate and this volume, a handbook.

The Family Handbook builds on the volumes that have preceded it in the Family, Culture, and Religion Project. Yet it takes the project in new directions.

This volume presses the question: What does this mean for practice? What does this mean for an abused child? What does this mean for a priest, a minister, or a rabbi writing a sermon? What does this mean for a couple looking forward to marriage? How can families be faithful amid changed patterns of work and child care and changed roles of genders and generations? By pressing such practical questions, this volume brings a clarity, focus, and good sense to the discussion of family issues that is too often lacking when politicians and scholars debate among themselves. This practical helpfulness is extended by a directory at the end of the volume that gives a myriad of resources, whether on fatherhood, finances, or finding family professionals.

A unique feature of this handbook is that it seeks to be practical in ways that are deep as well as immediate. Those who work with families will not only learn new techniques but also develop a sense of vocation for working with families. They will learn to see their efforts in a larger context. The material in Part 1 on contemporary perspectives on families and marriage ought not only leave the reader better informed but also with a renewed dedication to the task of working with families—seeing the work in its wider perspective. Likewise, Part 4 on families in history will leave the reader not only with a sense of perspective on the past but with a deepened understanding of the crucial role of religious communities in the continuing development of families in all their varied forms.

This volume is flexible as well as rich. It deserves to be in the library of all who work with families—social workers, therapists, lawyers, ministers, and health care professionals. It also has a place on the bookshelf of all those who wish to orient themselves to one of the most important social issues of the time, that of religion and family. Those who turn to this volume for this purpose will find here succinct statements by the most thoughtful people writing on these subjects today. Beyond this, the volume will have a variety of more specific uses. The articles on biblical exegesis by leading scholars would make the basis for a wonderful series of Bible studies. Such a study could be a faith-deepening experience for those who participated as well as a powerful tool for any religious community attempting to discern what its ministry to families should be. Likewise, this book could be a flexible resource in theological education in classes on pastoral or religious education but even more in the growing number of courses that are integrating practical subjects with the historical, exegetical, and theological disciplines. Thus this volume is radical in its intent, seeking not only to help and inform all those who work with families but also to enlarge our understanding of the importance of this work.

Don S. Browning
Ian S. Evison

Acknowledgments

We acknowledge with gratitude the generous support and interest of the Lilly Endowment in all stages of this project. We are grateful to the Divinity School of the University of Chicago for providing the institutional context that supported us in our work. This handbook benefited enormously from the yearly gathering of authors, editors, and other authorities on the family that joined them from time to time. Westminster John Knox Press deserves credit for their willingness to publish the series, including this volume, and their efforts in seeing it through to completion. Finally, a project of the scope of this handbook required ongoing attention to many details. An exceptional group of doctoral students provided this as well as wonderful infusions of energy. Our thanks to Christie Green, John Wall, Todd Yonkmann, and Claire Wolfteich.

Introduction

The Family Handbook is the culminating book of the Family, Religion, and Culture series. It extends the insights of the research of the entire project and the many books that have preceded this one. Yet a large number of new authors and many new insights have been added to this handbook. Handbooks are designed to help answer specific questions, provoke ideas, and provide hints about how to address a situation or solve a problem. This particular handbook is unique in its thematic scope and religious breadth.

Ministry to Families

This handbook contains features missing from most handbooks. In Part 2, we provide a large number of articles that should help ministers, laypersons, and professionals from other disciplines to enlarge the vision of ministries to families that churches and synagogues can provide. Informative and practical articles on a number of topics are included—for example, on ministries to those preparing to marry, to married couples, to youth and children as family members, to single parents, to the divorced, to fathers, to mothers, to stepfamilies, to gays and lesbians, to the abused, and to the elderly.

We present these models of ministry from an ecumenical perspective: articles have been contributed by Protestant, Catholic, and Jewish authors as well as by scholars who write from the viewpoint of one of the modern secular disciplines. We invite you not only to read what leaders in your own tradition recommend but to examine as well what representatives of other traditions propose. In attending to other traditions as well as our own, we hope all of us can come to a better understanding of our own traditions, become more understanding of others, and in the process gain new insights and possibilities for our ministries to families.

Theological and Moral Backgrounds

Besides practical help, this book offers theological, moral, legal, and historical insights on contemporary issues facing families. A great debate is taking place in our society on the present condition and future prospects of families. Controversies exist over what defines a family, what makes a family healthy, whether families are weakening or simply changing, and whether Judaism and Christianity have made positive contributions to families or whether they have been destructive—perhaps patriarchal, oppressive to women, and harmful to children. In order to define what ministry with families should be in our time, religious institutions must confront these issues. They must think about the theological, moral, and legal issues that concern families at the same time they are trying to help families spiritually and emotionally.

We address many of these major issues in Part 1. We also include in Part 4 several chapters on families in various historical periods—in ancient Israel, in the Greco-Roman world, in early Christianity, in medieval Christianity and the Reformation, and in the nineteenth and twentieth centuries—to suggest the richness and complexity behind modern religious and secular thinking about the family. Much of our society's confusion about its thought and practice concerning families results from our amnesia about the contributions, both positive and negative, of these periods. All of these issue-oriented and historical articles are worthy of study in small groups. An entire educational series could be developed on the basis of the historical essays.

Biblical Resources

The new ferment in family ministries both requires and enables examination of scriptural foundations. It requires new examination because previous biblical interpretation has bifurcated between finding "a plan" for the Christian or Jewish family and justifying a diversity of family forms. Neither approach has a broad base in scripture. Neither approach is particularly helpful to families in crisis.

Part 3 of the handbook offers an exceptional collection of short essays on key biblical texts regarding the family. Contributors to chapters 18 and 19, the most knowledgeable biblical scholars writing in English, look at a number of crucial texts in the Hebrew and Christian scriptures that have a bearing on life in families. Leo Perdue, who chaired the team of scholars writing our series volume titled *Families in Ancient Israel,* suggested passages and authors for the materials in the Hebrew scriptures. Carolyn Osiek and David Balch, authors of the book in the series titled *Families in the New Testament World,* nominated passages and authors for the articles on the New Testament scriptures. Together, these articles should provide an invaluable resource for sermon preparation, adult group study, or accessible reference when a perplexing point needs clarification.

A Directory of
Resources for Families

A Directory of Resources for Families concludes the handbook. Compiled by M. Christian Green and Todd Yonkmann, it is a comprehensive guide to the many organizations and services, both religious and secular, that are helping families in the United States. Our main point is to show the reader that many resources, reflecting different points of view, can be found. The directory aims to be an entry point into an exceptionally rich world of resources. A phone call or E-mail message may meet your need or may lead to a referral to an even better resource. Churches and individual families are not without resources of their own.

This handbook was assembled with two goals: (1) to help churches and synagogues prepare individuals for marriages and strengthened family living, and (2) to help all families to meet better the challenges they face and to live life more faithfully. We believe that marriages should be long-lasting, that families—especially those with children—should generally remain intact, that children deserve nurture and respect, that husbands and wives should treat each other with complete equality and respect, and that marital partners should have equal access to and responsibility for both public life and the domestic tasks pertaining to child care and household work. We recognize that the enormous pressures on families in modern societies often make this ideal difficult to attain. The turn to cultural individualism, the spread of market forces into family life, the generally welcomed yet stressful entrance of both fathers and mothers into the wage market, changing gender roles, discrimination and poverty, the help and interference of government programs, a stagnant wage economy, and a threatening youth culture—all make family life, even among the best prepared, difficult if not precarious. In this period of history, marital and family difficulties will likely visit us all, directly or indirectly. We have designed a handbook that we hope will help all families, regardless of their form or fortune. All families can be helped to do better.

Herbert Anderson
Don Browning
Ian S. Evison
Mary Stewart Van Leeuwen

PART 1

Families and Marriage: Contemporary Perspectives

1

Marriage

A Jewish Perspective

Almost from birth, all things in a person's life point toward marriage. On the eighth day of a Jewish boy's life, during the circumcision ceremony that enters him into the covenant, all present recite: "As this child has been entered into the covenant, so may he be entered into a life of Torah study, the wedding canopy, and good deeds." The ancient traditional greeting for an infant girl also prescribed for her marriage and good deeds, though not Torah study. (Now that women in some strands of Judaism also study the Torah, however, many modern Jews add that phrase to the female greeting as well.) Marriage precedes every other relationship. Celibacy, a superior state in other religions, was discouraged in Judaism. Marriage to a human partner was valued more highly than symbolic marriage to God. "Eighteen to the wedding canopy" was not a commandment but expressed the seriousness of marriage as the optimal way of adult life (*m. Avot* 5:24).

Everyone was drafted into the marriage enterprise: "What are the essential duties of father to son? . . . to circumcise, redeem, teach him Torah, take a wife for him, and teach him a craft" (*b. Kid.* 29a). "If an orphan wishes to marry [and has no means] the community should purchase for him a dwelling, a bed, and all necessary household utensils and then marry him off" (*b. Ket.* 67b). Similarly, the *mitzvah*, or obligation, of *hachnassat kallah,* of supplying a poor bride with the necessary accoutrements for marriage, was given great weight. It is a feature of the examined life, an obligation for which one will have to answer at the end of one's days.

What is the function of marriage? Procreation is a primary function. "Be fruitful and multiply" is the very first commandment (Gen. 1:28). The monthly twelve days of *niddah,* the period of sexual separation during menses and the week following, are timed to end at the peak moment of fertility. The Talmud concludes that the minimum number of children by which one can fulfill the biblical command is two; one should not depart from this earth leaving any less life than when one entered it. Lack of children after ten years of marriage was grounds for divorce, though that was neither law nor prescription. The Talmud relates the poignant story of a childless couple who prepare to divorce after ten years of marriage. The husband tells his wife that she may take back to her father's house whatever she wants from their household. She plies him with sweet wine, and after he has fallen into a deep sleep she has her servants carry him off to her father's house. When he awakens, she tells him that in fact he is the only thing that she wants. The story relates that they live happily ever after and are rewarded with children.

Procreation maintains biological life and also ensures the continuity of the covenant with God. Many human responsibilities in this covenant, including perfecting the world, cannot be fulfilled in one generation. The covenant depends on marriage and its procreative impulse. As a finite partner in relation to an infinite, eternal God, each human generation must hand down the covenantal tasks to the next. This explains in part, I believe, why the religious ceremonies marking the transmissions of the covenant—such as birth, bar mitzvah, and bat mitzvah—are not celebrated en masse as group events (for example, all thirteen-year-olds in a joint confirmation ceremony), but rather in very individualized, family-centered events, for these are the biological or adoptive issue of a particular marriage. The book of Genesis interweaves the story of receiving and transmitting the covenant with the earthy story of three generations of family life.

And yet, procreation and covenant are not at all the whole function of marriage. The Torah (JPS) states:

> It is not good that man should be alone. I will make a helper for him. (Gen. 2:18)

> This one at last is bone of my bones, and flesh of my flesh. . . . (Gen. 2:23)

> Hence a man leaves his mother and father and clings to his wife, so that they shall become one flesh. (Gen. 2:24)

Interestingly, the Hebrew word *davok*, "cleave," expresses the relationship between God and the Jewish people: "And you who cleave unto the LORD your God . . ." (Deut. 4:4).

When we separate the gendered language and hierarchical constructs—to which we shall return below—we are left with the scriptural essentials of a good marriage: mutuality; compatibility and companionship; intimacy and sexuality; primacy and exclusivity; and fidelity and permanence. The Torah spells out some of these parameters further: the basic material and sexual obligations of husband to wife are learned from the law of the bondwoman, who had the status of a wife in terms of these obligations: "And if he take for himself another wife, he shall not diminish [the necessary obligations to her] of food, clothing and satisfaction of her sexual needs. . . ." (Exod. 21:10).

And yet, immediately after this idealized version, Genesis presents an endless stream of untidy family tales. Everywhere there is deceit, pain, vulnerability, and frayed bonds. The very first couple fails the test of protecting one another. Abraham compromises his wife Sarah in King Abimelech's court to save his own neck. Jacob speaks with frustration, or maybe anger, as he pleads with his distraught wife, "Am I in God's stead that I have withheld from you the fruit of your womb?" (Gen. 30:2). Rebecca plots with her younger son Jacob against her husband Isaac to fool Isaac into giving the younger son the eldest's blessings. These stories teach us a lesson that should comfort ordinary mortals: No marriage is perfect, not even those of our foundational heroes. Nevertheless, the ideal marriage remains in place, held out to us as a model, something to strive for, to be reminded of at all times.

Where the Torah draws the general outlines, the Talmud gives detail:

Mutuality
(as symbolized by the phrase *ezer k'negdo,* "helpmeet")

Despite inequality and clear-cut role distinctions, there was a complementary aspect to the Jewish marriage, down to the most mundane tasks. For her husband a wife must "grind corn, bake, cook, suckle her child, make his bed, and work in wool" (*b. Ket.* 5:5). The *ketubah,* the traditional marriage contract (introduced circa third century B.C.E.), spelled out obligations of husband to wife: For his wife a husband must provide maintenance in proper style, payment for her medical and dental bills, ransom if she was taken captive, and payment in event of divorce. Even his funerary obligations were spelled out: "Rabbi Judah says even the poorest in Israel must not furnish less than two flutes and one woman wailer [for his wife's funeral]" (*b. Ket.* 4:4, 51a).

Respect and honor are even more important to mutuality: "He must love her as himself and honor her more than himself." "If your wife is small, bend down and whisper in her ear" (*b. Bava Mezia* 59a), which means consult with her on all matters. In the same place it is written, "One must always observe the honor due to his wife because blessings rest on a home only on account of his wife." Conversely, "He who has no wife lives without peace, without help, without joy, without forgiveness, without life itself. He is not a whole person; he diminishes the image of God in the world" (*Gen. Rab.* 17:3). The paean of praise for the Woman of Valor (Prov. 31) was introduced into the weekly home ritual of Sabbath eve. Prior to reciting the blessings over the wine, in a setting of family warmth and celebration, the husband sings to his wife and before all present of her manifold talents and exemplary character. It is an altogether romantic moment injected into sacred time.

The reader may observe that the dicta emphasize the husband's obligation to his wife. In a hierarchical society a wife's obligation to honor her husband needs no emphasis. These statements served as a corrective, a safeguard against abuse or excess, a way to maintain the balance. The sources were addressed primarily to men.

Compatibility and Companionship

Perhaps the strongest indication that Judaism perceives marriage as a vehicle for personal happiness is that it permitted divorce. The Torah establishes its legality: "When a man takes a wife and marries her and it comes to pass that she finds no favor in his eyes because he has found something unseemly [*ervat davar*] in her, then he writes her a writ of divorce. . . ." (Deut. 24:1). *Ervat davar,* the grounds for divorce, is somewhat ambiguous here. The Talmud explicates through a most interesting debate between the two great houses of study, Hillel and Shammai. The latter narrowly interprets *ervat davar* as adultery. (Christianity picked up this thread and forbade divorce except for adultery.) The house of Hillel interpreted the grounds broadly, including such indices of incompatibility as if she consistently burned his food or he permanently carried a bad odor from a profession such as leather tanning. The majority followed Hillel. The primary rabbinic view was that one should not be locked into a marriage absent feelings of love, companionship, and friendship.

Shared values are vital to a harmonious relationship. Therefore, initial choice of mate was—and is—crucial. The Midrash tells of a Roman matron who mocks a great sage: "What has your God been occupied with since the six days of creation?" He answers: "With finding mates for his earthly creatures." She replies, "What?! That is a simple task. I can do it myself." She assembles a thousand young men and women and pairs them off. Three days later they appear with broken bones and stories of friction. She apologizes to the rabbi, who comments, "Though it looks easy to make a match, even for God the task is as difficult as splitting the Red Sea" (*Gen. Rab.* 67.3).

"A man should be matched to a woman according to the measure of his deeds" (*Sot.* 2A). All other measures of compatibility were to be considered—character, family background, even genetic makeup. (See *Bava Batra* 110A, *Bechorot* 45B, *Pesachim* 49A.) "Look to the brothers" was the cautionary slogan, for brothers reflected the character of the spouse's family and also what the offspring might be like. Wealth, however, should not determine choice of marriage partner (*b. Kid.* 70A).

A young woman could not be given in marriage without her consent. This is based on the story of Rebecca, who is asked whether she will go to Abraham. So intent were the rabbis to ensure happiness for both partners that they overlooked the fact that in the biblical text, Rebecca is already betrothed when they ask her consent. Close readers of the text that they were, they would have come to an altogether different legal ruling, using that scriptural peg. For that reason, child marriages were discouraged. "A father is forbidden to betroth his daughter to another while she is still a minor. He must wait until she grows up and says, 'I want to marry Mr. X'" (*b. Kid.* 41 A13).

Intimacy and Sexuality

Judaism has been described as earthy. The sensuousness of the images of "one flesh" and "cleave unto his wife" is obvious. The sources interweave sexuality and marriage tightly. The sex drive was recognized and was properly channeled into marriage. "If a man has reached age twenty and has not married a wife, he will spend all the day long in sin. Is this really so? No, not sin, but erotic thoughts" (*b. Kid.* 29b). Likewise, "An unmarried woman runs the risk of becoming promiscuous" (*b. Sanhedrin* 76a).

Judaism is unique among religions born in antiquity in considering a woman's sexual needs. Already in the Torah we find the law of *onah,* the sexual obligations of husband to wife (Exod. 21:7–10). Generations later, the rabbis interpreted *onah* to mean both quality and quantity of sex. Rabbinic literature discussed openly frequency of sex as well as attention and foreplay. Obligation of frequency was linked to the husband's profession. For a camel driver who must travel in caravans for extended periods, once a month; for sailors, once in six months; for common laborers, twice a week; for men of independent means, every night (*b. Ketubot* 61b–62b). These obligations were not carved in stone; the emphasis of *onah* was to meet the wife's needs.

That sex was not merely for procreation is shown in the requirement that a man observe *onah* during a wife's pregnancy and lactation. No matter that some men resist intercourse with their pregnant wives because of the association with their mothers. The rabbis are explicit: A woman's sexual feelings must be respected during pregnancy as at other times. A man was enjoined to respond to his wife when she signaled her desire for him through adorning herself or through modest overtures. He was to be sensitive to her subtle hints at all permissible times.

Sex and intimacy of feeling are connected. "If a man is angry with his wife [when it is improper for him to have intercourse with her], he must do that which will appease her. . . . he may speak of such things to her in order to please her/make her willing. . . . he may not have intercourse with his wife unless she wills it" (*Shulkhan Arukh, Even Ha'ezer* 25:1, 2). "A man should not drink from this cup while his eyes are on another one. . . . Rebellious and wicked sons will be the product of sex under the following circumstances: marital rape; a disliked wife; where he wants someone else; where she hates him but is agreeable to intercourse; drunkenness, where in his heart he has divorced her; in a state of mix up or confusion; if she is fresh and brazen. . . ." (*Shulkhan Arukh, Orat Hayyim,* 240:1–4).

A medieval sage with romantic bent instructs: "Therefore you are to engage at first in matters which please her heart and mind and cheer her in order to bring together your thoughts with hers and your intention with hers. You should say such things some of which will urge her to passion and intercourse, to affection, desire and lovemaking, and some which will urge her to fear of heaven, piety and modesty. . . . You shall not possess her against her will or force her because in that kind of union there is no divine presence. . . . Rather you should attract her with charming words and endearments and other proper and righteous things as I have explained" (*Iggeret Hakodesh,* attributed to Nachmanides, chap. 6, "The Fifth Way Concerning the Quality of Intercourse").

Primacy and Exclusivity

"Therefore shall a man leave his father and mother. . . ." Though the Torah gives no explicit command to marry (judiciously so, because it is not given to everyone to marry) and does command honor to parents (Exod. 20:12), the

Talmudic rabbis set unequivocal priorities: A child should not marry against a parent's wishes, but when a clash between parent and partner is not resolvable, marriage wins. "If the father objects to his son's marriage or to the woman of his choice, the son is not obliged to listen to his father . . . for the belovedness of the partner is paramount" (*Yoreh Deah* 240.25. *Yoreh Deah* is one of the four tractates of the *Shulkhan Arukh,* the most authoritative Jewish legal compendium of the Middle Ages).

The language of the marriage ceremony is *kiddushin,* "sanctification, or setting aside as special, exclusive." One woman is set aside for one man. Both ceremony and language are male gendered. Polygamy but not polygyny was forbidden. Jewish law did not ban polygyny formally until the tenth century C.E. Yet it was practiced only in certain Middle Eastern countries where more than one wife was the cultural norm. None of the rabbis, who became the primary models for Jewish life, had more than one wife.

Fidelity and Permanence

The language of *davok,* "cleave," suggests a long-term relationship as well as intimacy. This same language is used to describe the steadfast relationship between God and the Jewish people. Equally important to the intergenerational nature of covenant as discussed above is its steadfastness. In the covenant with God, neither partner walks away when things go awry; likewise, in a marriage relationship, neither spouse pulls out during the inevitable periods of unevenness and sporadic failure. Divorce was permitted but was discouraged. The Talmudic tractate that deals wholly with divorce concludes: "The altar sheds tears for the man who divorces the wife of his youth" (*b. Gittin* 90B).

Did marriage in Jewish history and community always live up to this ideal? Of course not. No system is foolproof. No theoretical or practical guidelines for something as personal as marriage can possibly accommodate the variety in human nature. Over the millennia, Jews lived in many different cultures. Each had a different influence on how Jews organized their lives. All societies in prefeminist times were patriarchal and hierarchical. This shows up in the very language of our sacred texts. In the same Genesis in which we read that it is not good for man to live alone, we also read of the paradigmatic punishment for Eve in the Garden of Eden: "And he [your husband] shall rule over you." Even in the verses that set forth the elemental, positive qualities of a marriage—involving mutual care—the language is sexist: Woman is regarded as helpmeet to man. Though we know well that a marriage cannot succeed unless man also is a helpmeet to woman, the sources do not recognize this. In the Talmud, hierarchy is standard in such texts as the laws of divorce, which clearly favor men, and the laws of inheritance, according to which technically wives cannot inherit.

Yet the tradition was less sexist in practice than theory, more in ancient law and less in scriptural narrative; less in certain cultures than others, less in present than the past. The Jewish family was valued as the jewel in the crown of Jewish life, and this entity was wholly a product of marriage. Thus, marriage was closely monitored to meet a high standard. Words such as *honor, mutual love, gentleness, nurture,* and *dignity* can be found in many a source on marriage, hierarchical or not.

We cannot rewrite ancient sacred texts. We can, however, do two things: First, we can reinterpret the law to eliminate whatever pockets of potential discrimination still exist—such as in divorce law. To the extent that vulnerability exists in the area of divorce, the lofty truths about Jewish marriage are diminished. Second, we can extrapolate the essence of the function of a Jewish marriage and set this forth as the ideal model of marriage. The marriage model is not without flaws but is commendable in its design to continue human life into the future and to carry a sacred vision of that future. It is a unit capable of dispelling anomie and loneliness in the human condition. Marriage is likely to provide both great emotional happiness and deep physical pleasure. These are no small tasks. No wonder that God must be a partner in matchmaking!

—BLU GREENBERG

A Catholic Perspective

Since the twelfth century, Roman Catholics have maintained that marriage is not only a natural human institution blessed and confirmed by God but also one of the seven sacraments of the church. To name something a sacrament is to claim that what at first glance seems an ordinary human reality is also a place where we can encounter Christ in a saving way. Each of the sacraments is a graced encounter with an incarnational God who works through the everyday realities of life to love, to bless, to forgive, and to save. Thus, the sacraments are special moments of God's availability through which God's befriending love, perfectly embodied by Christ, continues to be experienced in the church.

This is especially true of marriage. To name marriage a sacrament means, first of all, that Christ is a partner to the marriage, just as present to the marriage and actively involved in its life as the spouses. The Second Vatican Council spoke of marriage as a life in Christ, indicating that it is rooted in baptism, takes its meaning from baptism, and is, indeed, a baptismal way of life. For Catholics, marriage is how spouses, who "put on Christ" at baptism, continue to live in Christ, grow in Christ, and be transformed by Christ.

This strong link between baptism and marriage also means that Christian marriage is a life of discipleship and gospel holiness. Christ is partner to the marriage not only to bless, strengthen, and encourage a husband and wife but also to help deepen them in such gospel virtues as love, patience, generosity, compassion, forgiveness, faithfulness, and joy. All the habits of goodness that are honed and sharpened through a lifetime of love are precisely the qualities that make spouses authentic and faithful disciples. For this reason, the Second Vatican Council rightly spoke of Christian marriage as a "training of salvation and of holiness" (*The Church in the Modern World,* 48). From a Catholic perspective, marriage is truly a gracious existence.

Perhaps most important, naming marriage a sacrament means that the entire life of marriage, even the most mundane and ordinary dimensions, has sanctifying possibilities. For Catholics, marriage is a saving way of life. It is the one relationship recognized by the church in which a very ordinary but powerful human love becomes, with God's help, a means to salvation. But Christ's redemptive love grasps everything in marriage and sanctifies it, which means that nothing in marriage is profane and nothing in marriage cannot be part of a graced and saving way of life. All of married life is susceptible to salvation and shaped to receive it. All of married life can contribute to the holiness and virtue of the spouses. Of course this depends absolutely on God's grace and the ready cooperation of the spouses, but if married life is truly sacramental, then everything that constitutes it, from grand gestures of love to the most monotonous routines, has supernatural bearing.

In addition to speaking of marriage as a sacrament, the Catholic church also considers marriage a special and distinctive vocation. First of all, a couple's marriage is a gift of God's love given for the sake of love. God is the author of marriage, and it is from the lavish generosity and creative goodness of God that every marriage begins. As a vocation, a man and woman's marriage rests not primarily on their own initiative but on the concrete and very personal way God has chosen to love them; thus, their marriage begins not so much in their choice, but in their acceptance of God's gift. And it is precisely because Christian marriage is founded on God's love that spouses can have confidence in what they are undertaking when they commit themselves to one another for life. God's love is the root and foundation of their love, and this means their love never stands on its own or depends entirely on themselves; rather, it grows from God's love for them and is continually supported and nurtured by that love. In other words, their faithfulness to one another relies on, and is bounded by, the higher faithfulness of God.

From a Catholic perspective, the whole purpose of marriage is for two people to be brought together to fullness of life and union with God through their love for one another. Marriage really is for the sake of love inasmuch as its primary aim is for a husband and wife to learn what it means to love God and neighbor by learning what it means to love one another completely and faithfully. In his pastoral letter on marriage and the family, Pope John Paul II wrote, "Creating the human race in his own image and continually keeping it in being, God inscribed in the humanity of man and woman the vocation, and thus the capacity and responsibility, of love and communion. Love is therefore the fundamental and innate vocation of every human being" (*Familiaris Consortio,* 11).

The universal human vocation is the call from God to learn love and to live in love. In the special vocation of marriage, spouses help bring to fullness the image of God in them as they grow in love, affection, trust, friendship, and communion with one another. This is why the Second Vatican Council spoke of marriage as "an intimate partnership of life and love" (*The Church in the Modern World,* 48). It is the communion of life whereby spouses grow in their friendship with God (a friendship Catholics call *charity*) through their friendship love for one another.

According to Catholic teaching, marital love is characterized by mutual generosity. At its best, marriage is a kind of friendship, and just as friendship requires people who want what is best for one another and truly seek each other's good, so too does marriage require spouses who find joy in working for the happiness, enrichment, and well-being of one another. Nothing frustrates marital love more than selfishness, fear, or loss of trust. Nothing kills marital love more than hardness of heart. It is only through mutual generosity, benevolent love and affection, and commitment to shared goods that the promise of marriage is achieved. In short, if the fullness of marriage is two-becoming-one, that perfect intimacy which is a communion of peace and love, it is reached by a lifetime of love characterized by generosity, patience, sacrifice, devotion, and delight. This does not deny that marriage should be individually fulfilling and satisfying, but it does say that genuine personal fulfillment in marriage is proportionate to the intimacy and communion spouses have with one another, and this is always the work of a mutual, generous, and benevolent love. When Christian marital love is marked by mutual generosity and service, it mirrors Christ's love for the Church (Eph. 5:32).

Finally, what is the Catholic understanding of the role of children in marriage? The Catholic church no longer teaches that children are the primary end or purpose of marriage, which would suggest that marriage was constituted and defined through children and not by the partnership-in-love of the spouses. However, Catholic teaching still speaks of children as the "supreme gift of marriage" (*The Church in the Modern World*, 50), first because marital love fittingly grows and deepens when spouses welcome children into their lives, and second because it is through the birth and care of children that spouses become co-creators with God and ministers of God's love in the world. Too, it is through parenting that spouses perform an important ministry in the church because they are a child's first teachers in the faith, and it is from them that children first experience the love and goodness of God.

Thus, Catholics believe good marriages are gifts to the church and absolutely essential for the life of the church.

Bibliography

Lawler, Michael G. *Marriage and Sacrament: A Theology of Christian Marriage* (Collegeville, Minn.: Liturgical Press, 1993).

Mackin, Theodore. *What Is Marriage?* (New York: Paulist Press, 1992).

Roberts, William P., ed. *Commitment to Partnership: Explorations of the Theology of Marriage* (New York: Paulist Press, 1987).

Thomas, David M. *Christian Marriage: A Journey Together* (Collegeville, Minn.: Liturgical Press, 1983).

—PAUL J. WADDELL

A Protestant Perspective

Transformation of marriage practices and perspectives lay at the heart of the Reformers' protest against Roman rites in the sixteenth and seventeenth centuries. Along with their elevation of faith over sacrament as the means of grace, they also desacramentalized marriage and returned it not to the families arranging a marriage but to the magistrates of an emerging state order. The Roman church had already identified the free consent of the partners as a necessary aspect of the contractual form of marriage settled in Roman law. Indeed, it made the validity of this contract the basis for its sacramentalization in the church. Marriage as sacrament had come to mean that the ordinary—indeed, according to Augustine, sinful—actions of marriage were enabled to be means of the grace safeguarded by the church. With the Protestant Reformers, marriage reemerged as a natural state more or less good in itself, entrusted to the partners in the marriage to make it a work of Christ's grace or of the church. Marriage and family would be a lay project of grace whose contractual form would be safeguarded by the state but whose actual content would be the work of believers themselves. The partners exercised the rights of citizens in contracting legal marriage and exercised a priesthood of all believers toward each other in the bonds of Christian marriage.

This removal of marriage from the sacramental system of the church tended to undermine marriage as a symbol of the divine mysteries of grace. The life of marriage and family might provide rich metaphors for grace, for God's love, for Triune fellowship, and for Christ's faithful relation to the church, just as it had in Hosea's writings in ancient Israel, but it would not itself be expected to be a symbolic vehicle of God's grace. Rather, it became more an ethical project and a source of natural human companionship.

To conceive of marriage as a Christian project and as a form of natural friendship, the Reformers fell back on biblical concepts rather than sacramental ones. Three of the most important have been vocation, covenant, and communion. The Reformers extended to all walks of life the capacity to be a valid response to God's call to sanctification. Marriage could be one of those arenas of vocational discipline. Thus, the sacramental task of simply being a symbol of God's nature was transformed into being the ethical task of systematically disciplining marriage to cultivate the particular virtues, actions, and patterns of life that might bring about greater sanctification for the partners. Moreover, the marriage would be seen not merely in terms of the couple but in terms of their common discipleship for the sake of the world's perfection. The ministerial couple, since Luther himself, has been a long-standing manifestation of this vocational ideal.

Over the centuries the idea of vocation became attached to jobs and careers of individuals. The very transference of vocation away from the sacramental life of the church now made of occupational advancement a kind of sacred path, first by the male breadwinner and then by the wife as well. Today, the notion of vocation that might have bonded the couple together in a common work now takes them apart in two career paths, with all the concomitant ruptures, tensions, and difficulties of contemporary family life. The original tension between family and vocational obedience that was institutionalized in monastic celibacy returns in secular form as the tension between work and family. The original vocational aim of world renewal and redemption is secularized as economic growth through jobs and career mobility.

To counter this individualizing tendency in vocational images, with their latent reinforcement of our present economy, we can turn to the second concept of marriage: covenant. Although the ancient Hebrews did not look on marriage itself as a covenant (a term reserved for political alliance), Protestants soon came to speak of marriage in this way. To some extent this usage merely picked up the old meaning of *contract* received from Roman law—a contract now to be administered by the state. *Covenant* for many Protestants simply meant a solemn promise by the couple before God and the church, reflected in the American confusion of the pastor's role both as state representative to validate the contract and as witness for the church—whatever that might mean.

However, a bridge having been made between marriage and the wider meanings of biblical covenant, the way was paved for marriage and family to emulate the community-building covenant into which Abraham and Sarah had entered. Marriage as covenant could then imply a wider obligation to build up a new community (for the Puritans, a new commonwealth) that would include obligations among generations, stewardship of land and resources, education for the common good, and philanthropic care of the needy. This richer notion of covenantal marriage flowed into communal experiments as well as into the covenantal theology of the Mormons (the Church of Jesus Christ of Latter-day Saints), who created their own new Israel in the deserts of Utah.

Such a full-blown understanding of marriage as covenant could, however, instrumentalize marriage and family to such an extent that it overwhelmed the natural human capacities tendered in the fragile bonds of human love. Moreover, biblical covenant, with its primarily hierarchical form, strained against the implicit equality of the spouses gained through their baptism, especially the capacity of either spouse to end the marriage. At the same time that Protestants fleshed out vocational and covenantal models of marriage to advance God's redemptive work, others, such as John Milton, began to emphasize marriage's natural purpose of companionship. Drawing on Genesis 2:18–25, Milton and others lifted up this friendship of mutual aid as the primary purpose of marriage, making procreation a secondary aim. Friendship, which the classicists had thought impossible between men and women, was now elevated to being a virtual Christian duty for the spouses—both a directive of nature and a discipline of Christian virtue. The friendship between spouses could be a participation in the friendship bond exemplified by Jesus in John's Gospel and by the love communion of the Johannine writings. As a possible worldly manifestation of the love bond of the Triune God, marriage as communion verged on being a new version of sacrament, a lead picked up by Roman Catholic theologians after Vatican II.

Such an understanding of marriage as communion has gradually become a secular ideal as well, just as the fissiparous forces of individualistic vocation and career pull the partners apart. However, the communion ideal can reduce the couple to an intimate enclave rather than being the nucleus of a generous worldly transformation. To help people pursue this friendship ideal in the midst of these pressures, pastors, churches, and secular counselors have expended enormous energies in marriage communication, enrichment, and marital counseling. However, these practices are inadequate when separated from the vocational issues of work organization and the covenantal obligations of wider communities of sustenance. We now face the challenge of reintegrating these three perspectives within Protestant tradition.

The task of a Protestant conception of marriage, then, is to hold all three of these together and to be open to a transformed sense of sacramentality that might emerge in other branches of the church. Cultivation of communion cannot be separated from the transformation of the workplace and of career patterns to make it possible for couples to pursue some semblance of a marital vocation. Development of this marital vocation cannot be separated from the cultivation of communities of covenantal obligation to care for future generations, for the land, and for the securing of peace among the nations.

Such a conception of marriage has import not only for conventional couples, who confront deep conflicts among their commitments to work, intimacy, and procreation, but also for our current controversies about same-sex marriages, whose proponents appeal first of all to the primacy of companionship as the aim of marriage. Added to this appeal then are vocational and covenantal purposes to build up community, steward the earth, and care for succeeding generations. Ironically, much theological opposition to such conceptions of same-sex marriage usually appeals to marriage as a "natural" structure governed by ordinary heterosexual impulses toward union and procreation—something Protestants originally affirmed over against a sacramental interpretation before discovering their own version of marital grace in friendship, discipleship, and covenantal community formation. A resolution of this controversy presses us to rethink our conception of marriage generally: how we define and relate its dimensions of nature and grace, as well as its purposes as sacrament, vocation, covenant, and communion.

Bibliography

Achtemeier, Elizabeth. *The Committed Marriage* (Philadelphia: Westminster Press, 1976).

Everett, William Johnson. *Blessed Be the Bond: Christian Perspectives on Marriage and Family* (Philadelphia: Fortress Press, 1985; Lanham, Md.: University Press of America, 1990).

Garland, Diana S., and David E. Garland. *Beyond Companionship: Christians in Marriage* (Philadelphia: Westminster Press, 1986).

Webber, Christopher L. *Re-inventing Marriage: A Re-view and Re-vision* (Wilton, Conn.: Morehouse Publishing, 1994).

Witte, John, Jr. "The Reformation of Marriage Law in Martin Luther's Germany: Its Significance Then and Now." *Journal of Law and Religion* 4/ 2(1986): 1–59.

Yates, Wilson. "The Protestant View of Marriage," in Arlene Swidler, ed., *Marriage Among the Religions of the World* (Lewiston, N.Y.: Edwin Mellen, 1990), 59–78.

—WILLIAM JOHNSON EVERETT

A Secular Perspective

Simply defined, marriage is the primary relationship within which a community socially approves and encourages sexual intercourse and the birth and rearing of children. It is society's way of signaling to would-be parents of children that their long-term relationship together is socially important.

The central significance of the institution of marriage to human societies is perhaps best understood by looking comparatively at human societies throughout history. Why is marriage our most universal social institution, found prominently in virtually every society? The answer lies in the irreplaceable role that marriage plays in child-rearing and generational continuity. As the eminent demographer Kingsley Davis (1985:7–8) has stated:

> The genius of [marriage] is that, through it, the society normally holds the biological parents responsible for each other and for their offspring. By identifying children with their parents, and by penalizing people who do not have stable relationships, the social system powerfully motivates individuals to settle into a sexual union and take care of the ensuing offspring.

There is good reason to believe that the marriage relationship is ubiquitous because it is partially rooted in human biology. In evolutionary terms, children whose parents cooperated to nurture them to maturity were more likely to survive and reproduce, and thus pass their genes along to posterity. Love has a biological basis. Unlike most animals, human males and females have a biological predisposition to have some emotional affinity for each other beyond the sexual act and to establish "pair bonds." There exists an "affective attachment" between men and women that causes us to be infatuated with each other, to feel a sense of well-being when we are together with a loved one, and to feel jealous when others attempt to intrude into our relationship.

Yet marriage is a social and not a biological institution, and as a social institution it was designed much more for the smooth functioning of societies than for the accommodation of adults in love. It is based on a fundamental realization: that all affective attachments between men and women, no matter how biologically based they may be, are notoriously fragile and breakable. Historically, the main function of the institution of marriage has been socially to strengthen these attachments with the goal of preserving extended kinship ties, assuring sound child-rearing, granting social status, and providing for the smooth transition of material assets between generations.

Especially fragile in the realm of attachment is the love interest of the male. To understand the male difference, and why human pair bonds are in many ways so fragile, we must turn to the new science of evolutionary psychology and consider the radically dissimilar sexual and reproductive strategies of males and females

(Wright 1994). Biologically, the primary reproductive function for males is to inseminate and for females is to harbor the growing fetus. Since male sperm are numerous and female eggs are relatively rare (both being the prime genetic carriers), a distinctive sexual or reproductive strategy is most adaptive for each sex.

Males, much more than females, have the capacity vastly to increase reproductive success by acquiring multiple mates. One man with one hundred mates could have hundreds of children, but one woman with one hundred mates could not have many more children than she could have with just one mate. Males, therefore, have more incentive to spread their numerous sperm more widely among many females, and females have a strong incentive to bind males to themselves for the long-term care of their more limited number of potential offspring.

The woman's best reproductive strategy is to maximize the survivability of the one baby she is able to produce every few years through gaining the provision and protection of the father (or, today, perhaps, the government!). The man can pursue two strategies: He wants his baby to survive, yes, and for that reason he may provide help to his child's mother. Yet it is relatively costless to him (if he can get away with it) to inseminate other women, and thereby help to further ensure that his genes are passed on. Using the popular terms suggested by evolutionary scientists Patricia Draper and Henry Harpending, male reproductive strategy can range from the relatively promiscuous and low paternal-investment "cad" approach, in which sperm is widely distributed with the hope that more offspring will survive to reproduce, to the "dad" approach, in which a high paternal investment is made in a limited number of offspring.

Why aren't all men promiscuous cads? Because, in addition to the pull of the biologically based pair bonding and parenting predispositions, virtually all human societies have established strong cultural sanctions that seek to limit male promiscuity and protect the sanctity of the family. It is likely that the chief function of the culturally elaborated kinship structures that human beings have devised, and which provide the social basis of premodern societies, is to protect the mother-infant bond from the relative fragility and volatility of the male-female bond. The famous anthropologist Bronislaw Malinowski (1930) pointed out the way in which kinship structures perform this function:

> In all human societies the father is regarded by tradition as indispensable. The woman has to be married before she is allowed legitimately to conceive. . . . An unmarried mother is under a ban, a fatherless child is a bastard. . . . The most important moral and legal rule concerning the physiological side of kinship is that no child should be brought into the world without a man—and one man at that—assuming the role of sociological father, that is, guardian and protector, the male link between the child and the rest of the community.

The main social institution that brings this about is marriage. As evidenced by the vows of fidelity and permanence that almost universally are part of the wedding ceremony, a manifest function of marriage is to hold the man to the union. Reinforced by ritual and public acknowledgment, the ceremony stresses the long-term commitment of the male, the durability of the marital relationship, and the importance of the union for children.

Thus while biology pulls men in one direction, culture has sought to pull them in another. Margaret Mead (1969) once said, with male biology strongly in mind, that there is no society in the world where men will stay married for very long unless culturally required to do so. The experience of modern societies surely lends weight to her statement.

Today, the institution of marriage is under assault and in decline. With each passing year, an ever smaller percentage of the nation's citizens are married. With each passing year, an ever larger percentage of the nation's children grow up in households that do not consist of two married parents. Kingsley Davis (1985:21), again, has noted that "at no time in history, with the possible exception of Imperial Rome, has the institution of marriage been more problematic than it is today." Consider these facts calculated from the U.S. Census: More than 50 percent of all first marriages contracted in the United States today are expected to end in divorce, and the nonmarital birth rate, which was 5.3 percent of all births in 1960, has jumped to a staggering 33 percent of all births (1994). More than one third (37 percent) of children today live apart from their biological fathers, a remarkable increase from 17 percent in 1960. Unlike in times past, when the paternal death rate was high, almost all of these fathers are alive and well.

The impact of marriage decline on children and youth has been devastating, as many recent studies and several national commissions attest (McLanahan and Sandefur 1994). The current younger generation appears to be the first in our nation's history to be less well off—psychologically, socially, economically, and morally—than their parents were at the same age. And because children from broken homes have a higher chance than those from intact families of forming unstable marriages of their own, the future for marital stability in America does not look bright. If both childhood experiences and adult risks of marital disruption are taken into account, only a minority of children born today are likely to grow up in an intact, two-parent family, and also, as adults, to form and maintain such a family.

If we wish to improve child well-being, and thus the quality of life for future generations, the institution of marriage must be strengthened (Popenoe 1996). It would be one thing if some alternative were in sight, a better institution in which children could be raised. But no such alternative has yet been devised or is known to exist. Modern societies should be doing everything possible to strengthen marriage through restoring the traditional dignity and worth of the institution, through providing incentives for people to marry and stay married, and through making the legal termination of marriage when children are involved somewhat more difficult.

Bibliography

Davis, Kingsley. "The Meaning and Significance of Marriage in Contemporary Society" in Kingsley Davis, ed., *Contemporary Marriage,* (New York: Russell Sage Foundation, 1985), 1–21.

Malinowski, Bronislaw. *Sex, Culture, and Myth* (New York: Harcourt, Brace & World, 1962).

McLanahan, Sara, and Gary Sandefur. *Growing Up with a Single Parent* (Cambridge, Mass.: Harvard University Press, 1994).

Mead, Margaret. *Male and Female: A Study of the Sexes in a Changing World* (New York: Dell Publishing Co., 1969).

Popenoe, David. *Life without Father: Compelling New Evidence that Fatherhood and Marriage Are Indispensable for the Good of Children and Society* (New York: Free Press, 1996).

Wright, Robert. *The Moral Animal: The New Science of Evolutionary Psychology* (New York: Pantheon Books, 1994).

—DAVID POPENOE

2

Family

A Protestant Perspective

Despite the human contingencies and social injustices that result in necessary and unnecessary departures, the Protestant ideal remains: The family in its essence is the culmination of marriage between man and woman as marked by the birth (or adoption) of a child in covenant love. The bringing of children into the world and their socialization through highly personal love are the main functions of the family, the essential fruit of marriage, the seal of a couple's union, and the opportunity for profound moral growth through motherhood and fatherhood. The interweaving of this ideal form of the family over several generations creates the extended family with grandparents, whose unique teaching function should always be valued.

Benefits for Children

The Protestant ideal of the family is shaped by the fact that children want and need a mother and a father in the context of a stable two-parent family. Although every case is unique, there is strong social-scientific evidence that, *on average,* mother and father together are better able to fulfill child-rearing duties, if only for the reason that more hands, hearts, and voices are available for a labor-intensive and emotionally demanding vocation. A wider circle of relatives can be supportive, but this is not a substitute for the attentive dedication of two responsive parents. Ample evidence points to the significant strain on many aging grandmothers who attempt to fill in the gap of fatherlessness. The view that diversity of family types is a sign of progress is contrary to the facts as far as children are concerned (Blankenhorn 1995).

Some single parents struggle courageously and do succeed in raising children of character and accomplishment in spite of the obstacles, while some married couples are neglectful and abusive toward their children. Given the sad realities of domestic abuse, Christians must be cautious not to stigmatize or stereotype the children of single-parent households, any one of whom may contribute more to society than many who enjoyed a responsive mother and father. There is no question that many men who would like to be good fathers cannot fulfill this desire because the economic underpinnings of their communities have been swept away; nor is there any doubt that sometimes divorce is justified. But Christians cannot accept the culture of "single-parent chic."

Current Theology

The ideal form of the family articulated above is more than an impressive im-age that, while easily acknowledged, need not be implemented. The Protestant family form has recently been beautifully described in the light of New Testament exegesis by Richard B. Hays, a Methodist (1996). His point, in articulating "the moral vision of the New Testament," is that scriptural teachings on the perma-nence of marriage and on the sanctity of motherhood and fatherhood need to be taken much more seriously as guides to action.

Over the last two decades, Protestant theologians have indeed tended to set aside any concern with the New Testament vision of the form of the family. John Patton and Brian H. Childs, for example, in their study of theology of the family and pastoral care, are representative of this trend toward formlessness: "There is no ideal form for the Christian family toward which we should strive. There is, however, a normative function: care" (1988, 12). While there is much value in their definition of care as a combination of appreciation, respect, com-passion, and solicitude, they refuse to "argue for or against any particular form of the family or for who ought to be living together and for how long" (1988, 12). For Patton and Childs, any form is acceptable if redemptive "care" is pres-ent, for however long.

Formlessness is one response to a tradition of marriage and family that is plagued by patriarchy and injustice. But such plagues do not mean that the two-parent family form can be rejected, for without it children will in general suffer, and an essential element of New Testament Christianity will be lost (Post 1994). The fact of patriarchy, made explicit in all the classical Protestant statements and the source of much oppression historically, continues to undermine the future of the Protestant family. But this headship patriarchy is giving way to the hard-won influence of feminism and gender equality both in the family and in society. The more traditional Protestant statements can at least be retrieved for their insistence on marriage and family as divinely sanctioned, as potentially filled with conjugal and parental love, and as essential to the building of a good society.

Marriage and family are important in the history of American Protestant so-cial thought. The literature of Protestant ethics gives far more attention to ho-mosexuality and abortion than to marriage and families. Courses in Protestant social ethics reliably take up the state, war, and property as key topics, wrongly assuming that in a just society the family will naturally prosper and does not need much discussion. Arguably, this omission could be due to the midcentury influence of Ernst Troeltsch, through whom the view was spread into social ethics that property relations are of primary importance and social relations of secondary importance.

The Protestant Challenge

If Blankenhorn is correct, many Protestant denominations have abandoned marriage as a vital area of religious attention, essentially handing the entire matter over to opinion leaders and divorce lawyers in the secular society. Such abdication of responsibility is tragic for American children (as well as for married Christians) and may help explain the popularity of more demanding conservative churches.

A socially responsive Protestantism should construct a new ethics of marriage and family that, informed by gender equality, addresses the issue of what spouses owe each other, their children, and outsiders near and far. In such a Christianity, family becomes a central concern of the church, but never so as to exclude or burden those who are called to singleness and never so as to tolerate patriarchal abuses. Practically, the church cannot succeed unless families support its beliefs and values; by the same token, families need the support of the fellowship of believers lest they become insular and exclusionary.

Finally, the Christian family should not be a haven of private separation from outsiders. Rodney Clapp rejects the public-private split typical of the modern bourgeois family, described as a "haven in a heartless world." Clapp is concerned that among evangelicals, Jesus has become a "domestic mascot," and Yahweh a "household god" (1993, 154). He recovers the notion of the Christian home as a mission base open to all sorts of comings and goings, consistent with the pattern of home churches so important in the formation of early Christianity. It is this public purpose that drives family activities, not the privatized ideal of intimacy. Clapp believes that the family, in order to avoid the problem of insularity, must be "decentered by the Church."

Bibliography

Blankenhorn, David. *Fatherless America: Confronting Our Most Urgent Social Problem* (New York: Basic Books, 1995).

Clapp, Rodney. *Families at the Crossroad: Beyond Traditional and Modern Options* (Downers Grove, Ill.: InterVarsity Press, 1993).

Hayes, Richard B. *The Moral Vision of the New Testament* (San Francisco: HarperCollins, 1996).

Patton, John, and Brian H. Childs. *Christian Marriage and Family: Caring for Our Generations* (Nashville: Abingdon Press, 1988).

Post, Stephen G. *Spheres of Love: Toward a New Ethics of the Family* (Dallas: Southern Methodist University Press, 1994).

—STEPHEN GARRARD POST

A Catholic Perspective

A Catholic vision of family is rooted in the crucified and risen Christ. Because the Catholic family is "in Christ," it has the privilege and the responsibility to "be Christ" for family members and others in society. An appropriate definition of how we act as Christ in a family context comes from psychologist Sidney Callahan, who states that families are called to share a common moral purpose: to care for one another and the wider community and to assume responsibility for one another (quoted in Coleman 1991).

Since the Second Vatican Council, the Catholic Church has been constructing a theology of the family that respects its crucial roles as moral agent and as living symbol of Christ in church and society. I believe that three elements of this recent teaching must be emphasized to gain a clear picture of the importance of the Catholic family in today's Church.

1. Recent Catholic teaching asserts that families are inherently holy. This does not occur as a result of church membership per se but because family actions and work, when motivated by faith in Jesus Christ, provide a concrete, day-to-day expression of the love of God.
2. Recent Catholic teaching underscores the idea that families are the smallest unit of faith: They are foundational or "domestic churches."
3. Recent Catholic teaching on the family reflects the challenge to live gospel values.

Families Are Holy

Recent Catholic teaching stresses that the family is inherently holy because it can reveal the presence of Christ in everyday life (*Gaudium et Spes,* art. 48; *Lumen Gentium,* art. 11). Families are sanctified not simply because they engage in activities of the Church as institution but because in and through day-to-day living, they share in Christ's paschal mystery. Through the ordinary events of life—sharing meals, sacrificing for each other, or caring for a sick family member or neighbor—families die to themselves and rise to new life in Jesus Christ. Every time a family reaches out to others—sometimes at great cost—Christ's love is revealed. The idea that ordinary family life is holy is a central element in the contemporary Catholic vision of family.

Families Are Domestic Churches

Catholic teaching underscores the concept that the foundation for faith begins not in the parish church but in the family. Families can function as the smallest unit of faith: They are truly "domestic churches" (McGinnis, in Coleman 1991). The idea that family provides a concrete expression of the body of Christ has its roots in Catholic tradition. It is found in the works of such diverse writers as Augustine, Gregory of Nazianzus, Hugh of St. Victor, Francis de Sales, and of others throughout the history of the Church. Furthermore, since Vatican II, when *Lumen Gentium* described the ancient idea that the faithful *are* the Church and reintroduced the phrase "domestic church" into the Catholic vocabulary, the Church has emphasized the role of the family as the primary agent of faith formation.

The notion that the family serves as the first faith community has two significant implications. First, it assumes that families have the potential and the right to demonstrate and teach faith to spouses, children, and other family members. Second, it presumes an awareness that the faithful, gathered in Christ, *are* the church. If families see the church simply as an institution rather than as an expression of who they are, difficulties can arise. In order to understand "domestic church" correctly, it is essential for Catholic families to realize that they are not called simply to embody a hierarchical institution; they are challenged to *be* the Church—the people of God, living members of the body of Christ.

Families Are Called to Live Gospel Values

Finally, recent Catholic teaching on the family reflects the challenge to live the gospel values of loving God and neighbor. The papal document *Familiaris Consortio* and a document from the National Conference of Catholic Bishops, *A Family Perspective in Church and Society,* articulate four tasks that help specify the ways that families can live these values: families form communities of persons; families serve life; families participate in the development of society; and families share in the mission of the Church.

The first task of the Catholic family is to *form a community of persons,* which takes place on several levels. Family community begins when a marriage in Christian faith takes place. Catholics believe that marriage is a sacrament, a symbol of Christ's love in the world and in the Church. This community continues through a relationship that respects the equality of husbands and wives. Because both male and female are created in God's image and likeness, both possess equal dignity, even if their marital roles are very different. Finally, the community of the family sustains itself by promoting an attitude of moral responsibility and care for the vulnerable, from the unborn to the very old. Catholic families cannot function with a "survival of the fittest" mentality. Instead, they are called to protect the rights of all. The notion that families are called to build a community is at the heart of Catholic teaching. Family is not simply a collection of individuals related by blood, adoption, or marriage; it is a community that serves as a model of love, compassion, and fidelity for the entire Church.

The second task of the Catholic family is *to serve life* generously. Openness to the possibility of new life is a basic element of Catholic teaching, but serving life goes far beyond procreation. Service to life builds on the foundation of the family community, for it is in the family that we first support efforts to uphold and nurture life. In daily life, families are challenged to make choices for life rather than against it. For example, parents can encourage an atmosphere of respect for all life; children can sacrifice time and talent to support family goals; adult relatives can serve as faith models to younger members of the family. As the book of Deuteronomy so clearly states: Choose life, that you might live! (Deut. 30:15–20).

A Catholic family does not simply exist for itself; rather it shares its talents and blessings with and for the church and world communities. Recent Catholic social teaching as well as Vatican II documents such as *Gaudium et Spes* remind us that part of the task of Catholic life in general, and Catholic family life in particular, is to *participate in the development of society,* the third task. A Catholic family vision asserts that families are called to be "the light of the world" (Matt. 5:14).

Families can participate in the development of society in very simple ways. For example, family meetings and shared decision making can provide an environment in which all members, young and old, experience participation. Moreover, all family members can become involved in projects that support the beliefs of the family.

Finally, Catholic families are called to *share in the mission of the Church.* While this includes participating in the life of the local parish, it also implies *becoming* church in the daily events of family life. Catholic families have unique opportunities to share in the mission of the church. For example, many couples attempt to grow as symbols of Christ's love to the Church and to the world through the sacrament of marriage. When they take time to share a family meal, and to give thanks for each other in the context of sharing food and drink, they participate in the eucharistic action of the Church. When they welcome a person, young or old, into their midst, one of the key elements of Christian initiation occurs. When they forgive one another as Jesus did, the ministry of reconciliation becomes real in family life. When families care for their sick, their hands are those of Jesus, healing those with infirmities. And finally, when persons serve as leaders for prayer and spirituality in their families, the ministry of orders comes alive in their hearts and homes.

These ecclesial actions take place in families throughout the world. The Catholic vision of family demands that we become who we are—the body of Christ—that we live as community and reach out to others in our church and world. It also challenges us to embrace the sacramental principle in our daily lives—to become living symbols of Christ in a world that so desperately needs his presence.

Bibliography

Coleman, John, S. J., ed. *One Hundred Years of Catholic Social Thought* (Maryknoll, N.Y.: Orbis Books, 1991). In particular, see articles on family.

Curran, Dolores. *Traits of a Healthy Family* (San Francisco: HarperCollins, 1983).

Heaney-Hunter, Joann. "The Domestic Church Proclaims the Gospel of Life," *Living Light* 32 (fall 1995): 27–38.

John Paul II. *Familiaris Consortio* (Washington, D.C.: United States Catholic Conference, 1981), art. 18–64.

National Conference of Catholic Bishops. Committee on Marriage and the Family. *A Family Perspective in Church and Society* (Washington, D.C.: United States Catholic Conference, 1988).

—JOANN HEANEY-HUNTER

A Jewish Perspective

Judaism perceives family as closely intertwined with individual self-fulfillment and with the building of a healthy society. Not only are these units closely interrelated, but the health of each depends upon the health of the other two. More particularly, family is the essential building block and prerequisite for the construction of human society.

Genesis in particular serves as a paradigm for Jewish perceptions of family and family ties. Genesis by no means suggests an idyllic portrait of family. On the contrary, it perceives family conflict as normative and urges working toward reconciling relationships within family units. Ultimately that reconciliation serves as the building block for wider social units and the construction of communities.

The opening chapters of Genesis narrate the creation of Adam. The Adam of Genesis 1 is majestic. He is enjoined to go out and conquer, to rule over nature and the universe. By contrast, the Adam of Genesis 2 is far more limited. He appears as a vulnerable creature, lonely and in need of human comfort. Rabbinic tradition, looking at this dual account of the creation of man, exalted the male-female unit as co-creator with the Almighty. To attain the status of majestic man, it was first necessary to create the family unit of husband and wife. In rabbinic tradition, marriage signified *shelemut,* or "wholeness." Through marriage, men and women were given the opportunity to become partners and co-creators with God.

Yet Genesis quickly proceeds to tell a tale of family breakup. Cain destroys the primeval family by murdering his own brother. Cain's reasons appear to lie in placing personal self-fulfillment over familial responsibility. Yet the tale of Cain's development serves as a biblical paradigm for repentance. Cain regrets his action, suffers punishment, and undergoes rehabilitation. Cain marries and has a son—one of the great mysteries of Genesis is whom Cain married—but the significance of his becoming a father lies in building a city, the earliest recorded form of civilization. It is as if fatherhood and family have taught Cain that social responsibility transcends personal needs for self-fulfillment. By becoming a "family man," Cain becomes a socially responsible citizen.

Perhaps the clearest illustration of this view in Genesis of the constellation of individual/family/community lies in the tale of Judah and his emergence from the sale of Joseph to leadership among the sons of Jacob, and by extension leadership of the Jewish people. Our first glimpse of Judah casts him as destroyer of Jacob's family. He is the architect of the sale of Joseph. Like Cain he appears to place personal self-fulfillment over responsibility to others. After the sale of Joseph, Judah leaves the family nest, perhaps a suggestion that he was responsible for the breakup of Jacob's family. He meets Tamar, who teaches him the importance of commitments and responsibilities.

With this lesson learned, Judah is able to take responsibility for the fate of Benjamin, his youngest brother. Judah demonstrates to Joseph that he indeed has changed. He no longer is prepared simply to cut the best deal for himself and ignore his commitments to other members of the family. Judah's concluding speech effectively "overcomes" Joseph, meaning that Judah has demonstrated his claim to leadership of the Jewish people through his taking responsibility for his actions and fulfilling his commitments to family members. He effectively shows Joseph what Joseph is not—a family man. By placing Genesis before Exodus, Scripture in effect suggests that building family is the prerequisite for the building of nationhood.

These tales of Genesis are didactic in several senses. First, they describe the family as a mediating institution between the individual and the broader society. The family is the setting in which individuals learn social responsibility to others. Second, it is assumed that conflict will take place within the family. If the solution to conflict lies in murder, as Cain thought, clearly the Jews and civilization generally are doomed. Rather, Judah's example teaches us about the willingness to pursue struggle within the family until reconciliation may be attained.

Last, Genesis approaches issues of sexuality in unabashedly moral language. Sexual relations are not evaluated on the basis of functionality; they are fundamentally moral matters. Therefore Genesis evokes a language of authority, demands, and judgment of behaviors—criteria that are often politically incorrect in contemporary American society. To be sure, Genesis contains examples of healthy sexuality; Jacob is perhaps the first romantic lover in classical literature. But Genesis, and later rabbinical commentary as well, insisted on the primacy of moral values and judgments in evaluating sexual behaviors.

Jewish tradition contains a wealth of resources that can cement family ties. Abraham Joshua Heschel understood this beautifully in defining the Sabbath as sacred time for families to be families together. Heschel saw the Sabbath as a twenty-four-hour retreat from our worldly experiences that provided us an opportunity to sanctify the time around us through personal relationships and family ties. The Sabbath, in effect, provided a structure by which families could be families together across the Jewish table. Divorce is much lower among religiously observant Jewish couples not because it is prohibited but rather because families celebrating Judaism together become stronger families in the process. Most important, the community has an educational responsibility to broadcast the message that for families to succeed will require enormous work and commitment.

Finally, in approaching family issues, Judaism underscores the well-being of children. On one level, that does mean discouraging divorce even as we acknowledge the reality of the single-parent home. Historically, Jewish courts spared no efforts to prevent divorce by reconciling conflicts. Yet they also recognized that divorce was often a necessary solution to a failed marriage. Our challenge today lies, first, in encouraging a greater bias in favor of marriage, especially in the therapeutic professions and the media culture.

Once divorce has occurred, the community can and should seek to strengthen the single-parent home. The values of tradition and religion can often serve as buffer and anchor in the turbulent world following divorce. Research on syna-gogues has demonstrated that the synagogue can often serve as a surrogate extended family, providing a message of continuity and stability for children of divorce.

Can we then speak of family values today? The state should not be regulating individual conduct, nor should the state intervene in the private relations within families except to prevent abuses. Yet the voices of society and the moral authority of the public square ought to be marshaled in a campaign to restore the primacy of family as a value. We should be willing to assert our cultural preferences for traditional norms such as marriage and the two-parent home while at the same time accommodating and reaching out to those who have chosen to lead their lives within alternative settings. We need have no nostalgia for the mythical nuclear family of the 1950s. Conversely, however, we have no need to redefine the family so as to recognize all possible living arrangements as being equally preferable. Recognizing what exists is not the same as stating what ought to be.

—STEVEN BAYME

A Secular Legal Perspective

Secular legal definitions of the family tend to dominate America today. Unlike many nation-states—which grant deference, sometimes even autonomy, to diverse religious or customary systems of family law—the American state holds preeminent legal power over the family. To be sure, American family law still reflects some of the basic ideas and institutions of Protestantism, Catholicism, and Judaism on which it was founded. Marriages are still contracted in churches or synagogues. Broken families still go to priests or rabbis for state-licensed counseling or mediation. Civil courts still refuse to compel Catholic and Jewish authorities to grant religious divorces. But, for the most part, the laws and policies of the secular state govern the formation, function, and dissolution of families.

American law today defines the family as a married couple—or a widow, widower, or divorcee—cohabiting with one or more natural children, adopted children, or stepchildren. It defines marriage as a monogamous, heterosexual union properly contracted between a fit man and woman of the age of consent. Historically, valid marriage contracts required the consent of parents or guardians, two witnesses, church consecration, and civil licensing and registration. Today, the marital contract normally requires only the formalities of licensing and registration. Historically, states imposed criminal prohibitions against same-sex and polygamous families. Today, prohibitions against same-sex couples have become dead letters in most states and are subject to increasing (and occasionally successful) constitutional attack. Historically, sharp distinctions were drawn between illegitimate children born out of wedlock and legitimate children born to or adopted by a married couple. Today, both the federal Constitution and state statutes accord such children equal protection under the law.

Defining the family is not an idle exercise in legal taxonomy. Numerous special rights and privileges attach to this institution and its members. A marital or family unit is subject to its own standards and forms of income, property, and inheritance tax. A person can be compelled to testify in court but may be exempted from testimony against a spouse, parent, or child. A woman may bring charges against a man who forcibly abducts her, but in several states the marital-rape exemption precludes such charges against her husband. Even an estranged spouse or natural child automatically inherits from a party who dies without a will, while intimate lovers or wards require special testamentary provisions. Federal and state laws are honeycombed with such special provisions for family members.

American law today retains the traditional presumption that one of the principal purposes of marriage is to beget and raise children. In many states, premarital conception of a child is a sufficient ground for marriage, even absent minimal formalities of marital formation. Sterility, frigidity, and impotence are sufficient grounds for dissolution of a marriage. A person who marries a widow, widower, or divorcee is automatically rendered a stepparent to his or her spouse's children and has a strong claim for adoption of these children.

Today, the state plays an active role in the care, protection, and education of children, even within the nuclear family. Historically, the parent-child relationship was largely beyond the purview of state law. Parents owed their children a minimal duty of care, which if violated led to criminal sanctions. Prohibitions against incest, battery, and cruelty set outer boundaries to parental conduct. But governance of the parent-child relationship was left principally to the individual family, as well as to the church, synagogue, and charity. The past three decades have seen an explosive growth of state laws governing adoption, child custody, child support, child abuse, juvenile delinquency, education of minors, and similar subjects. Abused minor children are plucked from their natural homes with increasing ease. State welfare agencies, and even adolescent children themselves, are suing delinquent parents and guardians with increasing success. The legal principle of "the best interests of the child" has begun to eclipse traditional legal principles of protecting paternal autonomy and preserving blood relations.

American law today generally treats spouses as equal parties in the marriage. A generation ago, American law still drew sharp distinctions between the roles and rights of the man and the woman. Husbands and fathers were treated as leaders and representatives of the family for purposes of marital property and commerce, inheritance, and taxation, among others. Wives and mothers were considered the primary nurturers, educators, and caretakers of their children and were often restricted in their ability to hold, use, or alienate marital property, or to enter into various legal transactions. Such presumptions and restrictions have now largely fallen aside. Husband and wife generally have equal rights and responsibilities in matters of work, commerce, and family finance. Father and mother are equally responsible for the care and protection of their children, both during marriage and thereafter.

No-fault divorce statutes, now in place in almost every state, provide a simple, though expensive, means for dissolution of a marriage. Until one or two generations ago, a suit for divorce generally required a showing of cause—adultery, desertion, cruelty, and the like. Today, such causes need not be alleged, though proof of them often triggers increased payments of alimony and other property to the victim and reduced rights of custody to the wrongdoer. Historically, divorce and annulment were subject to separate rules and procedures. Divorce was a judgment that a once properly contracted marriage was now broken. Annulment was a judgment that the putative marriage was null and void from the start by reason of an impediment—the impotence, imbecility, contagion, or other blemish of one of the parties. Today, most states treat both forms of dissolution under one divorce proceeding.

Contemporary American law has not been immune to the escalating costs of divorce, particularly to minor children and dependent spouses. Several states now mandate family mediation and counseling as a condition to hearing a divorce pleading in court. Divisions of common marital property often favor the once-dependent spouse. Most states still grant custody of minor children to the natural mother, but they have imposed on her a high burden of proof to demonstrate her parental fitness and have accorded fathers (and sometimes grandparents) increasingly liberal rights of visitation, supervision, and sometimes even joint custody of their children. Federal and state laws now mandate that noncustodial parents pay substantial portions of their income in the form of child support, and they punish delinquency in payment with unprecedented severity. Such legal changes, taken together, have helped to flatten the divorce rate and to preserve stronger relations and responsibilities among both divorcees and their children.

Bibliography

Clark, Homer H. *The Law of Domestic Relations in the United States,* 2d ed. (St. Paul: West Publishing, 1988).

Glendon, Mary Ann. *The Transformation of Family Law in the United States and Western Europe* (Chicago: University of Chicago Press, 1989).

Krause, Harry. *Family Law in a Nutshell,* 3rd ed. (St. Paul: West Publishing, 1995)

Regan, Milton C. *Family Law and the Pursuit of Intimacy* (New York and London: New York University Press, 1993).

Schneider, Carl E. "Moral Discourse and the Transformation of American Family Law," *Michigan Law Review* 83(1985): 1803.

—JOHN WITTE, JR.

3

Divorce and Remarriage

A Legal Perspective

When has a marriage failed? Legally a marriage has failed when the court declares that one party has demonstrated that statutory grounds exist to terminate the marriage. The grounds range from the traditional fault-based grounds of adultery and cruelty to the now-ubiquitous "no-fault" grounds. This wealth of allowable grounds for divorce in America developed through three stages that roughly parallel Roman Catholic, Protestant, and Jewish beliefs about marriage.

First was the Roman Catholic stage: The marriage ends only when one spouse dies, although separation from bed and board was allowed. If a marriage was invalidly contracted, the court's declaration that it never existed could annul it, but if a marriage was validly contracted, the court was powerless to end it.

Second was what might be called the Protestant stage: A court could end a marriage if one spouse proved that the other breached the marriage contract by dishonoring the sanctity of the union and its fundamental purpose of procreation. Adultery, refusal to bear children, refusal to support the family by desertion, and extreme cruelty were among the prohibited acts. The guilty party was punished by the imposition of the divorce decree and, if male, by the requirement to pay spousal support. If female, the guilty was punished by having her right to spousal support terminated with the marriage.

Finally, what might be called the Jewish stage began: no-fault divorce. In the Jewish tradition the marriage ends upon the statement of the husband that it is over. No reason need be given. The dominant ground for divorce in America today is no-fault, and the wife as well as the husband may seek divorce. Most states continue to provide for divorce on the basis of fault and have simply added a no-fault ground to the list of fault grounds. In addition, most continue to provide for annulment and for legal separation.

No-fault divorce is based on the assumption that the legal process of proving fault adds stress to an already stressful situation. The assumption is that the marriage is in fact broken when someone asks for a divorce and that the legal system has become a hoop through which the parties must jump to ratify legally a factual reality. It does not privilege continuance of marriage by making divorce an exception allowed in limited circumstances, a status difficult to achieve. It focuses on the happiness of the two individual partners, assuming that minimally restricting individual autonomy best advances society's interest. Because requiring alimony, child support, and property distribution guards society's economic interest, there remains no legitimate interest of society in maintaining the marriage of the parties despite their desire to end it.

No-fault statutes generally require the moving party to prove that there is an "irreconcilable difference" or that the relationship is "irretrievably broken." In interpreting the statutory language, some courts require proof that the marriage is broken and that reconciliation will not occur even if it is assisted by therapy or mediation. Other courts have decided that one party's declaration is sufficient to prove that the mutuality of the marriage is broken. The difference between the two is in the fact finding of the court. In the former the judge decides independently about the relationship of the parties; in the latter the judge does not.

One criticism of no-fault divorce is that the ease of gaining one may tempt an unhappy person to divorce rather than try to work through problems of the relationship. Since there are social costs in divorce—if nothing else, the cost of recordkeeping—states have imposed some barriers to overutilization. Georgia, for example, requires a thirty-day cooling-off period between the filing for the divorce and the grant of the divorce; however, the parties can appear at the perfunctory hearing through a single attorney authorized to represent both parties. California uses the device of not allowing the order of divorce to become final for six months, and Wisconsin requires mediation where there are children of the marriage.

The divorce revolution—allowing the parties to decide that the marriage is over without any outside interference—is not complete in states that require an evidentiary hearing to decide whether or not the marriage is irretrievably broken. The distinction is of practical importance. For example, if the wife has committed adultery and wishes to marry her paramour, but the husband, although very upset, does not want a divorce, a state like Missouri, where the court must agree that the marriage is irretrievably broken, might refuse the decree. In Florida, which recognizes as a sufficient ground the honest belief of one spouse that the marriage is over, the divorce would be granted.

The interests of the state and the church in the status of marriage differ. The state always wants to know who is married to whom because myriad intricate property interests and financial obligations depend on the answer to the question: everything from claims for spousal support to income tax obligations, from the right to decide medical treatment to the obligation to pay for it depends on marital status. By contrast, the interest of the church revolves around the relationship its members have with God and how marriage relates to the manifestation of that relationship in the world.

Legal doctrines of divorce are relevant only to those who are married. They do not apply to people living together without benefit of marriage. Nonetheless, the termination of any long-term, emotionally committed relationship is like a divorce. The issues of emotional support for the parties as they adjust their economic and social lives are substantially the same, and churches are in a position to provide leadership in recognizing that the partners in these nonmarital relationships are humans who have an equal claim to charity, support, and guidance.

Churches can reinforce and enhance the attempts of courts and the legal system to support the permanence of marriage and the seriousness of its commitments while nurturing healthy personal relationships. They can use their public voice to encourage people to take responsibility for their actions, to meet their commitments, and to consider the impact of their behavior beyond how it contributes to their transient sense of personal happiness. The church might do this by using rhetoric and liturgy that make clear that marriage is not to be cast aside lightly; though civil authority may be willing to change the status of marriage easily, the church views the covenant as requiring more than a minimal effort from the parties before they declare it a failure. In fact, the effort required might even be sacrificial.

Churches can continue to provide personal support through the familiar ritual of the liturgy and through individual counseling. Premarital counseling can help assure maturity and realism about marriage that may help make divorce a choice of last resort, not first. Churches can extend the counseling role when they provide communities that serve as extended family. A social ministry can provide protection to families. For example, when the stress of caring for children or elders makes a couple consider divorce as a form of relief, members of the church can provide an alternative by serving as temporary caregiver.

When a marriage begins to fall apart, the extended community can provide opportunities for a "reality check," an opportunity to explore what it will really be like if divorce were granted. Specifically in predivorce counseling, questions about how the person will live and what problems will really disappear along with the spouse can be addressed in a way that does not allow for fanciful answers. The extended community in which divorce is not the norm can also serve as a buffer against impulsive seeking of divorce.

For example, it is not unusual for a wife to throw her adulterous husband out—or to find that her failure to do so is viewed as a lack of self-respect (as evidenced by the intense media debate over Dick Morris's wife's decision to stand by him after the media revealed his relationship with a prostitute). The media, friends, and families all tell the injured spouse to "throw the bum out!" Yet she may desire to make the marriage work. This may require that she ignore the wishes and advice of those from whom she would ordinarily obtain the support she now needs. Churches can step into this void. They can bring to bear a long tradition of forgiveness and understanding, a sure knowledge that even the most egregious of sins need not be the basis for ending the marriage. The church can help advisers understand the power of forgiveness and the need to support the injured spouse who is trying to forgive.

Sometimes divorce is the best answer. When churches excommunicated the adulterer or refused the sacraments to one who deserted family, they declared publicly that some behavior would not be tolerated. Now the court declares that there is no fault in the breakup of the marriage, and the church may well allow the erring spouse to continue as a full member. There is no forum in which the innocent spouse can be vindicated or absolved. The lack of such a forum sometimes drives costly legal fights over children and property. Perhaps churches can help meet this need.

The legal system cannot effectively address the religious activities of divorcing couples when the activities are in conflict. This inability manifests itself in at least four situations. The first three involve children born of the marriage:

1. When children's understanding of their religious tradition brands the behavior of a parent—the divorcing wrong-doer—as sinful.

2. When differences between religious traditions of the parents lead to disagreements about religious upbringing of children. Prenuptial agreements may attempt to resolve the issue, but the solutions such agreements envisage may not be practical. For example, a Jewish father and a Catholic mother may have agreed to raise their children in the Catholic tradition, but this becomes impracticable if the children live with the father after the divorce.

3. When the parties find comfort in their religion during divorce and that "comfort" leads to a heightened commitment to their respective religious roots. The new religious commitment may place unexpected demands on the children after the divorce.

A fourth instance in which the legal system provides little assistance is when one party desires a religious divorce. For example, in the rabbinical courts today still only the husband may seek the divorce. Because the religious divorce can be granted only when religious rules are followed, a husband who does not want the divorce can prevent his wife from obtaining the religious divorce even though he has obtained a civil divorce. This presents a great problem for a deeply religious woman. In the world of civil obligation she is no longer married and has no claim against her husband or his property except that which the civil court has granted. Yet the wife is still married religiously and therefore cannot remarry a religious Jew. Because of the separation of church and state, the husband's refusal to obtain a religious divorce is not a ground for refusing to grant a civil divorce if the plaintiff husband has demonstrated that the grounds required by the civil statute exist. New York has addressed this problem by providing that a court may make it a condition of the grant of the civil divorce that the parties cooperate in obtaining a religious divorce *if the marriage was religiously contracted.* In states that have not addressed the issue, churches and synagogues must consider ways to allow the "abandoned" spouses to achieve conciliation with their religious traditions.

In sum, churches and synagogues can help provide the context for strong, secure marriages by creating communities in which everyone strives to honor the commitments of marriage, by counseling individuals, and by helping to model full understanding of the human condition, including ways for children

of divorce to reconcile the behavior of their parents with the child's understandings of religion.

Bibliography

Elon, Menachem, ed. *Principles of Jewish Law* (Jerusalem: Encyclopaedia Judaica, 1975).
Jacob, Herbert. *Silent Revolution: The Transformation of Divorce Law in the United States*
(Chicago: University of Chicago Press, 1988).
Wardle, Lynn D. "No-Fault Divorce and the Divorce Conundrum," *Brigham Young Uni-
versity Law Review* 79. 1(1991): 79–142.

—HARRIET KING

A Catholic Perspective

Questions raised worldwide concerning divorce and remarriage today confront all Christian churches. Not one of them, not even the Roman Catholic church, whose teaching on divorce and remarriage appears to be firm, escapes them. What should religious institutions do about divorce and remarriage? First, they should refocus their attention away from divorce and toward marriage, and contribute to the rebuilding of a family culture based on lasting marital relationships. Second, as one contribution to rebuilding marital relationships, they should pay closer attention to the ancient Orthodox practice of *oikonomia*. *Oikonomia* flourishes within a context of Spirit and Grace, not within a context of law; it grows out of faith in the Spirit of God and of Christ. It heeds the scriptural injunction that "the letter kills, but the Spirit gives life" (2 Cor. 3:6).

What does *oikonomia* have to say to the churches about divorce and remarriage? It admonishes them to be realistic, to understand that, though the gospel demands that marriages be lifelong, real men and real women sometimes do not fully measure up to the gospel. It instructs them that marriages, even marriages between Christians, sometimes die, and that when they die it makes no sense to argue that they are still binding. When a marriage is dead, even when the former spouses still live, *oikonomia* moves the churches to be sad—for the death of a marriage is always the death of a domestic church—but also to be compassionate, even to the point of permitting the remarriage of an innocent spouse. The ritual of that remarriage, however, is not on a par with the first marriage, now dissolved, as the liturgy makes clear.

There are prayers for the couple and there are petitions that the spouses be pardoned for their transgressions. Absent is the unbridled joy of the first-marriage ceremony; present is sorrow and repentance for its failure. Present too is the necessary confession that no one in attendance, including the church's minister, is without sin. The economy of Spirit and Grace is always threatened by sin; the Christian ideal is ever at the mercy of human frailty. It is precisely in such an economy that the church of Christ is summoned to minister and to be compassionate on behalf of the compassionate God.

A reasonable Christian objection arises at this point. Should not what the churches do about divorce and remarriage be based on the tradition in which they claim to stand, namely, the tradition of Jesus mediated to them in the New Testament? Yes, it should, and though this brief essay cannot fully examine that foundation, neither can it suggest what churches should do about divorce and remarriage without some brief consideration of the foundation.

Four times the Gospels report sayings of Jesus about divorce and remarriage: in Mark 10:11–12, in Matthew 5:32 and 19:9, and in Luke 16:18. Paul also acknowledges a command about divorce and remarriage, attributes it to the Lord (1 Cor. 7:10–11), and immediately goes on in v. 12 to make an exception to it on his own authority ("I and not the Lord"). The exception concerns a case that must have been common in Corinth, the case of an unbeliever unwilling to continue living with a recently converted spouse. There is no suggestion that their marriage is in any way invalid, and there is no suggestion that Jesus' remembered command does not apply to it. There is only the suggestion that Paul is making an exception to it. The reason he offers for the exception is of great interest, in the twenty-first century as in the first: "In such a case the brother or sister is not bound. It is to peace that God has called you" (7:15).

Paul made his exception to Jesus' command on the basis of a common situation in the church of Corinth. Matthew also made an exception, on the basis of a situation in his Jewish-Christian church—that is, a church composed of Jews who were followers of Jesus but who still adhered to the Jewish law. "Whoever divorces his wife, except for unchastity [*porneia,*] and marries another," he reports, "commits adultery" (Matt. 19:9). The meaning of that exceptive phrase has been, and continues to be, hotly debated in the churches, but I do not wish to enter into that debate. I wish to raise here a different question. Does the exceptive clause originate with Jesus or with Matthew; does it derive from the teaching of Jesus or from the authorship of Matthew? I submit, with the majority scholarly opinion, that the latter is the case, given the absence of the phrase in Mark, Luke, and Paul and given Matthew's recognized penchant for adding to the words of Jesus for his own purposes. I am interested in only one conclusion from that. Being fully aware of Jesus' position, Matthew, like Paul, did not hesitate to alter it in the light of the needs of his church.

This brief consideration leads to two conclusions. The first is that it is incorrect to speak of the New Testament *teaching* on divorce and remarriage, for there are several *teachings,* and unfortunately they do not all agree. The second is that not all these teachings derive from Jesus, though this is frequently and simplistically claimed as the reason that some churches, particularly the Roman Catholic, continue to oppose divorce and remarriage. Diverging accounts of divorce and remarriage, as of many other important human questions, are an integral part of the New Testament tradition, as the followers of Jesus sought to translate the meaning of his life, death, and resurrection into their concrete lives. There are diverging accounts, scholars now believe, because there were different Christian communities with different questions to be answered. That popular unwisdom later singled out one element in those diverging accounts—namely, the demand for indissoluble marriage—and allowed that single element to override all the others should not obscure the original divergence.

The process of interpreting the Lord's command concerning divorce and remarriage did not end with the New Testament church; it continued in the churches of both East and West. The East developed its doctrine of *oikonomia* related to marriage, and the West developed its law related to marriage, which continues in force today, especially in the Roman Catholic church. In the twelfth century, the Bologna canonist Gratian developed two pieces of legislation that continue to be a central part of that Roman Catholic law. The first was a continuation of Paul's exception, now called the Pauline Privilege, which remains today one of the bases on which the Catholic church grants the dissolution of a valid marriage. In a series of rulings that came to be misleadingly known as the Petrine Privilege, succeeding popes—Paul III (1537), Pius V (1561), and Gregory XIII (1585)—extended the Pauline Privilege to cases Paul never envisioned. The second piece of legislation was a compromise solution between the Roman and northern European answers to the question of when a valid marriage came into existence. Marriage is initiated by betrothal (consent) and perfected (or consummated) by sexual intercourse.

These two pieces of legislation became enshrined as the law of the Roman Catholic church with respect to the indissolubility of marriage. That church regards as indissoluble only the marriage that both is sacramental *and* has been consummated by sexual intercourse (Can. 1141). It holds all other marriages to be dissoluble, and it dissolves them on occasion "for a just reason" (Can. 1142) or "in favor of the faith" (Can. 1143). It does not require much insight to see that both these legal bases for dissolving a marriage go far beyond the Lord's gospel command. Good Jew that he was, Jesus could never have had in mind when speaking about marriage and divorce the medieval European notions of sacrament and consummation.

Several things are clear. First, in spite of every claim to be only following the Lord's command, the churches of both East and West have also followed Paul and Matthew in interpreting that command on the basis of their ongoing situations. Second, it is not true that the Roman Catholic Church never grants divorces. It grants them regularly in marriages that are not sacramental or not consummated, though it obscures that fact by naming the process *dissolution* rather than *divorce*. Third, though there is no warrant in the New Testament for such legal processes, there is ample warrant for *oikonomia,* a fact to which the Council of Trent attested. Despite hewing to a rigid line on the question of the indissolubility of marriage, the Council steadfastly refused to condemn the practice of *oikonomia* or to declare that it did not have equal claim to the gospel tradition and to the name Christian.

To conclude in plain English, the Orthodox practice of *oikonomia* is firmly rooted in the New Testament, more firmly rooted than the medieval marriage laws that are causing widespread suffering to many divorced and remarried Christians. The churches, including the Roman Catholic Church, should embrace it—adapting it if necessary to their ongoing traditions—as a way to alleviate that suffering and to attain the ecclesial peace and communion to which, Paul says, God has called us (1 Cor. 7:15). If divorce is a problem for the churches, and today it is a major problem, that peace and communion will create an ecclesial climate freeing the churches to focus on the unhappy, and sometimes brutal, marriages that inevitably lead to divorce. Those unchristian marriages, not the divorces to which they lead, are the real problems awaiting resolution.

Bibliography

Häring, Bernard. *No Way Out? Pastoral Care of the Divorced and Remarried* (Slough, England: Saint Paul Publications, 1990).

Kelly, Kevin. *Divorce and Second Marriage: Facing the Challenge* (New York: Seabury Press, 1983).

Lawler, Michael G. *Marriage and Sacrament: A Theology of Christian Marriage* (Collegeville, Minn.: Liturgical Press, 1993).

Malone, Richard, and J. R. Connery, eds. *Contemporary Perspectives on Christian Marriage* (Chicago: Loyola University Press, 1984).

Meyendorff, John. *Marriage: An Orthodox Perspective* (New York: Saint Vladimir's Seminary Press, 1978).

—MICHAEL LAWLER

A Protestant Perspective

As recently as the 1960s, divorce and remarriage earned a special taboo in the Protestant churches of the United States. The general rule said that the innocent party to a divorce could remarry, provided the cause was adultery or willful desertion. As a result of research by a number of people—especially in the Lutheran and Presbyterian churches—new guidelines were developed.

According to these new guidelines, there was generally no such thing as an "innocent" party. The real issue concerned "readiness for marriage." Was the past marriage really dead? Did the parties to a new marriage have that sense of repentance, commitment, and healing which would allow for a new marriage?

These new guidelines began with the assumption that "all have sinned and come short of the glory of God." To speak of an innocent party simply made no sense. Guidelines appeared in denominational constitutions. Some groups had a bishops' council that would review all marriage requests where a divorce had been involved. Others presented procedures whereby pastors had guidelines to follow with "fall-back" help if needed.

In those days, some of us recommended a period of counseling and then a meeting of the couple with a representative group of the parish governing body. Two things happened: Some churches did it well and received positive responses from the couples involved; the couples expressed appreciation for the sense of community and community support. Alternatively, some church judicatories would not take the responsibility. The reasons ranged from "we simply do not have the time" to "Pastor, you are the expert and that is your job."

As time passed, church constitutions changed, and the matter slowly dropped out of any document. The reigning attitude seemed to be that this was a question of congregational practice and not constitutional law. As a result, whereas once we had a theologically unsound base for a rule on the remarriage of divorced persons, we now have the chaos and inconsistency of as many rules and regulations as there are denominations, if not parishes. It is as though we rid ourselves of one devil, ten more inhabited the house, and the latter condition proved worse than the former.

The Problem

More than one divorced person could identify with the testimony of a former parishioner: "When I walked out of the divorce court with the paper in my hand," she said, "I felt that I saw one great word emblazoned in the sky: Failure." I refer here not to those who marry for convenience or out of impulse. In these few pages, I am talking about people of faith who married sincerely but whose marriages died. For more and more, the issue lies not so much in guilt as in a sense of failure, shame, and inadequacy.

Today's problem is exacerbated by two issues defined by David Harvey of Johns Hopkins University as typical of the postmodern condition: the reduction of space and of time. Lack of space to live one's life and "instant" everything require an opportunity for coming to terms with whatever happens to us, including divorce. The pressures on a marriage are tremendous. For all its growing secularism, the Puritan ethic of the past, joined by a Confucian ethic brought by the current influx of Asians, leads to little patience with oneself about this failure in marriage.

The psychiatrist, Donald L. Nathanson, has written that shame involves failure to live up to one's self-expectations (Nathanson 1992). The feeling of divorce as a failure lifts up the classic picture of the Adam and Eve story. Adam and Eve did not so much feel guilt for having disobeyed God as they felt embarrassment when discovered by God and thus sought to cover themselves.

Whereas those of us who wrote on the subject of divorce and remarriage in the fifties and sixties emphasized the need to have a forgiveness that dealt with guilt, today congregations need to emphasize a freedom that releases us from bondage to the shame—a shame that may express itself in anything from mild embarrassment to psychic withdrawal.

The couple that comes with a request for remarriage today, then, will bring a host of specific issues plus the "wounds" from the divorce experience that need healing. The church of today must be aware of the generic issue of shame, the possible guilt, and a forgiveness that allows freedom to meet both.

The Need

In any marriage, "readiness for marriage" stands as a key issue. The goals of preparation for remarriage therefore become the clarification of questions such as one's "call" or vocation for marriage, the genuine death of the prior marriage, and readiness for this new marriage; the replacing of shame or guilt with what I have called "the realization of forgiveness"; and the location of symbols that can make real the new relationship.

The keystone of this readiness lies in the move from the experience of the fall and death represented in Genesis 3 to wholeness and new life represented in the gospel. Paul summarizes the move when he writes to the church in Corinth (2 Cor. 5:16), "even though we once knew Christ from a human point of view, we know him no longer in that way." The goal of the premarriage conferences is a sense of being new creatures in Christ. "If anyone is in Christ, there is a new creation." In line with Paul's concept of the move from the First Adam to the New Adam, the key element is the freedom to leave behind what lies behind and move into the creativity of a new relationship.

The Process

The pastoral process then involves the following steps:

1. *A community context in which the process can take place.* This community may be a small discussion group, a formal

group from a church community, or, ultimately, a worshiping congregation that affirms this process through the service of worship.

2. *Premarriage counseling of both parties—separately and together.* This counseling gives the opportunity to explore individual feelings and concerns, to develop processes of interaction and communication between the two parties, and to discover those symbols that will make real the "new creation" of the coming marriage. This matter of developing such symbols too often is overlooked. The priest-in-charge cannot assume that the liturgy of the denomination automatically provides those symbols. The lighting of a candle, the use of anointing, some symbol that comes from the unique cultures of each person, the creation of the vows themselves—all become bases for creating symbols that work to make real this new marriage. It cannot be assumed that even the contemporary liturgies meet the need.

3. *An official community action.* The community needs to take some action that makes clear its backing and support. This action may be a formal motion on the books of the governing board to approve the remarriage itself. Because that approach suggests a presumption that many church groups do not wish to take, the official action may be more an approval expressed in the service of worship at which the marriage will take place than a formal action by a church body. This action then is lifted up in the service of worship itself by a litany or an act of the pastor who says something like, "As many in this congregation as do support and affirm these two as they come to this moment of marriage, please say, 'I do.'"

4. *The decision of the pastor or priest-in-charge regarding his or her participation.* In any decision for a particular service of marriage, four parties are concerned: the man, the woman, the pastor, and the community of faith. Too often, people assume that only the couple makes the decision. But the pastor or priest-in-charge also needs to make a personal decision. The pastor, as a person, may decline to participate in the marriage ceremony for reasons of conscience, concern about the couple, or even lack of rapport with the couple. A negative response on the part of the pastor does not necessarily mean, however, that the couple should not marry.

5. Finally, then, there must be *the public service of worship at which the liturgy allows both for making real and celebrating*

the act of marriage. And subsequent to the marriage itself, the couple needs to identify with some faith community as a community support for the marriage.

Conclusion

The fact of many divorces in our time should provide a caution flag for all who would either enter into a marriage relationship or facilitate the marriage. Yet the strength of marriages that, even today, endure for many years and provide a basis for family and personal growth must not be overlooked. Marriage is more than a cultural practice or an institution of society. In the Christian community, marriage is a process that reflects the mystery of Christ and the church. Marriage is a process in which the fullness of life comes to men and women in the midst of the pressures of this postmodern day.

Bibliography

The books of discipline and the books of worship or prayer of different faith groups.

Emerson, James G., Jr. *Divorce, the Church, and Remarriage* (Philadelphia: Westminster Press, 1961).

Nathanson, Donald L. *Shame and Pride* (New York: Norton Press, 1992).

Rambo, Lewis. *The Divorcing Christian* (Nashville: Abingdon Press, 1983).

Richards, Larry. *Remarriage: A Gracious Gift from God* (Waco, Tex.: Word Publishers, 1991).

Trafford, Abigail. *The Crazy Time: Surviving Divorce* (San Francisco: Harper and Row, 1982).

Wallerstein, Judith S., with Sandra Blakeslee. *Second Chance* (New York: Ticknor and Fields, 1989).

Wallerstein, Judith S., and Joan Berlin Kelly. *Surviving the Break Up: How Children and Parents Cope with Divorce* (New York: Basic Books, 1980).

—JAMES G. EMERSON, JR.

A Jewish Perspective

Frequent divorce in Judea in the fifth century B.C.E. disturbed the Prophet Malachi (Mal. 2:10–16). Centuries later, Rabbi Eliezer felt the pathos of divorce: "For him who divorces his first wife, the very altar sheds tears." Yet the rabbis recognized divorce as a relatively frequent occurrence. Moreover, the source of all Jewish law and mores, the Torah, gives divorce a legal status. The "certificate of divorcement" of Deuteronomy 24:1 is called the *get,* literally, "legal document."

A basic fact of Jewish divorce law is its asymmetry. The Bible allows husbands, but not wives, to initiate divorce (Deut. 24:1–2). Is this right? In a now-classic essay, Judith Hauptman recognizes the most straightforward answer: Whether this is "right" is beside the point; it just is (Hauptman 1972). The biblical law of divorce is clear. The tradition cannot erase it. Yet the tradition can and *should* deal creatively with it. Hauptman demonstrates that the history of Jewish divorce law is overall the history of increasing efforts to protect the wife by controlling the husband's exclusive rights of divorce.

First, the *ketubah* ("writing"), or wedding contract, guaranteed that should a husband divorce his wife, he would have to pay her a substantial sum, so that, as the Talmud put it, "it should not be a light matter in his eyes to send her away." Second, under certain conditions a woman had the right to ask the rabbinic court to force her husband to divorce her. The fundamental corpus of Jewish law compiled in the second century, the Mishnah, enumerates these conditions: infection with boils, contact with noxious materials, or contracting hideous odors at work. Jewish law grants the woman the right to petition for immediate divorce and payment of *ketubah* money on grounds of abuse or nonsupport—if the husband imposes stringent vows on her, forces her into asceticism, bars her unreasonably and consistently from social and family obligations, or even denies her certain foods or adornments.

The fact that the Bible says a husband divorces his wife when he "finds something objectionable in her" (Deut. 24:1) suggests that public opinion should constrain him from divorcing "without some fairly obvious good reason" (Gershfield 1967). Rashi, the eleventh-century expounder of the Bible and the Talmud, commented on the biblical law of divorce: "If thou hatest her, then sever the relationship. But act not cruelly by retaining her in the house if thou art estranged from her." As the Talmud knowingly put it two thousand years ago: "When love was strong, we could have made our bed on a sword-blade. Now that our love has grown weak, a bed of sixty cubits is not large enough for us."

The Bible discouraged rash divorce by the law that a man could not remarry his divorced wife once *she* had remarried (Deut. 24:2–4). In postbiblical times the requirement that a personalized divorce document be drawn up prevents the husband from acting in the heat of the moment.

The wife's behavior sometimes provided grounds for immediate divorce with no *ketubah* money: adultery, violation of religious laws and involving her husband in such violations, indecent appearance in public, loose talk with other men, and frequent use of vulgar and audible insults to his family (except his mother, for conflict between daughters-in-law and mothers-in-law was regarded as virtually inevitable by the sages of old). The husband still had to write the divorce document, but the rabbis could force his hand. The guiding principle for the husband became that "anyone who betroths [a woman] does so in implicit compliance with the ordinances of the Rabbis."

While the overall history was toward greater protection for the wife, the rabbis provided little limit to the grounds a husband could give for divorce. The Mishnah records a disagreement between the two most eminent schools of rabbis on the question of whether a man could divorce his wife for a slight annoyance:

> The School of Shammai says: A man may not divorce his wife unless he has found something improper [unchaste, lewd] in her. But the School of Hillel says: [A man could divorce his wife] even if she spoiled a dish for him [with the intention of aggravating him]. (*m. Git.* 9:10)

Hillel prevailed. A husband could divorce his wife on the slightest chance that he would remain unhappy with her. Yet the Bible does prevent a husband from divorcing his wife if he had wrongly accused her of immorality during their betrothal (Deut. 22:13–19) or if he had seduced her before marriage (Deut. 22:28–29). The Mishnah stipulated that a man could not divorce a mentally defective wife (*Yebam.* 14:1) or a wife in captivity (*Ketub.* 4:9). A man could divorce an insane wife only if he procured "the permission of one hundred rabbis." (The woman could not be divorced from an insane husband, since he could not give a valid bill of divorcement.)

A great tragedy in Judaism, which the rabbis have also tried to remedy, is the *agunah,* the woman chained to her marriage because her husband has abandoned her, refuses to grant a divorce, or is mentally incompetent to do so. Jewish folk literature abounds with sympathy for the *agunah.* An eleventh-century rabbinic decree declared that a man who refuses to grant his wife a divorce cannot be married by the rabbis. But what does a wife do if he doesn't care? In the nineteenth century, Reform Judaism dropped these old traditions of divorce, but Conservative and Orthodox Judaism still grapple with them. Children born of a second marriage in which no Jewish divorce is given are still regarded as *mamzerim* (bastards), and are restricted in their marriage options. In 1958, the Conservative Movement added a clause to its wedding contract in which both husband and wife agree that if their marriage is dissolved under civil law, *either* may appeal to the rabbinical court (*bet din*) of the Rabbinical Assembly and Jewish Theological Seminary for Jewish religious divorce and may sue a recalcitrant spouse in civil court to abide by that decision.

Simon Greenberg (1977, 157–218) has described rabbinic efforts to assist the woman in divorce as the prime example of Jewish ethical sensibilities: "It is one of the ironies of history that a biblical law which was unquestionably intended to protect the wife would become an instrument of inflicting grief upon her." The greatest ethical test of any Jewish man is whether, in the event of divorce, he mocks Jewish law, Jewish marriage, and Jewish divorce by refusing to cooperate or act according to Jewish ethical ideals.

Divorce is a major ethical test for both husband and wife in their roles as parents. Rabbi Earl A. Grollman (1969) makes a strong case for truthfulness ("Don't make promises that you can't keep"), for listening to children, for allowing them to express their feelings, and for patience. He warns ex-spouses not to deprecate each other in front of the children, take out aggressions against them, impose impossible standards on them to compensate for their own sense of guilt and failure, or make children in any way feel guilty for their tensions. He notes how, for centuries, rabbinic courts have exercised their own discretion in awarding custody of children. In ancient times, sucking infants were left with the mother. Boys returned to their father's home for their religious education by the time they were six years old.

Divorce tests both partners and synagogue because divorce can provide the occasion for people to lose ties to the tradition or their religious community. Rabbi Shlomo D. Levine (1981) offers ethical and emotional support to the divorced individual who attempts to find a meaningful Jewish life. Rabbi Levine reminds us that the Jewish bill of divorcement does not stipulate fault and that Judaism's commitment to "the worth and dignity of people" is particularly applicable under such "trying circumstances."

The single-parent Jewish family provides a particular test for the American synagogue. Sociologist Barbara Kalin Bundt (1982) observes that in many ways the synagogue can become the other parent. She advises that "instead of putting effort into single-parent family programs, a congregation might examine existing programs which would allow these families to be reintroduced rapidly into the total synagogue structure."

Single-parent families, like all families, must observe Shabbat, Yom Tov, and other rituals at home to cement relationships and reinforce identification with Judaism, and to foster the God-faith. A synagogue family must feel like a family.

Divorcing spouses and their respective communities must meet the tests of divorce with the understanding that, while divorce is sad, even tragic, it is a *mitzvah*, a commandment, a ceremony sanctioned by biblical tradition and even sanctified when carried out according to the laws through which the Jew has best felt the presence and guidance of the God of Israel. Rabbi and sociologist Allen S. Maller (1978) observes that, while people may make mistakes in choosing marital partners or grow apart, and while the divorce decision may be mutual or one-sided, remarriage is also a *mitzvah*. Trying again fulfills God's will that one "be willing to trust someone else again" in order to "revitalize faith in one's self also." In Judaism divorce is an attempt to bring dignity and compassion to the individual's attempt to build a new relationship on the foundation of a new status. (For a full treatment of this topic with extensive citations of the sources alluded to in this article, see Elliot B. Gertel, "Jewish Views on Divorce," in *The Jewish Family and Continuity,* Steven Bayme and Gladys Rosen, eds. [Hoboken, N.J.: KTAV Publishing House, 1994].)

Bibliography

Bundt, Barbara Kalin. "The Divorced-Parent Family and the Synagogue Community," *Conservative Judaism* 35/2 (winter 1982): 74–77.

Gershfeld, Edward M. *The Jewish Law of Divorce* (New York: National Council of Jewish Women, *Report,* 1967).

Greenberg, Simon. *The Ethical in the Jewish and American Heritage* (New York: Jewish Theological Seminary, 1977).

Grollman, Earl A., ed. *Explaining Divorce to Children* (Boston: Beacon Press, 1969).

Hauptman, Judith. "Women's Liberation in the Talmudic Period: An Assessment," *Conservative Judaism* 26/4 (summer 1972): 22–28.

Levine, Shlomo D. *The Singular Problems of the Single Jewish Parent* (New York: United Synagogue Commission on Jewish Education, 1981).

Maller, Allen S. "A Religious Perspective on Divorce," *Journal of Jewish Communal Service* 55/2 (winter 1978): 192–94.

—ELLIOT B. GERTEL

4

Advances in
Reproductive Technology

A Protestant Perspective

Like the Mississippi River following the spring snow melt, the family landscape is being flooded with new technologies having to do with baby-making or not-making. The explosion of progress in reproductive technologies is creating choice in a dimension of life we previously consigned to destiny, namely, pro-creation. Fertile women can stop baby-making with Norplant, RU486, or abortion. Infertile couples can still make babies with the help of artificial insemination by husband (AIH), artificial insemination by donor (AID), in vitro fertilization (IVF), donor eggs, frozen embryos, and surrogate motherhood. Soon we will be able to enact quality control regarding the health and perhaps the genetic makeup of future children with the aid of prenatal genetic testing, genetic engineering, nuclear transplantation, egg fusion, cloning, selective abortion, and in utero fetal surgery. A woman can become a mother at age 62. And if experiments in ectogenesis and interspecies gestation prove successful, a woman will be able to become a mother without herself becoming pregnant.

Technology and choice quickly translate into markets. The already nascent reproductive industry is likely to expand as new technologies open up new possibilities for baby-stopping, baby-making, and baby-selecting. Infertility clinics will soon expand the range of services they offer, and their clientele may expand to include fertile couples and perhaps even individuals who are willing to pay for designer babies.

Under market conditions, will babies become commodities? This fear is based not so much on the prospect that children will be bought and sold; rather, what is at stake is the value children will have for us when they are the result of engineering or selection in order to manufacture a superior product. Of course parents want their children to enjoy good health. But choice at the level of reproductive technology means selecting the healthy baby and discarding the unhealthy. Of course parents may yearn for a child with certain genetic traits or talents or abilities. But choice at the level of genetic testing to achieve only acceptable embryos or engineering for superior genetic configurations may lead to the perfect-child syndrome, wherein the neighborhood children born the old-fashioned way may be led to feel inferior. Or, worse, something might go wrong—technology is seldom perfect—and something less than the perfect child will be produced, causing the parents to deprive the child of unconditional affection.

The possibility of treating children as commodities raises the specter that human dignity will be threatened. So, based upon observations of how Jesus behaved with poor and diseased outcasts, and also upon the theology of the incarnation—wherein God loves the imperfect world enough to become a part of it—I submit the following as a fundamental principle: God loves each of us regardless of our genetic makeup, and we should do likewise. What this means for families in our churches is this: Regardless of how a child is brought into this world and regardless of how good or bad a child's genome is, the welfare and flourishing of the child become our first ethical priority.

Even those less interested than I in basing an ethic upon Jesus might hold some reverence for the Enlightenment commitment to human dignity, to Immanuel Kant's dictum that we treat each person as an end and not merely as a means. My central concern here is that children—perfect or imperfect, created by choice or by destiny—receive unconditional love from their parents and equal opportunities in society. I cede a certain presumptive primacy to the babies being made by reproductive technology, so that they are treated as ends in themselves and not merely as means for attaining some other social or parental values. I want an ethic that successfully places the love of children foremost and that orients all secondary concerns for parental fulfillment and technological means toward this end.

This position has some correlates, one of which is the debunking of the inheritance myth. According to the inheritance myth, we assume that the biological connection between parents and children defines their relationship. This assumption played a big role in ancient tribal and agrarian cultures. It frames the background for the description of family life in the Bible. And it is the default position in our society today, in which governments use DNA testing to try to make deadbeat fathers pay for their abandoned children.

Yet I see no reason for granting Christian support for the inheritance myth. On this point I take a stand against those who would prop up the inheritance myth by appeal to sociobiology or Roman Catholic natural law. Why? Because Jesus said that we should love the person who is other, including our enemies. Enemies may lie outside the tribe, outside the family, outside kinship connections. The significance of this for procreative ethics is that no special priority should be given to children whose DNA carries their parents' genes. We need not argue on the basis of the inheritance myth that collaborative or third-party parenting via AID or surrogate motherhood is intrinsically immoral on the grounds that the resulting children do not share the genes of their social parents. Or, to reverse the direction, children who are adopted or who have been produced by reproductive high technology deserve the same love and dignity given to those produced by their parents' coital sex.

For some families a distance will open up between the genetic makeup of the parents and the genomes of their children. Donor semen or donor eggs or both mean that a baby will be born who does not carry strictly the biological inheritance of his or her social parents. In an extreme case a child could be born with two fathers and three mothers: one father for the donor semen and a second one committed to raising the child. One mother to donate the egg, a surrogate mother to bring the infant to term and to give birth, and a third mother committed to raising the child. Who are the real parents? The real parents are the ones who love the child and dedicate themselves to the child's flourishing, regardless of genetic continuity or discontinuity, regardless of health or disease.

We live in an era of inescapable choice, and the array of choices regarding how we bring new children into the world is expanding. Also expanding is the array of genetic configurations that high-tech babies will add to their social families. There is no escape from choice. An ethic that tries to eliminate choice by appeal to some sort of biological essentialism or theological naturalism—a conservative ethic that forbids the use of reproductive technology on the ground that biological continuity between parent and child is somehow definitive or divinely ordained—will fail to provide guidance for people in a society awash in choice. What is called for on the part of our churches is ethical leadership that will help establish criteria for choosing. The central criterion I put forth is this: the love of children. Procreative decision making should begin with the welfare and flourishing of the child as its first consideration; this trumps all other considerations, such as the desires of the parents or questions about whether reproductive technology should or should not be used. Treating the child as an end and not merely a means for achieving parental fulfillment confers dignity upon the child, a dignity we hope the child will grow up to claim.

From the point of view of the Christian faith, the dignity of our children and hence the dignity of all of us is not to be found in our biological inheritance. Rather, our final dignity is eschatological; it accompanies our fulfillment in the image of God. Rather than something with which we are born that may or may not become socially manifest, dignity is the future end product of God's saving activity, which we anticipate socially when we confer dignity on those who do not yet claim it. The ethics of God's kingdom in our time and in our place consists of conferring dignity and inviting persons—inviting the children we bring into this world—to claim dignity as a prolepsis of the kingdom's future fulfillment.

—TED PETERS

A Catholic Perspective

The clearest statement of Catholic teaching on reproductive technology is found in an "Instruction" issued by the Congregation for the Doctrine of the Faith (CDF) in March 1987. The English title of this work is *Instruction on Respect for Human Life in its Origin and on the Dignity of Procreation: Replies to Certain Questions of the Day*. As the subtitle suggests, the document seeks to answer questions about Catholic teaching on reproductive technology. It also seeks to offer moral guidance on assisted reproduction generally. Since the CDF is one of the offices of the institutional church designed to assist the pope as he discharges his role as moral leader, and since the Congregation's specific role is the oversight of Catholic theology, including Catholic moral theology, the CDF is part of the *magisterium*, or teaching authority, of the hierarchical church. The Instruction should thus be understood as the officially sanctioned teaching of the Catholic Church. Although an instruction does not carry the same weight as other types of teaching documents—for example, encyclicals—it is considered an authoritative teaching and should be taken very seriously by Catholics confronting difficult reproductive decisions.

The Instruction itself consists of an introduction, three substantive sections, and a conclusion. This article briefly summarizes the conclusions reached on specific reproductive interventions, the basic arguments supporting these conclusions, and some responses to this teaching.

Section 1 of the Instruction takes up the manipulation of human embryos made possible by modern reproductive medicine. Specifically, the Congregation considers three basic questions: Is prenatal diagnosis morally acceptable? Are therapeutic procedures carried out on human embryos acceptable? Is research and experimentation on human embryos acceptable? The answers to all three questions are rooted in church teaching on the status of the embryo. Because the Catholic Church teaches that a human embryo is a person from the moment of conception, any manipulation of the embryo must safeguard its life and integrity and be directed to the good of the individual. Thus, prenatal diagnosis is acceptable if it aims at preserving life, for example, by facilitating an early therapeutic intervention. By contrast, prenatal diagnosis undertaken with the expectation of aborting a defective embryo would be unacceptable. Moreover, recent techniques for screening preimplantation in vitro embryos, commonly referred to as preimplantation genetic diagnosis (PGD), would also be unacceptable. Since PGD involves discarding defective embryos rather than placing them in a uterus, it is considered a form of abortion and is therefore wrong.

The answers to the second and third questions also depend on church teaching on the status of the developing embryo. Because the embryo should be treated as a person, therapeutic interventions—fetal surgery, for example—is acceptable so long as there is not a disproportionate risk to the fetus. Likewise,

experimental forms of therapy on the fetus can be used when there are no reliable alternatives. However, research or experimentation on embryos that is
not directly therapeutic is unacceptable. Indeed, any use of human embryos
that does not respect their integrity as individuals is morally unacceptable.
Thus, cloning, freezing, or otherwise manipulating embryos in ways that reduce them to mere biological materials is morally wrong.

Section 2 takes up specific forms of assisted reproduction and is divided into
those that involve only the partners in a marriage (homologous artificial procreation) and those that—like donor insemination, in vitro fertilization with
donor eggs, and surrogacy—involve third parties (heterologous artificial procreation). Although the Congregation concludes that forms of assisted reproduction that involve third parties are more seriously wrong than those that
involve only the spouses, both are thought to be morally problematic. Why are
they problematic? There appear to be two lines of argument provided in answer
to this question.

The first line of argument has to do with Catholic teaching about the nature
of the person and about the meaning of procreation. Because a person is, in
church teaching, a "unified totality" of body and soul, it is important not to treat
a person in a way that reduces the person to either mere body or mere spirit.
And that is the problem with reproductive medicine: It approaches human reproduction as if it were nothing more than the union of bodily material,
namely, gametes. The first line of argument is thus that reproductive technology is dehumanizing because it treats human reproduction as merely material.
Because it reduces human procreation to the union of gametes, reproductive
medicine is unconcerned with how this union is brought about. For the
Catholic Church, however, how this union takes place is important. According
to the Church, a conception that results from the union of gametes in the lab
is fundamentally different from a conception that is the result of a loving act of
sexual intercourse. The former involves the reduction of a person to a function;
the latter involves a quintessentially human act that is at once physical and spiritual. By allowing for noncoital procreation, reproductive technology diminishes the full significance of human reproduction. It turns our bodies into mere
instruments of our wills and disembodies procreation in a way that sets the
stage for the objectification and commodification of reproduction.

The second line of reasoning used to oppose interventions in the reproductive process is related to Catholic teaching on natural law, specifically to
Catholic teaching on human sexuality. Drawing upon church teaching that
there is an intrinsic structure to human sexuality that requires sex, marriage,
and procreation to be united, the Congregation concludes that assisted reproduction frequently violates the integrity of human sexuality. This is perhaps
clearest with procedures that require using donor gametes—because one of the
partners is procreating with someone other than a spouse—but it is no less true
when a married couple uses their own gametes. Consider, for example, artificial insemination with the husband's sperm. Although this is not as problematic as donor insemination, it is still wrong, the Congregation says, because it

separates sex and procreation in a way that violates the natural law. Just as artificial contraception is wrong because it violates the structure of human sexuality by separating sex from procreation, so artificial insemination with husband's sperm is wrong because it separates procreation from sex.

Given how closely Catholic teaching on reproductive technology is tied to church teaching on abortion and contraception, it is not surprising that the position articulated in this Instruction has been controversial. For example, many Catholic theologians believe that the church drew the line between acceptable and unacceptable interventions too narrowly when it ruled out artificial insemination with husband's sperm (AIH). Given that the church teaches that one of the goods of marriage is children and that the child conceived through AIH would be the genetic offspring of the married couple, how, it is asked, can AIH be wrong? Although church teaching on reproductive technology continues to be discussed among theologians, perhaps the most interesting response has been that of the American Fertility Society (AFS), the professional organization of health care workers in the field of reproductive medicine. Before the CDF released its Instruction, the American Fertility Society had undertaken a review of the ethical issues raised by reproductive technology and had issued its own policy statement on the ethics of assisted reproduction. Because the Vatican reached quite different conclusions on the issues, the AFS felt compelled to respond and thus issued a second document that specifically responded to Catholic teaching.

Bibliography

Lauritzen, P. *Pursuing Parenthood: Ethical Issues in Assisted Reproduction* (Bloomington, Ind.: Indiana University Press, 1993).

Pope John Center. *Reproductive Technologies, Marriage, and the Church* (Braintree, Mass.: Pope John Center, 1988).

Shannon, T. A., and L. S. Cahill. 1988. *Religion and Artificial Reproduction* (New York: Crossroad, 1988).

Vacek, E. V. "Vatican Instruction on Reproductive Technology," *Theological Studies* 49(1988): 110–31.

Wallace, M., and T. W. Hilgers. *The Gift of Life: The Proceedings of a National Conference on the Vatican Instruction on Reproductive Ethics and Technology* (Omaha: Pope Paul VI Institute Press, 1990). (Includes the text of the Instruction)

—PAUL LAURITZEN

A Jewish Perspective
Stewards of the Earth

Reproductive technology has opened the doors to parenthood for thousands of families who once would have remained childless, yearning for the joyfulness, solidity, and generativity that children bring as gifts to relationships. For all religious traditions that share a concern for the relief of human suffering, such technology might seem to be an unfettered good. For Jewish families, many of whom live one generation from the shadow of the Shoah (Holocaust) and the loss of millions of children, this question can be even more heavily freighted. In fact, the case that first drew our attention to surrogacy as a solution to infertility was the Baby M case, which had at its heart the yearning of a lone heir of Shoah survivors to sire genetic offspring.

Can the new advances in reproductive technology be seen as merely a logical and welcome miracle of science? Or is the manipulation of genetic material and the mechanics of pregnancy an unjustified encroachment into terrain that is not quite properly our own, acting, as the charge is so often made, *as* God instead of acting on behalf of God's command?

Thinking as a Jew:
Text and Tradition

Religious ethics helps us to see an answer to this dilemma that is arguably somewhere in the middle. The context for the discussion of Jewish ethical response is traditionally the source texts of the *halakah,* or Jewish legal tradition. Jews turn to texts as first source to enter a conversation about meaning and value of action that is rooted both in history and faith. In these traditional sources each voice constructs an ongoing social world and a moral meaning for the tragedies and dilemmas she or he faces. Like us, the writers of these texts struggled to lead contending and questioning Jewish lives, and like us, they faced mortal decisions that shape both personal and social narrative.

You might wonder why we start with *halakah.* Why not start with a general discussion of ethics and values? The answer is that Jewish ethical reasoning cannot be fully separated from the religious legal system of *halakah.* Reflection and analysis about ethical questions are based practically and theoretically in real narratives and historical and cultural context. Arguments about principles are made analogically from precedents, and the reader is supposed (across oceans of exile, and centuries of history) to think about how the stories match stories of her own. These disputes, and the tradition of dispute itself, rather than a set of rules applicable to specific dilemmas, are preserved. There is no one final Jewish "truth" about a rule of conduct. Every author reflects on views held in tension, on majority and minority viewpoints, and on what are called "counterhistorical" and "intertextual" meanings (different texts reflect on and influence each other) in a tradition that values nuance in text and, above all, the argument.

What Kind of Knowing Is Wisdom?

Advanced reproductive technology (the technological manipulation of the components of human life, persons, and genetic material to facilitate and assist reproduction) is neither an unqualified good, nor an unredeemable evil. Serious ethical problems worry us as we confront technologies so powerful, but the task of the society, community, and family that use these tools involves both limit-setting and meaning-making—hard to accomplish in the face of the seductive potency of the laboratory siren call.

Scientific answers call us to scientific solutions. But Jewish law asks us if perhaps how we construct a family calls for a different kind of knowledge, not solely about synoptic wisdom but moral wisdom (Kerkes 1996). The *halakah* of the Talmud suggests reality has a moral order, and such a moral order reverberates with loss and its meaning. The condition of exile itself, the "wrestling" with God that is the task of all adult Jews, is an agonistic, not an easy path; living a good life is a serious matter, "being hard, requiring constant struggle against serious adversity" (Kerkes 1996). Unlike scientific questions ("What physically blocks my achievement of a specific goal?"), religious knowledge also asks, "What does God want of us when we are challenged in this way?"

Finally, devotion to scientists and physicians as moral arbiters has not proven to be completely justified. The specter of the Shoah haunts at the margins the entire discourse on reproduction in Jewish life. It does so in two ways that frame the borders of our very Jewish reflections on the moral limits of science and health. On the one hand, most Jews in this immediate post-Shoah generation feel a near-moral obligation to restore the terrible losses to Jewish population that occurred at the hands of the Nazis (Tendler 1982). But on the other, the use of eugenics by the Nazi regime in the attempt to create a master race of genetically superior families (Levinson 1988) raises the fear that genetic manipulation will go beyond therapeutic uses to enhance to an ideal type, with other types first marginalized and then pathologized (Zoloth-Dorfman 1997).

The Fence Around the Torah:
A World of Limits

Jewish tradition supports neither unbridled autonomy nor sanguine consequentialism. Both of these points not only create a specificity of response to the use of reproductive technology, but create a stance about the notion of limits that questions some of the very premises of the use of reproductive technology. Jewish thought, human creatures, and human families live in both existential and literal exile. Our collective human exile, marked by our exit from an edamic reality, is to a world of limits—of temporality and specificity. Temporality shapes each human life, the seasons of harvest and growth, lunar cycles. For each event ordered by the natural world, rabbinic law proscribes detailed human restraints. Eating, consumption, sexuality—all seen as unequivocally good acts—are not unregulated. Limits are not tragedies, but social realities.

Infertility and Fertility Therapy

To have stewardship over the earth does not necessarily mean keeping it unchanged (Zoloth-Dorfman 1998). Jews are taught that healing is a matter of present and persuasive obligation. The pronatalist enthusiasm for reproductive technology is potentiated by a conviction and commitment to the dreams and visions of medical technology. Judaism does not yearn for a faith healing, nor for a simpler, less interventionist era in medicine. In our thinking about the range of therapy for infertility, most Jewish commentators (Dorff 1988; Rosner 1986; Feldman 1974) find their way to creative uses of the texts, and even elaborate physical maneuvers, to justify vigorous efforts to assist reproduction. In fact, the most strictly religious hospitals and clinics in Israel are among the most aggressive prescribers of fertility therapy, including the ready use of Clomid as a pregnancy enhancer, creating multiple births with each pregnancy. Religious Jewish communities throughout the world have among the highest birth rates in part because of this practice, and in part because of the decided emphasis on procreative sexual union within marriage.

But there are limits even to this enthusiasm. Death, illness, and barrenness are cause for sorrow, for action, and for prayer, but not seen as extraordinary or catastrophic. Barrenness in a pronatalist tradition motivates action, but action within a limited sphere of possibility. The world is not regulated by nature only; persons interfere with history, persons are entitled to heal by prayer, potion, and social behavior. Nowhere is this more true than in the realm of fertility. The barren matriarch is a recurrent theme of the Torah, a yearning for simple maternity at the heart of a personal journey of the encounter with spirituality. Classic biblical texts regard the infertility of parents as a spiritual and physical test: since God is a partner with persons in all creation, the relationship to God is at stake in the traditional dramas of biblical infertility. The rabbinic response was more pragmatic. While surrogacy (Sarah and Hagar) and manipulation by external medical means (mandrakes in the case of Rachel) are noted, the anger, upset, and generational conflict are also a concern. The rabbinic view of the absolute responsibility of men to father children as a part of the appropriate adult spiritual journey includes adoption as a reasonable alternative, as well as becoming a teacher and in that sense bearing the responsibility of the next generation.

In this view, infertility is not a disease of the woman for a physician to cure, but a social concern about adult obligation and what can be expected of the community in response. Classically the guidance of the child's learning, not the physical act of procreation, is regarded as significant. Children are not yet another commodity that one must "have" to be whole. Parenting is a construct of clear and mutual obligation—an obligation to the next generation that is a commanded act of faith.

Genetic Testing and Intervention

Today's reproductive technology goes far beyond the use of fertility drugs and surgery to create preimplantation embryonic life. How far can we reach in the pursuit of not only children, but perfectly endowed children? In some sectors of the Orthodox world, couples are screened genetically prior to their arranged marriages, and genetically unfavorable unions are simply not arranged. Such practices are seen not as new theory but as refining technology that dates from the *Shulkan Aruch* (*Even Ezer* 2:7): "A man should not marry a woman from a family of lepers or epileptics." And testing is widely used for Tay-Sachs disease, a disease that affects children with a devastating and slow neurological destruction. Attempts to manipulate genetic traits occur commonly through the Talmud (*Yebam.* 64b, *Nid.* 31a, *Ber.* 20a) as rabbinic authorities reflected on sexual and social practices that seemed to result in healthy and well-born offspring. But such efforts had their limits. Judaism is remarkable in its approach to the disabled child once born. Unlike Hellenistic traditions in which a child's personhood and admittance into the society depended upon his acceptance by a patriarch, rabbinic codal authority prohibits infanticide; genetic misfortune could be avoided, but children bearing the misfortune could not be destroyed.

Jewish values caution against the seduction of overreaching pride in the construction and manipulation of the natural world. This thread, running throughout the Torah and rabbinic texts (for example, the story of the Tower of Babel and the cautionary midrash about the Golem) is held in tension with the repeated mandate to heal. In this motif, the rabbinic authorities base their injunctions on the explicit metaphors of agriculture and stewardship. The physician's task is to heal (Dorff 1985), yet the claim to infallibility would be hubris. This middle ground is precisely that upon which to locate our response to reproductive technology.

Surrogacy

While tradition limits manipulation of genetic information, there are even stronger limits on such practices as surrogacy. Limits on the use of another are among the clearest in the Jewish tradition. Thus, one of the most ethically problematic issues in advanced reproductive technology is the use of surrogates to achieve pregnancy. Surrogacy in the biblical narratives creates one of the fundamentally difficult relationships in the struggle of the Land. The devaluation of Ishmael's worth as a child once a "real" heir is created sends him into the desert. And other questions can be raised by surrogacy. Jews are prohibited from making unfair contracts. Contracts that are unduly burdensome are unenforceable. The use of the womb of the other, aside from all the questions of technical "adultery," suggests just such a contract. Offering the use of one's body for money, particularly for procreative use, commodifies a central experience of a woman's life, which is seen of course not only as a physical act, but as a profoundly spiritual one, a faith journey, after which specific prayers are written, rituals created, and spiritual obligations expected. Children are not a commodity, not property. The restrictions on their generation are drawn with care: intercourse is not permitted at some times, and procreative intercourse prohibited for some women at specific times. Creation itself is a relationship, girded and guided by the holiness of family itself. Families, however, exist within larger communities of purpose and restraint. And families cannot use the vulnerable, even to serve legitimate ends. When the contract for surrogacy involves the differential between the wealthy with resources to buy, and the poor with desperation to sell, the conditions that regulate the contract are even stricter, and the moral objections ever stronger.

Conclusion

For most American Jews, this level of Talmudic deliberation is curious, but only marginally important. However, the value that is placed on children and family life deeply affects even Reform or secular Jews (Gold 1988). The yearning for children, the yearning to control the state of befallenness and chanciness of human life resonates through Jewish tradition. Jewish ritual life centers on family celebration; the assumption is made religiously and textually that Jews approach and worship God as members of both families, and of a community of others who are in families. The biblical stories unfold around the drama of children. Matriarchs and patriarchs move through history and faith journeys blessed and encumbered. A Jewish journey of faith is not a solo flight: it is, from the moment of Creation, a choice against aloneness with relationship, an answer to the query of spiritual Presence with the promise of partnership, of presentness of one's own. It is this blessing, the declaration of the goodness of the creation of women and men, embodied and imperfect, creaturely, in a nexus of other created lives, that the Torah records as God's blessing to us: *Ki Tov* (very good!).

Such stewardship presents the necessity of trouble: the travail, the labor of children is also the moral recognition that we bear them in a world of limits. In so doing, it is part of our obligation to worry about the future, to watch the world with care, to prune, and to harvest. Reproductive technology calls us to the highest possible level of attention, reminding us that every medical gesture must remain clearly in our moral control.

Bibliography

Dorff, Elliott. *"Choose Life: A Jewish Perspective on Medical Ethics,"* *University Papers* 4/1 (Los Angeles: The University of Judaism, 1985).
Feldman, David. *Marital Relations, Birth Control and Abortion in Jewish Law* (New York: Schocken Books, 1974).

Gold, Michael. *And Hannah Wept* (Philadelphia: Jewish Publication Society, 1988).

Kerkes, John. *Moral Wisdom and Good Lives* (Ithaca, N.Y.: Cornell University Press, 1996).

Levenson, Jon D. *Creation and the Persistence of Evil* (Princeton, N.J.: Princeton University Press, 1988).

Rosner, Fred. *Modern Medicine and Jewish Ethics* (Hoboken, N.J.: KTAV/Yeshiva University Press, 1986).

Tendler, Moshe David. *Pardes Rimonim: A Marriage Manual for the Jewish Family* (New York: The Judaica Press, 1982).

Zoloth-Dorfman, Laurie. "Mapping the Normal Human Self: The Jew and the Mark of Otherness" in *Genetics* (New York: Pilgrim Press, 1997).

——— "Promises of Exiles" in *Religious Conversations on Population, Consumption and Ecology* (New York: State University of New York, 1998).

—LAURIE ZOLOTH-DORFMAN

5

Work of Families:
Roles of Families

The Nature of Parenting

In the United States, postmodern culture is neither "child-friendly" nor "parent-friendly." Many communities have become "toxic" for children. A cacophony of expert voices debates about conflicting approaches to raising children. Beleaguered parents scramble to do what is best for their offspring. Nearly every sector of society acknowledges the challenge.

Within the maelstrom, confusion and concern are giving way to cautious hopefulness and cooperative action. Converging descriptions of the challenges facing parents and communities as well as emerging common languages for positive responses bode well for the future care of children.

Common Ground

While diverse opinions regarding the direction and forms of good parenting abound, at least two broad agreements are emerging on critical aspects of the task. Research and common experience reveal effective child rearing to be a personal, corporate, and public partnership that is grounded in parental and community commitment, confidence, and competence.

Persons raise children. Good child rearing requires commitment from each parent and caregiver. Raising a child occurs within personal relationships requiring significant one-to-one-interaction.

Communities raise children. Parenting and caregiving occur within an intricate web of relationships. Peers, families, and neighborhoods are the many "faces" of caregiving and create an atmosphere that shapes a child's very being.

Societies raise children. Public policies, private and public institutions, mass communication, and cultural values have an impact on children, parents, and caregivers. The outcome of every child's journey to adulthood is profoundly affected by the character, decisions, and behavior of the community, the state, and the nation.

We know that there are varying approaches to effective parenting. Parents and communities of differing ethnic, socioeconomic, and religious backgrounds provide a rich array of good possibilities.

While healthy communities and societies committed to children are crucial to good child rearing, the focus here is on individuals and their primary life relationships—with parents, caregivers, and families. Consideration is given to communities only by pointing out the importance of parents engaging the specific resources most critical to constructing the network necessary for "good-enough" parenting (Winnicott 1988). Single parents, nuclear families, blended families, and extended families all can parent well if they are surrounded by supportive people and resources with which they work cooperatively.

Across cultures and over the generations a variety of family forms have been the primary contexts for parenting. The Old and New Testaments reflect this variety. Within the Scriptures there are clans, extended families, and Levirate marriage (in which the brother of a husband who dies with no male heir is obligated to provide a son through sexual relations with his dead brother's wife). In some situations one finds polygamy, but in most monogamy is the rule.

In the biblical revelation the purposes for families and parenting remain consistent. However, the forms often change with the circumstances so that care for the generations can be sustained, whatever the situation. The Bible understands families and parenting as essential historical structures and tasks, mediating against fragile, isolated existence on the one hand and oppressive totalitarian life on the other. Families and parents are necessary crucibles, providing relationships in which children can be nurtured in freedom and accountability.

Recent research (Blankenhorn 1995) and common experience reveal similar conclusions. Children benefit when both parents are constructively engaged in caregiving. All else being equal, healthy families with both parents present are the best and least complex crucibles for child rearing, especially when they are surrounded by a supportive community. Extended families are the most supportive contexts for these two parents. In more cases in postmodern American culture these two parents will be in a nuclear family.

Although their situation is considerably more complex, parents in healthy blended families do well when they are intentional. So too do coparent families (where both members of a divorced couple are actively engaged in parenting) and single-parent families, especially when they are surrounded by supportive communities.

Studies show that both fathers and mothers make critical contributions to parenting, especially when they are supportive of each other and each significantly engaged in caregiving (Scales 1996). Men and women will of course enact their roles as parents out of their unique sexual identity, but if they are committed and competent, both mothers and fathers are capable of handling major caregiving responsibilities. In single-parent families, other committed, competent males or females can become "surrogate" fathers or mothers. The critical issue in all these relationships and structures is faithfulness or intentionality worked out with confidence through commitment and competence.

Intentional Parenting

Child rearing is intentionally working out life with the child in the presence of others. The first responsibility of parents is to tend their own life and relationships with a maturity and competence that enhances their own health and contributes toward a life-giving environment for the child. Although a parent must make sacrifices for his or her child, to be an effective caregiver over time is to make good choices concerning one's own well-being. Parental commitment and competency in family and peer relationships contribute toward the positive social, psychological, moral, and spiritual climate in which a child's life unfolds. Effective parenting emerges from a basic decision and thousands of day-to-day choices to be healthy and strong for the sake of the child.

Judeo-Christian faith communities have understood child rearing to be framed and focused by their relationship with God. As the prime cocreators with God of new human beings, parents have a high and unique calling. Parents are to tend the child on behalf of God. This child shares in the mystery of life that flows from God, is sustained by God, and is accountable to God.

Parents are also to tend the child on behalf of the community. The community has a stake in the child's potential whether as a constructive community contributor or a destructive social liability.

Parents also tend the child on behalf of the child. The child's character and potential will be greatly influenced by early life with parents who have significant impact on that 10 percent of the child's essence that isn't genetically coded.

Finally, parents tend the child on behalf of the future, because children carry the next generation's character, courage, and imagination in their youthful potential.

Parents are to be guided in their high calling by the faithfulness with which God relates to God's people. God is steadfast. God makes and keeps promises. God cares. God persists. God is there with and for humankind, Israel, Jesus Christ, and the new community that bears Christ's name. So it is to be among the generations and between parents and children. Faithfulness is a dynamic concept. It is grounded in loyalty and in promised persistence. It is active. It means becoming involved in the well-being of the other. It is steadfast love, a promise to care consistently for the child.

For men and women of faith, parenting is grounded in core convictions that give confidence and direction as well as establish accountability.

A Guiding Vision

In the many and long days of tending both the mundane and extraordinary tasks of child rearing, parents consciously or unconsciously operate from governing values that reflect a particular view of children and their development. The more realistic and true these governing values, the more constructive the parenting; the more clear and compelling the vision of childhood and adulthood inherent in these governing values, the more effective the parenting.

Some argue that a child is like a stone to be sculpted; others, like a plant to be watered and pruned; still others speak of a child as an animal to be trained. While all of these similes contain helpful insights, none expresses the complexity that is the growing child. A child is a real, developing person needing support and guidance. Out of the significant relationships with their parents and caregivers these mysterious, impressionable, yet active young "life agents" are forging identity, character, and industry. To parent is to evoke from the child his or her essential worth and ability but also to contribute toward that worth and ability. In this vision of the child, the message from the parent to the child is this: You are a person who is lovable, capable, and forgivable.

A child is lovable because God has created each child with inherent dignity and loves him or her as God's own. Parents communicate this dignity and love when they recognize and celebrate the mystery of the child's spirit. Children whose parents treat them with respect learn to respect themselves. The more parents value a child's uniqueness and elicit that child's gifts, the greater value and confidence the child finds in himself or herself. As a parent works with a child to set realistic expectations, encourages that child in living up to those expectations, praises the child for successes and holds the child accountable for failure, that parent assists in the conversion of the child's latent abilities into effective life skills. Children need challenges and coaching in order to become confident of their unfolding potential for independence, interdependence, and resiliency.

Every child has limitations and experiences failure, even failure to live up to his or her own expectations. When grace is regularly experienced as acceptance and "forgiveness with accountability," that child's dignity and abilities are secured and strengthened. Children who don't experience such grace become driven perfectionists or give up; others who live without this acceptance and forgiveness become fragile or belligerent.

For women and men of faith, parenting might well be guided by a vision of the growing child and the emerging adult secure in the identity of a lovable, capable, and forgivable human being.

Bonding, the Basic Building Block

Because parenting is essentially relational, its basic building block is the connection that a parent forges with the child. This crucial attachment with the child is a strong and multifaceted bond that establishes the parent or caregiver as a regular, "life-determining other" in the child's existence. Without this bond the child flounders. Without this bond the parent's effectiveness is greatly diminished.

Bonding is an intense, ongoing interaction with the child that etches the caregiver's presence and behavior in the child's memory and focuses his or her life. When adequate, this bond communicates the safety, sufficiency, and support that leads the child to trust this "good-enough other" and forms the child's own identity and worth. This bond establishes the psychological, social, and moral underpinnings for the child's personhood and the context for the parent's ongoing efforts.

Bonding can be cultivated. This attachment has an emotional component: it is a parent developing a deep connection with the child; it is a parent valuing the child and giving an expression of value to the child. Sometimes this sense of value is spontaneous, seemingly innate and irrational. At other times it will need to be cultivated by searching for something in the child's makeup or the parent's own commitments that leads the parent to cherish the child.

Bonding has a physical component. To bond with a child is to be in the child's presence, to be smelled, seen, and heard by the child. Parents strengthen their bond with a child through respectful, loving touch, especially through timely hugging and holding of the child.

Bonding has a volitional component. Strong parent-child bonds are created and sustained as parents make commitments to consistently, compassionately be with and for a child when he or she needs the parent the most. Through these regular rhythms of intentional care, the child experiences the parent and the "significant world" to be dependable and trustworthy.

Bonding has a spiritual component. When a parent allows a child to see in action that parent's deepest convictions, values, and emotions, the child identifies with the parent's humanity and is allowed a window into the parent's spirit.

Whatever else a parent seeks to be or do with his or her child, this foundational bond will be crucial to their interactions.

The Arts of Parenting

Most concretely, parenting will take place in the regular rhythms of working out life with the child. The words and behaviors of everyday exchanges define the parent-child relationship and nurture the child. These words and behaviors are the arts of parenting through which parents and caregivers become the midwives of human personhood. Both fathers and mothers can enhance the knowledge and skill associated with these arts. A sample of these skills portrays the concrete, mundane nature of "good-enough parenting."

Affirming: To affirm is to acknowledge a child's presence and value. At a deeper level it is discovering the unique and valuable in a child and celebrating these dimensions with the child and others. At a still deeper level, affirmation is acceptance of a child even when the child is unruly and unhappy. Parents can learn to distinguish between a child's behavior and a child's being. Misbehavior can be firmly discouraged and changed at the same time that the child is loved and accepted as a person.

Confronting: To confront is to help a child face reality, whether painful or not. Confronting is not accusing or blaming; it is allowing children to experience the consequences of their destructive behavior. Descriptive language needs to be used. Consequences need to be clearly understood. Options can be explored. Children can be coached as they work through difficulties to solutions or restoration. Parents can teach children appropriate skills and demonstrate good conflict-resolving behavior.

Consoling: To console is to join the child in struggling through disappointment and difficulty back to normalcy. Children do not have the perspectives born of experience that balance and buffer life's traumas. They often hurt deeply over matters that adults might consider trivial. To console is to hurt with the child, to be present with and support the child in his or her hurt. A parent will need to wonder about the way the child sees the matter and how the child thinks of responding. Ways of coping can be explored. To console is to walk with the child to a better place.

Guiding: To guide is to point the way for a child. While there are times when children need to be controlled or forced, more often they need to be instructed, shown, or trained. Guides ask questions, provide information, and demonstrate. Guides not only teach skills, they model what they are teaching and provide occasions for children to practice and grow in competence. Children need parents to coach them in moving from dependency to competency and interdependence.

Listening: Every child communicates. Actions, words, moods, silence, and passivity are all channels through which children give themselves to others and create their own identities and relationships. To listen to a child is to receive that child. Paying close attention to a child's language, behavior, and moods allows parents to receive the messages that their children long to have understood. Listening is the active observation and consideration that leads to genuine and appropriate parental response.

Disciplining: Authoritative parents discipline with respect, truth, and love. For authoritative parents, discipline begins with mutual respect for the worth and dignity of both parent and child. They recognize that every human being has choices within limits prescribed by society. Authoritative parents present these choices and allow children to choose and be responsible for their choices. They explain expectations and rules. They accurately and carefully go over natural and logical consequences. They don't keep children from either the positive or the negative results of their behavior. They provide support as the child wrestles to find a way to live responsibly with his or her self and society.

Parenting is not primarily adding an additional layer of esoteric theories or the frenetic pursuit of special activities; it is essentially developing the art of constructive interaction with the child in working out life itself.

Faith and Values

Many within the religious and scientific community understand families and parents in particular to be key contributors to a child's faith and values. Deuteronomy 6:4–9 admonishes the Israelites to recite the *Shema* to their children and talk about it when at home or away, when lying down or getting up; these words are even to be posted on the doorposts and gates of their houses. Martin Luther, a leading figure in the Protestant Reformation, wrote that parents are apostles and pastors to their children. Family-systems theorists have found that every family system generates an ethos and a mythos that communicate values and beliefs to its children.

Parents can intentionally nurture the values of their children as they work out everyday life together. By establishing a positive emotional climate in the family, parents communicate respect, honesty, and trust. As parents model just and cooperative use of power and establish clear and fair rules, they immerse children in experiences and relationships that build wholesome character. Through shared participation in caring for others, both parents and child discover the joy and satisfaction of service.

Families are one of God's communities where the story of God's truth and love creates the knowledge, the experience, and the life of faith. Parents can tell God's story and be instruments of God's Spirit. They can help children integrate God's story with the child's life through regular sharing of the parents' own faith journey. When parents speak candidly of God's participation in their struggles with life, they are portraying God's connection with life to their children. Lively rituals provide parents and children ongoing experiences of celebrating and integrating their faith stories. Listening to parents pray introduces children most immediately to the living God; praying with the child and teaching the child to pray empower the child to exercise his or her own relationship with God.

Being "Good-Enough Parents"

Parents and child often hurt and fail one another. A child ignores a mother's warnings about drugs. A father verbally abuses his daughter. Parents and children fail to spend enough time with one another, and their relationship becomes shallow and distant.

The love of God speaks of forgiveness and acceptance that go beyond the fear of punishment. It provides healing that comes from understanding and living with imperfection. The gospel speaks of forgiveness that can reconcile parents and children alienated from one another.

Parents do not always know the best way to raise children. Some haven't had good models. Some have been given knowledge and skills that prove destructive. Well-meaning parents can approach parenting with debilitating goals. Children can be stubborn and closed.

Both parents and children can receive forgiveness. Both can sense God's deep love for them and be opened to God's truth. Each can learn new ways. All parties to the parent-child relationship can accept their own and each other's limitations.

Child rearing can overwhelm and wear down parents. Parents can easily respond in frustration with degrading insults or abuse. The shame resulting from these experiences diminishes the worth and life of the child, the parent, and the family. Insults cannot be withdrawn, but they can be stopped and acknowledged, and forgiveness and healing sought. There can be support and new beginnings for both parent and child. They can understand that parents and children do not have to be perfect and that child rearing does not have to be accomplished alone. Within God's forgiveness and the networks of the community, parents can find new beginnings and partnerships that provide the child with the "good-enough parenting" the child needs to become lively and resilient (Bowlby 1973).

In the scriptures, religious communities are sometimes portrayed as extended families of faith. In these families of faith parents and children can find truth and love, daily repentance and renewal, as well as networks of support as they care for each other and tend a new generation.

Bibliography

Anderson, Herbert, and Susan Johnson. *Regarding Children* (Louisville, Ky.: Westminster John Knox Press, 1994).

Blankenhorn, David. *Marriage in America: A Report to the Nation* (New York: Institute for American Values, 1995). [The report was included in David Popenoe, Jean Bethke Elshtain, and David Blankenhorn, eds., *Promises to Keep: Decline and Renewal of Marriage in America* (Lanham, Md.: Rowman & Littlefield, 1996).]

Bowlby, John. *Child Care and the Growth of Love* (London: Penguin Books, 1973).

Glenn, H. Stephen, and Jane Nelsen. *Raising Self-Reliant Children* (Rocklin, Calif.: Prima, 1989).

Patton, John, and Brian Childs. *Christian Marriage and Family* (Nashville: Abingdon Press, 1988).

Scales, Peter C. *Working with Young Adolescents and their Families* (Minneapolis: Search Institute, 1996).

Thompson, Marjorie J. *Family: The Forming Center* (Nashville: Upper Room Books, 1989).

Winnicott, Donald. *Babies and Their Mothers* (Reading, Mass.: Addision-Wesley Publishing Co., 1988).

—ROLAND MARTINSON
SHARON A. MARTINSON

The Tasks of Men in Families

The overarching task for the twenty-first century is to reconnect manhood and fatherhood in the lives of Western men. Both the Million Man March and Promise Keepers are mass efforts to reestablish men's responsibility to their families and society. These movements are energized in part by the disconnection many men have felt between their own manhood and fatherhood.

For many centuries Western fathers working on family farms and in home-based trades held significant responsibilities for the education and socialization of their children. The concepts of fatherhood and manhood were well integrated. But then the Industrial Revolution rapidly removed many men's work functions from the settings of their homes and families. With this economic change came a radical shift in men's relationships with their families, especially with their children. Men began to emphasize their role of providing income for the family and to de-emphasize other roles.

They began to image their task in the family solely as being that of the "breadwinner." This word did not appear in our vocabulary until about 1860. It is also interesting to note that until the nineteenth century all parenting literature and advice was directed to the father, the primary parent then, but over a relatively short period of time, fathers were demoted to the position of "secondary parent." For example, in 1860 the California Supreme Court ruled that mothers rather than fathers were in a better position to serve the best interests of the child. Thus manhood became associated more and more with work, and fatherhood was linked more with the by-product of work, that is, with the provision of income for the family.

In more recent years prominent economic forces have significantly altered men's roles throughout the world. For example, in traditional East African societies men had three main functions: providing meat through hunting, protecting the village, and initiating and educating the boys. Now, however, hunting is no longer permitted, the government's police and military forces protect the people, and the boys are educated and socialized in schools. The demise of the hunter, warrior, and initiator/educator tasks and the movement from a focus on the clan to a focus on the nuclear family has been very rapid. East African men have had to struggle to achieve the economic opportunity to provide for their families in a new way, the educational background to protect their families psychologically and emotionally, and the collective wisdom to discover different methods of caring for boys and guiding them into responsible adult roles.

The Protestant canon of the Old Testament ends with these words about the anticipated return of Elijah: "He will reconcile fathers to sons and sons to fathers, lest I come and put the land under a ban to destroy it" (Mal. 4:6, NEB). Then this prophecy is connected with the birth of John the Baptizer

(Luke 1:16–17). God's *shalom* includes reconciliation between fathers (parents) and their sons (children). The Malachi text is rendered: "He will turn the hearts of parents to their children and the hearts of children to their parents. . . ." The love and concern of parents turned toward children is an apt picture of God's *shalom* and a fitting image for the task of men in the years ahead.

Richard Louv in *FatherLove* (1993) identifies five dimensions of fatherhood that he encourages each man to embrace: breadwinning, nurturing, community building, helping the family find its place in time and history, and sharing his spiritual life with his wife and children. These five line up very well with the five functions of fathering that anthropologists have recently named: provision, caregiving, protection, endowment, and formation.

Each of these five dimensions can form a basis for identifying the tasks of men in the family of the twenty-first century and turning the hearts of men toward their children. It is worth looking at them more closely.

Provision

Providing for one's family has been the mark of a good man for many centuries. However, we now understand that doing this must not be an end in itself. Most men do not talk as much as women do about conflict in balancing work and home life. Men lose out on much that can enrich their lives when they spend an inordinate amount of time at work, away from their families. Yet they may feel they have no alternatives. Can we name one man who as he is dying says, "I wish I had spent more time at my work"?

If men discussed with each other the conflict between work and family, they could become more active in shaping workplace policies that would conflict less with family welfare. Their companies would also benefit because men who have effective relationships with their children have fewer health problems and have qualitatively better relationships with their work colleagues.

Caretaking

Several studies have shown that children whose fathers are involved in their lives grow up being more socially competent, have more compassion for others, are more self-directed, and are more persistent in solving problems. On the other hand, a high correlation has been noted between absent fathers and children's drug abuse and delinquent behavior. The nurturing of fathers often takes the form of providing structure that is consistent and dependable. The nurturing of sons by their fathers appears to be crucial to creating functional adult men with secure masculine identities.

One of the more profound changes for men in recent years is the increased number of fathers who are present in the delivery room. This initial bonding between fathers and their children is likely to increase the nurturing that these men provide for their offspring. One study of fathers who abused their children did not find a single case of an abusing dad who was present at the delivery of his child.

Perhaps the saddest result of paternal absence from the nurturing of children is the effect that it has on the father himself. When men turn over most or all of the caregiving of children to women, they experience themselves as outsiders looking in or as intruders in the family. However, a group of men who participated in their children's preschool activities reported feeling like "real men" when they were involved in fathering activities.

Support for men who are reclaiming involvement in their children's lives is now available through the National Center on Fathering, *The Dads' Newsletter,* and various support groups for fathers. Men need to encourage each other in their nurturing activities in order to overcome the tremendous social pressure to remain silent about this aspect of their lives.

Protection

Today men who arm themselves and join militia groups to protect their families and values are frightening to the general public. Fortunately they are few. A better approach for men in the twenty-first century is to seek to protect their families through becoming community builders. Communities where fathers are absent are often run and manipulated by gangs of young men who move in to fill the void. Louv (1993) gives three challenges to men regarding community building. He encourages men to do the following: network with each other to break through the fear, despair, and helplessness that they may feel regarding their communities; involve their children in the community and world around them and also to be a prominent presence in their children's activities; and become politically involved in building the community for their children and their future.

Endowment

All of us hunger to have a place in our family history and to be connected across the generations. This is something that the book and television series *Roots* provided for African-American people. The Old Testament presents this important sense of connection across the generations. In the ancient Hebrew seder ritual the youngest child of the family would ask, "Why is this night special?" The father would then tell the story of the Passover. Throughout the centuries fathers have told stories to pass on the family and community traditions. Men can still help children connect across generations through telling stories about the past and by teaching family values and ideals.

It is also important for all of us to sense our place in the future. Fathers can be instrumental in helping their children visualize a future for themselves. Erik Erikson referred to this task as being generative, first imagining and then working toward a future-oriented goal.

Perhaps this is the most precious gift that parents can give to their children.

In past centuries endowment to descendants included the giving of land and the teaching of a trade. Some parents can still endow their children with material wealth, but all parents can and ought to help their young people know their place in time.

Formation

Fathers took a significant role in the formation or guidance of their children until about one and a half centuries ago, when men began to defer to their wives in carrying out this task. A significant aspect of formation is helping each child become acquainted with spiritual values. The spiritual world takes us beyond the isolated family or individual parent into a more universal sphere. Our spiritual formation connects us with the whole earth and the cosmos.

Men who become tuned into their own spiritual centers and wholeness are in a position to help their children feel connected with eternity. Men cannot give physical birth to a child, but they can and ought to help children experience a spiritual birth. It is in this spiritual dimension that fatherhood and manhood are most effectively joined. Men who are isolated and separated from their families, communities, and themselves are not capable of participating in the spiritual formation of their children. But men who are spiritually centered and whole become visionaries for their children and the children of their community.

Conclusions

With the rapid increase of women in the work force and the development of dual-career marriages over the last three decades, men are now needing to broaden their understanding of their positions and tasks in the family. This current economic change may prove to be as influential on family structure and roles as was the Industrial Revolution. The relevant question today may well be: "Whose face is turned toward the children?" An opportunity is now offered for men to reenergize their caregiving, protection, endowment, and formation functions in the family. Men will need support and encouragement to become reconciled with their fathering roles, with each other as accountability partners, and with the church from which they are often as estranged as they are from their families. The imago of father in our society needs a reframing that is less destructive and negative. As older men hold younger men in their hearts and younger men respect older men, the imago of father will be healed and will become positive.

Four elements are contained in each response to fulfilling male tasks in the family: the man's internalized self-concepts, the current modifying constraints in the environment, the integration of these previous two, and finally the development of men's roles over time and history. Those who are involved in pastoral care interventions will need to take these four elements into consideration when establishing a plan of ministry with men today. When the hearts of fathers are turned to the children—their own and those in the community—then they will participate in God's *shalom*.

Bibliography

August, Eugene R. *The New Men's Studies: A Selected and Annotated Interdisciplinary Bibliography,* 2d ed. (Englewood, Colo.: Libraries Unlimited, 1994).

Betcher, R. William, and William S. Pollack. *In a Time of Fallen Heroes* (New York: Macmillan Publishing Co., 1993).

Blankenhorn, David. *Fatherless America* (New York: Basic Books, 1995).

Lamb, Michael E., ed. *The Father's Role: Applied Perspectives* (New York: John Wiley and Sons, 1986).

Louv, Richard. *FatherLove* (New York: Pocket Books, 1993).

—THEODORE STONEBERG

The Tasks of Women in Families

How should we conceive the tasks of women in families? I approach this question as a Calvinist layperson working in psychology and gender studies, and as a supporter and beneficiary of women's legal, economic, and social gains from the "second wave" of feminism. My resources for answering it include the Hebrew and Christian scriptures (using a hermeneutic that emphasizes the biblical drama of creation, fall, redemption, and future hope), academic theory and research (particularly from the social sciences), and women's individual and corporate experience—of which feminist writings past and present are an important if partial record.

I begin with some considerations from social science, since this allows me to make an important point about terminology. The word *tasks* in this article's title is closely related to the more standard term *roles*—as in phrases like "professional roles" or "gender roles." But asking for an analysis of women's family roles (or men's, for that matter) risks oversimplification. The concept of roles is central to both classical psychoanalytic theory and its offshoot, sex-role theory, according to which there exists an unchanging "essence" of masculinity and femininity, grounded in biology and/or religiously revealed or other metaphysical truths. This point of view is reflected in Freud's insistence that "anatomy is destiny" and that women's natural spheres of activity are "*kinder, kuche, und kirche*": children, cooking, and church.

Both theories hold that, because of human finitude, perversity, or both, people do not grow into their "essential" masculine and feminine roles naturally but must also have them reinforced, and both psychoanalytic and sex-role theory pay a great deal of attention to how this happens, particularly in childhood. Classical Freudians emphasize the process by which the child comes to identify with the same-sex parent, particularly through the resolution of the Oedipus complex, while sex-role theorists stress the processes of social learning: the rewards, punishments, and role-modeling opportunities afforded by children's parents, peers, and other significant adult figures.

Critics of these approaches do not dispute that human behavior is limited by biology—so that, for example, in certain settings the constraints of pregnancy and lactation will affect the range of women's behavior, just as men's on-average greater upper-body strength will affect theirs. Nor is it disputed that identification, reinforcement, and role-modeling account for some of the observed behavioral differences between women and men. One recasting of psychoanalytic theory, known as feminist object-relations theory, holds that identification is indeed an important process in the development of gender identity and style. But its proponents suggest that this occurs earlier than the Oedipal stage, in infancy when children of both sexes bond and identify with their primary caretaker, who is usually female. This is less problematic (at least in the short run) for girls, who proceed to acquire culturally feminine habits by simply continuing to bond with their mothers. But boys—particularly ones who lack involved male parent figures—eventually conclude that to become masculine, they must reject what their mothers represent, that is, whatever is perceived to be feminine. The result, according to feminist object-relations theorists (and a supporting body of empirical research, both intra- and cross-cultural), is that women on average grow up more relationally—and hence domestically—inclined and more secure in their gender identity, whereas men are more likely to develop a fragile gender identity and to take refuge in abstraction, misogyny, and the avoidance of womanly traits and activities in order to compensate (Chodorow 1978).

The recently developed "critical theory" tradition in social science suggests further reasons why Freudian and sex-role theories cannot explain all the complexities of gender. Both fail to account for the diversity of gender roles across cultures and within cultures across time, and also for the diversity of behavior shown by individual women and men in various settings. Moreover, whereas sex-role theorists treat men's and women's ascribed roles and traits as equal in costs, benefits, and social value, critical theorists have emphasized that the activities and characteristics ascribed to men almost always have greater cultural value and power than those ascribed to women (Connell 1987).

To exemplify the limits of the earlier theories, consider two daughters from the same family. Both may have been equally socialized for "feminine" roles and both may marry, yet one works in the (male-dominated) police force while the other chooses the stereotypically feminine field of nursing. To complicate matters, the second daughter may have a reputation for directing her nursing supervisees in an authoritarian, "masculine" fashion, while her sister in the police force is known for her "feminine" empathy and her mediation skills in dealing with potentially violent situations. And on the home front, the policewoman is known for her spotless household and the fact that she earns more than her husband, while her sister's domestic disorganization and her husband's millionaire status are legendary. Is each one's degree of femininity—and success in "womanly tasks"—to be defined by her personality traits, her paid work, her behavior at home, or her economic status relative to her husband? And how are we to account for the discrepancies among these if sex roles, once acquired, are permanent and consistent features of our adult lives?

The failure of Freudian and sex-role theories to answer such questions has led contemporary social scientists to conceptualize gender in more *relational* and dynamic terms. Whereas role theory tends to treat marital life as the sum of separate parts—rather like two railway tracks moving in parallel—critical theorists might prefer the image of a canoe on a lake. In such a situation, although all occupants may be paddling diligently, they are not strictly equal, since the person in the stern, just by virtue of being in the rear "ruddering" position, has more power over the boat's direction. And yet if the person in the bow stops paddling, or shifts weight, the other must somehow adapt—willingly or reluctantly—if the boat is to keep upright and moving.

This metaphor captures the notion in critical theory that gendered behavior within marriage (as elsewhere) is a relational dynamic: something its members are constantly negotiating, sometimes with small and almost unconscious shifts and sometimes with much energy and controversy, as the past several decades of feminist activity have shown. Gender, on this reading, is more a verb than a noun—something we *do,* rather than *have.* And in contrast to the passive image of people simply "absorbing" gendered behavioral norms via the mechanisms of identification and conditioning, critical theory stresses the agency of all the people involved. For even if the person in the stern (historically the husband and father) has more power over the direction of the vessel, the other persons in the boat are never without influence. They can shift their weight, change the side they paddle on, stop paddling completely for a time, or even insist that, at the next stop on dry land, the passengers rotate places! Some may even leave the canoe and seek a different mode of transportation if such a shift cannot be negotiated to their satisfaction.

The picture that emerges from critical theory is one in which women and men are more alike than different—"neighboring sexes" rather than opposite sexes, as Dorothy Sayers noted half a century ago in her witty essay "Are Women Human?" And it is a picture that is affirmed by the scriptural record, considered in its redemptive-historical sweep. For when we look at what Reformed theologians call the "cultural mandate" of Genesis 1:26–28, we do not find God saying to the first female "Be fruitful and multiply," and to the first male "Subdue the earth." Both members of the primal pair are called to accountable dominion, sociability, and fruitfulness. Made equally in the image of God, both are called to unfold the potential of creation in all areas of life, to work out together God's call to stewardship, justice, and fidelity, albeit in ways that take account of differing settings and times in history.

We cannot, of course, simply stop with a creation theology of gender relations; we must also factor in the effects of human sin. Various feminist theologians have suggested that God's description of the results of the fall in Genesis 3:16 (the woman's "desire shall be for [her] husband, and he shall rule over [her]") portends the differing ways that women and men tend to distort the image of God in themselves. Men's practice of legitimate, accountable dominion too easily degenerates into self-seeking domination—of the earth, of other men, and of women and children—while women's exercise of legitimate, creational sociability can degenerate into social enmeshment. The woman's complementary flaw to the man's domination is thus the temptation to cling to and idolize relationships even when they are distorted by abuse and injustice (Plaskow 1980; Van Leeuwen 1990).

In spite of all this, God's cultural and social mandates continue for both sexes, and in the third, redemptive act of the biblical drama we see them coming together again after being tragically warped and divided along gender lines. Particularly noteworthy is Jesus' refusal, on several occasions, to endorse the prevailing assumption that women's status depends primarily on their childbearing and domestic functions (for example, Matt. 12:46–50; Luke 10:28–42;

11:27–28). Additionally, Paul's sermon on love in 1 Corinthians 13, his sermon on the whole armor of God in Ephesians 6, and his list of the fruits of the spirit in Galatians 5 show no hint of a rigidly gendered division of traits: together they address the essential components of the generic Christian character.

None of this means that a gendered division of labor is always wrong. What a biblical theology of gender relations does affirm is that whatever tasks we embrace as women or men, single or married, are secondary and flexibly subordinate to the shared creational calling to "fill the earth and subdue it" and the shared redemptive calling to fulfill the Great Commission and to work toward the restoration of God's kingdom *shalom* in all areas of life, whether public or domestic. However, if the feminist reading of the differential effects of the fall is correct, then marriage should also be a forum for overcoming those effects, women helping men to develop their relational capacities more fully, and men helping women to pursue vocational visions that go beyond social-reproductive tasks such as the preparation of food, the maintenance of shelter and clothing, and the physical and emotional care of family members throughout the life cycle.

This is admittedly a different view of family life than the one which, since the Industrial Revolution, has read back into Scripture a rigid gendering of public and domestic spheres—with women assigned to be "angels of the home" and men the "captains of industry"—then confidently claimed the result to be the "traditional" (or even "biblical") family. But in the long sweep of history, the truly traditional family has been one in which workplace, dwelling space, and child-rearing space largely coincide, as in a family farming operation or a small family business (Degler 1980). If feminist object-relations theorists are correct, we have paid a heavy psychological price by effectively reducing parenting to mothering, and fathering to breadwinning in locations geographically removed from the home. Such arrangements, as noted above, tend to produce misogyny in boys deprived of hands-on male models, who by their continued presence and care could have helped reassure their sons that they were masculine enough to get on with the more important business of being human. And the "reproduction of mothering" that results from the public/private division of labor by gender may result in girls and women who do not develop their public selves and who too easily translate the misogyny of the surrounding culture into low self-esteem and various forms of vulnerability—economic, physical, emotional, and sexual.

How does all of this translate into practical counsel for family life at the dawn of the third millennium, and particularly for women in families? I offer the following observations:

1. A growing body of empirical research supports the notion that marital satisfaction is higher on average when both partners are involved in child-rearing *and* breadwinning tasks. When partners have an intimately shared, ongoing task in child care, there is less likelihood that they will

grow apart over the years, that women will suffer depression from the cumulative effects of isolation and economic dependence, and that men will over-rely for self-esteem on their success in the public arena. A wife's greater involvement in the waged workplace eases the husband's burden of having the entire household economy depend on him, and fathers' ongoing involvement with children reaps positive benefits: their sons are able to show more vulnerability, and their daughters more competitiveness than is the case in families with a more clearly gendered division of labor (Rivers and Barnett 1996).

2. However, two qualifiers to the above generalization need to be noted. When both partners are in the waged workforce full time, not only is the risk of burnout higher, but the otherwise shared task of child rearing tends to be turned over to full-time professional child care workers. Thus, unless the couple are among the minority in which both have the same kind of waged work, the danger of progressive estrangement is just as great as in families where the husband is the full-time wage earner and the wife a full-time homemaker. Moreover, the effect of maternal waged employment on children has less to do with the type and amount of work itself than with the degree of choice mothers perceive themselves to have. When women, by reason of economic or other pressure, are in the waged workforce more than they want to be, both they and other family members express dissatisfaction. But the reverse is also true: When women are reluctant full-time homemakers, both their own level of satisfaction and that of other family members is lower than in families with wage-employed mothers.

Both qualifiers underscore the need for flexibility in making decisions about marital tasks. Although all family members benefit from fathers' and mothers' participation in both public and domestic arenas, the way tasks are best allocated depends more on individual differences within families at different stages of the family life cycle than on some unchanging essence of "womanliness," "manliness," or "ideal family life." To return to our analogy from critical theory, there is more than one way to get a canoe successfully to its destination. What is important is that all the people in the vessel learn all the skills necessary, and that the positions are shared in a way that takes account of individual and corporate needs, desires, and energy levels throughout the voyage.

3. In a fallen world, the question of justice in marital rela-
    tions cannot be neglected. Critical theorists and feminist
    theologians of both sexes have underscored the reality of
    men's historically greater power in both public and pri-
    vate life, and the ways in which this power is abused. I
    note this not to romanticize women's suffering (as some
    "difference feminists" tend to) nor to suggest that male
    sexism is the original sin and women are the pristine new
    creation, but merely to affirm that a creation theology of
    the goodness of marriage needs to be tempered by a real-
    istic respect for the existence of sin.

    Gender injustice runs the gamut from men's physical,
    sexual, and emotional abuse of women, through family
    desertion and the resulting feminization of poverty, to the
    cumulative unfairness of women's "second shift"—that is,
    men's reluctance to balance women's entry into the waged
    workforce with a more equitable sharing of domestic
    tasks. Although there is evidence of accelerating change
    for the better in these areas, counselors still need to be
    alert to women's greater vulnerability in the family con-
    stellation. And although there is evidence that on average
    it is better for children to be raised in intact families, di-
    vorce must often reluctantly be accepted as the lesser of
    two evils where chronic male abuse or irresponsibility
    characterizes a marriage. Poor women in particular need
    access to resources in both public and nongovernmental
    sectors that can empower them for economic security and
    the development of skills that enable not only families but
    women within them to flourish.

4. Family life is vulnerable to idolatry even (or perhaps es-
    pecially) when it is satisfying to everyone involved. Thus
    "it is a salutary rebuke to the church's overvaluing of fam-
    ily life to remember that Jesus was seen as a family-
    breaker" (Clapp 1993, 192). Women, no less than men,
    need to regard family life not only as creationally valuable
    in itself but as a potential launching pad for mission to a
    hurting world, and as secondary to the kingdom family in
    which membership is based not on blood ties but on
    shared allegiance to a religious vision of personal and so-
    cietal redemption. Churches and other religious bodies
    thus need to find a balance between the tasks of strength-
    ening families and calling them to involvement in the
    wider community. Evangelicals have typically erred on
    the side of the former, liberal churches on the latter. There
    is great need for a recovered biblical synthesis of the two.

Bibliography

Chodorow, Nancy. *The Reproduction of Mothering: Psychoanalysis and the Sociology of Gender* (Berkeley and Los Angeles: University of California Press, 1978).

Clapp, Rodney. *Families at the Crossroads: Beyond Traditional and Modern Options* (Downers Grove, Ill.: InterVarsity Press, 1993).

Connell, Robert W. *Gender and Power: Society, the Person, and Sexual Politics* (Stanford, Calif.: Stanford University Press, 1987).

Degler, Carl. *At Odds: Women and the Family in America from the Revolution to the Present* (New York: Oxford University Press, 1980).

Plaskow, Judith. *Sex, Sin, and Grace* (Washington, D.C.: University Press of America, 1980).

Rivers, Caryl, and Rosalind C. Barnett. *She Works, He Works: How Two Income Families are Happier, Healthier, and Better Off* (San Francisco: Harper San Francisco, 1996).

Van Leeuwen, Mary Stewart. *Gender and Grace: Love, Work, and Parenting in a Changing World* (Downers Grove, Ill.: InterVarsity Press, 1990).

—MARY STEWART VAN LEEUWEN

The Tasks of
Grandparents in Families

The rapidly changing dynamics and demographics in American family life over the past fifty years provide a new frontier for grandparenting. There was a time when grandparents lived in close proximity to their adult children and were considered a normal part of extended family life. Grandparents were often relied upon by their adult children for their experience and wisdom in the rearing of grandchildren.

Where grandparents were once looked to for intergenerational stability and identity, they are today more likely to be expected to provide child care for working mothers. Some grandparents have had to become parents again. There are 3.2 million grandparents raising their children's children. These grandparents have stepped in to rescue their grandchildren from the incapacity or inability of their sons or daughters to function effectively as parents. These grandparents have had to make radical adjustments in their own lives and take on responsibilities for which they have more wisdom but less energy.

Perhaps the most difficult challenge for grandparents in today's society is to observe the radically different lifestyles and parenting dynamics practiced by our adult sons and daughters with our grandchildren. Today's parents are more independent, less open to advice, and more involved with their own peer group than with their parents. They tend not to look to grandparents as mentors and models for their own parenting and family life. Often, they will intentionally break with a family tradition of parenting as a way of establishing their own independence.

Anxious about their own financial burdens and stressed by the fast-paced life of their children and the cost of their education, parents find it hard to include the grandparents in the family life cycle. When grandparents cannot be physically present, they often lavish grandchildren with gifts as a way of staying in touch. In 1992 grandparents spent $8.3 billion on gifts for their grandchildren.

In our contemporary society the mold for grandparenthood has been broken. Grandparents today are, on average, younger, more mobile, more active, and less involved in the day-to-day activities of their adult children and grandchildren. The structure of family life has undergone radical change. And along with those changes the role of grandparents in families has also changed. Experts on child rearing have replaced grandparents with new scientific theories about parenting. Increased mobility in the work force, migration from rural to urban and suburban centers, and the high rate of divorce has meant that grandparents are often less involved in daily family living.

Divorce creates another set of problems for grandparents. Divorce not only separates children from one of their parents, it also can separate children from their grandparents. With the remarriage of a parent, children often acquire a new set of grandparents, resulting in "top-heavy" family structures. This can be confusing for the children and awkward for the grandparents. And when grandparents divorce, who receives "custody" of the grandchildren?

Conflict between parents and their married sons and daughters can also lead to alienation, with the result that grandparents are denied access to their grandchildren. Some grandparents have sought legal recourse in their attempt to have a relationship with their grandchildren. A grandparents' bill of rights has even been proposed in support of those who have been denied contact with their grandchildren. While these situations are unusual, they reflect the fact that grandparents may be the neglected casualties in the disintegration of the family structure.

All of these factors can leave grandparents anxious, confused, and helpless. Participation in parenting decisions is often taken as unwanted intervention. The culture gap widens the generation gap, and many a grandparent has retreated, wounded and hurt. Because being a grandparent is a form of love, it will always involve risks and hurts, as do all loving relationships. Grandparents learn to live with less than optimal circumstances in order to create room for what is possible.

First-time grandparents find themselves thrust into a new role without preparation and without a traditional context in which to fit comfortably. How does one shift gears from being a parent to a grandparent? It is not as though being a grandparent comes naturally. For most of us, entering into the role of grandparent is uncharted territory. The exhilaration of having the first grandchild is often accompanied by a shock of dismay at suddenly being called "grandma" or "grandpa"!

However fulfilling it is to see one's own adult children hold their own newborn child, we sense immediately that our relation with this son or daughter who has now become a parent is significantly changed. The arrival of a child is the beginning of a "new family" and marks a generational transition more sharply than when an adult child leaves home and marries. The father or mother of a married son or daughter is still a father or mother with the addition of a daughter- or son-in-law. But when an adult child becomes a parent, our role as parent is displaced, and we have become grandparents.

There are pitfalls as well as pleasures in being a grandparent. What used to be advice when given to one's own child may now be received as criticism when offered with respect to a grandchild. Learning to give advice, whether asked for or not, with practiced indifference to whether the advice is followed can be the key to effective relationship with the parents of one's grandchildren. By respecting the rights of parents, one preserves the privilege of being a grandparent.

The number of grandparents in the United States is rising rapidly. While more than 58 million Americans are grandparents today, by the year 2005 there will be more than 76 million grandparents. Nearly half of these grandparents will come from the present population of baby boomers. The need for grandparents is greater than ever! Grandparents will need to discover how to meet this need and what shape their role should be in the family life of their children and grandchildren.

First of all, we must understand that grandparents represent a valuable and rich resource for the contemporary American family. This is a resource not available through social services, community support groups, and professional experts. Grandparents perform an important task because they are a repository of values and beliefs; they are living symbols of family continuity and stability; they are a source of unconditional love and acceptance; and they are mentors in the task of facing life and death with courage and faith.

A Repository of Values and Beliefs

The task of being a grandparent is not so much that of being a religious teacher as of living a consistent life of personal faith that embodies the teachings and practice of the Judeo-Christian tradition. Where grandchildren are brought up in a religious tradition different from that of the grandparents, this task becomes more difficult. There is often a temptation to make an issue of the differing religious tradition and belief system with the result that a conflict or division arises in this area between the grandparents and the parents. Though such a stand can be viewed as a form of adherence to one's own religious convictions, it can become an obstacle and even a deterrent to the spiritual development of the grandchildren.

When the apostle Paul sought to encourage the younger Timothy, he reminded him of the faith that "lived first in your grandmother Lois and your mother Eunice and now, I am sure, lives in you" (2 Tim. 1:5). Here we have an instance of a three-generation religious faith within the very first century of Christianity. More than an allusion to a historical fact, Paul's reminder to Timothy of his grandmother's faith was meant to inspire and encourage his own faith in a time of much opposition, confusion, and uncertainty.

Grandparents need to be reminded that their first priority is to live out their own religious beliefs in such a way that the value of having faith is transmitted to grandchildren through the conduit of a shared family story. What grandparents can provide is an ongoing narrative of life lived with the assurance of God's faithfulness toward us in such a way that grandchildren can take up that story in their own faith tradition. Even where the religious tradition of the parents is the same as that of the grandparents, it is the shared family narrative of God's faithfulness based on the biblical stories that provides a resource for grandchildren in their own discovery and pilgrimage of faith.

Living Symbols of Family
Continuity and Stability

What children need today are family icons, not cultural heroes. An icon is like a figure that is familiar and yet carries a transcendent, luminous quality. Some software programs use icons as a user-friendly way of making accessible the mysterious and hidden power of the computer. In somewhat the same way, grandparents can make the hidden wisdom of life user-friendly.

For the small child, a grandparent is viewed in a different way than is a parent. Grandparents are the nearest that a child comes to experiencing a reality that stands outside of their daily life and yet is approachable and familiar. Parents are bound into the child's small world as extensions of the child's needs for survival and security. Grandparents move back and forth across that boundary, shedding their light upon the family and, at the same time, providing for the child a luminous icon extending into the past and pointing to the future.

The task of the grandparent is to preserve that role not by attempting to become another parent to the child but by capturing the life of the child in a relation that is as free as a fairy tale and as cozy as a warm hug. When adult sons and daughters become parents and have their own families, they need grandparents as icons of continuity and stability as much as do their children. More than good advice on raising their children, parents need from grandparents a "river that runs through" life, providing a sense of continuity and stability amidst change and uncertainty.

But relationships with grandchildren must go beyond stories about the "good old days." Grandparents are a repository of stories and anecdotes that must be remembered, told, and recorded. It is important for grandparents to find ways to interest their grandchildren in their family history. This may be done by making sure that the oral history that grandparents carry with them is recorded—in writing, tapes, pictures, or other means—so that it will be available when there is more interest in such information.

Grandparents need to remember that their role is often an invisible and unrecognized one. As grandparents, we are providing a scaffolding for the building of lives we may never see. When we remember our own grandparents, we see that this is true.

A Source of Unconditional Love
and Acceptance

Everyone needs someone who believes in them and loves them unconditionally. Grandparents can provide this for their grandchildren in a special way. While it is true that parents often accuse grandparents of spoiling their children by giving expensive gifts and "breaking the rules," children have need of someone who mediates pure grace. Self-worth is not like a safety deposit box, locked up and sealed to prevent any loss. Rather, self-worth is more like a bucket of water that we carry every day with some holes in it, some larger than others! We need our bucket constantly refilled and, when it can be done, we need to have some of the holes plugged or at least made smaller.

The self-worth of a child is constantly under assault. Failures come by the dozen, at school, with friends, and at home. Without expectations, a child has no sense of motivation. But with every bright expectation there is a shadow of failure. Parents are caught in the cycle of behavioral problems and the need to discipline. Grandparents have a different role, equally difficult, but clearly essential.

Grandparents face the difficulty of supporting parental rules and discipline while, at the same time, offering the child a special relationship. It is in the special relationship, not in breaking the rules, that a grandparent provides the kind of love and acceptance that a child needs. Without playing favorites, grandparents can give each grandchild the feeling of being a "favorite" person.

When children receive attention and affirmation from grandparents, it comes as unmerited favor, rather than as a reward for some performance. This is the same quality of love that is conveyed by the theological word *grace*. We all need to learn to receive grace in order to live "grace-filled" lives. Grandparents have a special role in developing the capacity to receive grace in children and thus preparing them for the grace of God. This is especially important when so many children today suffer from lack or loss of parental love. Grandparents can provide a stream of grace that reminds the child that he or she is both the object of God's love and a person who receives and appropriates the grace of God.

Mentors in the Task of Facing Life and Death

In former years, when grandparents spent their last years and sometimes their last days in the family home, children were initiated into the reality of death as part of the structure of life. The death of grandparents put a human face on death for the child, as it were. The passing of a generation was a ritual that embraced all members of the family, preparing each for their own journey.

Today, few people die at home, and children rarely experience the dying of a family member. People simply disappear from the child's world when they die, leaving the child to cope with a loss that has no power to shape his or her own encounter with mortality.

One important role of grandparents is that of mentoring their children and grandchildren in the task of entering into life with both a vision for living meaningfully and dying with dignity and hope. I well remember going as a boy with my parents to the local cemetery near the farm where we lived. There we walked among the grave sites and read the names of my grandparents; the stories told brought them to life again.

One of my earliest memories is of my grandmother lying in her coffin in the parlor of our farm home during the two- or three-day interval between her death and the funeral service. At that age I had little sense of what death meant. But I understood that this too was part of our family life. Grieving a loss without surrendering to despair and hopelessness is a capacity that must be learned. Who better to mentor us in the crucial passages of life and death than grandparents?

Preparing to be a grandparent and acquiring the skills of being an effective grandparent begin with the intentional formation of rituals and rites of passage in which grandchildren can participate. This is a lifelong task. The benefits begin immediately, and the rewards accrue to the generations that follow. The Fifth Commandment exhorts us to "Honor your father and your mother." It is the First Commandment that carries a promise for this life and, by implication, for generations to come (Eph. 6:2). Grandparents are also fathers and mothers; to honor them is to find the glue that can bind our broken families together. This is a promise!

Bibliography

Anderson, Ray S. *Unspoken Wisdom—Truths My Father Taught Me* (Minneapolis: Augsburg, 1995).

Carson, Lillian. *The Essential Grandparent: A Guide to Making a Difference* (Deerfield Beach, Fla.: Health Communications, 1996).

Gutowski, Carolyn. *Grandparents Are Forever* (New York: Paulist Press, 1994).

Kornhaber, Arthur, with Sondra Forsyth. *Grandparent Power! How to Strengthen the Vital Connection among Grandparents, Parents, and Children* (New York: Crown Publishers, 1994).

O'Connor, Karen. *Innovative Grandparenting: How Today's Grandparents Build Personal Relationships with Their Grandkids* (St. Louis: Concordia Publishing House, 1995).

—RAY ANDERSON

Families, Work, and Economic Pressures

Few, besides certain neoliberal economists, claim that family life can be completely reduced to economics. Still, our families and households are deeply shaped and affected by work, and by the broader economic circumstances, values, and assumptions in which our activities as workers are enmeshed. Considering how work and economic concerns permeate the atmosphere of family living, talk about them in churches and synagogues is surprisingly rare. The absence of vital conversation about economy and work in our congregations is a serious concern. Without it, members are deprived of a moral and religious vocabulary for interpreting central aspects of their daily lives.

We in religious communities badly need to find ways to break the silence and spark such conversation. A good place to begin is by exploring the history that lies behind the work experiences of families today. Contemporary household economies are embedded in a long story of changing institutional patterns and beliefs about the purposes of work and economy and their relation to family flourishing.

Historical Background

The connection between the familial household and economic activity has ancient roots, reflected in the etymology of the word *economy*—*oikos-nomos*—Greek for the laws and management of a household. In ancient Greece, the household, or *oikos,* was the private realm of family and work, oriented around material survival and maintenance. Economics had a widely accepted purpose: managing the acquisition, production, distribution, and consumption of material resources to ensure sufficiency for all household members. To this end, assets such as human competencies and physical strength, time, money, raw materials, and finished products were to be wisely administered. Work, primarily a means to material survival, also enabled persons to develop and exercise abilities and to contribute to the community.

For centuries, families were centers of economic activity, and work and economy were embued with normative, communal meanings. Christian theologians even employed the term *economy* to describe the creating, saving, and consummating work of God in Christ Jesus. This divine *oikonomia* was reflected in the interdependence of all members of the created order, and in God's ordering and redeeming "management" of all God's "household" toward its proper end and destiny. Christian churches ministered to families in settings where both the integration of economy and family, and economy's provident function in relation to families, were assumed.

Modern Challenges

In the modern West, profound changes in family and economy brought new challenges to pastoral ministry. First, modern economics narrowed the meaning of *oikonomia* to market exchange, whose goal is not livelihood for all members but individual profit (Meeks 1989, 37). Since the eighteenth century, workers have been swept up in successive waves of change as production, transportation, and communications have been reinvented in industrial, technological, and most recently, computerized modes. Simultaneously, urbanization transformed the majority of family households from sites of production to "units of consumption." A further change has been the sharpening distinction between private household and public economy, and the gender roles connected to each realm. Among the middle class in the nineteenth and twentieth centuries, the public-private distinction became associated with a particular gender-based division of labor. Women—"housekeepers"—were best-suited and responsible for the private, domestic household, and men—"breadwinners"—for wage-earning in the public realm. The lesser public value accorded to domestic, women's labor in this scheme was reflected in popular vocabulary, as "to work" came to connote something done outside the home, for wages.

In the twentieth-century United States, the landscape of the family-economy relation continued to shift. More men moved from self-employment into waged labor; child labor declined as a source of household income; the geographical distance between domicile and workplace increased. In the later twentieth century, perhaps the most important change has been the streaming of women into the full-time waged workforce, and its still-unfolding impact on both the domestic and the public economies.

On the threshold of a new millennium, families continue to experience economy and work as dynamic and volatile. Among the "signs of the times" for middle- and working-class North American families are financial pressures and longer work hours because of declining real wages; job insecurity because of rapid skill obsolescence and corporate outsourcing and downsizing; conflicts between time and energy demanded by paid work and by home and family; anxiety about providing for children or elderly parents; lack of respect and power in the workplace; the cultural devaluation of unremunerated homework and the consequent neglect of children and neighborhoods; turmoil concerning roles of women and men in domestic and public economies; and the complex effects of race and class on work and economic opportunity.

Below the Surface:
Competing Moral Interpretations

Winding through this confusing contemporary scene are competing interpretations of the very meaning and purposes of work, economy, and family life. Families are presented, both overtly and subtly, with at least two powerful, opposing answers to the fundamental question: Where and how are survival, sufficiency, and flourishing to be attained? Consumerist, market-driven society offers one answer: Survival and well-being, always precarious, must continually be earned by producing, achieving, and acquiring. Work and consumption are the arenas in which one's basic identity and self-worth are grasped or lost. Family functions chiefly as a pit stop on the fast track of work-and-spend, whose most significant activities are consuming and refueling. Religious communities propose a different, more traditional response: Survival, security, and well-being rest in accepting and sharing the love and life of God and others. Family is a primary arena for cultivating this orientation to persons and life. Production, acquisition, and possessions are limited, strictly instrumental goods. When treated as ends in themselves—as market culture tempts us to do—they become idolatrous and addictive, exercising a false hold over our attention and energies that in the end will only exhaust, disappoint, and defeat us.

Families lacking a vital relation to strong countervailing communities of economic interpretation (whether religious or humanist) too often absorb these contradictory messages in circumstances that reinforce, willy-nilly, patterns and values purveyed by market culture. The dominant economic culture tends to obscure alternative ways of seeing and acting for one simple reason: at the end of any given day or week, family members find themselves with little time and energy to imagine, much less enact, anything different. Adults, many in dual-worker or single-parent households, often suffer from time pressures that siphon energy away from family or community life. Middle-class mothers and fathers trying to juggle career and family are pulled between the qualities required for career success (including mobility, a prime commitment to oneself, efficiency, a controlling attitude, and a goal-oriented, time-pressured approach to tasks) and those needed for good parenting (such as stability, commitment to others, a tolerance for chaos, an ability to let go, and an ability to tie the same pair of shoelaces twenty-nine times with patience and humor) (Hewlett 1991, 85–86). A cultural mood that connects happiness and status to financial achievement and material security encourages workers exhausted by "competing urgency systems" to devote their off-work time to privatized pursuits revolving around consumption. Whether relaxing in front of the television with a beer, or making weekend getaways to Aruba, the upshot is the same: families are tempted to devote their best energies to acquiring, spending, and consuming. Neither religious sensibility nor public virtue fits easily into a life pattern etched between workplace, mall, and single-family dwelling. It is no surprise when civic engagement declines, as well as church involvement.

A religious perspective insists that as families succumb to the narrow orientation proffered by modern economic culture, relying on it to fulfill every need and desire, then do individuals and their most cherished relationships, including family bonds, languish. The damaging results are seen in puzzling contradictions that mar our daily lives. We seek close and intimate family bonds but are frequently isolated from others. We long to integrate work, home, and civic community but instead find fragmentation and disjointedness. We want family lives that are engaged with what really matters, but too often we find ourselves

living off superficialities, concerned more with appearances or the latest amuse-
ments than with the stuff of genuine character, beauty, or nobility. We have a
nagging sense that we were not simply "born to shop" or to work or to consume,
but the lens formed by the conspiracy of market economy and consumer culture obscures alternatives from view. Frenetic work-spend-collapse schedules
erode families' capacities to break free of this constricted pattern to discover a
different and fuller view (Kavanaugh 1992; Schor 1991).

What Can Religious Congregations Do?

Grappling with work pressures amidst a consumer economy that tends to
override other sources of meaning and direction, families find their spiritual
bearings threatened and their moral integrity and confidence assailed. Religious
communities have a crucial role to play in helping families pierce the gilded veil
of materialism and recapture their capacity to engage in work and economy
from a firm spiritual and moral base.

At first blush, faith communities seem admirably equipped to provide such
assistance. Jewish and Christian scriptures are filled with exhortations concerning work's necessity and dignity, the folly of idolizing wealth or material
security, and the need to set one's heart on the only treasure that lasts (for example, Isaiah 44; Luke 12). In communal worship, people's works and achieve-
ments are on one hand sanctified and offered up to God's glory, and on the
other revealed as relative values superseded by the dignity of the persons behind the works, and supremely, by the Divine. Yet, as we have noted, concrete
work and economic concerns confronting families receive little explicit or consistent attention in our congregations. If effective connections between faith
and family economic life are to be made, creative initiatives must be aimed, first,
at prompting people to talk about their experiences of work and family and to
begin putting them in religious perspective; second, at educating and supporting families in humane, community-minded viewpoints on work and economy;
and third, at cultivating dispositions and practices that enable families to become active resisters, subverters, and transformers of idolatrous economic patterns both within their homes and in society. Drawing on varied media
(preaching, catechesis, study, liturgy, community activities, social action), religious congregations need to forge strategies for fomenting among families renewed, religiously grounded ways of seeing, judging, and acting with respect
to work and economy. By so doing, parishes and synagogues can serve as "holding communities" (Miller-McLemore 1994, 185–95) and transformative bases
for families in these important areas of life.

Breaking the Silence

As a beginning, congregations might consider ways to help families cultivate
their "seeing" concerning work and economic matters. A perverse genius of any
false worldview is its ability to distract and lull, preventing those under its thrall

from looking more closely and engaging in the honest conversation that would empower people to see "the way things are" concerning work and economy more clearly. In several U.S. cities, movements for congregation-based community organizing have germinated out of local churches' efforts to gather people for conversations concerning, simply, what family and work are like for them these days. Discussing work, money, and economic issues threatens an influential middle-class ideal that links individual dignity with economic self-sufficiency and the ability to keep financial matters completely private. Even to talk with fellow believers concerning family and work experiences discomfits many of us. One place to start conversation is to ask each other why this is so. What does our silence seek to protect?

Celebrating a "Community of Work"

Taking a different tack, a local congregation might gather information about the work that people in their community do, have done, or might be preparing to do. Imagine compiling a portrait of a congregation as a community of workers. A core of volunteers surveys members of each household to ask about three arenas of work, and the competencies and responsibilities persons exercise in each: domestic work; volunteer civic, church, and community work; and waged work inside or outside the home. Members are invited to meet and discuss the findings. People who do similar work could identify themselves to one another. Older or retired members might be introduced to younger colleagues from the same lines of work, and dialogue fostered. In congregations where there is a great deal of mobility, with many members moving in and out, that phenomenon could be considered in light of the kinds of jobs, socioeconomic circumstances and values, and fears and hopes for children that might precipitate such movement. Through this sharing, an initial vocabulary for conversing about work and economy in a faith setting could emerge, along with bonds of communication and trust that provide a foundation on which to build.

Making the Deeper Connections

Grassroots-directed initiatives like this can enable members to discover and affirm the relevance of core religious teachings for their family and work lives. Despite conflicting cultural trends, the priority of persons over their labor, production, and wealth may be brought home. Congregations that explicitly recognize and affirm the significance of families' daily work and economic experiences can underscore their connections with central religious motifs in liturgy, preaching, and communal outreach.

In seeking to enlighten and empower families in their economic activities, *stewardship, solidarity with the poor and marginalized,* and *Sabbath* traditions are among the potent, biblically grounded motifs on which faith communities may draw. To elaborate briefly only on the latter, the ancient Jewish practice of honoring the Sabbath, and Christians' of Sunday rest and worship, breaks the work-spend cycle. Its beneficial and subversive strategy is captured in the reversed imperative: "Don't just do something; sit there!" Taking time for prayer, liturgy, reflection, and attentive (versus distracted or anesthetizing) family recreation allows us to pause and look up from our preoccupation with material and work issues. It is also an indispensable condition for cultivating and maintaining a spiritual or interior life, something antithetical to the world of an external locus of control and attractive surfaces touted by market and advertising culture. The habit of living mindfully, of incorporating a contemplative dimension into the everyday, can renew and fortify families grappling with economic pressures and demands, and create the space to envision alternatives.

Discerning the Spirit's Movements in Society

While embracing the treasures of their traditions, and opposing corrupt tendencies in economy and society, faith communities need to remain alert to movements of the Spirit in elements of contemporary culture. These movements are particularly evident in contemporary struggles for justice among groups historically separated and subjugated because of their sex, race, or class. Religious strictures against greed are complemented by growing societal awareness that sufficiency for the poor requires curbing wasteful and incessant acquisition by the affluent, protecting natural resources, and challenging unjust distribution of wealth and economic power. On another front, feminists emphasize that efforts of families to deal with work pressures will not have lasting impact "without a deeper desire for change on the part of American men and women." There needs to be "a personal and cultural crusade to deconstruct and restructure adult generativity" in ways that honor a just and life-giving partnership between family and work, domestic and public economy for men and women alike (Miller-McLemore 1994, 194). Religious persons striving to forge just familial and economic lifestyles need help in separating the wheat from the chaff both in the wider culture and in certain strands of their religious traditions. Congregations need to create opportunities for this ongoing, concrete discernment.

Conclusion

Judaism and Christianity sustain rich images and values concerning work and economy, which in turn imply judgments and practices that religious communities need to help families recognize and embrace. These judgments and practices bespeak an ideal consonant with the aspirations of families beyond the boundaries of our congregations. But, because it is also an ideal in serious tension with dominant values of contemporary economic culture, a vital religious ministry will not be confined to helping families "handle" their economic and work situations. It will assist families in uncovering, resisting, and reconceiving those elements of economy and culture that conflict with genuinely

God-centered and hence authentically human paths for making a living together.

Bibliography

Hewlett, Sylvia. *When the Bough Breaks: The Cost of Neglecting Our Children* (New York: Basic Books, 1991).

Kavanaugh, John R. *(Still) Following Christ in a Consumer Culture* (Maryknoll, N.Y.: Orbis Books, 1992).

Meeks, M. Douglas. *God the Economist: The Doctrine of God and Political Economy* (Minneapolis: Fortress Press, 1989).

Miller-McLemore, Bonnie. *Also a Mother: Work and Family as Theological Dilemma* (Nashville: Abingdon Press, 1994).

Raines, John, and Donna Day-Lower. *Modern Work and Human Meaning* (Nashville: Abingdon Press, 1986).

Schor, Juliet. *The Overworked American: The Unexpected Decline of Leisure* (New York: Basic Books, 1991).

U.S. Catholic Bishops. *Economic Justice for All.* (Washington, D.C.: United States Catholic Conference, 1986).

—CHRISTINE FIRER HINZE

The Role of Churches in Relationship to Government on Behalf of Families

A Theoretical Perspective

According to Catholic social teaching—the tradition that I draw upon in this section—the family is the primary source of the material and spiritual well-being of persons in society. In the words of John Paul II, the family is "the basic social community, or 'cell of society.'" However, Catholic theory also holds that, in a well-ordered society, the family never carries out this role alone but rather in relation to other associations. According to John Paul, "the public authorities must do everything to ensure that families have all those aids—economic, social, educational, political, and cultural assistance—that they need in order to face all their responsibilities in a human way." In order to address the issue of the role of churches and the government on behalf of families, therefore, it is necessary to look at the full range of associations and institutions in civil society. In addition to churches and the government, the economy and a wide array of voluntary associations have roles as well.

The principle of subsidiarity, always present but first defined in modern Catholic social teaching by Pius XI in 1931, regulates when it is appropriate for which association to help families to meet basic needs. In brief, the insight of the principle of subsidiarity is that those persons and institutions most intimately related to the problem at hand have the first and most direct responsibility for attending to the problem. Other institutions may indirectly support the efforts (the Latin root *subsidere* means "to support") but are to intervene more directly only when the efforts of those persons and institutions closest to the situation are not adequate. In the case of meeting the needs of families, this means that the first line of responsibility rests with the families themselves, with the aid of the economy (to provide a family wage as a result of work performed), the state (to shape the various institutions to enable them to perform their own tasks as well as possible), the church (to provide meaning for life and service to humanity in the name of Christ), and voluntary associations.

The economy is the primary source for providing for the material needs of the family. The key material function of the economy is to produce wealth in such a way that unemployment is at a minimum and workers receive a just wage. An economy that fails to meet either of these purposes adequately puts severe strain on families and places greater pressure on other institutions—the state, the churches, and voluntary associations—to help provide for the material well-being of families. Since the collapse of world communism in the late 1980s, the focus on the relative merits of socialism versus capitalism has shifted to a focus on which form of market economy best serves the above function.

Pope John Paul II, for instance, has argued that for the sake of the common good there need to be limits on the market. The market requires "a strong juridical framework which places it at the service of human freedom in its totality, and which sees it as a particular aspect of that freedom, the core of which is ethical and religious." An unrestrained market both leads to an increasing gap between rich and poor and jeopardizes nonmarket-driven values in society. As a result, although it can produce greater overall wealth, the market can also fail to meet the requirements of an economy to meet the basic needs of employment and a just wage.

Often overlooked is the fact that activity in the workplace is also a source of the development and even flourishing of the *whole* person, and not simply of the meeting of material needs. Here, the market economy can provide the context of great freedom and creativity, especially for persons of the entrepreneurial class. However, particularly when unstable, it can also be the source of great anxiety because of job insecurity. Moreover, the market can also generate menial jobs that pay, as we have noted, less than adequate wages. Insecure and menial employment, and not only unemployment or lack of adequate wages, are impediments to human flourishing and create a greater need for response on the part of other institutions.

Although debates over welfare have focused on the state's role as a provider of material goods when the economy and other associations fail to do so adequately, this is not its first role. According to Catholic social teaching, the state's primary task is to provide the conditions within which the other associations within civil society can function appropriately. It might, for instance, set a legal limit on the market concerning a minimum wage so that families can earn an adequate income to serve the educational and material needs of their members. Tax-exempt status for churches and nonprofit service associations is another case of the state enabling other institutions to serve better their own aims, as well as that of the common good. The state expands its role to include the meeting of the material needs of families only when the other institutions, even with appropriate enabling laws, cannot do so. There is a two-sided risk here that is difficult to balance: if the state involves itself too frequently and forcefully, then the ability of other institutions to perform their appropriate roles can atrophy. Moreover, like the economy, the state also has a role that serves the nonmaterial needs of persons in society. Participation in the political order allows persons and families to be agents in the shaping of the society in which they live. The practice of such agency itself contributes to human flourishing. This is why Pius XII in his 1944 Christmas Address distinguishes between a "people," whose members display "the consciousness of their own responsibility, the true instinct for the common good," and the "masses," who "are inert of themselves and can only be moved from outside." The state can become so structured for the provision of services that it compromises its role as a context for the practice of agency. The opposite risk, however, is that if the state does *not* involve itself adequately in the provision of services when other associations fail, families suffer in the meantime.

In addition to families, the economy, and the state, civil society includes a variety of what have been called "voluntary associations." These may be political (for example, the Wabash College Young Republicans) or economic (for example, the Junior Chamber of Commerce of Tulsa, Oklahoma), but it is helpful to identify them as distinct from the state or the market, each of which has an existence quite apart from whatever voluntary associations persons may form. Among these associations are service organizations—for instance, Catholic Charities, USA—that help to meet the needs of families. In accordance with the principle of subsidiarity, the proximity of voluntary associations to persons means that in most cases they are the institutions of resort prior to the state. Indeed, vibrant activity in voluntary associations can lessen the demand on the state to intervene directly on behalf of families.

Although churches are often referred to as voluntary associations, it is important to keep in mind the very important ways in which they are different. To be sure, the purpose of constitutional disestablishment is to structure society so that persons can attend to religious matters with no coercion of conscience. But from *within* a religious perspective, it is precisely through the conscience, formed in community, that God draws persons. In its 1965 document, *Dignitatis humanae,* the Second Vatican Council affirmed that in a pluralistic democracy, the *juridical* doctrine of religious freedom is the most appropriate means for facilitating persons' responsiveness to God. It is important to note, however, that juridical freedom in a constitutional democracy and the freedom of the act of faith dovetail or coincide *only* on the practical legal level; they are not synonymous. The freedom of the act of faith is structured by God's invitation to persons to the life of faith. This context does not allow the person to stand outside as a complete self, consider a variety of alternatives, and then decide on one of them on the basis of weighing pluses and minuses. From *within* the religious perspective of the relationship of faith, one does not choose among a variety of options as an already complete person; one is called to become oneself through a relationship with God, and that call is recognized and realized through reception into a particular community of faith. For the life of faith, the question of freedom is not "which one of these options" but "yes" or "no" to the one option offered. A "yes" affirms the relationship with God, who becomes the primary locus of loyalty and source of obligation. In a constitutional democracy, juridical freedom *protects* the freedom of faith. The U.S. Constitution does so through the free exercise clause of the First Amendment. Here, the state is saying that it acknowledges and protects the fact that religious communities have modes of relating to the world that other kinds of associations—including the state—do not share.

The sense of givenness of membership in a religious community is crucial because the sacrifices required in aiding needy families is of such magnitude—and will be even greater with the reduction of welfare benefits in the United States—that only a community that has a significant *claim* on us can move us to provide such aid. It is the very nature of voluntary associations that if their activities do not match our own personal vision, then we can discontinue our membership. Quite often, our personal visions do not include the degree of sacrifice called for by the needs of others. To the degree that they have a claim on us, churches can prompt us to reshape our vision to include greater personal sacrifice for our neighbor.

In light of the importance of the givenness of church membership understood theologically, it is particularly disconcerting that American views of such membership is becoming increasingly patterned after the voluntary association. Denominational identity is of decreasing importance for persons. Even among Roman Catholics, where there is less of a propensity to change denominations, there is an increasing tendency not to attend the geographical parish but to investigate a variety of Catholic worship options in a wide region and to attend the church that best fits with the person's preferences. As these trends continue, the churches become less communities that make claims on us than what sociologist Robert Bellah calls "lifestyle enclaves" (Bellah, 154). Such enclaves are less capable of service to families than is the church that makes a claim on us.

In order to gain another view on our contemporary situation, it is helpful to bring Catholic teaching to bear on "conservative" and "liberal" viewpoints as these are generally understood in American political discourse: the "right" and the "left." Conservatives often invoke the principle of subsidiarity to set limits on the state. Properly understood, however, subsidiarity also concerns situations where other social spheres—including the market economy—overextend themselves to the detriment of society in general and the family in particular. The logic of the market can affect families such that their members begin viewing each other in cost-benefit terms rather than in the familial terms of love. (The prenuptial contract is a case in point and an instance of the market violating the principle of subsidiarity.) Liberals tend to appeal to subsidiarity in order to make the case *for* direct state intervention in the provision of material and other goods to meet basic needs to the neglect of entertaining other options such as public-private partnerships. In general, conservatives are more sanguine about the impact on families of reducing the direct role of the state in the provision of goods and about the ability of churches to step into the breach; liberals are less concerned about how a state that takes on the bulk of the responsibility for providing services contributes to the atrophy of intermediate associations, including churches.

The shifting of American sympathies toward accepting more conservative ideas (President Clinton's incorporation of such ideas into his own agenda is the foremost evidence of such a shift) places the churches in a situation where it is unclear that they can meet the demands placed on them. The growth since the New Deal era of the state as a provider of goods to meet basic needs has created a greater dependency on the state on the part of intermediate associations. Indeed, the major religiously affiliated charitable organizations receive considerable government support. Recent cutbacks in this role of government have revealed the dependency. Such cutbacks will indeed hurt families, particularly those that are most needy. The question remains whether churches that have become both more like lifestyle enclaves and more dependent on government support for their charitable services can marshal timely responses to what will undoubtedly be an increase in the unmet needs of families.

Bibliography

Bellah, Robert. *Habits of the Heart* (San Francisco: Harper & Row, 1985).

John Paul II. *Centesimus annus* (One Hundred Years). In O'Brien and Shannon 1992.

———. *Familiaris consortio* (On the Family). (Washington, D.C.: United States Catholic Conference, 1982).

———. *Laborem exercens* (On Human Work). In O'Brien and Shannon 1992.

———. *Sollicitudo rei socialis* (On Social Concern). In O'Brien and Shannon 1992.

O'Brien, David J., and Thomas A. Shannon, eds. *Catholic Social Thought: The Documentary Heritage* (Maryknoll, N.Y.: Orbis Books, 1992).

Pius XI. *Quadragesimo anno* (After Forty Years). In O'Brien and Shannon 1992.

Pius XII. "True and False Democracy" (Christmas Address of 1944). In *The Major Addresses of Pope Pius XII, Vol. 2: Christmas Messages* ed. Vincent A. Yzermans. (St. Paul: North Central Publishing, 1961).

Second Vatican Council. *Dignitatis humanae* (Declaration on Religious Freedom). In *The Documents of Vatican II,* ed. Walter M. Abbott. (Piscataway, N.J.: America Press/New Century Publishers, 1966).

Whitmore, Todd David. "Strangers, Enemies, or Neighbors?: American Restlessness and the Decline of Civil Society." *Papers of the Henry Luce III Fellows in Theology* (Atlanta: Scholars Press, 1996).

Wuthnow, Robert. *The Restructuring of American Religion: Society and Faith since World War II* (Princeton, N.J.: Princeton University Press, 1988).

———, ed. *Between States and Markets: The Voluntary Sector in Comparative Perspective* (Princeton, N.J.: Princeton University Press, 1991).

—TODD DAVID WHITMORE

A Practical Perspective

A critical debate swirling throughout this nation is the appropriate role of government in ensuring the welfare of its citizens. Conservative forces have done much to fix the consciousness of the nation on the divisive, destructive aspects of the so-called welfare state. Governmental intervention of almost any sort is viewed by many as counterproductive and undesirable.

The watchword of the 1980s and 1990s by which conservatives voiced their belief that social welfare work was not the role of the government but should be tended to by charitable agencies is volunteerism. The poor, the oppressed, and the disenfranchised surely exist, but it is not the responsibility of the government to alleviate their plight. An individual must have the initiative and fortitude to do that on his or her own. The assistance that families may need should flow from those organizations chartered to address such matters, for example, the YMCA, Catholic Charities, soup kitchens, and job banks. Churches should, in turn, perform a supportive role by preaching a work ethic laced with evangelism to extricate people from spiritual bondage and reduce their lethargy.

The essential question is, What is an appropriate role for government and churches in addressing family needs, and what are the responsibilities and rights that belong chiefly to the individual and family?

First and foremost, government has the responsibility to ensure the safety and rights of every family, regardless of culture, background, or economic circumstances.

Government alone has the legal and constitutional mandate to be sure that all families are given equal protection and encouragement under the law. Within this category rests a number of issues. Family-leave laws are an example. Meeting the needs associated with catastrophic illnesses, pregnancy, and care of children and the elderly require universal, comprehensive solutions. The individual corporations, churches, and para-church organizations that understand and address these problems cannot provide a fair, equitable solution for everyone. Government must set standards and enforce policy that addresses the alleviation of these concerns, regardless of a family's economic strength.

Another role of the government is to protect its citizens from the abuse of power. The regulatory power of government must be exercised if families are to live in communities free of toxic contaminants. Regulations to ensure air and water quality and to control the effects of tobacco and alcohol are examples of necessary governmental protections.

The third area where government must intervene on behalf of families is to encourage those independent institutions that are working to undergird and strengthen the stability and well-being of families, namely religious and charitable institutions.

Government can support religious institutions by providing resources and offering technical assistance to them in their delivery of services. This would mean that government, as an encourager of private institutions, would reduce the amount of bureaucratic structure, requirements of overly detailed paperwork, and overly restrictive guidelines so that independent agencies would not be intimidated from carrying out their important support role.

How can churches assist families with the responsibilities that remain in the family's jurisdiction? Before we can understand the church's role in this area, we must first be clear on the nature and purpose of the church.

The New Testament provides an excellent example of the mutual dependence of religious institutions and the family. Luke 2:22–40 describes the presentation of Jesus in the temple. This material describes the crucial interaction of church and family in matters of holistic growth.

Jesus was brought to the temple by Mary and Joseph, in fulfillment of the law of Moses. A woman was considered unclean for forty days after the birth of a male child. At this ceremony a lamb and a pigeon were presented as a burnt offering and as a sin offering. Should the person not be able to provide the lamb, two turtle doves or pigeons would suffice, this being known as the offering of the poor (Leviticus 12:8). Mary and Joseph present the poor person's offering, and their time of purification is ended. Simeon, an elderly man, takes the baby in his arms and blesses him, acknowledging that he is the Messiah of God. Simeon then says, "Lord, now lettest thou thy servant depart in peace" (Luke 2:29, RSV). Also in the temple is Anna, a prophetess of great age who "gave thanks to God, and spoke of him to all who were looking for the redemption of Israel" (Luke 2:38, RSV).

Several insights concerning the church as family can be lifted from this text. The identity of Jesus was set in the temple. The religious community formed his earliest self-understandings. Learning about one's place in the world begins from one's birth. This text implies that if the church joins with the family to share responsibility for personality formation, the potential for healthy growth is heightened.

The extended family, according to the text, also plays a key role (the extended family being social and religious, not just biological). Both Simeon and Anna are elderly. Each takes part in the fixing of this child's identity by establishing that the baby is specifically blessed of God. A fascinating interweaving of growth for child, family, and extended family takes place in the religious context of the temple.

In light of the challenges that face families today, churches could choose to do nothing. They could simply maintain the traditional worship and evangelism programs while families deteriorate before their eyes. Conversely, churches might choose to plunge headlong into efforts to reprogram and restructure budgets so that volunteerism becomes the primary mission. This would mean curtailing worship, Christian education, and mission budgets in order to hire job counselors, psychologists, and social workers. A better solution, however, is for the church to face these tenuous times by striking a creative blend of crisis intervention and volunteerism, concurrent with a long-term strategy of political action and advocacy for families, without abandoning worship, missions, and Christian education.

Many churches throughout the nation are grappling with the issue and attempting to model constructive engagement. The first pillar of this constructive engagement is the role of advocacy. By whatever means necessary the church must lobby incessantly for the correct and appropriate role of government in our society. Government in a democratic society must not exist just to protect the haves against the have-nots. What takes place too often is that legislation is passed by legislators who have little or no knowledge of its implications for the community.

Constructively engaged churches would develop and implement watchdog groups to examine the spate of proposed and pending legislation to assess the impact of such measures on public education, economic well-being, housing, and transportation. Some instruction in forming such groups may be necessary, and the religious denominations that hold similar views could be consulted for ways to perform this task effectively and efficiently. Within the local churches, recent retirees and high school and college students could staff editorial boards where critical and important matters could be assessed and materials appropriately disseminated.

Beyond the role of information sharing comes the next level of advocacy: social action. Churches will also need social justice committees to spearhead letter-writing campaigns, organize selective patronage responses, carry placards, and walk picket lines as the need arises to bring political pressure on the powers that be. Children and the poor have few lobbyists. Churches can move aggressively in this important area.

Living in the center of a society where family disintegration is the watchword of the times calls for emergency measures and strategies. We do not need poorly designed programs that are high on good intentions but lack depth.

Practical programs that work to rebuild families will need to model the best theological, psychological, and sociological principles. The breakdown of the family did not begin in isolation, and its restoration will require a holistic understanding of intra- and interpersonal dynamics.

The next level of the church's involvement with families encompasses the tasks of the socialization and education of its members. The story of Jesus' presentation in the temple affords a helpful example of interaction between family and religious community. The religious environment of the temple was the site where the infant received his name.

Receiving one's name is the assumption of identity. Churches can assist families in addressing the problems of low self-esteem, a major issue for families in crisis. The process of establishing identity can be accomplished by educational programs in which families receive instruction in clarifying values, determining personal boundaries between family members, and self-empowerment. Families in crisis will often experience disempowerment through the realities of broken and strained relations. Children of divorce, abusive homes, or impoverished circumstances will be inclined to blame themselves for the family's condition and to take their identity from the realities they encounter. They will feel and act as though they are incomplete because of the overwhelming psychological and social needs they encounter daily. Church educational programs can assist these children who are at risk by intentionally working to give them their rightful names. These children are not "bastards," they are not simply from broken homes, they are not just poor or oppressed. They are God's children and bear God's name. Intentional strategies to rebuild self-image should be a component of a church's regular educational offerings.

In the temple, the infant Jesus received the blessings of the elders. Churches can provide much-needed assistance for families by creating intergenerational mentoring programs and opportunities. At-risk adolescents can benefit from big brother–big sister initiatives; after-school programs can provide safe space where youngsters gather and receive tutoring and physical fitness instruction and benefit from being in a caring environment.

The third component of Luke's account of the temple dedication is the offering of two turtle doves, a sacrifice of the poor. A profound sense of the economic realities of life is involved here. The gift of a child requires a tangible fiscal response. Although the sacrifice of the turtle doves indicates the family's indigence, the presentation of these turtle doves requires a financial commitment. They must first be purchased and then presented as an offering. Regardless of the family's economic circumstances the child must be viewed as a person of worth and value. Families at all financial levels must be encouraged to invest in their family's future.

Churches could serve families by providing instruction in financial management and planning that features investment in children. Rituals like baptisms, first communions, and infant dedications could all be opportunities for families and friends to invest in children's futures. Savings accounts could be initiated or investment clubs for higher education could be established. Instruction in investing in children's futures affirms the child's essential worth and value to family and community.

Economic issues, however, have broader implications. In tight financial situations families need assistance with the basic realities of survival. Churches can provide an essential service at society's breaking points by offering families such opportunities as buyers' clubs, credit unions, investment possibilities, and job counseling. Families that perform well economically are much more likely to be stable, well functioning, and healthy.

Families need support and nurturing from many quarters. The government holds almost exclusive responsibility in some areas, but families and individuals hold sway in other realms. Between these two poles exists the church's sphere of influence. When the church offers important assistance at the breaking points, when government provides fundamental protection, and individual families accept their responsibility, then the disintegration of the family will slow dramatically, and the negative realities of family brokenness will be overturned.

—WALLACE CHARLES SMITH

PART 2

Approaches to Special
Situations of Family Ministry

6

Marital Preparation

A Catholic Perspective

Preparing couples for marriage is a primary pastoral concern in the Catholic Church in the United States. Significant personnel, time, and development of materials in parishes and dioceses are directed to marriage preparation. A 1995 national study of couples married for one to eight years who had participated in a preparation process in the Catholic Church found that the great majority of them judged it valuable for their married life (*Center for Marriage and Family* 1995). A minority of couples, however, said that the preparation in which they were involved was not helpful, and some found it useless. Marital preparation in the Catholic Church is, then, always a work in progress.

Pre-Cana Conferences began in 1946 in the Chicago Archdiocese and were among the earliest programmatic approaches directed to preparing couples for marriage. In 1981 the letter *On the Family* from Pope John Paul II gave a mandate to all church leaders worldwide: "The Church must promote better and more intensive programs of marriage preparation in order to eliminate as far as possible the difficulties that many married couples find themselves in, and even more in order to favor positively the establishing and maturing of successful marriages." By 1995 all 175 Catholic dioceses in the United States had marriage preparation policies and programs; nearly all the 330,000 couples married in the Catholic Church in that year were involved in some marriage preparation process.

Each Catholic diocese, and in some cases, each parish, determines its own approach to preparing couples for marriage. National and worldwide resources, movements, and guidelines influence the design of these local programs. *Faithful to Each Other Forever: A Catholic Handbook of Pastoral Help for Marriage Preparation,* produced in 1988 by the United States Catholic Conference, provides overall direction. This handbook says that marriage preparation is to be viewed and developed as a lifetime, four-stage process.

1. *Remote preparation* is to begin in early childhood and involves all those family and environmental factors that influence and predispose the individual in positive and negative ways for marriage. In practice, this remote stage is often overlooked as an explicit part of marriage preparation.
2. *Proximate preparation* is to begin at puberty. It deals with the developmental and formational issues during adolescence

and young adulthood. To the mid-1990s, limited resources have been directed to the proximate stage of marriage preparation, but many in the Church are becoming aware that attention to this stage may be crucial to the prevention of many later problems.

3. *Immediate preparation* is to take place in the months directly prior to the wedding. This stage is popularly considered to be the whole of marriage preparation. It has received the most directed resources and evaluation by the Catholic Church.

4. *Pastoral care after marriage* is the final stage of marriage preparation. Marriage is considered an ongoing process; therefore, input for new issues at new life stages, help for couples in crisis times, and support in the dailiness of the marriage is needed. Many parishes do not approach pastoral care after marriage as seriously or systematically as they do immediate preparation.

Immediate Preparation

The approaches to immediate preparation for marriage can be examined by an overview of its purpose, content, processes, and realities.

Purpose

Immediate marriage preparation in the Catholic Church strives to help a couple make the best possible decision about their readiness to marry. The Church's role is not to judge if a couple is to marry but to assist them in this judgment. Readiness to marry involves the couple's knowledge, understanding, and acceptance of each other. It involves skills and the capacity to live out a marriage commitment and some grasp of the meaning of marriage as a Christian covenant. Marriage preparation is intended to provide a situation in which couples have the time, the environment, the resources, and the assistance needed to examine and to build their readiness to enter such a marriage.

Content

Marriage preparation varies somewhat across dioceses, but its basic intent is to help a couple know more about self, the other, marriage, and the skills needed to put together a successful marriage relationship. Books, videos, leaders' manuals, and inventories are available in these categories: *Match*—Family-of-origin issues, personality differences, expectations of marriage roles, friends, and interests. *Skills*—Communication and conflict resolution patterns and styles. *Bonders*—The basic connectors of money, sex, religion, children, extended family, and commitment. In recent years, special applications have been made in materials to two-job or two-career marriages, second marriages, inter-church marriages, and marriages taking place after cohabitation.

Research with couples married one to eight years indicates that the most help-ful content in their marriage preparation concerned communication, commit-ment, conflict resolution, children, and church (religion, values, and sacraments).

Processes

Approaches to marriage preparation in the Catholic Church vary.

The facilitator: The 1995 Creighton Center on Marriage and Family Study indicates that a *team* of clergy and married lay couples is the most valued and successful. Church policy calls for such a team approach. However, clergy working alone with the couple is the most common approach (26 percent of all preparations).

The amount: Most Catholic dioceses require that marriage preparation begin a minimum of six months before the marriage. Some require only four months; a growing number are moving toward nine months. A few require one year. The intensity of the marriage preparation as measured by the number of sessions also varies, and this also influences the way the preparation is valued. Too few sessions (one or two) or too many (twelve or more) are correlated to a low valu-ing of the preparation.

The format: Most couples meet privately with clergy or parish staff. Many parishes and dioceses use a self-diagnostic inventory to help couples focus on their specific issues and give the clergy or lay facilitators a profile to help them tailor the preparation process to each couple. FOCUS is the inventory used by the greatest number of dioceses; PREPARE and PMI are also used.

A large percentage of dioceses and parishes follow the inventory with an ed-ucational program. Weekend programs such as Engaged Encounter are very common and provide for an intense, reflective process; these are highly rated by couples. Also common and rated highly are private sessions with the en-gaged couple and a mentor couple or a format bringing three to five engaged couples together with a leader couple. Diocesan or regional Pre-Cana days are common: these are single or multiple large group sessions with a team of pre-senters. In general, in follow-up research, participants rate such large group ses-sions less highly than other formats.

Some Realities

Marriage preparation in the Catholic Church is generally mandatory. Current studies indicate that although some couples would not attend preparation pro-grams if they were not required, the overall rating of mandatory programs is no lower, after the fact, than the value rating of completely voluntary programs.

Some areas for improvement in marriage preparation in the Catholic Church are evident. More involvement of married couples in the preparation process is required if there is to be a quality "team approach." Improved training in mar-riage preparation work for both lay leader couples and for clergy is generally agreed to be an ongoing need. While clergy generally see the value of marriage preparation, they sometimes get "burned out" on it or are not prepared to do it well; there may be need to designate some clergy as "specialists" for marriage preparation. Quality control and good selection are key in the choice of married couples as presenters or mentors; every willing leader couple is not necessarily an able couple.

Minority couples seem to do best in programs designed to incorporate unique cultural attitudes about marriage. Many minority couples need to be prepared for both the marriage model from their cultural background with which they will usually begin their married life and the model they may subsequently move into because of inculturation into the predominant society.

Bibliography

Center for Marriage and Family. *Marriage Preparation in the Catholic Church: Getting It Right. Report of a Study on the Value of Marriage Preparation in the Catholic Church for Couples Married One through Eight Years* (Omaha: Creighton University, 1995).

John Paul II. *On the Family* (*Familiaris Consortio*) (Washington, D.C.: United States Catholic Conference [USCC] Office of Publishing and Promotional Services, 1982).

U.S. Catholic Conference. *Faithful to Each Other Forever. A Catholic Handbook of Pastoral Help for Marriage Preparation* (Washington, D.C.: United States Catholic Conference [USCC] Office of Publishing and Promotional Services, 1988).

—BARBARA MARKEY, N.D.

A Jewish Perspective

Helping Jewish couples to prepare for marriage has been primarily viewed as the responsibility of the officiating rabbi. The focus and intensity of such preparations has varied depending on the rabbi involved. Today there is a slow but growing realization of the value of additional formats for Jewish premarital counseling, including group counseling.

Until recently, Jewish premarital counseling has consisted of individual couple counseling by the rabbi. The time devoted to such counseling varies depending upon the rabbi's goals, attitudes, and abilities. One can distinguish between a minimalist, intermediate, and maximalist approach to such counseling.

In the minimalist approach, a rabbi will spend time explaining the steps and meaning of the Jewish marriage ceremony, as well as interviewing the couple to obtain ideas and information to be incorporated into the rabbinic address to the bride and groom on the wedding day. Such rabbis view their role exclusively as that of an officiant.

At the other end of the spectrum, the maximalist approach assumes that although the rabbi must certainly help the couple to prepare for the wedding, the marriage itself is of paramount concern. Rabbis who follow this approach take the task of premarital counseling very seriously. They schedule a number of sessions with the couple at which they discuss a full variety of issues related to married life, including communication, relations with in-laws, finances, and intimacy. Many rabbis have adopted a middle course, supplementing their focus on the wedding ceremony with attention to the Jewishness of the couple's home. They spend one or more sessions exploring with the couple how Judaism might strengthen their marriage and their connection to the Jewish community. Topics might include the couple's expectations about children and their Jewish education, affiliation with a synagogue, Sabbath and festival observances, and rituals in the home. More traditional rabbis may raise with the couple the observance of *kashrut* (Jewish dietary laws) and *taharat hamishpaha* (the laws of "family purity" that regulate a couple's conjugal life). Also included in such meetings might be traditional prewedding rituals such as the *aufruf* ceremony in the synagogue on the Sabbath preceding the wedding and the bride's immersion in a *mikvah* (ritual bath) before the wedding day.

In recent years, the case for the maximalist approach to Jewish premarital counseling has grown. Within the Jewish community there is a dominating concern for "Jewish continuity" and a growing realization that it is insufficient simply to encourage Jews to marry those within the faith. After two Jews have made the decision to marry, serious efforts are needed to help assure the success of the marriage. In generations past, the comparatively lower rate of divorce among Jewish couples contributed to a lesser sense of need for serious premarital counseling. This is no longer the case.

Very slowly, the process of premarital counseling for individual couples is being augmented by the rise of group counseling. *Time* magazine's cover story on February 27, 1995, was about efforts to make marriages more permanent, and it highlighted the proliferation of intensive marriage preparation programs. While Catholics have a Pre-Cana program, Jews have had nothing like this mandatory group process for engaged couples. There have, however, been some positive beginnings within the Jewish community.

Making Marriage Work, housed at and sponsored by the University of Judaism in Los Angeles, is the oldest and most intensive group premarital program in the American Jewish community. It includes twelve hours with a psychologist, four hours with a rabbi, and two hours with a financial planner. The program has been in existence for more than ten years and has served over eight hundred couples.

A different model of group counseling is the program in Baltimore run by Beth El Congregation and the local Jewish Family Service. It consists of two sessions co-led by rabbi and social worker and is available only for Beth El members at whose wedding the Beth El rabbi officiates. Session 1 focuses on family background, listening skills, and models of marriage. Session 2 emphasizes religion, sexual communication, and money issues.

A third model is that piloted in northern New Jersey under the joint sponsorship of the Board of Rabbis of Morris/Sussex Counties and the Jewish Family Service of Metrowest. It consists of three two-hour sessions with rabbi and social worker, including half of one session with a financial planner.

The Baltimore and New Jersey models emphasize the presence of rabbi and social worker/psychologist together at each session. This assures that Jewish teachings are integrated into all facets of the workshop (for example, discussion of economic priorities, sexual relations, communication patterns) and that guidance, inspiration, and support from Jewish sources are interwoven with open-ended discussion and structured exercises. This partnership harnesses to the goal of marriage preparation the professional expertise both of rabbis and those with specialized training in couples/family therapy.

There are a number of significant benefits to the group setting. By leaving details of the wedding ceremony to the officiating rabbi, premarital counseling groups emphasize the importance of preparing for the marriage rather than for the wedding. A group setting allows a sharing with others in a similar life situation. Potentially, it expands the couple's Jewish social circle. Furthermore, placing premarital counseling in a group context helps it to be perceived by couples as a supportive or educational endeavor rather than a "therapeutic" one, thus avoiding a potential stigma that might inhibit participation in what is a voluntary process.

Some rabbis feel that they simply do not have the time to devote to a maximalist counseling approach with individual couples. Others do not feel qualified to do so and see intensive premarital counseling as the domain of the social worker or psychologist. Such concerns are alleviated by group premarital workshops co-led by a rabbi and a social worker/psychologist.

Currently, the Rabbinical Assembly (the international organization of Conservative rabbis) is exploring ways of establishing a group of Jewish premarital workshops throughout its North American regions. If fully implemented, this program could solve a major impediment to serious premarital counseling. Many rabbis find that the weddings at which they will officiate involve children whose parents are affiliated in the community. However, the couple does not necessarily live where the wedding will take place, thus often precluding more than one or two meetings with the rabbi to plan the ceremony. A network of premarital counseling groups throughout the country would allow for networking—for example, a couple that lives in Texas but is being married in New Jersey could be counseled in Texas.

A series of obstacles need to be overcome if group premarital counseling programs are to become more widespread. These include making the cost affordable for couples and overcoming possible resistance to multisession commitments. Ultimately, the success may depend on widespread rabbinical support, so that a significant number of rabbis will ultimately require it for couples, just as Pre-Cana is required for Catholics.

Efforts to further premarital counseling groups make an important statement about the Jewish community's desire to respond in a Jewish way to the human needs and concerns of its engaged couples. Counseling groups can contribute to the success of a new marriage and show a couple how their religious tradition can enhance and sanctify their relationship. Simultaneously, workshops can bolster a couple's communal affiliation and strengthen their connection to the Jewish tradition.

—RALPH A. DALIN

A Protestant Perspective

Premarriage preparation by Protestant ministers is generally regarded as the work done with couples prior to a wedding. Although it is sometimes referred to as premarital counseling, this pastoral work is most often a mixture of education, counseling, theological reflection, and liturgical planning. Because of its multidimensional character, *premarital* or *prewedding work* is the most accurate term to delineate this pastoral activity of helping couples prepare for marriage.

The importance placed on premarital work has varied significantly among ministers. Some have taken marriage preparation very seriously and insisted on a number of private sessions with a couple before the wedding. Others have met with couples only long enough to establish that they are ecclesiastically and legally eligible to marry. More recently, as the focus has shifted to determining the psychological compatibility of the couple, some ministers have referred couples to counseling centers or to individuals with psychological expertise in order to explore the strengths and liabilities of their relationship in response to the expectations and demands of marriage.

The methods used by Protestant ministers in premarital work have changed over the last decades as the understanding of its purpose has changed. Prior to World War II, the emphasis was largely instructional. The focus was on developing an understanding of the Christian view of marriage, the place of religion in the home, some reference to money and sex, and the meaning of the wedding rite itself. In their overview of the development of premarital counseling, Robert F. Stahmann and William S. Hiebert have noted that since World War II the role of clergy has shifted toward an examination of the emotional readiness and maturity of the couple for marriage. This aspect of premarital work has increased in importance as the divorce rate has increased. The seriousness with which pastoral ministers took their psychological gatekeeping responsibility was complicated by the increase in the number of people without religious affiliation asking to be married.

Measuring Relationship Maturity

The use of psychological tests in premarital work was one consequence of this shift in emphasis toward helping couples become aware of the maturity of their relationship. Some used standardized inventories like the Taylor-Johnson Temperament Analysis or the Sex Knowledge Inventory. Others developed their own inventory that would emphasize the dimensions of marriage that they regarded as most important. Although some screening is inevitably perceived to be present whenever psychological tests are used, the aim of these inventories was at minimum to help couples identify areas of potential conflict prior to the wedding. The inventories often determined the content of premarital pastoral conversation. If a couple was simply not suited for marriage, the hope was that they would themselves decide to postpone the wedding. Ministers will occasionally refuse to perform a wedding if they regard the couple as unsuited or at least not ready for marriage.

In recent years, the PREPARE Inventory (from PREmarital Personal and Relationship Evaluation) has become the instrument most frequently used by Protestant clergy in marriage preparation. The purpose of PREPARE is to help the couple explore the strengths of their relationship and areas of growth, modify unrealistic expectations of the intended spouse or of marriage itself, discuss their own family of origin with each other, practice conflict resolution, and initiate a process whereby each couple commits to work on the marriage over time. Studies have shown the value of using some type of premarital inventory with couples, especially if the results of the inventory are utilized in learning communication and conflict resolution skills. David Olson and others who developed PREPARE have found that premarital work is most effective when it can begin *at least one year before marriage.*

Allowing at least one year for explicit marriage preparation also makes it more possible to focus on marriage education as a part of the process. Churches generally teach about marriage through preaching, ordinary church school and catechetical instruction, and many forms of modeling marriage through community life activities. Marriage education, as the primary purpose of premarital work, may be individually focused, or it may occur in a group context. The wedding service itself often provides the outline for instruction about the Christian understanding of marriage. Herbert Anderson and Robert Cotton Fite, in a book entitled *Becoming Married* (1993), have proposed another method. They suggest that couples be invited to explore the Christian perspective in general in order to identify particular themes like hospitality or justice for the formation of a family that would be included in the wedding as well. From this perspective, the educational aspect of premarital work seeks to help couples discover Christian themes for family living rather than begin with explicit family themes in Christian teaching.

Premarriage education in Protestant churches may not always begin with Christian ideals or norms about marriage. Rather, it may seek to help couples define the type of marriage that will work best for them and then provide the relational skills that are necessary to achieve the marriage goal they have set for themselves. Customary topics of sex, money, religion, gender roles, and in-laws give way to developing communication skills, clarifying expectations of marriage, and teaching the art of compromise and the necessity of conflict resolution. Couples are often reluctant learners in this educational adventure. Couples before the wedding are not readily disposed toward reflecting honestly and critically on a relationship that is still in the process of being formed. For that reason, when the educational focus is on the dynamics of marital living, it may be more effective to emphasize "in-marriage training" after the wedding rather than premarriage education before. This emphasis on the usefulness of education in marriage and family living after the wedding also corresponds with an understanding of becoming married as a process that happens over time.

Leaving Precedes Cleaving

The process of becoming married has at least two fundamental movements. The first is leaving one's home of origin, and the second is forming the marital bond. These two movements are reflected in the biblical mandate that leaving precedes cleaving ("Therefore a man leaves his father and his mother and clings to his wife, and they become one flesh" [Gen. 2:24]). Until recently, the emphasis of premarital work had been on examining and encouraging the new relationship being formed. Little attention was given to leaving home. Although most people physically leave home some time before they marry, the emotional separation is seldom finished by the time of the wedding. Planning the wedding often becomes a significant moment in the events of leaving home. The development of family-systems theory has occasioned a renewed emphasis on the lingering impact of our homes of origin, particularly in our living in marriage. Anderson and Fite have suggested that one purpose of premarital work is to continue the process of emotional separation and help each partner understand the legacy of values and patterns of family living that he or she brings to forming a new family.

Historically, the process of becoming married was marked by two ritual moments that were separated in time. The betrothal was first. It was a public ritual that acknowledged a couple's intent to marry and initiated a period of separation. The wedding itself was the second ritual moment and marked the couple's incorporation into marriage. If the process of becoming married includes leaving as well as cleaving, consideration of the need to separate should be part of both premarital work and the wedding ritual. More attention needs to be given to the public nature of the wedding ritual. Marriages are more likely to endure when they are sustained by communities of people committed to remaining married.

The frequency of remarriage has not been included sufficiently in reflecting on methods of premarital work. Some of the issues are the same although often intensified: exploring the expectations of marriage, understanding the Christian meaning of being married, continuing the process of emotional separation from one's home of origin, and learning communication and conflict resolution skills. Every post-initial marriage, however, is born in grief. What needs more attention with people who are remarrying is the lingering sadness in children (where they are present) and in people for whom the dreams of the first marriage were lost. Since most people remarrying will not bring up grief, ministers need to have it in mind as a special topic for premarital work a second time.

Purposes of Premarital Work

Everyone will agree that the church needs to do whatever it can to prepare people for marriage. We may also find general agreement about the purposes of premarital work. There will be differences, however, in what may be realistically regarded as the most helpful marriage preparation in a brief time of heightened emotionality. In his book *Marriage Savers,* Michael J. McManus has proposed a four-month period of intense preparation that includes mentoring, taking a premarital inventory, and attending an Engaged Encounter. While there is no doubt about the usefulness of attending to the relationship that is being formed, its value is limited. Couples are turned toward one another and generally not receptive to input from outside. If we understand becoming married as a process that happens over time, it will be easier to expand the time frame for premarital work to include in-marriage education.

There is a conundrum among many Protestant ministers regarding weddings and marriage that goes something like this: In the culture, weddings are very important even though the rate of divorce suggests that staying married is difficult. People spend great sums of money to have a perfect wedding. In the church, many pastors will admit privately that they hate weddings even though marriage as an institution is regarded as part of God's plan for creation requiring a lifelong commitment.

The church and its ministers have both an opportunity and a responsibility to strengthen marriage. Like the process of being married itself, premarital work takes more time and requires more energy (both before and after the wedding) than we expect. The methods vary, but the aim of prewedding work should be constant. It is to help two people to form a bond that honors the uniqueness of each other while weaving a common future together in God.

Bibliography

Anderson, Herbert, and Robert Cotton Fite. *Becoming Married* (Louisville, Ky.: Westminster/John Knox Press, 1993).

Cavanagh, Michael E. *Before the Wedding: Look Before You Leap* (Louisville, Ky.: Westminster John Knox Press, 1994).

Harris, Roger, Michele Simons, Peter Willis, and Anne Barrie. *Love, Sex, and Waterskiing: The Experience of Pre-Marriage Education in Australia.* (Adelaide: Centre for Human Resource Studies, 1992).

McManus, Michael J. *Marriage Savers: Helping Your Friends and Family Avoid Divorce* (Grand Rapids: Zondervan Publishing House, 1995).

Olson, David H., David G. Fournier, and Joan M. Druckman. *Prepare, Enrich: Counselor's Manual* (Minneapolis: Prepare-Enrich, Inc. 1994).

Stahmann, Robert F., and William J. Hiebert. *Premarital Counseling: The Professional's Handbook,* 2d ed. (New York: Lexington Books, 1987).

—HERBERT ANDERSON

Some Secular Approaches

Typical goals of the various approaches to marital preparation include easing the transition from single to married life, increasing couple stability and satisfaction for the short and long term, and improving the quality of couple and family relationships. In secular settings, the two primary methods and contexts used in marital preparation are family life education and premarital counseling.

Family life education programs are found in high schools and colleges, and more recently through community adult education courses and extension programs. Such courses and programs are usually structured so that participants gain knowledge about marriage and relationships and can learn to apply it in practical ways. Therefore goals may include information about marriage (marriage statistics, marital satisfaction, and stability factors), skill development (communication, problem solving, decision making), exploring values and attitudes (marital expectations, roles, beliefs), and family background (homogamy, parenting). Specific goals in family life education classes differ because of the varying ages and developmental levels of the participants. At the high school level, because most of the participants have not yet selected a marriage partner and are not ready to enter marriage, the focus would be less on the nature of specific relationships and relationship issues and more on developing knowledge about marriage, gaining general interpersonal skills, exploring values and attitudes regarding marriage, and considering information about mate selection from a family studies perspective.

At the college level, marriage preparation programs are found in courses in departments of family sciences, sociology, human development, psychology, religion, and the like. Textbooks often focus on marriage and the family with only a portion of the material dealing specifically with marriage preparation. Evidence points to the fact that college-age dating couples who take such a class together are more interested in marital preparation, study more, and find the course material more relevant than students in such a class composed of noncouples.

In community education programs, the experience is usually less structured than in college academic settings because no academic credit is given for the course. Thus instructors may more freely use materials from sources beyond textbooks, including popular magazines and books for a lay audience. Discussion of topics and experiential exercises, along with structured skill training, would be commonly used in these classes.

Premarital counseling programs are intended to help couples learn about themselves as individuals and as a couple, and to provide them with information and skill learning. Although the majority of premarital counseling is done in church settings, a significant amount is done in other contexts, such as college and university counseling centers and training clinics, community mental health centers, and governmental family service agencies, and by mental health professionals in private practice. As would be expected, premarital counseling occurs when a couple is in a relationship and is seeking to strengthen that relationship or seeking to evaluate it. Thus, premarital counseling is educational, remedial, and preventive.

Much premarital counseling is done in groups. One advantage of the group format is that it is economical: more couples can be served by fewer counselors or leaders. Also a group experience provides a couple with the opportunity to compare and contrast their relationship with others'. This can "normalize" premarital and marital adjustment in very healthy ways. Groups also provide feedback from others, and partners can observe how their future spouse interacts with others in that setting. On the other hand, limitations of the group format include the fact that one couple may dominate the group, and the specific need(s) of some couples may not be addressed because of time constraints or program design. It may be that some individuals or couples do not disclose or interact as freely in a group setting, either because they are afraid of a group situation or because they are not able to talk comfortably in a group setting.

Advantages of individual couple marital preparation are that the counselor can focus attention and energy on only one couple instead of dealing with group processes and issues. Topics can be personalized to meet the couple's specific needs and situation. Also, in individual couple counseling, the couple must focus on their own issues and skills and cannot be sidetracked by issues of other couples.

A word should be said about expectations regarding marital preparation. It is important that expectations be clear to all involved. What are the couple's expectations about the marital preparation program, course, or counseling that they are entering? What are the counselor's or leader's expectations about the process? Are there specific goals because of the context of the marital preparation experience such as imparting specific information or values? The marital preparation counselor or leader needs to make the goals and the process clear and assist the couple (as individuals and as a couple) in clarifying their expectations as they begin the marital preparation process. Not to do so could lead to confusion or a less meaningful experience than if expectations are clarified.

Whether a group or individual format is used in marital preparation, the following should be kept in mind in an attempt to meet the goals and needs of the couple and marriage preparation provider:

1. Instruments that assess personality, couple type, strengths, areas of concern, and marital expectations are useful. Such information can be helpful to the counselor and may be appropriately shared with the couple as part of the program. Also, assessment information gives those who wish to study the process and outcome of their marriage preparation intervention a means to do so.

2. Certain topics have been shown to be important for inclusion in secular marital preparation programs: marriage as

a commitment; family of origin and individual backgrounds; future relationship(s) with family of origin and
in-laws; temperament and personality of self and partner
(adaptability, humor, and so on); roles in marriage; leisure
and recreational interests; friends; educational, work, and
career goals and expectations; affection, nurturing, and
sexuality; children and parenting; religious or spiritual values and expectations; financial and resource management;
perceived strengths as individuals and a couple; plans for
the wedding.

3. Specific skills can be taught or enhanced effectively in
   marriage preparation programs: communication skills,
   conflict resolution skills (including dealing with power
   struggles in the relationship), decision-making skills, and
   financial management skills.

4. It is important to recognize that marital stability and marital satisfaction are not the same. Solid marital preparation
   can help couples understand and anticipate this and realize that satisfaction varies for all marriages from time to
   time.

5. Marital preparation extends beyond the wedding. There is
   significant adjustment in the early months of marriage. An
   effective marital preparation experience can build into the
   program a series of sessions that occur after the wedding,
   perhaps six months to a year later. These sessions can follow the format of the original meetings and may well include information from the field of marriage enrichment.

6. Tremendous adjunct resources are the many self-help
   books, audiotapes, and videotapes that can assist in marital preparation and enrichment. Counselors may be able
   to recommend resources that they know well, or the couple may wish to make selections that appeal to their needs
   and interests.

7. Evidence is that some 30 to 45 percent of those seeking to
   attend marital preparation programs have been previously
   married. These couples generally have higher expectations about marital preparation, that is, they are more motivated and have more specific questions than those
   entering a first marriage. In addition to the topics suggested above, the remarital preparation provider should
   include such areas as dealing with issues from the previous marriage(s), dealing with a "new" family, defining and
   clarifying extended family relationships and roles, defining stepparenting roles, discipline of children, and rela-
   tionship(s) with ex-spouse and in-laws.

Bibliography

Fowers, B. J., K. B. Montel, and D. H. Olson. "Predicting Marital Success for Premarital Couple Types Based on PREPARE," *Journal of Marital and Family Therapy* 22(1996): 103–19.

Stahmann, R. F., and W. J. Hiebert. *Premarital and Remarital Counseling* (San Francisco: Jossey-Bass, forthcoming).

Stanley, S. M., H. J. Markman, M. St. Peters, and D. B. Leber. "Strengthening Marriages and Preventing Divorce: New Directions in Prevention Research," *Family Relations* 44(1995): 392–401.

—ROBERT F. STAHMANN

7

Ministry with Couples

A Jewish Perspective

Contemporary American society promotes a sense of rugged individualism. Though in some ways laudable, this individualism is alienating. Our culture encourages us to spend huge blocks of time in front of the television, artificially connected to our environment. In our passion for secularization and worship of technology, we have experienced a diminution of the sacred. The spiritual fragmentation experienced runs deeper than the images flashing across our television screens at eight-second disjointed intervals. It is manifested in a lack of connection to our environment and ultimately to each other.

The traditional family has been shaken by the stresses that these pressures impose. Marriages are dissolving at an alarmingly high rate, and resultant family disruptions destabilize our society.

Young couples entering a marriage often find themselves living in a community that is distant from their family of origin. Though marriage assumes a healthy break from the parental orbit, and the affirmation of individual creativity and independence, the importance of the support that extended family gives is not to be discounted. This is true especially if the couple is separated by hundreds or thousands of miles from an extended family support system. E-mail and the telephone are very poor substitutes for the real interconnectedness of extended family, a connection endangered when couples first establish their nascent family unit.

These phenomena are compounded by the decline in sacred ritual. Historian of religion Mircea Eliade tells the story of a primitive tribe whose communal life centered around a sacred pole. When the tribe traveled, the pole would go with them. Whenever they settled down, this very pole was placed at the center of their encampment. It was the tribe's means of being oriented to the world, making the world understandable to them. One morning they awoke and found the pole broken in half. They then wandered in confusion, became exhausted, collapsed, and wanted only to die. This story illustrates how ritual can help maintain our orientation in the world, and how essential it is in preserving faith. When deprived of a primary way of ritualizing their experience, the tribe in question became disoriented, suffering emotionally and spiritually.

Modern-day couples live in an era in which ritual is devalued. Ritual moments and celebrations, if recaptured and reinvigorated with relevance and meaning, can strengthen the couple as they face the difficult challenges of adjustment leading to the creation of family. One of the goals of the contemporary synagogue is to bring couples and families into closer contact with community and the sacred by exposing them to shared ritual moments.

Synagogue programs focusing on ministry to couples are varied. I briefly present two such programs sponsored by the Reform Temple of Forest Hills, an urban congregation located in central Queens, a borough of New York City. The two programs ministering to couples are the Young Marrieds' Havurah and Side by Side.

The Reform Temple of Forest Hills established the Young Marrieds' Havurah as a means of involving couples in synagogue life. In general, *havurah* is a small group (operating within or outside of the synagogue) in which individuals come together regularly for either prayer, study, or observance of Jewish rituals and life cycle events.

This particular havurah meets monthly. The havurah comprises five to fifteen couples who celebrate, either in their homes or within the synagogue, holy days such as Purim and Hanukkah. They also take trips to various cultural and socially oriented Jewish events in the New York metropolitan area. Programs also include study sessions and participation in Sabbath services. The group sponsors a yearly congregational Friday evening Sabbath dinner. They plan and lead the service with the input of either the rabbi or cantor.

In our experience, for the group to be successful, the clergy needs to take a proactive role. This role is primarily motivational and advisory. The clergy makes sure that each year one or two couples take on an advisory responsibility. A steering committee is formed, and the clergy willingly gives programmatic ideas, is available to teach, lead discussions, and assist the group in Jewish ritual experience. The Young Marrieds' Havurah brings young Jewish couples within the synagogue community, but it has also succeeded in welcoming the interfaith couple. This openness enables such couples to experience Jewish community and ritual experience within an accepting, nonthreatening environment. It is not unusual for the various couples in this havurah to form friendships that range beyond involvement in the synagogue's activities.

Within the havurah, these couples find a real sense of community and experience more intimately the various holiday and ritual moments through hands-on involvement. Through this group, both the couple as family unit and the synagogue are strengthened.

A second ministry to couples sponsored by the Reform Temple of Forest Hills is the Side by Side program. The target population for this ministry is both temple-affiliated and unaffiliated couples with children. Partners usually range between the ages of 25 and 50. The program's goal is to interest unaffiliated couples to engage more actively in Jewish life through holiday celebrations, weekend retreats, and shared Jewish family experiences.

The long-range objectives of this ministry are for participants to build stronger ties to the Jewish community. It is hoped that participants experience a sense of extended family. In addition, it is hoped that unaffiliated members of the community will demonstrate greater interest in Jewish affairs and decide formally to join the synagogue. To this end, fifteen unaffiliated couples from the community were recruited through fliers, newspaper announcements, and recommendation by neighbors. These couples were matched with twenty couples already participating in Temple activities.

Ten Friday evening services were scheduled throughout the year. This program was designated Temple for Tots, which includes an abbreviated service filled with music and story telling. A Shabbat dinner follows. This creates a warm, welcoming experience. This format enables couples with young children to experience not only the familial but also the communal aspect of the Sabbath. The program's success far exceeded the organizers' expectations. The participation of both affiliated and unaffiliated couples was enthusiastic. The lighting of candles, the kiddush (the blessing over the wine), the motzi (the grace before the meal), and the blessing of the children taking place before the Sabbath meal—these moments were embraced by the participants, who came to experience a greater sense of grounding and confidence in these home celebratory rituals.

The Side by Side program also included a Sabbath weekend retreat in the Berkshires. The purpose of the weekend was to build a sense of community withn the context of a Sabbath experience. The retreat was open to couples of any age, and singles were also included. The result of these yearly retreats has been the experience of a greater sense of community within the temple family and a renewed sense of commitment on the part of those attending this phase of the program. It was further noted that couples who were cut off from their nuclear families found within this community experience a renewed sense of extended family.

Ministering to couples within a synagogue setting has proven to be a challenging and rewarding ministry. The results not only strengthen the identity and religious growth of the couple but revitalize and reinvigorate the synagogue community.

Bibliography

Dosick, Wayne. *Golden Rules: The Ten Ethical Values Parents Need to Teach Their Children* (San Francisco: HarperCollins 1995).

Friedman, Edwin H. *Generation to Generation: Family Process in Church and Synagogue* (New York: Guilford Press, 1985).

Grishaver, Joel Lurie. *Forty Things You Can Do to Save the Jewish People* (Los Angeles: Aleph Design Group, 1993).

Reisman, Bernard. *The Jewish Experiential Book: The Quest for Jewish Identity* (New York: KTAV Publishing House, 1979).

Schulweis, Harold M. *For Those Who Can't Believe* (New York: HarperCollins, 1994).

—MAYER PERELMUTER

A Catholic Perspective

Catholics' understanding and experience of ministry and church are in a process of vibrant transformation. Increasing numbers of Catholic laity are responding to a "call to ministry," pursuing ministerial/theological or social/psychological studies, and then taking formal positions as pastoral associates, chaplains, pastoral counselors, or youth ministers. Many other Catholic laity would not use the language of call or ministry yet are increasingly involved in sharing their gifts in and through the church. Ministry is coming to be viewed as that life-giving exercise of one's unique gifts, a means by which to experience God's presence more fully, which flows from the commitment to being church. Church then continues to be diocesan, deanery, and parish structures, but it has also become couples working with other couples in premarital preparation programs or in remarriage and interfaith marriage programs, families committed to being the primary religious educators of their children, and individuals, couples, and families coming together to hold, support, learn from, and celebrate with each other. This evolving sense of ministry and church is especially evident in the church's successful ministry to couples.

The Catholic Church has implemented broad initiatives for preparing couples for marriage, including a mandatory waiting period of six or more months from declaration of intent to wed until the actual wedding, administration of an inventory such as FOCUS or PREPARE, and a required daylong or weekend retreat. Couples are being asked to think harder about this major developmental step in their lives; they are helped to clarify and share their expectations for the future and to look at their family-of-origin models for marriage. One diocese invites engaged couples and their parents to a special once-a-year liturgy with the bishop for a blessing of their relationship. This event draws over 125 couples per year (from a possible 500 couples) and seems to speak especially to those couples for whom faith is an important part of their lives. Couples are often provided with resources for the journey: an initial subscription to a marriage newsletter, a small desktop calendar with a reflective quotation concerning relationships for each day, workbooks for a "do-it-yourself" marriage enrichment program. Some pastors regularly invite back all the couples married that year for a social evening with some enrichment design.

A somewhat unintended benefit of the Church's heavy commitment to engaged couples is the involvement of many married couples in the process. It is often a married couple who administers the premarital instrument, becomes a mentor couple to the engaged couple, and accompanies them through the wedding and possibly afterward. Mentor couples invariably report deep satisfaction through this "ministry." In many cases the mentor couples gather with each other and become an ongoing community/church. Some such groups have met monthly for years.

Interfaith marriages make up 30–40 percent of weddings in the Catholic Church today. Premarital preparation for these couples requires special attention. Dioceses struggle to determine the best way to serve such couples, but one effective approach has been to provide leadership by an interfaith couple(s). Similar levels of faith appear to be a very important variable in successful interfaith marriages. The church is also recognizing the need for special premarital preparation for couples who are remarrying. Most of these couples pursue a second marriage following divorce, and all have struggled or are struggling with deep experiences of loss and associated intense feelings. Dioceses report that this group is especially motivated and that it is not unusual for an ongoing support group to form out of the premarital group experience. One diocese reported an especially successful day centered on the reflections of a young college-age woman from a divorced family, which led to extensive group questioning and dialogue.

How does the church minister to couples across the life cycle? On the one hand it appears that the major resources of time, energy, and finances go toward entrance into marriage rather than ongoing support of marriage. Excellent marriage enrichment programs such as Growth in Marriage, the Couple Communication Program (CCP), Relationship Enhancement (RE), Training in Marriage Enrichment (TIME), or most recently Imago Relationship Therapy see minimal use in church settings. However, the church continues to minister to couples in many other ways, especially around family rites of passage. The Elizabeth Ministry seeks to gather women to share their experiences of childbirth. Baptism of an infant becomes an opportunity to reflect with a couple on the resources of their faith (the possibility of community, the meaning of ritual, symbol, and sacrament) and to help them begin to fashion their own family spirituality. First reconciliation and communion for children become the occasion to develop an increased family understanding of forgiveness and thanksgiving. The church is learning how these sacramental moments are for the whole family and not just the child. Family-centered religious education in addition to child-centered religious education is attracting new interest in numerous parishes. Such programs help families be better attuned to the Scriptures and liturgical rhythms and are intended to support the value of parents as primary religious educators of their children.

Couples and families are developing an increased sense of a *marital or family spirituality*. Retreat centers are beginning to offer couples' retreats and in a few cases spiritual direction for couples. Couples are recognizing their relationship as a vocation, as their unique means to experience and realize God's presence and mystery, love and forgiveness in their lives. Their communications, conflict resolution, and decision making take on new meaning as they perceive the divine in their midst. In some ways this phenomenon is far from recent. Many couples and families in the 1950s and 1960s participated in groups like the Christian Family Movement (CFM) and built a strong sense of community with other families and a close relationship with a clergyman. The communal experience and the close relationship with the priest nurtured an identity of faith and ministry within the couple and the family. It also provided the priest with a unique connection to marital and family life. CFM continues to be quite active in a small number of parishes within dioceses.

Other initiatives support a growing sense of marital and family spirituality. Many parishes and dioceses celebrate in ritual those couples married for a number of years, typically marked by decades or half decades. Couples report the powerful impact of being with couples who have been married forty or fifty years. Valentine's Day is the occasion of one parish's yearly highlighting of the vocation of marriage. Couples are invited for a special dinner and celebration and tend to return in increasing numbers each year. Some parishes offer Sunday morning adult education sessions on marital-family spirituality, possibly including book discussion sessions built around texts such as H. Borys's *Sacred Fire: Love as a Spiritual Path* (1994), O. and S. Levine's *Embracing the Beloved* (1995), W. Wright's *Sacred Dwelling: A Spirituality of Family Life* (1989), or E. Boyer's *Finding God at Home: Family Life as Spiritual Discipline* (1988). Some parishes and dioceses observe November as Family Month, with preaching addressed to marital and family spirituality; often the homily is given by a married couple.

For couples struggling with their marriage the traditional resource of the Catholic Church has been Catholic Social Services (CSS), the clinical arm of Catholic Charities. Couples in conflict were typically referred to CSS by their pastor or were self-referred. At times inappropriate referrals were made to Marriage Encounter (ME), although ME was designed primarily to make good relationships better and not to repair struggling ones. Two new programs have been designed specifically for couples experiencing severe conflict. The programs may or may not be connected with Catholic Social Services. Recovery of Hope is a half-day program that features witnessing by couples who have been through severe conflict themselves. The program seeks to facilitate a significant shift in the couple's perspective on their conflicts and to provide them with the resources of a counseling staff. Retrouvaille has similar goals but extends to a whole day or weekend.

What other directions will ministry to married couples take? Initiatives will likely continue to come from both the grass roots as well as diocesan and parish structures. Energized by their own needs and resources, invested couples will continue to launch successful programs for remarriage couples, interfaith couples, and couples of minority cultures. Diocesan family life directors will continue to listen to and respond to couples' needs in the areas of time management for dual-career couples; the challenges of balancing autonomy and intimacy, individual and couple roles; conflict resolution/anger management/violence containment; values discernment in a materialistic, consumer society; long-term commitment in a short-term culture; and parenting issues in remarriage families. There is much good news about the church's ministry to couples. Perhaps most exciting is the growing sense that ministry involves sharing our gifts and needs with each other and that this process builds community and church in our midst.

Note

The author thanks the four directors of family life ministry who generously shared their experience and vision reflected in this paper: Frank Hannigan in Chicago, Mary Stubler in Green Bay, Randy Nohl in Milwaukee, and Jane Cosmo in Manchester, New Hampshire. In addition the author extends appreciation to Carol Eipers, director of the religious education office in Chicago.

Bibliography

Borys, H. *The Sacred Fire: Love as a Spiritual Path* (New York: HarperCollins, 1994).

Boyer, E. *Finding God at Home: Family Life as Spiritual Discipline* (New York: Harper and Row, 1988).

Hays, E. *Prayers for the Domestic Church: A Handbook for Worship in the Home* (Leavenworth, Kan.: Forest of Peace Publishing, 1979).

Hendrix, H. *Getting the Love You Want: A Guide for Couples* (New York: Harper and Row, 1988).

Levine, O., and S. Levine. *Embracing the Beloved: Relationship as a Path of Awakening* (New York: Doubleday, 1995).

Linn, D., S. Linn, and M. Linn. *Sleeping with Bread: Holding What Gives You Life* (New York: Paulist Press, 1995).

Wright, W. *Sacred Dwelling: A Spirituality of Family Life* (New York: Crossroad, 1989).

—PAUL GIBLIN

A Protestant Perspective

Exciting, effective ministries with couples express faith assumptions about marriage and renew the central importance of marriage for the nurture of spouses, families, churches, and communities (Popenoe et al. 1996). Everett (1989) describes four major symbolic models for marriage (sacrament, vocation, covenant, and communion) that guide faith and practice in marriage.

Ministries to couples are grounded in marriage as the vow between a woman and a man who publicly "espouse" each other without reservation. In this pledged vision, spouses live out their values, expectations, and assumptions in all aspects of life (Hunt 1987). Marriage ministries enable couples to choose their future, use their resources, increase their strengths, and eliminate negatives across their life journeys (Hunt and Hunt 1994).

Four major categories of postwedding ministries are couples' classes, mentoring, marriage enrichment, and marriage counseling.

Couples' Classes

Ministries to couples have existed for decades as local church "couples' classes" that meet on Sundays or at other times for study, fellowship, and support. Thousands of couples have nurtured each other through these ongoing groups, which often form with newly married couples who continue together across their lifetimes.

Couples' classes may address any marriage issue, including finances, parenting, sexuality, career, and Bible study. Couples' groups provide fellowship (often with child care) and support and initiate service and outreach projects to other couples and families in the community.

Marriage Mentoring

Couple-to-couple mentoring is fast becoming a major new marriage ministry. The Caring Couples Network (CCN, phone: 615-340-7170), established in 1995 by the United Methodist Church, incorporates basic principles of couple mentoring, friendship, marriage enrichment, and outreach to implement marriage ministries in local churches. The CCN team consists of married couples working with their pastor (and pastoral staff in larger churches) and with consultants (therapists, attorneys, family finance experts, and other professionals) to minister to engaged and newly married couples, couples with children, and couples with serious difficulties, such as substance abuse, violence, and losses. The CCN team's ministries are described in a handbook and video (available from Discipleship Resources, phone: 800-685-4370).

Michael McManus's *Marriage Savers* (1995) extensively describes many excellent programs for strengthening good marriages and saving troubled marriages, providing contact addresses and telephone numbers and directions for churches to join together in establishing community marriage policies concerning weddings, marriages, and family concerns.

Marriage Ministry, originated by Father Dick McGinnis in St. David's Episcopal Church in Jacksonville, Florida, developed seventeen action statements for couples concerning Christian example, commitment to God, commitment to partner, changes in oneself, trust and nurture, and marriage as a continuing process and lifelong journey (McManus 1995, 204).

Retrouvaille, an outgrowth of Catholic Marriage Encounter, addresses couples facing divorce. The Recovery of Hope program, established by the Mennonites, offers both half-day and weeklong intensive interventions for deeply conflicted couples. On a Saturday morning, three couples who have recovered from major marriage crises share their stories, and then attending couples are given opportunity to consult with therapists about therapy and other options.

Marriage Enrichment

Marriage enrichment includes many types of weekend and other formats for couples to learn communication and conflict resolution skills, exchange support, and renew their enthusiasm and vows. The Association for Couples in Marriage Enrichment (A.C.M.E., phone: 800-634-8325), founded by Dr. David and Vera Mace in 1973, provides leadership training for couples and outreach programs.

Marriage Encounter, initiated by Father Gabriel Calvo in the Roman Catholic Church in Spain in 1962, also has several Protestant denominational expressions. In weekend retreats and other settings Marriage Encounter provides information about all areas of marriage interaction and private time for spouses to nurture each other and build stronger marriages.

Some denominations have created their own marriage enrichment programs, such as the United Methodist Celebrating Marriage program initiated in 1981. Other enrichment programs are Getting the Love You Want, developed by Harville Hendrix, and Christian PREP, adapted by Scott Stanley from research on PREP, a marriage communication training procedure originated by Howard Markman.

Among many resources are Christian Marriage Enrichment, founded by H. Norman Wright; Couple Communication, founded by Sherrod Miller; and the Prepare/Enrich inventories developed by David Olson and associates. As committed Protestant Christians, these leaders have developed programs and resources that many churches use.

Marriage Counseling

Marriage and family counseling, as part of pastoral care, has long been a ministry of pastors and staff. Some local churches sponsor counseling centers or join with other churches in an ecumenical pastoral counseling agency, sometimes with satellite offices in churches across a metropolitan area. Couples and individuals who are trained as lay counselors (Tan 1991) or through the Stephen Ministries may provide marriage counseling in some churches.

Couple counseling is a term used by those who wish to make counseling services available to all couples, wedded or not. However commendable this effort is, it obscures the important foundation of pledging oneself to one's spouse in a wedding that clearly marks the desire of the partners to benefit from church wisdom and support for marriage (Popenoe et al. 1996).

Toward Comprehensive Marriage Ministries

Churches need to increase their ministries that enable marriages to succeed in being the healthy key to family wellness. Also needed are ministries to single parents and stepfamilies, to troubled and failing marriages, to families with violence and substance abuse, and to families with other dysfunctions.

Available tools and techniques include training in communication skills, conflict resolution, goal setting, sexual intimacy, finances, career-family interfaces, and parenting training. Newsletters, books, videos, and other media resources contain information about marriage ministry and leader training.

Every local church needs to provide marriage ministries. Information about many training opportunities and resources is published in the ACME newsletter, *Marriage* (sponsored by International Marriage Encounter), *Marriage Partnership* (sponsored by Christianity Today, Inc.), and other sources.

Bibliography

Everett, William J. *Blessed Be the Bond: Christian Perspectives on Marriage and Family* (Lanham, Md.: University Press of America, 1989).

Hunt, Richard A. "Marriage as Dramatizing Theology," *Journal of Pastoral Care* 41/2 (1987): 119–31.

Hunt, Richard A., and Joan A. Francis Hunt. *Awaken Your Power to Love* (Nashville: Nelson Press, 1994).

McManus, Michael J. *Marriage Savers,* rev. ed. (Grand Rapids, Mich.: Zondervan Publishing House, 1995).

Popenoe, David, Jean Bethke Elshtain, and David Blankenhorn. *Promises to Keep: Decline and Renewal of Marriage in America* (Lanham, Md.: Rowman and Littlefield, 1996).

Tan, Siang-Yang. *Lay Counseling: Equipping Christians for a Helping Ministry* (Grand Rapids, Mich.: Zondervan Publishing House, 1991).

—RICHARD A. HUNT

8

Ministry with Children
and Youth

Typically, the question that religious educators ask is, How can we pass on our tradition to our children so that they understand and live according to it? When this is the key educational or formational question, the responses tend to be unilateral and hierarchical. The authorities of a community bring the tradition to its children, and the children receive the tradition. This is increasingly alienating children and youth today; growing up in a pluralistic environment, they are less willing to have tradition imposed upon them in this manner. Families and communities today who are seeking more egalitarian relationships require a more mutual process of educating and forming their young people. The question before these families and communities is, How can we let our children know that the tradition belongs to them and that they are part of its unfolding into the future? How can we actively include children and youth in the ongoing play with and even argument over the story and practices of our faith?

"Traditioning," as I understand it, is not something that we do to and for our children, it is something in which we invite them to share with us. We let them know that they are part of the story by welcoming their wrestling with the story and listening carefully to their insights and interpretations of the story. This is one of the most important practices of faith, and it has implications for how young people live their lives with others in this world.

Theologian Letty Russell asks the question, "What might a church that struggled to practice a sharing of authority in community look like?" She poses the image of a round table where authority is shared and hospitality is extended to all, including those typically marginalized. In a "church in the round," partners in faith come together to work for justice, and it is the kitchen table that symbolizes the hard work of welcoming those at the margins. Although Russell herself does not name children and youth as persons on the margins, I extend her discussion to these least of us. And I ask that we welcome them to the kitchen table to join us in the hard work of being a community.

This Belongs to You:
Wrestling with the Word in the Kitchen

In a kitchen scene in Olive Ann Burns's novel *Cold Sassy Tree,* we are made privy to the practice of including children and youth in the story of faith. The novel, set shortly after the turn of the century, revolves around the life of fourteen-year-old Will. Will's beloved grandmother recently died, and Will himself, through a freak accident, has narrowly escaped death. His near-death experience causes Will to become reflective, and he muses out loud to his grandfather about the trouble he was having making sense of the inequality of suffering and hardship around him.

> "Grandpa, uh, why you think Jesus said ast the Lord for anything you want and you'll get it? 'Ast and it shall be given,' the Bible says. But it ain't so." I felt blasphemous even to think it, much less say it out loud.
>
> Grandpa was silent a long time. "Maybe Jesus was talkin' in His sleep, son, or folks heard Him wrong. Or maybe them disciples tryin' to start a church thought everbody would join up if'n they said Jesus Christ would give the Garden a-Eden to anybody believed He was the son a-God and like thet." Grandpa laughed. Gosh, I'd get a whipping if Papa knew what was going on with the Word in his kitchen. "All I know," he added, "is thet folks pray for food and still go hungry, and Adam and Eve ain't in thet garden a-theirs no more, and yore granny ain't in hers, and I ain't got no son a-my own to carry on the name and hep me run the store when I'm old. Like you say, you don't git thangs jest by astin'. Well, I'm a-go'n study on this some more. Jesus must a-meant something else, not what it sounds like."

In this conversation, Will deeply engages his faith tradition, and his grandfather plunges in with him. For many in Will's community, including his father, such a discussion could not go on, for it would be considered blasphemous. Grandpa wisely does not censure Will's struggles with tradition, nor does he give him pat answers to quell his questions. In his somewhat irreverent way, Grandpa realizes that the kind of questioning and pondering "going on with the Word in our kitchen" is holy ground. And thus, with an old man's help, a youth is fully welcomed into the church in the round.

Allowing the questions, doubts, and insights of young people to be part of the traditioning process is valuable for all involved. Young people are drawn to a tradition that welcomes their grappling, and older members have to rethink the issues of faith as the next generation poses its pressing questions. Grandpa listens and reflects "a long time" before offering his honest thoughts. Though his theological ramblings seem a bit crude, Grandpa permits a conversation that not only allows for risky exploration but opens up to future possibilities. Grandpa does not know all the answers, but he does not dismiss the questions. Studying "on this some more" is not only an affirmation of Will's question but an invitation to go even deeper. Rather than being whipped for wrestling with the Word in the kitchen, Will was joined.

Very often, listening to the questions and doubts of young people enables us to share with them important aspects of the faith tradition. One year when I taught seventh-grade Sunday school I noticed how often the kids asked questions that were not related to the planned lesson for the day. I decided to capitalize on this; we spent an entire session listing all the questions they had about Christian faith. I then tossed the curriculum and planned our lessons around their questions. Each week I focused on one of their questions by bringing to them some of my thoughts and the thoughts of other forebears in the faith (and I wasn't afraid to let them know different saints have thought differently on the various issues); then I would listen for their responses and further questions. It was one of the most rewarding years for me as a teacher. Certainly this is not always a feasible strategy, but it is a very effective one when used.

In addition to welcoming the questions of our youth, we can also reveal to our youth some of the key questions and debates that have shaped the history of our faith traditions. For instance, our creeds and practices were shaped by important conflicts. Rather than simply teach youth to memorize the resolution that has become our tradition, we can take them through the sides of the debates and allow them to engage the controversies.

We welcome young people to the story not only by allowing them to converse with the tradition but also by promoting their wrestling with God. My own children, in fact, have taught me a lot about such wrestling. My youngest son, Paul, has always been closely connected to God—and full of "chutzpah" in his dealings with God. He is the first to thank God for God's presence in our midst and the first to challenge God when God seems absent. One night our family was reading together Genesis 3, the story of Adam, Eve, and the serpent in the garden. Paul, who along with his older brother and sister has numerous snakes and reptiles for pets, was probably predisposed to reading the story from the serpent's vantage point. I was not surprised that he took a liking to the trouble-making reptile in the story. "You know, Mom, the serpent has a good point there. Why would God not want Eve to have her eyes opened and to know good and evil? Shouldn't we have our eyes opened?" Our family then embarked on a conversation about questioning God, struggling with God over commands that seem unfair, and confronting God and others with our awareness of evil. This young child who had heard about Abraham arguing with God, Jacob wrestling with the angel, and the Syrophoenician woman chastising Jesus knew that God could handle his brazenness. I thanked God then and there that my own eyes were opened by the spontaneous question and inquiring vantage point of my child! When a child knows that God listens to his questions, including his bold questioning of God, the child truly belongs to God; when a child knows that the community listens to her questions and learns from her insights, the child truly belongs to the round table and its story.

We can more adequately symbolize and practice the full integration of children and youth. In many Protestant churches, it is the practice to invite the children to come up as witnesses when new babies are baptized. This is a touching ritual, and it reminds the whole community of the generation to come. This practice, however, stops short of what it should do. When the congregation repeats its vows to the newly baptized baby, the children stand mute with their eyes glazed. A baptism can include vows that the children take to commit themselves to nurturing the new one; this signals to them early that they are an integral part of the people who have come before and the people who will come after. It lets them know that they matter.

When welcoming young people into the tradition, we need to address the historical inequality between girls and boys, men and women. Family ministry that seeks to prepare young people for egalitarian families whose members express mutual regard for one another must pay special attention to gender issues. Many faith traditions and their sacred Scriptures have excluded girls and women from the traditioning process, and efforts must be made to rectify this exclusion. When girls are encouraged to bring their questions and insights to their communities, wrestling with patriarchy and sexism becomes an integral part of what goes on with the Word in the kitchen.

Girls, This Belongs to You Too

Communities of faith can welcome girls into the argument of tradition and the story of faith by paying attention to both the instructional process and its content. Studies of group behavior, including classroom dynamics, suggest that males and females exhibit different manners in their speaking, and that (Western European) men's style is the valued pattern. Boys and men are more likely to use highly assertive speech, impersonal and abstract examples, and competitive or adversarial interchanges. These not only are favored but are perceived to be more intelligent and authoritative behaviors. Girls and women are more likely to hesitate and qualify their speech ("I'm not sure, but maybe sometimes it is the case that . . ."), end with "tag" questions ("This is really important, don't you think?"), share personal experiences, and belittle their contributions ("This is probably not important, but . . ."). The more tentative style of women invites more interruptions from male conversation partners and less attention and notice from leaders and teachers. Indeed, a point made by a woman in a deferential style may go unnoticed and then repeated by a man and engaged or praised by a leader. The fact that teachers may ignore, neglect to call on, expect less of, and forget to credit women for their contributions contributes to discouraging and sometimes silencing women in discussion settings. On top of all this, girls and women may be doubly bound; if they learn the code of the male, they may be perceived as inappropriately pushy, aggressive, and unfeminine.

Leaders attuned to these dynamics, which begin in elementary years, can make efforts to listen to girls, to acknowledge their responses, and to give them credit for their contributions to a discussion. This does not mean that leaders should be patronizing or condescending to girls; quite the contrary. As long as girls' contributions are acknowledged and their intelligence respected, girls will eagerly engage in hearty discussion. We need not take their tentative conversational style as evidence of lack of knowledge; instead we should value it for its inviting and collaborative effects (Hall 1982; Hess 1997). Most important, female role models can dispel the stereotype that girls should not engage in passionate and heated discussion about important issues.

With regard to content, leaders in communities of faith can recover the stories of heroines of faith and can prepare for and invite wrestling with the patriarchy in the tradition. There are some spunky, assertive women in our traditions whose stories should be shaping our daughters' identities, but all too often these stories go unnoticed. Puah and Shiprah resisted Pharaoh's murderous orders in Exodus, Deborah was a great leader of Israel in Judges, Vashti refused to parade her beauty before a court of drunken men in Esther, and Mary the sister of Martha studied at the feet of Jesus in the Gospels.

In addition to celebrating the liberating narratives in our traditions, we can invite girls to wrestle with difficult texts that subordinate or demean women. We can teach young people some basic interpretive principles that allow them to listen to and talk back to these texts. Put simply, they can go behind the text, read between texts, look over the text, stand in front of the text, and talk back to the text. *Going behind the text:* First, we can teach young people to read the texts in light of the cultural situation of the time. Where does the text simply reflect the cultural assumptions about women? Where does it push the edges of the cultural assumptions in a way that we can follow a trajectory toward liberation? *Reading between texts:* Second, we can teach them to read intertextually. How can texts be compared to one another? Where do we need to hold conflicting themes in tension? Where does one theme have priority over another? *Looking over the text:* Third, we can teach young people to read the parts of the canon in light of the theological whole. What are the overarching theological themes that take priority in our tradition? How do these themes complement or even correct specific texts? *Standing in front of the text:* Fourth, we can teach young people to see some texts (those that Phyllis Trible calls "texts of terror") as mirrors of the suffering women have endured; we read them to remember and resist such suffering in the present. *Talking back to the text:* Finally, we can teach young people to question the stories of faith and cry out to God when they perceive that their tradition has canonized oppression. These are strategies that welcome young people into the story and that empower girls in particular to join the community of faith.

Ministry with young people today requires that we help prepare them for the future. In addition to a future of gender equality, North Americans look to a future that is diverse and pluralistic. The kind of qualities that welcome young people into a tradition can be stretched to enable them to engage those who are from other traditions.

Guests at the Kitchen Table:
Interfaith Dialogue and the Future

As we welcome children and youth to the table, it will be important that we teach them how to show hospitality to those whose culture and faith are different from theirs. On the one hand, we can hope that children who have been welcomed will "learn what they live." A community that neither presses for conformity (an imperious quashing of difference) nor settles for surface tolerance (a vacuous celebration of difference) is life-giving and future-serving. When we create an environment that is open to difference and intense dialogue, we prepare our children for a pluralistic world.

Having been treated with respect themselves, our children and youth will be inclined to respect others. The hope is that they will share with confidence the tradition they cherish, and they will be open to the questions and challenges that others bring. Having already questioned and wrestled with their tradition, they will not be unnerved by the difficult questions that others raise. Likewise, they will listen to others share their own stories, and they will also respectfully question and engage others in genuine dialogue.

On the other hand, just as we intentionally involve our children and youth in wrestling with their tradition, we can also actively prepare them in interfaith dialogue. We can give them the skills to name their own beliefs *and* allow others to name their beliefs. Those who have no knowledge of or commitment to a tradition cannot enter into dialogue, for they have nothing to offer. Genuine dialogue requires the hospitality of listening and the generosity of sharing; dialogue partners are simultaneously open to learning and ready to teach.

Studying on This Some More

Many of our communities of faith are losing their children and youth. This is tragic, for it is our young people that prompt us to do what Grandpa had to do, "study on this some more." This loss does not have to be. Children and youth who are invited to shape the future of our communities will sit at the table with us. Yes, they will squirm and flout traditions as they sit with us. But that's their job—and it's an important one. How else are we going to have our eyes opened?

Bibliography

Hall, Roberta M. "The Classroom Climate: A Chilly One for Women?" (Washington, D.C.: The Project on the Status and Education of Women; Association of American Colleges, 1982).

Hess, Carol Lakey. *Caretakers of Our Common House: Women's Development in Communities of Faith* (Nashville: Abingdon Press, 1997).

Russell, Letty M. *Church in the Round: Feminist Interpretation of the Church* (Louisville, Ky.: Westminster/John Knox Press, 1993).

—CAROL LAKEY HESS

9

Ministry with Single Parents

Recently there has been a renewed emphasis on the message that growing up in a single-parent home is detrimental to the health and well-being of children. This research sometimes decries single parenthood and champions "traditional family values." Such polemics against single-parenthood often ignore the crucial needs of the children and parents in single-parent families.

In 1970 there were 3.8 million single-parent families in the United States. The 1990 Census reported that there were 10.1 million, 15 percent of all families. In single-parent households, 6 percent of the family heads were widowed, 38 percent divorced, 34 percent never married, and 22 percent separated. Women headed 8.7 million single-parent families, and men headed 1.4 million. The number of one-parent families has grown dramatically. Single-parent households headed by men are increasing at a faster rate than those headed by women.

The Single-Parent Family

Like other families, single-parent families struggle with making ends meet; they struggle with changing roles, rules, and relationships within their own family network; and they interact with the larger society. Yet single-parent families have distinctive features. Associated with every single-parent family is a drama or story that has resulted in there being a single parent. Another distinctive feature is the lack of a partner with whom to raise children and run the household. Poverty often attends single-parent families. Children from single-parent families have more academic and behavioral problems.

Avoiding Stereotypes and Ghettoization

Before reviewing responses to these factors, we need to consider the pluses and minuses of focused programs for single-parent families. While single-parent families need specialized church programs and ministries targeting single-parent families, such programs can stereotype and ghettoize. A support group for children from single-parent families can cause the children to feel "marked." If these children participate also in a larger youth group, the processing in the smaller group is unavailable for processing with and through the larger group. The potential for cliques and alienation is increased. A focused ministry for single parents can ignore issues common to all parents and thereby deny single parents beneficial information, resources, and experiences. Focused programs can isolate single parents and may provide them only limited support. On the other hand, focused ministries can attend to distinctive needs. Religious bodies should both provide special programming and include single families in the general family ministries of the church.

The Church as Partner

The image of partner best expresses the optimal role of the church in single-parent family ministry. The church does not assume the role of the nonresident parent: The church cannot and should not attempt to be spouse to single parents or the second parent to their children. The church is a partner that covenants with single-parent families to enhance their family life, to strengthen their connection to systems outside of the family network, and to nurture and support their family faith journeys. The image of partner also applies to the church's ministry with two-parent families. They also need the church's supportive and caring ministries. As a partner the church provides spiritual support and moral guidance for the difficult task of building healthy families. The church can be a partner by providing companionship for parents who struggle to balance work and household responsibilities. Sharing the joy and pain of being a part of a family strengthens and enhances family members' capacity to celebrate and endure their life together. The church is a corporate or collective partner, whose many members are needed to support children and their families.

Singleness

In what I consider to be the best practical workbook for helping single parents, *The Single Parent Experience,* Beverly Barnes and Jennifer Coplon (1980) identify seven groupings of single parents: Separated, Divorced, Widowed, Divorced Father with Child Custody, Never Married, Adoptive Single Parent, and Foster Single Parent. An eighth has emerged recently: Grandparent. Specific issues accompany each of these groupings. In some, tremendous grief prevails; in some, domestic responsibilities are absent or are faded memories; in still others there is the uneasy, sometimes volatile interaction between the parents. Effective ministry with single-parent families must address these various elements. Individual counseling is often needed as the single parent copes with recent and unexpected singlehood. Periodically holding groups for those who have experienced grief and loss gives opportunities for them to grieve the losses of spouses and marriages, of the single lifestyle, or of a retired life free of daily responsibilities for children. Single parents also need to gather with other single parents for sharing and support. The church may support a formal meeting of Parents Without Partners or arrange informal gatherings of single parents around a particular issue, crisis, or need. One church in Chicago was planning a day care center. In preparation they invited single parents within the congregation to meet and offer their suggestions and reflect on their needs for day care. The meeting was an opportunity to contribute to the development of the day care center, to share experiences, and to exchange support.

Going It Alone

Often single parents must produce income, care for children, keep on top of the family's schedule, respond to emergencies, and manage the household alone. Overwhelmed by these responsibilities, the single parent is susceptible to isolation and loneliness. Satisfying the single parent's need for interpersonal relationships—platonic and romantic—is complicated. Spending time with others can generate feelings of abandonment, guilt, envy, or jealousy in the children. The church can encourage members to offer times of respite and breaks from the responsibilities of managing the single-parent household. Youth activities should not be solely times to take the kids off a parent's hands, yet providing a break can be a valuable secondary goal to the primary goal of faith development activities.

Children in single-parent families need another set of ears and alternative relationships as they grow and develop. The church can help children identify others in their family or in the church to whom they might turn. The church that fosters the gift of opportunities to get away and to borrow another set of ears or another shoulder relieves the loneliness of the single-parent family, whether this is done through special programs or not.

Poverty and the
Single-Parent Family

Children in single-parent families are the poorest people in the United States. While 11 percent of children in two-parent families live in poverty, 60 percent of the children who live with never-married mothers are poor. "The single parents are disadvantaged from the beginning," says Timothy S. Grall, a Census Bureau statistician. "They are not as well educated, and disproportionately Black and female. Financially, Blacks and females tend to earn less" (Cooper, 26). Those doing pastoral counseling with poor single-parent families should adopt a comprehensive care approach including one-on-one and family counseling, and in addition economic empowerment through job training, employment counseling, and money management. This counsel and assistance can be given in various ways. Linking with municipal, state, and federal job training programs, churches can help single-parents increase the earning capacity in the home. Advertising jobs in the church bulletin or having parishioners offer job placement counseling also helps single-parent families. Some churches, as a part of their preparation for childbirth classes, offer guidance about how to set up and manage household budgets to avoid debt and extreme financial difficulty.

Children at Risk

Children from one-parent families are about twice as likely to drop out of school as children from two-parent families; they are less likely to graduate from college, more likely to become teen mothers, and somewhat more likely not to be employed or to be attending a work training program in young adulthood. Churches can help these high-risk children with both direct services and advocacy. A sense of belonging and positive peer influence are important to children from single-parent families. They should be sought out and encouraged to participate in group gatherings. In these groups guidance in values and activities that nurture a sense of well-being and accomplishment are possible. The absence of a second role model could be addressed through a mentor program in which an adult from the congregation is identified as a person whom a child can trust and turn to when needed. Such a program could be formally or informally established. In either case the child and the other adult would know they have a special relationship that augments the relationship between the child and his or her single parent.

In an effort to "reform" welfare, government bodies have deprived single-parent families of money for food, clothing, and housing, increasing the vulnerability of children already at highest risk. Churches should lobby federal and state legislatures not to solve welfare's problems by worsening the plight of children.

Conclusion

To minister to single-parent families, religious bodies must attend to the complexity of what they share with other families and what they do not. Only thus can they build effective programming and faithful communities that nurture and support those families in our midst who are at highest risk.

Bibliography

Barnes, Beverly C., and Jennifer K. Coplon. *The Single-Parent Experience* (Boston: Resource Communications [in cooperation with Family Service Association of Greater Boston], 1980).

Cooper, Mary Anderson. "Beyond Stereotypes: Women as Heads of Households—A Look at Poverty, the Single Woman, Her Household—and Public Policy," *Church and Society* 83 (March/April 1993): 24–37.

Hardey, Michael, and Graham Crow, eds. *Lone Parenthood: Coping with Constraints and Making Opportunities in Single Parent Families* (Toronto: University of Toronto Press, 1991).

Kissman, Kris, and JoAnn Allen. *Single Parent Families* (Newbury Park, Calif.: Sage Publications, 1993).

—HOMER U. ASHBY, JR.

10

Ministry with Stepfamilies

While the details of statistical reports vary, the pattern is clear. A large percentage of all children in the United States and Great Britain have been, are being, or will be raised in a home where at least one of the adults is not the biological or original adoptive parent. To put it another way, there are huge numbers of stepfamilies, defined as marital partners with children from a previous relationship.

Stepfamilies are more numerous and more complex than the "normal" nuclear family. A variety of authors note approximately seventy-two different ways of becoming a stepfamily and approximately sixteen different types of stepfamily households. The variety has to do with a number of things, including present composition and previous circumstances. For instance, in a stepfamily household a husband or wife might introduce the children by saying, "Those are his, these are mine, and those are ours." Furthermore, the circumstances prior to the members' coming together under one roof might include death, divorce, abuse, escapes from danger or persecution, relatively friendly separations, or court-ordered placements. The ages of children may vary widely, and those ages have identifiable developmental issues that affect the marital relationship and life within the present home, not to mention the developmental issues of the parents. Some children may be grateful for this new home and the harmony it seems to bring, while others may yearn for their previous situation and resent the present one. Some stepfamilies have only one parent present, and a child or children may not even be the biological or original adoptive child of that parent.

A parish pastor must be careful not to presume that stepfamilies are simply variations on the "normal" first-marriage family constellation. The typical extended stepfamily has 60–100 people in it, because of the proliferation of aunts, uncles, grandparents, and so on who are brought into the picture by the "step" marriages. Furthermore, the leader of a congregation needs to know that the divorce rate within stepfamilies exceeds that of first marriages. That increase is, no doubt, directly related to the complexity and strain of stepfamily life.

What, then, are some of the considerations for congregations developing approaches to respond helpfully and faithfully to stepfamilies? Several suggestions are made here: References to stepfamilies should become part of the "normal" language of the community; grief should be acknowledged as a primary experience in the history and early years of the life of stepfamilies; educational and support groups should be formed to help stepfamily members adjust to the gap between expectations and reality; pastors and congregational leaders should be trained to understand and recognize the complexities of stepfamily life and the ways in which they exceed those in the family life of first marriages; and stepfamilies should be viewed as resources for a congregation working to create a community that values diversity.

Making Public Acknowledgment

Pastors, church leaders, and church members as a whole know that stepfamilies are numerous, but they often don't say it out loud. Any congregation that seeks to be inclusive of stepfamilies should acknowledge their existence openly and regularly. They should be treated as a normal variation rather than as something unusual. Along with the complexities mentioned above, it is not unusual for members of stepfamilies to carry some level of anxiety about the attitude of the church toward their circumstances. Guilt over a divorce, sensitivity to being "unusual," or awareness of old stereotypes of what a family "should be" may contribute to stepfamilies' discomfort in the life of a congregation, even after years of involvement.

A congregation can be welcoming and responsive in a number of ways, often so simple that we overlook them. Pastors and worship leaders can use illustrations in sermons and other announcements that include stepfamilies. To be mentioned is to be included. The same can be done by church school teachers and planners.

The point here is simply to claim stepfamilies as a part of congregational life in the same ways that we claim so many other forms of family life—retired couples, siblings living together, single-parent families, and so on. All too often the absence of references to stepfamilies results in feelings of being singled out by omission. And, of course, the references should be positive. Not only should we incorporate them by reference, but we should expect to gain much from their experiences of change, adaptation, and claiming new hopes for the future.

Responding to Grief

Stepfamilies are usually born of grief. Partners who find each other and bring children from previous relationships have lost a great deal. Whether by death, divorce, or some other tragic circumstances, dreams and hopes have been shattered. Rebuilding is taking place against the backdrop of loss. This is not just true for the marital partners. Children, too, have lost. They have usually lost a parent—either by death or by divorce—or at least time spent with the more absent parent. Furthermore, they may have lost former living space; rituals and pastimes are changed; images of what life would be like in the future have been disrupted and altered.

Congregational leadership may assume that grief is a part of the life of stepfamilies, particularly in their first years (note the plural). Sermons and class sessions become opportunities to refer to the "normality" of grief in families that are rebuilding and seeking to blend. Pastoral care and counseling should be cognizant of grief and address it in premarital, marital, and familial care. Support groups for stepfamily members would do well to include grief—the acknowledgment of it, responsiveness to it, and the study of it—as a key component of their work together.

Reducing the Gap
between Expectations and Reality

Again, because of the grief that lies in the background of stepfamilies, idealistic expectations for a new family are powerful. In particular, previously divorced husbands and wives look to the newly constituted family as the opportunity for fulfillment of dreams lost in the previous marriage. Children formerly abused or neglected yearn for a household that feels unflaggingly secure and harmonious. At the same time, children who are angry at disruption and separation from their earlier lives often seek, consciously or subliminally, to "prove" that this new situation won't work. The possibilities for disappointment, anger, and resentment are voluminous. And the greater the expectations, the bigger the fall as the normal routines of any family life combine with the complexities that stepfamily life brings.

In order to prepare for or help repair the pain of disappointment, congregations may offer a number of resources. First, the educational ministries of the church can regularly emphasize the importance of mediation, conflict resolution, and problem-solving skills. And those skills should be taught and modeled as a normal part of living. Theological connections can and should be made. Our theological understanding of human nature prepares us for the frequent occasions in which human beings, particularly in families, misunderstand and disappoint each other.

Second, pastoral support groups should be designed for stepfamilies. Such provisions become both demonstrations of the care that comes from the larger congregational family and "safe places" for stepfamily members to equip themselves for their life together.

Training Leadership
for the Sake of Stepfamilies

Seminary training in the past has been more likely to equip pastors for the "normal" issues of "first-marriage" life. Congregations and church leaders should encourage pastors to attend training events and become current in the literature on stepfamilies, their lives, and their unique issues. Pastors have an opportunity to be genuinely welcoming to stepfamilies, whose struggles and hopes are deep-seated.

Valuing Stepfamilies
as Congregational Resources

The stepfamilies' unique difficulties and complexities have been noted. As in all of human life, however, those very problems become resources if helpfully viewed and understood. Stepfamilies are confronting existentially the very issue that congregations struggle with as well: how to incorporate persons from different experiences, practices, even beliefs and values into one living, breathing unit of human cooperation and support. The skills and lessons learned in cooperation, patience, and respect within stepfamilies can benefit us all. Therefore, congregations would do well to seek out occasions when both parents and children can serve as teachers and encouragers to the rest of us. In fact, families further along their road are primary resources to whom a church can turn to provide encouragement for persons in earlier stages of forming new and blended families.

Along with this suggestion, however, comes a warning. It is important not to segregate stepfamilies into a separate "program" of the church. To do so would be to miss the richness they have, or will have, to offer. Indeed, stepfamilies, in their formation from experiences of grief and in their determination to find family again, have a great deal to teach us about hope.

Bibliography

Carter, Elizabeth A., and Monica McGoldrick. *The Changing Family Life Cycle* (New York: Gardner Press, 1988).

Einstein, Elizabeth A. *The Stepfamily: Living, Loving, and Learning* (Ithaca, N.Y.: E. Einstein, 1994).

Papernow, Patricia L. *Becoming a Stepfamily* (San Francisco: Jossey-Bass, 1993).

Visher, E., and J. Visher. *Old Loyalties, New Ties: Therapeutic Strategies with Stepfamilies* (New York: Brunner/Mazel, 1988).

————. *How to Win as a Stepfamily* (New York: Brunner/Mazel, 1991).

—WILLIAM ARNOLD

11

Ministry with Families with Homosexual Sons or Daughters

A Jewish Perspective

The purpose of pastoral/rabbinic counseling is to help a congregant cope with an issue that threatens to get out of hand, using the rich resources of the congregant's religious tradition to foster health and balance. Jews come to their rabbis with a range of issues, from marital problems and divorce to child-parent relations, employee-employer strains, or conflicts with friends or relatives. What is problematic to one person may not be to another. Hence, counseling begins with the perception of a problem. The essential question is one of perspective, of how a reality is understood, not of the reality itself. Whether homosexuality is perceived as a problem will vary from individual to individual. Some experience their homosexual identity as a cause for distress; some fear being repugnant to the people or the community they love. For others, their sexual orientation isn't so much a hindrance as it is a new way of expressing their identity in the world. For some parents, issues of shame ("How do we tell our friends?") or of failure ("Did we cause this?") stimulate the need to seek counsel. Finally, for religious Jews, the question of maintaining our ancient covenant with God is at stake: is there room for God and Torah in the life of a Jewish homosexual? Is there room for the Jewish homosexual in Judaism?

Perspectives in the Jewish Tradition

In Jewish tradition, perception of homosexuality (and, hence, of counseling objectives) is inextricably connected to perceptions of God's will in the Torah, as well as to a larger nexus of values about family, community, tradition, human dignity, and freedom.

Orthodox Jews understand the Torah both literally (each and every word is God's) and diachronically (what it means is what is meant, and vice versa). Hence, the biblical prohibition in Leviticus 20:13 ("If a man lies with a male as one lies with a woman, the two of them have done an abhorrent thing; they shall be put to death," NJB) includes all male-male sex, in all places, and for all time. Some Conservative Jews add a sense of historical gradualism, so that the modern Western insistence on heterosexual unions provides additional support to viewing homosexuality as a problem to be solved.

More liberal Conservative Jews understand the Torah as the vehicle through which God communicates. The Bible is God's Word, but not God's words. The

Torah is understood to reflect the perspectives of its human recipients, who share an active role in its formulation and its transmission. Reform and Reconstructionist Jews understand that the Torah records a human understanding of what it means to live in covenant with God. For each of these latter three coalitions, the broader principles of the Torah (such as the assertion that all people reflect the image of God) direct how its laws are to be understood and applied. These coalitions prefer readings that prioritize God's love, justice, and compassion over readings that give greater weight to ritual or conventional concerns. These latter three segments of Jews situate the Torah in a historical context, understanding it as addressing first its own age and context. Applying its teachings for other times or places requires an act of *midrash* (of interpretation) even when we seek to apply its *p'shat* (contextual meaning).

Shared Commitments

All Jewish religious groups share a fundamental commitment to the rule of law; its expression of moral and social norms is an essential tool for human betterment and for receiving God's guidance. All Jewish groups are committed to maintaining the dignity of each person (regardless of whether they approve of particular behavior) and to showing compassion to all. It is important to affirm this broad consensus. The inherent tension between these two commitments, and the deep passion about homosexuality, leads many conservatives to deny that liberals are committed to tradition and to normative standards, and leads many liberals to deny that conservatives cherish human dignity and compassion. The debate is hot enough without vilification or distortion. The chasm separating the two sides concerns theological presuppositions, and issues of emotional comfort and temperament, not a lack of commitment to rules, tradition, human dignity, and compassion.

Divided Consequences

For those who read the Bible as God's timeless verbal gift, the fact that Leviticus condemns male-male sex as a *to'evah* (an abomination) and as a capital crime ends the discussion. Homosexuality is a sin and must be treated as a sin. Rabbinic counseling should love the sinner and discourage the sin. Concern for the dignity of the homosexual involves speaking in a civil manner, patiently explaining reasons for the Torah's prohibition, and encouraging the homosexual to repent of his or her orientation. Since most Conservative thinkers have recognized that orientation is largely beyond conscious control, they seek primarily to limit behavior, encouraging the Jewish homosexual to live either as a heterosexual or as a celibate. Only in those ways can the homosexual live in accord with God's teachings. Since God's teaching leads to human betterment, the homosexual who lives this way will enjoy a richer, fuller life. Counseling a homosexual along these lines expresses the truest love and compassion for the individual and preserves social good by affirming the heterosexual family as the sole acceptable *norm* for the community. By and large, then, the Orthodox and the prevalent (so far) Conservative position treats homosexuality as a sinful action and as a sickness to be overcome.

For the more liberal Jews (and indeed for most homosexuals, even religious ones) this position seems cruel and unreasonable, even if its adherents intend to be neither. To demand that an adult live a celibate life, surrendering the responsibilities and joys of committed relationship, children, and companionship is—within a Jewish context—unthinkable. Jewish sources—ancient, medieval, and modern—all affirm that marriage exists for health and for companionship, as well as procreation. To deny those blessings to a homosexual merely because of the gender of the companion makes God and Torah seem unjust and harsh.

Consequently, a growing number of Jewish religious leaders are reading the Torah anew. Reflecting an *a priori* insistence that God is just, compassionate, and loving, these sages insist that any reading of the Torah that is not just, compassionate, and loving cannot be God's will, however much it may reflect the *p'shat*. Strategies for reading the Torah vary, as they have across the ages. Some (Rabbi Arthur Waskow, for example) resort to close textual reading. Noting that the Torah prohibits "lying with a male as one would with a female," he insists that the qualifying phrase ("as one would") changes the meaning of the entire sentence. He therefore reads it as saying that two men should have sex differently, not simply acting as though one man is a woman. Male-male sex, for Waskow, must appreciate the maleness of both partners. Some (Rabbi Rebecca Alpert) call for flatly confronting Leviticus by proclaiming "the two consecutive weeks in the spring during which these words are read as Jewish Lesbian and Gay Awareness Weeks." Responding negatively to the Torah's words shifts the authority from the words to the response, from the book to the community, which is precisely where Rabbi Alpert wants to vest authority.

For most of these Conservative, Reform, and Reconstructionist Jews, homosexuality is not itself a problem, but reconstruing Jewish tradition and welcoming the homosexual is. For them, counseling the homosexual entails affirming that Jew as homosexual, seeking to connect the individual back into the Jewish community, and helping to fashion a way of living as a homosexual consistent with Jewish values and Jewish traditions. Counseling Jewish parents of a homosexual involves letting them grow in their understanding of homosexuality, persuading them that they did not cause their child's orientation (and, hence, don't get the credit for it), and encouraging them to be open and proud with their friends.

Derekh Ha-Beinoni:
A Middle Path

There is a third alternative, one that eschews both the literalism of the first reading and the shift of authority of the second. In my own view the Torah is authoritative but historically rooted. The voice of God, then, emerges in context. The message is God's, and the words are ours, the particles through which the light of God becomes visible. Learning to distinguish dust from light is the essential act of engaged, faithful *midrash*.

I hold that the Torah is best understood against the backdrop of its age. In antiquity, the categories of "homosexual" and "heterosexual" did not exist. Adult free men were to express their masculinity by taking sexual pleasure; and all others (slaves, prisoners, women, children, animals) existed as sexual objects. In such a world, the great revolution of the Torah was to insist that people could not be used, that no one was an object. Sex with children was prohibited. Rape was criminalized. Marriage was ordained. Sex with animals was outlawed. Each of these breakthroughs added to the edifice of human dignity in the sexual realm. Sex is to be a gift, freely given and freely received, within the context of commitment and monogamy.

In antiquity, expression of homosexuality—as with sexuality in general—was integrally linked to gender and socioeconomic definitions of power. Men were to have power and impose it; women were not. The biblical prohibition of male-male sex must be read in that light. Hence, the preferred reading understands the levitical prohibition as prohibiting male-male sex as an illicit imposition of power. Indeed, both biblical examples of *mishkav zakhur* speak of rape, and the preponderance of rabbinic examples deal with rape, pederasty, or anonymous sex. Such instances are indeed abominations, and the levitical prohibition rightly prohibits them.

Sexuality in a broader social context of equality became a possibility only with modernity. The Torah (indeed the entire Hebrew Bible) nowhere explicitly addresses this. We can retain the authority of Leviticus by upholding its prohibition of sex as power. But we need not construe reciprocal and committed homosexuality under the same rubric. God's compassion and love and justice are most apparent when we read the Torah as sanctifying such commitment and love. Monogamy is the royal road to monotheism, both for gays and for straights.

Counseling shows a Jewish homosexual that there are positive and negative expressions of homosexuality as there are of heterosexuality. As a rabbi, I remain a servant of God's will as it unfolds from the Torah. I diverge from the literalists by affirming that traditional rabbis have always insisted that the Torah itself gives them the power to define what the Torah means and how it is to be applied, even at variance with a verse's contextual meaning. I diverge from the extreme liberals by insisting that authority is vested not in the community but in God's revelation (how the community interprets and applies the Torah). I allow the gay Jew to grieve the wounds of internalized gay-hatred (and Jew-hatred) and transcend them. Loving God and loving Torah have nothing to do with one's sexual orientation but everything to do with how one lives life. A gay Jew is not exempt from the sacred covenant that our people affirm: a life of Torah, commandments, and good deeds. As God's servant, I create a trusting space in which that Jew can experience the healing power of God's great love. I encourage that gay or lesbian to live an active life in the Jewish community, without hiding and without shame—with a Jewish partner who can share life's joys and tribulations.

Bibliography

Artson, Bradley Shavit. "Judaism and Homosexuality" *Tikkun* 3 (March/April, 1988): 52–54,92–93.

———. "Gay and Lesbian Jews: An Innovative Jewish Legal Position," *Jewish Spectator* 55 (winter, 1990–91): 6–14.

———. "Homosexuality as Family-Centered Judaism," *Jewish Spectator* 57 (winter 1993a): 30–31.

———. "Enfranchising the Monogamous Homosexual: A Legal Possibility, A Moral Imperative," *S'vara: A Journal of Philosophy and Judaism* 3 (spring 1993b): 15–26.

Balka, Christie, and Andy Rose. *Twice Blessed: On Being Lesbian, Gay, and Jewish* (Boston: Beacon Press, 1989).

Brooten, Bernadette J. *Love between Women: Early Christian Response to Female Homoeroticism* (Chicago: University of Chicago Press, 1996).

—BRADLEY SHAVIT ARTSON

A Catholic Perspective

In 1976 the Vatican's Congregation for the Doctrine of the Faith issued a critical statement that situates all Catholic conversation about homosexuality: "(T)he human person is so profoundly affected by sexuality that it must be considered as one of the factors which give to each individual's life the principal traits that distinguish it. In fact, it is from sex that the human person receives the characteristics which, on the biological, psychological and spiritual levels make that person a man or a woman, and thereby largely condition his or her progress towards maturity and insertion into society" (*Declaration on Sexual Ethics,* n 11).

More recently the *Catechism of the Catholic Church* focused this belief by encouraging "Everyone, man or woman, [to] acknowledge and accept his sexual identity" (n 2333). The *Catechism* recognizes the fact that the number of persons with a homosexual orientation "is not negligible" (n 2358), and since such persons do not choose a homosexual orientation (n 2358), it is important and pastorally critical for homosexual people to be ego-syntonic rather than ego-dystonic about their sexual identity.

While some authors (for example, Nicolosi and Socarides) take a different view about such an acknowledgment, the church affirms that "some people find themselves through no fault of their own to have a homosexual orientation" (*To Live in Christ Jesus,* National Conference of Catholic Bishops, 1976, n 4). Consequently, homosexual people, "like everyone else, should not suffer from prejudice against their basic human rights" (*Ibid.*). It is for this reason that the 1986 *Letter to the Bishops* on the question of homosexuality teaches that the homosexual orientation "is not a sin" (n 3).

The church takes no official position on the origin of a person's homosexual orientation (for example, genetic factors, prenatal hormonal influences, early conditioning), and so parents and children should refrain from making judgments in this regard. The church encourages us to acknowledge the fact that some people are homosexual and to live in a way that honors and respects every individual with his or her sexual identity.

The church condemns all forms of homophobia: "It is deplorable that homosexual persons have been and are the object of violent malice in speech or in action. Such treatment deserves condemnation from the Church's pastors wherever it occurs" (*Letter to the Bishops,* n 10).

As parents, family members, and youth, we are called on to confront our fears about homosexuality and "to curb the humor and discrimination that offend homosexual persons" (United States Catholic Conference 1990, 55).

The church embraces the necessity of supporting the child with a homosexual orientation. The child or young person should not be coerced into being "restored" to heterosexuality. The Catholic Church therefore does not endorse various forms of conversion ministries.

The church is also sensitive to the fact that acknowledging one's homosexual orientation is extremely difficult. It thus encourages parents to seek the necessary help for all family members when a child is struggling with sexual identity issues. Every person is to be viewed as a child of God and is never to be rejected, scorned, or ridiculed. This counsel is especially problematic in certain ethnic groups that refrain from any discussion of sexuality and that create an atmosphere of hatred and violence toward persons with a homosexual orientation.

While the church does not sustain an official position on adoption of children by gay and lesbian people, it does affirm these critical points: children must be guaranteed a permanent and stable environment in which to live and mature; all parents must provide a loving home environment for a child and must not use adoption as a means of simply fostering gay rights; and a child must always be seen as a gift and never an object of possession.

The church has a long-standing respect for the virtue of chastity, a human characteristic that fosters goodness in our sexual lives. This virtue must be encouraged in all people, heterosexual or homosexual. We must all seek to assimilate attitudes of fidelity, integrity, honesty, self-control, and modesty.

The Catholic Church makes these recommendations to parents with a gay or lesbian child: accept and love yourselves as parents in order to accept and love your son and daughter; do not blame yourselves for a homosexual orientation in your child; do everything possible to demonstrate love for your child; accepting a child's homosexual orientation does not have to include approving all related attitudes and behavioral choices; urge your child not to abandon the church community but to seek spiritual help and guidance from a wise mentor or teacher; and seek for yourselves understanding and inner peace, perhaps through support groups with other parents of gay and lesbian children.

Bibliography

Coleman, Gerald, S.S. *Homosexuality: Catholic Teaching and Pastoral Practice* (New York: Paulist Press, 1995).

Reid, John. *The Best Little Boy in the World* (New York: Ballantine Books, 1973).

Siker, Jeffrey S., ed. *Homosexuality in the Church* (Louisville, Ky.: John Knox Press, 1994).

United States Catholic Conference. *Human Sexuality* (Washington, D.C.: United States Catholic Conference, 1990).

—GERALD COLEMAN, S.S.

An Evangelical Protestant Perspective

The discovery that a loved one is gay can be devastating for other family members. They are often thrown into a period of grief and mourning, similar to that experienced at the death of a loved one. This grief may be centered on a deep sense of loss. The grief is especially acute in conservative families where homosexuality is believed to be immoral.

Pastors and other spiritual leaders facing this crisis in a parish family often feel unequipped to help. Their lack of knowledge on this topic may cause feelings of insecurity; the topic itself may trigger discomfort.

We feel confident that the average spiritual leader *does* have the knowledge and counseling skills to be of concrete assistance in this situation. Based on the authors' years of intervening in this specific family crisis, we offer the following guidelines:

* *Concentrate your concern on the person in front of you rather than on the gay loved one who is not present.* Typically, a nongay family member will seek spiritual counsel on how to influence the life of the gay loved one. It is extremely common, for example, to face a mother who has great concern for a gay son who needs "fixing." Gently remind the mother that her son cannot be helped until he comes himself seeking spiritual counsel. Then focus on the issues facing the mother, such as her grief, her fears, and her future relationship with her son.

* *Help family members understand their emotional reaction to this situation.* Discovery of a loved one's homosexuality can be devastating. The closer the relationship, the greater the sense of trauma. The relationship will never be perceived in quite the same way again, and this is a valid loss to grieve. If the person has strong spiritual beliefs, then it can be an even greater blow. (Doesn't God promise to protect Christian families from these types of situations?) Deep, prolonged grief is a normal reaction, and it can be of immense comfort for the person to hear that truth. Grief is a process through which this person will move over time. Sometimes the most effective statement for that person to hear at the beginning is, "You can feel better than you do today, no matter what your loved one chooses to do in the future."

* *Focus your counsel on the underlying issues, not the homosexual "symptom."* Often it can be helpful to remove homosexuality from the picture entirely for a few moments. For example, a son moving in with his gay lover is, in many ways, similar to a son cohabiting with a girlfriend. How would the parent deal with the latter situation? Or if the son was presenting symptoms of becoming addicted to drugs, how involved in intervention would the parent become? Discussing principles related to nongay situations can be extremely helpful.

Be a calm, active listener. Many nongay family members are deeply ashamed to share this family situation with someone else. Be compassionate and gentle, affirming the person without showing disgust or shock. Family members often feel deep shame about their loved one's lifestyle choices. They need to see God's compassion in you. This reaction on your part will enable them to share more deeply. The counselor should also encourage them to share this situation with close friends who can be trusted. Family members need to start building their own support system outside of the professional counseling room.

Instill realistic hope. Christians often have only one desire: To see their gay loved one abandon homosexuality as soon as possible. Give them a balanced picture. God is certainly able to help a gay person change, and many thousands have done so. But change is a process that takes time. And change is motivated by that person's convictions and desires, not the desires of other family members. The first step is to maintain a loving relationship with the gay person without compromising one's own moral beliefs. Again, it can be helpful to discuss how family members would deal with a situation of heterosexual immorality to guide them in formulating an appropriate response to the gay loved one's actions.

Encourage family members to pray for their gay loved one. Prayer is a powerful tool to influence a loved one's heart motivations. Years ago, I (Anita) wrote out a simple prayer for my gay son and made it available to other parents. I was surprised at how many requests came in. Spontaneous prayer may not be part of that person's religious tradition, so many find it helpful to have a written prayer. Encourage them to write out a prayer that expresses their love and concern toward the gay person.

Be prepared for difficult questions. Many pastors and counselors are asked very difficult questions with little or no time to prepare answers. Questions may arise on AIDS, child custody cases, causative factors in homosexuality, or the eternal destiny of a gay loved one. Sometimes information is given out of limited knowledge and even personal fears and biases. Saying less is always better in cases of doubt; offer to find out reliable information and get back to the person asking the question.

Have specific information on homosexuality available. Family members may be too ashamed to seek out books and other information on this topic, so collect some helpful resources. Exodus International (P.O. Box 77652, Seattle, WA 98177; phone: 206-784-7799) has information on Christian ministries that offer support to men and women seeking freedom from unwanted homosexuality; these agencies also offer support and counsel to family members who view homosexuality as an undesirable condition. Exodus also has free resource lists on available books, tapes, and videotapes from a conservative Christian viewpoint on this topic.

Bibliography

Davies, Bob, and Lori Rentzel. *Coming Out of Homosexuality: New Freedom for Men and Women* (Downers Grove, Ill.: InterVarsity Press, 1993). Realistic but hopeful counsel for Christians struggling with unwanted homosexual desires.

Johnson, Barbara. *Where Does a Mother Go to Resign?* (Minneapolis: Bethany House Publishers, 1994). A Christian mother struggles to cope with multiple family tragedies, including the discovery of her son's homosexual involvement.

Worthen, Anita, and Bob Davies. *Someone I Love Is Gay: How Family and Friends Can Respond* (Downers Grove, Ill.: InterVarsity Press, 1996). Practical answers for all the common questions asked by family members and friends.

—ANITA WORTHEN
BOB DAVIES

A Mainline Protestant Perspective

John told us in stages that he is gay. On a sunny autumn afternoon, as we jogged together, he spoke tentatively about what he was discovering about himself. He was eighteen years old. As a father, I was pleased that John trusted me enough to talk about his sexuality. I remember stammering something like, "Don't make up your mind about this right now. You'll be learning about sex throughout your life." What I did not understand at the time is that sexual orientation is not something about which one decides. Nor did I realize that John's discovery about himself had been going on for some time, gradually and in secret.

Two years later, John, his mother, and I were having dinner on one of his visits. We now lived in Chicago, but John had stayed in Minneapolis. He spoke of a men's group he had been attending and then took from his billfold a photograph of his special friend. It was the photo of a handsome young man. Showing us the picture of his special friend was part of John's "coming out" to his parents. We were stunned. Our son was a homosexual. Although we did not understand the full meaning of his disclosure, John seemed to us more comfortable with himself, more authentic than he had been in the past.

Over the last eight years, since that first tentative disclosure on the jogging path, we have learned a great deal from our relationship with our gay son. All of us, including John's older brother, have come to understand ourselves and our family better. Some of this awareness is the result of understanding homosexuality better. We still wonder what some of our friends would think of us if they knew our son is gay. We are also aware of occasional lingering grief because of what seemed initially to be a great loss. Gradually, however, these feelings have faded with our acceptance of and gratitude for a son who is a wonderful human being.

This is not to say that we are clear or comfortable with all the issues that surround homosexuality. We were fearful then and are fearful now that our son might have to suffer in a society that does not accept homosexual behavior. Our reticence to be completely public about our son's orientation is out of respect for John more than fear or shame. From our experience and the experience of many other parents of gay and lesbian children, we have discovered that having a gay son in the family is a story that continues to unfold.

When parents first learn of a son or daughter's homosexual orientation, they need to remember that this is the same child they watched grow up. Parents who are angry because they feel they have been deceived, or ashamed because they think they should have known, may overlook the self-sameness of their child. What gay children may do to please parents (for example, dating) can be interpreted later as betrayal. In the beginning, I needed to remember that the seventh-grade son with whom I played catch in the front yard is the same person who has come to know himself as a gay man. He is the same son we have known all along. Now, however, he more fully understands himself and is willing to share that understanding with us.

It is important for parents to be aware that their son or daughter has taken a big risk in making known to the family his or her sexual orientation. The fact that a young person would take that risk is a sign that some trust already exists within the family. It also reflects a healthy desire on the part of lesbian daughters and gay sons to stop hiding and pretending. A young person's coming out, which at first may be devastating news, can in fact help make an entire family more honest in its dealings with one another. Once this new level of honesty has begun between parents and grown children, however, it needs to be continued. Sometimes the homosexual orientation of a child is problematic in a family only because once revealed, it is buried again and becomes a family secret. A common lament heard from gay and lesbian people is that after they worked up the courage to tell parents, "the subject never came up again." As in all aspects of family living, honesty begun needs to be continued.

Parents need to take time to process this new information about their child. It takes our children a long time to realize they are homosexual. Parents also need time to assimilate this new information. At the same time, parents need to understand that it may be urgent for their daughters and sons that their parents accept them. This vulnerability is particularly apparent when the child struggling with his or her sexual orientation is in adolescence. When parents are aware of the vulnerability of their children, they will work harder toward an accepting response.

Our assimilation process was helped particularly by talking with other parents of gay and lesbian children through an organization known as P-FLAG (Parents, Families and Friends of Lesbians and Gays). P-FLAG is a national organization with local chapters in many cities in the United States. (For specific information and locations, contact P-FLAG, 1101 14th St. N.W., Suite 1030, Washington, DC 20005; phone: 202-638-4200.) Talking with other parents of gay children provides support, diminishes fear and guilt, and helps avoid secrecy. The friendships we have made at P-FLAG have enabled us to move toward acceptance. Anne and I have never left a meeting without saying that it is good to be in the company of other good parents who love their children. Not all parents, however, wish to talk to other parents about their child's orientation. For us, it has been an opportunity to learn and to grow.

With the permission of a gay person, it is helpful to plan orderly ways in which the larger family can be told. In our own situation, it was an unplanned event that made John's orientation known throughout our wider family. At a large luncheon gathering of women in the family organized by a matriarchal aunt, each woman was asked to tell what was new in her family. When it was Anne's turn, she simply said, "Our son John is gay." In one luncheon and with one sentence, the whole family network was told the news. Our son thanked his mother for her courage. Her honesty at the luncheon made it easier for John to be open to the family about his sexual orientation.

Not every family's response to the revelation of a child's homosexuality is positive. Most are not. As a pastor, I have walked with families who agonized over their awareness of a child's sexual orientation. What we have come to consider a gift, other families have seen as judgment or shame. Denial, anger, and confusion are common family responses to a homosexual child's longing for love, understanding, and acceptance. Because of our experience with John, I now invite families to be patient with themselves as they assimilate this new information from a son or daughter. I invite them to promise to remain a family even though they do not know what it will look like in the future. And I invite them to continue the journey toward a transformation of the heart and mind, even though they do not know if or how this is possible. That transformation will be greatly helped by actual personal involvement with others who are in the same situation.

The discovery that a child is gay is an invitation for a family to embody reconciling love. Our family continues to grow in understanding of and love for one another. Our continuing relation with gays and lesbians and their parents and friends enables this continued growth. Parents of homosexual sons and daughters need a safe place to tell their story without judgment or fear of rejection. It is my hope that some day a congregation will be such a community. Meanwhile, we are on a journey that challenges us to be family in ways we have not known before. Along the way, we keep learning that the truth does set us free.

Bibliography

Bernstein, Robert A. *Straight Parents, Gay Children: Keeping Families Together* (New York: Thunder Mouth, 1994).

Dew, Rob Forman. *The Family Heart: A Memoir of When Our Son Came Out* (Reading, Mass: Addison-Wesley, 1994).

Fairchild, Betty. *Now That You Know: What Every Parent Should Know about Homosexuality* (Orlando, Fla.: Harcourt Brace, 1989).

Switzer, David K. *Coming Out as Parents: You and Your Homosexual Child* (Louisville, Ky.: Westminster John Knox Press, 1996).

—MARK P. WIBERG

12

Ministry with the Elderly

What are some current promising directions in family ministry with the elderly today, and what are some of the more important issues raised by them?

Directions

Family ministry with the elderly falls into two main categories, which overlap somewhat in practice: *melioristic ministries* and *crisis ministries.*

Melioristic Ministries

Melioristic ministries aim broadly, and with progressively diminishing ambition, to make things better for the family of the aging person, to maintain the elderly person in his or her present condition, or to mitigate the effects of the decrements of aging.

Clergy have sometimes been criticized for the vagueness of the melioristic approach. Nevertheless, this approach to "the whole person" is rightly focused and is a great improvement on that of the past in which the future of the soul alone was often too narrowly in focus.

Several melioristic ministries have the characteristic of providing the elderly with a surrogate family. In our day the elderly often live at a distance from their children or other family members, and even when this is not the case, they may seldom see them. Groups, both specialized and more general, can perform this function.

A common form of this ministry in my area is what I shall call the Group. The Group goes by many names, such as the Fiesta Club, 50 Plus, and Leisure Agers. It ranges in size from twenty-five to three hundred and is found in both large and relatively small churches. Typically, the Group meets for lunch about once a month at the church. Inspirational speakers, guest entertainers, testimony and commentary by members (particularly by bereaved members and those who have suffered other losses), worship (with an emphasis on familiar hymns and songs), and observance of members' birthdays and special liturgical days (such as Ash Wednesday and Maundy Thursday), and above all, socialization, characterize these groups. The groups also engage in outside activities, the most popular of which are community projects, such as Habitat for Humanity, and chartered bus trips to regional attractions.

Such groups in multi-age churches typically include all persons above the age of fifty, while churches in retirement communities are more likely to have separate groups for couples and singles. Smaller support groups, especially for those suffering losses, are also of great importance.

A second form of melioristic ministry which has a surrogate family character is that of intergenerational programs in multi-age churches. Some particularly useful activities of this sort contain liturgical, educational, and interpersonal components, often taking place on Sunday evenings under such names as Logos Club. These events may be rather fragile and somewhat difficult to maintain.

We can see from these examples that such activities have some, but not all, of the characteristics of family life. They possess the interpersonal interactional potential of families, even though not on the scale of intensity found in families. Members care about the destiny of the Group, though not at the level of involvement of family members whose very existence may depend upon the destiny of the family.

A third important melioristic ministry is the ministry to the homebound, including the functionally shut in—who do not get out, even though physically able—and their family-member caregivers. Under such evocative names as Mitzvah Squad and Care Crew, some churches and synagogues in retirement communities and some multi-age congregations provide various forms of assistance to the homebound and their caregivers. These include telephone checks (in which other homebound are sometimes engaged), shopping, cleaning, and respite care. One large multi-age church is leading the way with a community-oriented volunteer training program, funded in part by a grant from a national foundation. More of such programs will be needed in the future. Social workers are employed by some churches to assess needs and provide care, although the current trend is toward hiring visiting nurses to provide more needed services.

Crisis Ministries

Liturgical and pastoral care ministries to bereaved families remain the most conspicuous and significant crisis ministries with families. More intense efforts to follow the bereaved, particularly widows and widowers, throughout their period of mourning, no matter how long it may be, are needed.

Clergy mediation of decisions concerning assisted living is a widespread and particularly useful form of crisis intervention. Assisted living is any situation in which an elder receives help in the daily affairs of living. This can include an elder living with an adult child or an elder living in a retirement center with assistance, ranging from almost none to skilled nursing care. Some clergy actively seek to assist in these decisions, while others are reluctant to get involved but do so because of pastoral care relationships with one or more family members. Others rely primarily on visiting nurses or social workers, becoming involved as a secondary resource.

Care should be taken in this ministry of mediation to preserve as much of the autonomy of the elder as possible, while also giving due consideration to the actual burden of caring for the elderly placed upon adult children or other relatives. Attention should be paid as well to their feelings and attitudes—especially to those of guilt—and to the inherent possibilities for exploitation. Rabbi Levi Meier, commenting on the Fifth Commandment, has emphasized the respect and personal service due parents with diminished mental capacity, though he exempts children from the latter in cases of irreversible senile dementia, thus helpfully addressing their sense of guilt (Meier 1977).

Although few clergy wish to become involved in family disputes other than those that may involve a move to assisted living, and few have the time and training to do so, the option of referral for family therapy involving the elderly should be kept in view. Hargrave and Anderson (1992) have shown that intergenerational family therapy involving the elderly as a focal person can be helpful.

Issues

Goals

Family ministry with the elderly governed by misty melioristic visions has the advantage of not being overly specific, when the basis for such specificity may be beyond our knowing. Melioristic ministries have the disadvantage, however, of allowing our prejudices and anxieties to gain the upper hand in our efforts. Our sympathies are frequently, but not always, with the apparently overburdened children who cannot persuade their curmudgeonly parent to move to some form of assisted living—a parent, moreover, who may be employing threats of altering his or her will in order to hold on to some sense of centered existence. But we owe our empathy no less to the parent than to the child who is becoming in some respects "the parent."

Reflection on models of family interaction can help. We are accustomed to think in terms of autonomy versus dependency, but both should be seen as submodels of a more general *interdependency*. No one is completely autonomous, and all are in some respects dependent. Malcolm Johnson has argued a strong case that one-way dependency of the elderly on society is exaggerated (Johnson 1990). I would add that children frequently remain in some respects emotionally dependent on even the most demented parents. Interdependency does not have to be a fully conscious model embraced by both parties to be the dominant one.

Inclusivity versus Exclusivity of Groups

Briefly, I wish to stress the advantages of inclusivity of gender and marital status in groups of the elderly as surrogate families. These allow for a greater range of socialization and hence of improvement in personal status and outlook. Singles' groups may still serve a purpose where more traditional values predominate.

Risks of Intervention

How actively should clergy become involved in family disputes, especially in those not immediately focused upon the question of a move to assisted living? Though many considerations enter into such decisions, including competence and available time, personality variables may be decisive. One must have a tolerance for a high degree of interpersonal turmoil if one seeks active involvement in family disputes involving elderly members and yet wishes not to be drained by such interventions. Nevertheless, relief for pained and knotted families, as well as satisfactions for the caregiver, can be great.

Reliance on Other Professionals

Is the reliance on visiting social workers and, increasingly, on visiting nurses the best approach to the homebound and their family caregivers? These professionals have relevant knowledge, yet they lack the authority of the clergy and the set-aside layperson, who are often perceived to represent more adequately the church and the benign power of its tradition.

Conclusions

Traditional ministries to the bereaved elderly should be emphasized and should be continued for longer periods for the deeply grieving than is often the case. Family members who are providing care for the homebound require more attention, and more use should be made of trained laypersons for the ministries involved here. Churches and synagogues should become more conscious of their role in providing surrogate families for the elderly who live apart from their families, or who may be estranged from them. Mediation of assisted living decisions can provide a genuine service in time of crisis, and family therapy is an important resource in many family disputes and tensions involving the elderly.

Note

In preparing this article, I received considerable help from people representing religious institutions in the greater Phoenix, Arizona, area, to whom I am grateful for their time and keen insights. The representatives interviewed and their institutions (listed alphabetically) are Rabbi Seymour Moskowitz, Beth Emeth Congregation, Sun City West; Dr. Dosia Carlson, Church of the Beatitudes (United Church of Christ), Phoenix; Rev. Lester W. Hoffmann, Community Church of Joy (Evangelical Lutheran Church), Glendale; Dr. Robert E. Palmer, Desert Palms Presbyterian Church, Sun City West; Elder Agnes R. Poole, Faith Presbyterian Church, Sun City; Rev. Brian R. Paulson, Orangewood Presbyterian Church, Phoenix; Rev. Paul J. Kohler, First Presbyterian Church, Peoria; Rev. Earl Deon, St. Clement of Rome Roman Catholic Church, Sun City; Rev. Richard Schowalter, Shepherd of the Valley Lutheran

Church, Phoenix; Chp. Mary Smiley, Unitarian Universalist Church of the Sun Cities, Sun City.

Bibliography

Gillespie, B. J. "The Black Church and the Black Elderly: A Bibliographical and Historical Essay," *Journal of Religious Studies* 10/2(1983): 19–30.

Hargrave, T. D., and W. T. Anderson. *Finishing Well: Aging and Reparation in the Intergenerational Family* (New York: Brunner/Mazel, 1992).

Johnson, Malcolm. "Dependency and Independency," in *Aging and Society,* P. Coleman and J. Bond, eds. (London: Sage Publications, 1990), 209–28.

Meier, L. "Filial Responsibility to the Senile Parent," in *Spiritual Well-Being of the Elderly,* J. A. Thorson and T. C. Cook, eds. (Springfield, Ill.: Charles C. Thomas, 1977), 161–68.

Van Meter, M.J.S., and P. Johnson. "Family Decision Making, Long-Term Care for the Elderly, and the Role of Religious Organizations: Interventions for Religious Professionals and Organizations," *Journal of Religion and Aging* 1/4(1985): 73–88.

—JAMES N. LAPSLEY

13

Ministry with Families Troubled by Abuse

Family violence in the United States is significantly more prevalent than most of us believe or want to believe. In the United States in the mid-1990s, 2.1 million women are battered by their husband or partner in a given twelve-month period, an average rate of one battery every fifteen seconds. In this period 75 percent of married women report having received threats of violence from their partners; 50 percent are estimated actually to fall victim to wife abuse of one form or another; and 13 percent suffer partner abuse that is chronic and severe. At the same time, an estimated 2.5 million children in the United States are sexually abused each year, 90 percent of them by a relative or friend close to the child, 50 percent of them by a parent or stepparent. And it is currently estimated that one in five to one in three girls, and one in sixteen to one in eleven boys, are physically or sexually abused by the age of eighteen.

Such statistics can of course be misleading, and family violence in particular is difficult to gauge because it tends to be shrouded in denial and secrecy. But the sad and uncomfortable truth is that family abuse is common, it is usually unrecognized and suffered in isolation, and it pervades every social class and ethnic group. For religious leaders family abuse can be especially difficult to confront because it flies in the face of spiritually informed family ideals, and it is easy to refer the problem to the province of trained psychological specialists. Yet it is more than likely that abused wives and children sit every Sunday in our pews hoping for pastoral support, understanding, and help. Family abuse is in fact not only a psychological but also a spiritual and a profoundly social problem, and religious leaders can do much to address it.

The kinds of abuse that exist in families are so various that we can focus here on only two of the more prevalent: wife abuse (physical battery) and the sexual abuse of children. This means we will not address the important issues of child physical abuse, child neglect, the effects of wife battery on children, wife rape, elder abuse, sibling abuse, husband abuse, and a host of other kinds of violence that can occur within families. Nor will we have the space to examine the complex cross-cultural and cross-racial differences that characterize family abuse.

A Brief History of Abuse in the Family

Wife and child sexual abuse have existed for all of history, but it is probably safe to say that they have not been acknowledged as a "social problem," as opposed to a merely private one, until very recently. Violence toward women and children has its roots in the West in a long history of family patriarchy. Biblical Jewish and Christian families were held together by a powerful paterfamilias who ruled over his immediate and extended kin in all family affairs. The Council of Toledo in 400 A.D. decreed that if a wife disobeyed her husband, he would be permitted to beat her, keep her bound to the house, or force her to fast, although "not unto death." Medieval and Renaissance towns made similar decrees, on the reasoning that while husbands were subject to lords, princes, and religious authorities in the public realm, in the private realm of the home they alone were "lord."

Reformation Christianity enhanced the status of the family as a religious and spiritual calling, but it still followed the medieval view of women as the more sinful marriage partner. While it affirmed an *original* equality of men and women, it saw women as being demoted by the Fall to an inferior status on account of Eve's carnality. The English Common Law that grew up after the Reformation made husband and wife legally *one* entity, so that most punishment of wives for wrongdoing was performed by husbands rather than the state. It was viewed as only fair that since a husband was publicly responsible for his wife's behavior, as well as his children's, he should be able to take a stick to them to keep them in line. The expression "rule of thumb" is thought to come from a 1768 English law that permitted a husband to beat his wife only if the stick used was no thicker than his thumb.

In 1883 Maryland became the first state in the United States to outlaw wife-beating. A decreased social tolerance for wife-beating seems to have come about from a combination of factors like the first women's movements raising awareness of the problem, a growing bourgeois culture of self-restraint, and women gaining authority in the "separate sphere" of the home. Even through the mid-twentieth century, however, wife and child abuse continued to be generally considered both a strictly private issue and highly unusual, "deviant" behavior, and as late as 1975 a national poll indicated that only 10 percent of Americans considered child abuse a serious problem.

The 1970s saw a profound shift in which Americans came to view wife abuse and child sexual abuse as broad social problems. This increased awareness came from factors like the women's movement bringing private family issues into public debate, a post-World War II cultural focus on children, a renewed concern with violence stemming from a series of race riots and political assassinations, and a general view that family life was somehow in crisis. In the mid-1970s social scientists began to reveal surprisingly high rates of wife abuse and child sexual abuse. In 1974 Congress enacted the Child Abuse Prevention and Treatment Act, and the first book was written on wife abuse, Erin Pizzey's *Scream Quietly or the Neighbors Will Hear*. In the 1980s Congress enacted the National Domestic Violence Prevention and Treatment Act, although wife rape was not made illegal in all fifty states until 1993 (stranger rape had been illegal since 1848).

Despite these gains, women and children who are victims of abuse are still not well protected in our society. Nearly 90 percent of defendants charged with domestic violence are never prosecuted. Assaults by family members are "undercharged" as misdemeanors rather than felonies in 30 percent of cases, whereas if the assault had been committed by a stranger it would have been a felony. Many judges and police still view domestic violence as a private issue in which they should not become involved. And victims of family abuse still lack strong social and cultural supports to help them escape the powerful physical and emotional control their abusers exercise over them.

Understanding Wife Abuse

Those who work with women physically abused by their husband or partner generally agree that such abuse is caused not fundamentally by anger, stress, or anxiety but by the abuser's desire to claim and maintain *control*. Anger, stress, and anxiety may be *occasions* for violent behavior, as also may consumption of alcohol or drugs, but wife abuse is about the abuser using physical and psychological violence to manipulate and control his victim's thoughts, feelings, and behavior, whether he is aware that this is what he is doing or not.

To understand how control drives wife abuse we can identify a rough five-part wife-battery cycle, which represents the gradual robbing of agency, humanity, and empowerment from the victim. The cycle is described in detail in McKenzie's *Domestic Violence in America* (1995). *Initiation* into abuse involves the abuser becoming increasingly prone to verbal abuse and criticism, taking unilateral control over significant family decisions, and repeatedly invading his partner's personal space. *Intimidation* then begins to establish the abuser as "entitled" to control by violence through pushing, grabbing, and threatening gestures, with the effect of making the victim feel increasingly more helpless, anxious, and imprisoned. *Venting* establishes clear domination over the wife through egregiously abusive acts like punching, kicking, choking, and rape, and intense verbal and emotional abuse, causing the wife to feel she has little will left of her own and often to enter into massive denial. *Latency* generally ensues, in which the batterer seeks to convince his victim that the violence is over, and a period of calm sees renewed affection and understanding and the abuser expressing contrition and empathy. *Loss of control*, the final stage, sees the abuser compulsively driving the victim into utter submission through intensely cruel battery, rage, and often the use of weapons. If she survives, the victim at this stage either finally leaves or enters into what is known as the "learned helplessness" of giving up trying to redeem the situation and feeling demolished as a human being.

Why do women stay in abusive relationships? Why is it that an estimated two-thirds of battered women end up being battered severely more than once, one-third more than five times, and many as often as once a week? The answer is complicated and multifaceted, but it centers on the battered wife's systematic *disempowerment*. Battered women feel helpless when their usual techniques for problem-solving fail to bring the violence to an end. Most adapt to abuse by focusing narrowly on the immediate avoidance of violent attack. Many quite rightly fear revenge for leaving. Battered women are also physically and emotionally exhausted. Under violent conditions they are prone to manipulation by the abuser's frequent apologies and promises to reform. Many furthermore feel pressured by social expectations for women to change their partner's negative behavior. They may be made to feel ashamed or guilty in our society for getting themselves into an abusive situation, and this may in turn cause them to avoid exposing the abuse to others. And many face genuine material impoverishment if they leave, or have nowhere to go.

More than all this, however, battered women generally lack the support they need from outside the home. Friends and family are often in denial that abuse could be happening to someone they know. Or they may misguidedly play into the victim's self-blame by encouraging her to try harder to make the relationship work. Likewise police and judges often do not understand the need for abused wives to find safety and for the abuser to be held accountable. Ministers and counselors frequently deny the seriousness of the problem or are reluctant to become involved in "private" affairs.

Wife abuse can be ended or treated in a variety of ways. Most important, the wife may leave the home to stay with a family member or friend or at a shelter. In a "safe place" outside the abusive environment she can get medical help, pursue legal action, have her material needs met, and begin to put her life (and those of any children) back together again. Abused women can also join support groups that help them take back control of their lives and renew their sense of empowerment. Such groups help by letting the victim know she is not alone, providing emotional release from the trauma, deescalating self-blame, resolving anger, helping to grieve, validating her feelings, communicating respect and acceptance of her as a person, showing warmth and care, and helping her break with the past and get on with rebuilding her life. They also provide a context for abused women to overcome social isolation.

The most effective treatment for abusers seems to be men's group therapy. Of men who complete group therapy, 53 to 85 percent do not batter again in the subsequent year (the lower end of the percentages is the report of victims). Good group therapy aims to help abusers see violence as learned and socially sanctioned, identifies and confronts resistances and avoidance tactics, and in a supportive way keeps the focus on the responsibility for the violence on the abuser himself. One tool often taught in group therapy is the "time out" in which men learn to recognize the warning signs of violent behavior, express their need to leave the potentially violent situation, and cool off until such a time as they can communicate nonviolently.

Some couples may be able to resolve the problem through marital therapy. Marital therapy works only if the violence has already ended and the victim can feel assured that it will not resume, something many believe cannot happen for at least two years after the violence has ended. Therapy for an abusive couple begins by contracting for nonviolence, which includes the abuser's taking full responsibility for his actions. It can then seek to develop anger- and stress-management skills for the abuser, new ways for the couple to communicate, a deeper understanding of the abuse, nonstereotypical sex roles that do not justify the woman's victimization, and the healthy empowerment of both partners.

What Religious Organizations Can Do
to Address Wife Abuse

While therapy for wife abuse victims and their abusers can and should be referred to trained specialists, churches and synagogues stand in a unique position to help abused women both spiritually and practically. Unfortunately, statistics show that women who escape their abusers rank the help they received from clergy at the bottom, and that women who turn to their clergy for marital guidance stay longer with their abusers and the abuse does not subside. It may be that ministers have a particular investment in acknowledging only the loving side of family life, or are prone to deny violence in their ranks because it seems like a failure of the church, or even subtly promote theologies that encourage women to take suffering upon themselves and to forgive their abusers too readily.

Theologically, battered women are particularly susceptible to interpreting their suffering as a required Christ-like means of redemption. An abused woman's undeserved pain can be accounted for either as necessary for eventual liberation or as her punishment by God for being undeserving. The minister can helpfully point out that in fact her suffering is not redeeming her from violence but playing into her partner's sinful manipulation, and that far from condoning suffering, Jesus healed it when he had the opportunity, especially the suffering of women. What is more, Jesus' suffering was unique and was undertaken not to enslave but to liberate, a cause for hope in God's kingdom in this world. "For surely I know the plans I have for you, says the LORD, plans for your welfare and not for harm, to give you a future with hope" (Jer. 29:11).

Religious leaders can also take a "prophetic" stance toward wife abuse which removes its stigma from women and places it instead on the community that enters into complicity with violence against women by failing vigorously to decry it. A prophetic voice empowers women by insisting on gender-neutral language in its services, recovering stories of women sympathetically from its Scriptures and traditions, including women in the total structure of the church, and condemning battery as violence against the trust and covenanted love of the entire religious community. Most of all a prophetic stance bears witness to the fact of violence in the home, refuses to play into the abuser's desire that such violence go ignored, and makes it clear to abusers that their actions are a sin against their wives and God.

Practically speaking, ministers can first and foremost make their churches safe places for battered women to seek help. They may do so by addressing domestic violence in sermons, prayers, litanies, group discussions, and study groups. They may become more informed about battery by obtaining information from the National Domestic Violence Hotline (1-800-333-7233), and ensure that staff and pastoral care providers are appropriately trained. Bible studies can be organized around passages that feature violence against women like 2 Samuel 13 and Judges 19.

Ministers can also develop a process of pastoral support and referral. They can write up a church policy about family abuse; be prepared to offer abused women a place to stay; know what to do in a crisis situation; create a fund to pay the emergency shelter expenses of victims; have emergency resources available like child care, clothes, toiletries, and food; and ensure that women are accompanied to court. In addition, ministers might make sure the church library has books on wife abuse and publicize them in newsletters; arrange women's self-defense classes and assertiveness training; discuss violence in premarital counseling; put up posters with information on wife abuse referral; and assist local shelters with fund-raising efforts and clothing. They may also help abusers by referring them to men's groups and counselors.

Understanding the Sexual Abuse of Children

If wife abuse traps women in a manipulative system of *control,* child sexual abuse traps children and adult survivors in a terrifying *secrecy.* The profound secrecy surrounding child sexual abuse is played into by all parties: the abuser, the child herself (or himself, although 81 to 95 percent of victims are girls), and third parties who could potentially help the child. While it would be instructive to explore the relation between child sexual abuse and the serious and pervasive problem in our culture of the physical abuse of children generally, the discussion here will be limited to sexual abuse and the uniquely profound secrecy associated with it.

Because 90 percent of sexually abused children are abused by someone whom they respect and depend upon, most sexually abused children cannot tell anyone that abuse has occurred without great material and emotional risk to themselves. Only 42 percent of children tell anyone of their sexual abuse within a year of its occurrence, and 36 percent never tell until adulthood, if at all. Because of their limited life experience, abused children are easily coerced into thinking that their pain and feelings of helplessness are normal. What is more, sexually abused children are reluctant to believe that an adult they depend on for love and nurturance—whether it is a parent, stepparent, teacher, or other care-giver—could be so "bad" as to cause them so much pain. Abused children tend unconsciously to "split off" or "repress" the adult's bad actions from their image of the adult as dependable and good and to protect themselves from massive psychological damage by assuming that their pain must somehow be their own fault.

The secrecy surrounding child sexual abuse is compounded further by how difficult it can be for third parties to face the horror and pain of the victim's experiences. Child sexual abuse raises disturbing issues of identity and power at the heart of everyone's private life, especially for those who may themselves be survivors of abuse. Our discomfort is attested to by the popular myth that child sexual abuse is usually committed at the hands of strangers, when strangers in fact make up only 10 percent of abusers. Furthermore, even the most sensitive parent or caregiver finds it easier to believe the mature and reasonable explanations of an adult than what a child may have revealed to them.

Child sexual abuse is defined as *any* involvement of an adult in sexual activity with a person under the age of eighteen. Because there is an inherent imbalance of power between minors and adults, it makes no difference if child sexual activity is consented to or invited by the child. Furthermore, child sexual abuse need not be committed by force, and indeed in the majority of cases is induced by persuasion, bribery, or deception, all of which play on the child's need for adult care. Nor does it have to involve physical touching, but can include masturbating in front of a child, looking at sexually explicit movies with a child, or talking with a child about sex for the purpose of deriving pleasure.

The effects of sexual abuse on children can be various. Children feel fear, shame, guilt, or anger, which in the long term can lead to low self-esteem, extreme anxiety, or depression. Children may develop an inability to trust reality, undergo extreme mood swings, or feel self-destructive. Symptoms of child sexual abuse can include sleep disturbances, strong reactions to physical contact, a sudden regression in behavior, withdrawal, aggressiveness, compulsiveness, early overt sexual behavior, physical reactions to stress like headaches and joint pain, spacing out, holes in memory, and violent flashbacks. Child sexual abuse can lead in adulthood to eating disorders, the abuse of alcohol or drugs, vulnerability to sexual assault, and suicidal tendencies. It can create difficulties in adult interpersonal relationships such as aversion to certain or all kinds of sexual touch, being unable to trust, and having problems maintaining intimacy.

Therapeutic treatment for a sexually abused child focuses on reducing the child's feelings of guilt; placing responsibility squarely on the abuser; addressing the child's fears, anxieties, and feelings of helplessness; and rebuilding self-esteem. Therapy can also address physical issues like damage to reproductive organs, the possibility of pregnancy, and naming the parts of the sexual anatomy. Treatment is especially complicated in cases where the abuser is a family member, for the child has to sort out many negative and positive feelings toward the abuser, address particularly profound issues of trust and vulnerability, and deal with reactions of other family members or the family's possible break-up.

What Religious Organizations Can Do to Address Child Sexual Abuse

Religious leaders can effectively help address child sexual abuse in several ways. First and foremost they can help to relieve the secrecy that surrounds child sexual abuse by being an open and accepting avenue for treatment referral. They can make themselves more approachable to survivors of child sexual abuse by becoming educated about its prevalence and nature, preaching about it, holding study groups on it, and developing referral contacts. Few clergy have the psychotherapeutic credentials to treat child sexual abuse effectively themselves, but they can mitigate some of the barriers of shame, guilt, and denial that keep so many from seeking the trained help they need and deserve.

Religious leaders can also provide significant treatment "support." They can resist the tendency to deny the prevalence of child sexual assault and listen openly and believingly to the stories of its survivors. By simply listening they convey the message that they, their church, and God are not destroyed by the survivor's feelings but rather know the survivor to be lovable and worthy. They can affirm that God is standing beside the victim in all her pain and doubt and, as Cooper-White eloquently puts it, is "continuously stirring the waters of healing within her soul." All this conveys that the abuse was not the survivor's fault, no matter what she thought or did at the time, and helps begin to unravel the years of shame and self-blame. Religious leaders can also assure the survivor that no secrets are too deep to be hidden from God's healing power, which reaches even to parts of the soul the survivor herself may not be able to find.

In providing support to survivors of child sexual abuse, ministers face several unique problems. First, as we saw above with regard to wife abuse, the Judeo-Christian tradition can be viewed by those who are abused as sanctioning their suffering in the service of a transcending redemption. Survivors need to face their suffering in such a way as to get over self-blame and accept as legitimate their anger at the abuser. For the same reason, survivors should not be made to feel obliged to "forgive" their abusers too easily. Second, ministers ought to be aware of the ways in which their sacred texts and traditions have adopted patriarchal standards that lend support to child abuse, standards that disempower children as much as they disempower women. Ministers can support abused children by witnessing against the patriarchal abuse of power and trust. Finally, ministers must face the problem that abusers often relate their pain to a religious feeling of not having been able to maintain their "sexual purity." Survivors may need to have it affirmed that their abuse was brought on strictly by the coercive and selfish motives of the abuser.

Bibliography

Adams, Carol J. *Woman-Battering*. Creative Pastoral Care and Counseling Series (Minneapolis: Fortress Press, 1994).

Adams, Carol J., and Marie M. Fortune, eds. *Violence against Women and Children: A Christian Theological Sourcebook* (New York: Continuum, 1995).

Cooper-White, Pamela. *The Cry of Tamar: Violence against Women and the Church's Response* (Minneapolis: Fortress Press, 1995).

Fortune, Marie M. *Keeping the Faith: Questions and Answers for the Abused Woman* (San Francisco: Harper and Row, 1987).

Gelles, Richard J., and Claire Pedrick Cornell. *Intimate Violence in Families,* 2d ed. (Newbury Park, Calif.: Sage Publications, 1985).

McKenzie, V. Michael. *Domestic Violence in America* (Lawrenceville, Va.: Brunswick, 1995).

—JOHN WALL

14

Ministry with Families Experiencing Loss

Much of the literature written on grief and grieving presumes that the primary mourner is an individual. We individualize grieving even further when we insist that each person's grief is the unique and particular response to the loss of a unique and particular relationship or object. Without discounting the importance of this individual emphasis, grief is also a systemic or communal reality. Families and groups and communities to which we belong need to mourn their losses. That is what is usually meant by systemic grief. The ability to grieve its losses is crucial for the vitality of any human system. For that reason, to paraphrase Judith Viorst, the families we are and the lives our families live are determined—for better or worse—by our loss experiences.

The grief families experience when loss occurs is more than the sum of individual grief and needs to be expressed in ways appropriate to the human community as a whole. Each family will have its own ways of grieving shaped by its *legacy of loss*. A family's legacy of loss is a combination of its history of losses and patterns of responding to loss when it occurs. Families are likely to get into difficulty as a social system when they are unable to grieve. Furthermore, the inability of human systems like families to mourn also makes it harder for individuals within those communities to grieve their own particular losses.

Two recent publications make this point about the family as the primary mourner. *Living Beyond Loss: Death in the Family,* edited by Froma Walsh and Monica McGoldrick (1991), not only introduced loss into family therapy literature but suggested that the ability to accept loss is at the heart of healthy family living. In *Grief as a Family Process,* Ester R. Shapiro (1994) suggests that families develop ways of coping with actual or anticipated loss in order to remain balanced. If a family's adaptation to loss is inflexible or rigid in order to maintain equilibrium, it will develop an intergenerational legacy that makes it more difficult for subsequent generations to respond to loss. A family that cannot grieve its losses is likely to be troubled in some way.

Some time ago, Norman Paul observed that when families do not grieve, that grief is usually buried somewhere in the emotional system. Families may be unable to grieve because they are overwhelmed by too much loss or because there is shame connected with the loss, as in miscarriage or suicide or death because of AIDS. Families may be reluctant to express the loss they experience when balance in the system is threatened. In any event, buried or hidden grief in a family frequently leads to what Paul called a *fixed family equilibrium*. In order to ensure that grief remains secret and hidden, family stories are not told, emotions are flattened, the past is disconnected from the present, or children are permanently kept in a dependent position. When there is trouble in a marriage or a family, it is appropriate to look for buried grief.

The following story illustrates how grief may be buried for generations. Great-great-grandfather Smythe was hung as a horse thief in Oklahoma in 1860, after which the family changed its name to Smit and moved west. Only two people in the family remembered about great-great-grandfather. For four generations, the dominant family pattern was to avoid shame at all cost, but nobody knew quite why. The family myth was about adventure and courage, not shame. Then Kevin, the great-great-grandson of a horse thief, died of AIDS, and somebody said this was the family's second moment of shame.

In order to help a family mourn its losses, it is necessary to help a family be aware of the legacy of loss it has received from preceding generations. The history of loss in a family may be identified in a variety of ways. There may be patterns of loss that repeat across the generations when deaths occur at an early age or under similar circumstances over time. Some loss is so secret that we know only the patterns of communications that have kept families from grieving for generations. The coincidence of birth and death creates a particular dilemma for families. The joy of birth and the sadness of death are difficult emotions to express simultaneously. As a result, a child born under the shadow of sadness may become the bearer of the family's expressed grief. One of the ways to help a family cope with unresolved grief is to ask about its history of loss.

How a family responds to loss is the second part of a family's legacy of loss. The family is a group of individuals who have regular interaction with one another that presumes some membership. As a human system, the family as a whole is greater than the sum of its parts. The parts have assigned roles that are interdependent. Communities function best when those roles are clear and flexible. Those roles are maintained by rules and myths that need to be equally explicit and adaptable. The assignment of roles in human systems is not always conscious, nor are the rules that govern them always explicit. Families may be more aware of beliefs or operative myths that affect how rules or roles are chosen or enacted. How families respond to loss will be determined by the way these beliefs, roles, and rules function in a family.

Every family has a theory or even a theology about change. For some, change is good; other families insist that stability can be established only through continuity. What families believe about change will affect how they respond to the losses that come with change. Family beliefs set the tone and establish the limits for acceptable behavior in a family when loss occurs. Families that pride themselves on their durability will encourage one kind of response to loss. ("When the going gets tough, the tough get going.") If privacy is highly valued, family members are more likely to grieve alone. ("Smile and the world smiles with you; cry and you cry alone.") It may be necessary to make their operative beliefs about change and loss explicit in order to assist families in their grieving.

Families often have rules about the expression of intense emotions that may impede their expression of grief as well. Families also have rules about not upsetting grandmother or not speaking ill of the dead or becoming irrational or telling a secret or disagreeing with father that will limit the freedom of a family to mourn. When the rules that govern a family's interaction inhibit grieving, processing the rules or encouraging rules to be broken becomes part of the family's work of grieving. A third issue is something persons in the helping fields often discover about families when there is grief or pending loss. Whether a family is open or closed to the outside world will determine how easily they will let others share in their grief. A closed system is more likely to bury the grief because it is too much for a family to endure without the outside help they have already decided to reject.

Roles affect a family's grieving in two distinct ways. One is about who will do the family's work of grieving and how it shall be done. The second has to do with the family's need to reassign the role that has been lost with the departure of a family member. The family member with the role of the "responsible one" may insist on making all funeral arrangements and then later be angry at other family members for not allowing him to grieve. Other families have one person who does its emoting so others cannot. Because the family is an interdependent reality, roles will be redistributed as the system reorganizes itself when one member is lost. Families are looking for replacements for the lost person whenever they say things like "Who will make us laugh?" or "Who will organize Thanksgiving dinner?" or "Who will bring us together as mother used to do?" Sometimes families assign roles that are not age-appropriate to children or insist that people take up responsibilities they are ill suited for simply to avoid reorganizing the system when death occurs.

The tasks of grieving, difficult enough for individuals, are complicated even further when the family is the mourner. First, *the family must acknowledge the reality of the loss or death that has occurred.* Families that have a history of denial in general are likely to modify the reality of the loss in order to protect some members or cover shame and rage or postpone thinking about how the family can possibly endure when this one has died. It takes time for families to arrive at a common understanding of a death because the loss will mean something different for each family member. Each one had a different relationship with the deceased. When members cannot imagine being a family without the presence of the lost person, the family as a whole is likely to deny the reality of the loss.

The second task when the family is the mourner is *to share the emotional pain of grief as fully as possible.* Immediately after a death has occurred, the family is likely to huddle together for comfort. As feelings about the loss begin to differentiate, the family faces the toughest task of grieving: to tolerate different and even conflicting feelings among its members. Because the loss often means something different for each family member, we need to honor those differences and avoid misinterpreting their meaning. Silent mourners, for example, should not be accused of not loving the deceased. When a child dies, each parent is mourning a different loss even though the same child died. Marriages frequently disintegrate when a child dies, simply because couples allow their differences in grieving to push them apart. This task in grieving will challenge a family's ability to tolerate and even honor different emotional responses to the same event.

The third task *requires that a family reorganize itself, taking into account the loss that has occurred.* Under the stress of grief, some families insist on reverting to role assignments that people may have long outgrown. If a family is unprepared to make role changes or reorganize itself, it may also postpone coming to terms with the reality of the loss. Grief for a missing family member may be compounded by grieving for the system as a whole that now seems inadequate to meet the survivors' needs. For that reason, adaptation to loss in a family is facilitated by cohesiveness of the family unit for mutual support, balanced with tolerance of and respect for different responses to loss by various family members.

Communal grief, such as that experienced by a family when loss occurs, requires greater attention to rituals that will legitimate and create safe environments for the process of grieving. Individual grieving is most often done spontaneously, as one is reminded of the loss by events or persons in our daily living. Family grieving cannot count on informal meetings or conversations. The family members need to intend to be together so that their grief can be shared. In order to support the full and free expression of grief within a family, it is important to build boundaries around the inevitable chaos of systemic grief. Such an environment will accept ambiguity and resist secret keeping. The key to family mourning is the willingness to share grief over the acknowledged loss.

The prophet Jeremiah creates a picture of the land of Judah that is painfully contemporary. "Death has come up into our windows, it has entered our palaces, to cut off the children from the streets and the young men from the squares" (9:21). In response to the close presence of violence, the prophet Jeremiah urges the mourning women to raise a dirge and teach it to their daughters (9:20). Men today have a similar responsibility. If fathers, as well as mothers, have learned to lament and have taught their daughters and sons to lament, families will be more effective mourners. Families that do not learn to lament are consigned to isolation and apathy. Being better grievers is therefore not an end in itself. Learning to mourn is a prelude to loving others more deeply because love and grief come from the same source. For that reason, we might say that the family that grieves together will more likely stay together.

Bibliography

Attig, Thomas. *How We Grieve: Relearning the World* (New York: Oxford University Press, 1996).

Mitchell, Kenneth R., and Herbert Anderson. *All Our Losses, All Our Griefs* (Philadelphia: Westminster Press, 1983).

Shapiro, Ester R. *Grief as a Family Process: A Developmental Approach to Clinical Practice* (New York: Guilford Press, 1994).

Sprang, Ginny, and John McNeil. *The Many Faces of Bereavement: The Nature and Treatment of Natural, Traumatic, and Stigmatized Grief* (New York: Brunner/Mazel, 1995).

Walsh, Froma, and Monica McGoldrick, eds. *Living Beyond Loss: Death in the Family* (New York: W. W. Norton, 1991).

—HERBERT ANDERSON

15

Families and Popular Culture

The entertainment media are a force in American life far too powerful for churches to ignore. By the age of six, the average American child will have spent more time watching television than that child will spend speaking with his or her father in a lifetime. And over the course of that lifetime, this average citizen will have invested more hours in a television set than will have been devoted to all the jobs he or she has ever held. This may seem hard to believe, but consider the facts: we begin our work life sometime after the age of eighteen, but we begin our TV watching well before the age of two. Most people retire from work at some point in their sixties, but few of us ever retire from television. We also take vacations from work—weekends, holidays, extended family trips— but hardly anyone bothers to take a vacation from the tube.

When we consider the huge proportions of time that we invest in this activity (nearly one quarter of our waking hours), we realize that churches and synagogues have been strangely silent on this subject. Perhaps our religious leaders feel powerless to interfere with the addictive relationships that most members of their congregations have developed with the entertainment media. But without an honest and effective response from religious institutions, the pervasive and dysfunctional influence of popular culture will continue to undermine all the positive messages that Judaism and Christianity seek to convey. To respond more aggressively to Hollywood's challenge, religious institutions and leaders should stress four primary points:

1. Messages matter.

The entertainment media represent far more than a "harmless waste of time." Every television show, motion picture, and popular song conveys messages— some of them blatant, some of them subtle, but all of them combining for an overwhelming cumulative impact. *None of this material is morally neutral,* and organized faith should take the lead to teach skills of evaluation and emphasize that media messages matter.

Clergy should urge consumers to go beyond questions about which entertainment offers the most glamorous stars or most dazzling special effects and begin to ask which items of entertainment will help us *achieve our goals,* bringing us closer to becoming the people we know God wants us to be. This is not to say that a single film or television program will instantly ruin or corrupt us, any more than a single hot fudge sundae will instantly make us overweight or clog our arteries with cholesterol. If, however, we begin eating five hot fudge sundaes every day, both our cardiologists and our tailors will notice. By the same token, it's the *accumulation* of destructive messages—hour after hour, year after year—that threatens to harm us, rather than some isolated example of awfulness.

Born-again Christians, like American nonbelievers, watch a lot of TV and movies, including trash TV or films that are saturated with sex and violence. Clergy should stress the fact that we are responsible to the Almighty for *all* our days and ways—including the entertainment images and ideas we allow to enter our minds, our imaginations, and our very souls.

2. The world God made is better than the world TV portrays.

The most devastating impact of our immersion in media isn't the encouragement of violence or rude behavior or irresponsible sex. It's the intensification of our great national epidemic—the epidemic of whining. We seem to live in a crybaby culture in which pessimism is pervasive, despite the fact that by any objective measure we in the United States in the last decade of the millennium are one of the most fortunate generations in the most blessed country in the history of the earth.

Why are we tempted toward collective self-pity—especially when all studies of the phenomenon indicate that our sour mood has little to do with personal experience? As Robert J. Samuelson points out in his book *The Good Life and Its Discontents* (1995), all recent surveys reveal that people are generally happy and satisfied in their own lives, but when asked about the general state of the country, they're convinced things are dreadful.

This "I'm okay, but everybody else is in trouble" syndrome is directly attributable to the influence of the media, which endlessly emphasizes the dark, the dysfunctional, and the decadent. Consider the daily messages of the news business, which ought to be called the *bad* news business. If an inner-city father works hard at three jobs to support his family and makes his weary way home each night to kiss each of his sleeping children, that's not news. If, however, the same father one night returns home and stabs or shoots those kids, then he will be featured at the very top of the next evening's local news. By the same token, TV series and movies only rarely focus on life's small triumphs or daily joys, since it is much easier to grab and hold our attention with tales of crisis and tragedy, emphasizing the bizarre and the dangerous. This is especially true given the progressive desensitization of audiences through their exposure to images of violence.

To counteract this influence, churches and synagogues must affirm the fact that the reality of the nation around us is far better and far brighter than the distorted and disturbing images shown in the media. Religious institutions are well positioned to combat the prevailing sense of self-pity and paranoia, since the most effective answer to pessimism isn't enforced optimism but *gratitude*. If Americans can learn regularly to say "thank you" for the manifold blessings they enjoy, they will move beyond what Robert Hughes has aptly termed "the culture of complaint" (1993).

We all recognize in our personal relationships the deleterious consequences of an inability to express thanks when they are due. If we owe a debt of gratitude to a parent, spouse, or business associate, but some sense of pride or stubbornness prevents us from expressing our appreciation, then that unpaid debt can become a poison that withers every joy.

3. The basic problem is the nature of the medium, not just the substance of its message.

Religious institutions can step forward to impress on congregants that the fundamental problem with watching television isn't just a few dubious programs with destructive content but the very structure and essence of the medium itself. To understand this point, play a modest thought-experiment. Imagine that crusaders for better television succeeded beyond their wildest dreams, and that everything on the tube except for the very finest material— PBS, C-SPAN, A&E, and so forth—has been eliminated. If your child watched twenty-six hours a week (which is the average level of TV watching today) of this sanitized version of television, would you then feel totally comfortable with his pattern of consumption?

Of course not. Twenty-six hours a week sitting passively in front of a box would *still* be a destructive influence on a youngster's school work, socialization, and physical development, regardless of the substance of the programs he watched. The old idea that television can help children learn must be questioned. It even needs to be asked whether large amounts of the best TV (like the beloved *Sesame Street*) are good for children. Surely, television programming achieves a negative cumulative effect on children when watched in excess.

Network TV shifts to a new image on screen at an average rate of once every nine seconds. The entire medium is built around what TV screenwriters call "beats": a series of jolts and surprises inserted into programming every few minutes in order to keep the audience titillated and tuned to a particular show. Though the vision of reality may be intensely negative with its emphasis on violence and misfortune and family breakdown, it is still colorful and lurid and exciting. Is it any surprise that many people—particularly young people—turn from their hours of television watching each day and then find the real world dull and slow-moving by comparison? Even the best shows on the networks are built around a schedule in which a life challenge is raised dramatically and then neatly solved a half hour (or at most an hour) later. In this way television contributes mightily to the sense of restlessness so palpably present in our country today. The entire purpose of the commercials that represent such a significant proportion of what we see during a broadcast day is to make people *impatient*, to stir them to want a given product without delay.

Of course, these characteristics of the medium itself directly contradict the fundamental purposes of religious teaching. Television encourages a short attention span; faith demands that we expand our horizons and take a long view of our lives and our place in the universe. TV emphasizes this moment; religion tells us to remember that there is something even beyond this life. Media culture values superficial glamor and excitement above all; faith requires that we look below the surface and consider the soul. The advertisers on the tube strive to make viewers fretful and unsettled, desiring more and more material possessions; both Judaism and Christianity strive to give their adherents a sense of peace and fulfillment with what they have. (The Talmud asks, "Who is happy?" and answers, "One who rejoices in his portion.") Hollywood is currently obsessed with "thrill-ride" movies, breathless entertainment that provides so many sensory distractions that no thought or reflection is possible; our faith traditions ask us to reflect more on life and truth. The media stress fun, which is fleeting and insubstantial; religion emphasizes happiness, which must be earned and has a chance to last.

We must advance the idea that these contrasts go beyond the entertainment industry's current obsessions with violence or graphic sex and that they involve the irreducible essence of electronic media themselves.

4. What we need most is not better TV, but less TV.

Those of us who are part of the fabled Baby Boom generation will vividly remember the years in the late 1950s when, prodded by the surgeon general of the United States, the public first became widely aware of the dangers of cigarette smoke. The initial response to these revelations was a much-publicized attempt to make cigarettes less harmful by attaching better filters or reducing the level of tar and nicotine. Only years later did we as a society acknowledge that even with these improvements, smoking remained a threat: what we needed was less smoking, not better cigarettes.

Regarding the issue of television, we are right now at the same level of consciousness that we achieved when we first suspected that cigarettes might threaten health. Attempts to clear violence and sexuality from the media are similar to the old attempts to bring down the levels of tar and nicotine; yes, they're worthwhile, but they hardly represent a long-term answer to the problem. The only meaningful response to the influence of the media isn't to change the *quality* of the TV we watch but to reduce the *quantity* of TV we watch.

Religious organizations should play a leading role in this effort. A number of congregations across the country already sponsor "Turn Off the TV" weeks for young people, and they all report that after the experience of living without the tube for just seven days, a significant number of the participants in such programs permanently alter their viewing habits. Such efforts should be encouraged and expanded and probably coordinated with national "Turn Off the TV" week, which occurs every year in April.

In addition, Sunday morning sermons provide a special opportunity for influencing congregational behavior because the Christian Sabbath happens to be the day that every major newspaper in the country publishes a listing of the TV schedule for the week to come. Clergy should encourage their church audiences to plan their viewing—to go home and review the schedules, deciding as a family which TV shows are worth watching. A yellow highlighter can prove helpful in marking down those programs you don't want to miss. Then the family should compile this information, posting a copy of their viewing schedule on the door of the refrigerator and on the side of every TV set in the home.

Sticking to such a predetermined plan is the best way to reduce the dominance of television in our lives. The main problem with our viewing habits isn't the relatively few shows we anticipate and enjoy; it's the idle hours we spend fiddling with the remote control, "channel surfing" from one meaningless program to another, wasting big chunks of time before we finally reach the unavoidable conclusion that "nothing good is on!"

Finally, religious leaders should also champion the radical idea that even beyond the necessity of reducing the amount of TV viewing, it is possible for a family to survive *without* television altogether. Increasing numbers of Americans are finding that life is sweeter, and the communication between family members is vastly improved, when all TV sets are removed from the home. Religious organizations can help to provide "support groups" to encourage those brave people who are willing to take that step; like all other recovering addicts, those who are trying to shake their dependence on the media can benefit greatly from the fellowship of others in the same situation.

One way of making a smooth transition to life after television is to replace your conventional TV set with a "video monitor" (a TV set with no cable or antenna to receive broadcast signals). This expedient means that you have far greater control of the substance and the timing of what you watch. You don't have to depend on broadcasters to provide quality programming; you can go to the video store and find it yourself. You can also offer such videos on a schedule that your family determines, rather than arranging your life according to the schedule of some network. Using video in this way allows you to own and control the tube, rather than letting that tube own and control you.

The average American devotes thirteen uninterrupted years to TV during his or her lifetime. Would we want this investment recorded on our gravestones: "Here lies our beloved husband and father who selflessly devoted thirteen years of life to his television set"?

Our churches and our synagogues should find the courage to ask—and to answer—these vital questions.

Bibliography

Hughes, Robert. *The Culture of Complaint. The Fraying of America* (New York: Oxford University Press, 1993).

Medved, Michael. *Hollywood vs. America: Popular Culture and the War on Traditional Values.* (New York, HarperCollins, 1992).

Samuelson, Robert J. *The Good Life and Its Discontents* (New York: Time Books, 1995).

Winn, Marie. *The Plug-in Drug: Television, Children and the Family* (New York: Viking Penguin, 1985).

—DIANE MEDVED
MICHAEL MEDVED

16

Families and Violence

A Chicago mother still struggles to understand how two children could have dropped her five-year-old son from an apartment building to his death—all because he would not steal candy. She lives with a terrible loss and a haunting view of human failure and sin. Children in Sarajevo grow up in orphanages, torn from their mothers and fathers by civil war. What will they learn of love and community? Residents of a rural town in Iowa ask how one of their own could have shot and killed his estranged wife and five children and then turned the gun on himself. They wonder how a family could have gone so wrong, and they wonder whether they could have prevented the tragedy.

Violence threatens the stability and well-being of families all over the world—in urban, suburban, and rural areas. In the face of this destruction of human life and community, in the face of the resulting grief and suffering, what are churches to do?

This article focuses on one type of violence: the interpersonal violence that threatens many families in the United States and other Western industrialized nations. The United States, though relatively free of political violence, leads industrialized nations in violent crime—by far. Juvenile violent crime is a particularly severe problem. The Federal Bureau of Investigation reports that murder rates by young people aged ten to seventeen nearly tripled between 1983 and 1993, when it reached an all-time high. Reports of child abuse, spouse battering, and even abuse of elderly parents remind us that our most intimate relationships are not immune from this violence. They may be particular danger spots that, given our sense of the sanctity of the private sphere, often go undetected. While the number of homicides committed by American adults has declined by almost 50 percent in the last fifteen years and rates of juvenile violent crime finally have edged down from their peak in 1993, violence remains a great threat to families.

The Response of Religious Groups

How can churches and other religious groups help? First, they must recognize their limitations. Interpersonal violence is a complex problem. Weak families, lack of supervision of youth, inconsistent punishment or harsh physical punishment of children, poverty and socioeconomic inequality, prejudice, substance abuse, and the availability of guns all increase the levels of interpersonal violence in the United States. Religious groups cannot end violence single-handedly. Yet they can help to curb violence outside and inside the family and especially to reduce the impact of violence on children.

The efforts of religious groups will be most authentic and valuable when they include reflection and discussion about violence as a moral and a spiritual issue. What contributes to violence? Who bears responsibility? What is a good and just response to violence? How can religious people promote an understanding of the sacredness of human life, of the importance of justice and human dignity? Jewish and Christian groups, for example, can point to the Hebrew prophets who teach that doing justice is a requirement of faithfulness (Micah 6:8) and that peace is the fruit of justice (Isa. 32:17). Christians can reflect on violence in light of Jesus' insistence on the importance of reconciliation (for example, Matt. 5:21–24), and the Beatitudes' promises to the peacemakers and to those who hunger and thirst for righteousness (Matt. 5:6, 9). Religious groups also need to acknowledge the ambiguous messages about violence in their traditions, including theology that portrays God as avenging and destructive. Most religious groups justify some forms of violence, whether it be in teachings on "just war" or support of the death penalty. As religious groups confront interpersonal violence in our streets and families, they need to continue to wrestle with violence as a moral and spiritual issue. Is it ever justified? How can it be avoided or at least curtailed? Religious groups also should honestly acknowledge the violence that has been perpetrated in the name of religion (holy wars, murder of heretics, domestic abuse), and their inadequate responses to violence—against women, minorities, the disabled, the elderly. This self-examination will help churches to articulate the moral and spiritual dimensions of violence and their response to it.

Religious communities can help families protect themselves from interpersonal violence and prevent family members' own violent behavior. Each church or synagogue needs to assess its own particular situation—the types of violence experienced in its neighborhood, its own resources, its ability to make an enduring commitment to tackling the problem. As a community of faith, it will discern the ways that it can best respond to the problem. Religious groups may be able to help combat violence simply by nurturing the faith and sense of community among its members and neighbors. Research by Joy Dryfoos (1990), Peter Benson (1993), David Lester (1987), and others indicates that religious belief and participation may reduce some violent and delinquent behaviors. Church attendance, for example, has been correlated with lower suicide and homicide rates. It also may promote resiliency in vulnerable youth, helping them to avoid destructive behavior in spite of difficult life situations by providing coping skills, community, order, and a sense of meaning.

Churches and synagogues are among the few intergenerational communities existing today, and as such they are in a position to nurture supportive relationships among people of all ages. These relationships can provide mentoring for the young, giving them caring adults to turn to if they lack such figures in their own families or when parent-child tensions inhibit communication. Adults can provide informal supervision or structured youth activities in the after-school hours, when most juvenile crime occurs. Intergenerational ties also can protect the elderly, many of whom live alone and may be particularly vulnerable to violence.

Ministering with Families through Life Cycle Transitions

Churches have important points of contact with families at key transitional points in the life cycle: marriage, birth of a child (baptism), entrance into adolescence (confirmation or baptism), illness, and death. These transitions can unsettle families, opening them to guidance and support from the community. Clergy and laypeople ministering to people at these times can help strengthen family networks and raise awareness of violence both within and outside the home. For example, some premarital counselors inquire into how couples resolve conflict and ask them to consider how through their own marriage and through their relationships with other married couples they might promote nonviolence. Preparation for baptism could include an honest discussion with parents of the frustrations of child-rearing, and ways to avoid using violence against children. (For a more extensive discussion of ministry with abusive families, see chapter 13 and the directory in this volume.) Churches usually have fairly sustained contact with young adolescents preparing for confirmation or baptism. The process of preparing these teens to assume the Christian witness could emphasize the Christian call to love and the "ministry of reconciliation" (2 Cor. 5:18). How can young adolescents carry the gospel in the environments *they* face every day? How should they approach the outsider at school, the opposite sex, or an opposing sports team? How can they resist the pressure to drink, do drugs, or join a gang? Prayer about and reflection on violence in light of faith also can be an important part of regular liturgies and Bible studies.

In fighting violence, religious groups often identify and build on existing resources in their communities. Churches have joined with schools, community organizations, police, and local businesses to improve basic social services, to foster economic development, and to develop neighborhood watches, youth programming, drug prevention campaigns, and gun turn-ins. St. Sabina's Roman Catholic parish, for example, created a business training program called "Something Good for the Hood" to provide summer jobs for teenagers on Chicago's South Side. The Congress of National Black Churches helps local churches to form partnerships with public and private organizations to reduce drug-related violence and crime in African-American neighborhoods. In taking this community-organizing approach to violence, religious groups move beyond their own congregations into the local community, to minister to the whole person beginning with the most fundamental needs.

Teaching Alternatives to Violence

Some religious groups also teach alternatives to violence and embody a spirituality of peace and justice. The historic peace churches, such as the Quakers and the Mennonites, have made conflict resolution their special task. They understand the promotion of peace and justice as central to Christian faith and see con-flict resolution as finding the ability to forgive and to restore a relationship as well as to solve disputes. Conflict resolution programs also attend to cultural diver-sity, reduction of prejudice, and management of anger. Churches can help their members resolve conflicts nonviolently. In addition, they can support and learn from community mediation centers, court mediation efforts, and peer mediation programs in public schools. (A variety of resources on violence and conflict res-olution are available from the Mennonite Central Committee U.S., 21 South 12th Street, P.O. Box 500, Akron, PA 17501-0500.)

Some churches strive to develop a spirituality of peace and justice through their worship, youth programming, and adult education. They seek to form people whose faith is rooted in a commitment to the God whose peace "sur-passes all understanding" (Philippians 4:7) and who live out that faith by seek-ing more just families and communities, more peaceful inner spirits and outer selves. Numerous resources are available for this spiritual formation and reli-gious education. For example, the Presbyterian Church (USA) and the Evan-gelical Lutheran Church of America together have published a handbook entitled "Youth in Peacemaking." They each also offer collections of worship materials and other teaching aids emphasizing peacemaking (to order, call Dis-tribution Management Service PC [USA], 800-524-2612, or ELCA Distribution Service, 800-328-4648). The Episcopal Church offers a *Youth Violence Preven-tion Resource Packet* (to order, contact Youth Ministries Office, The Episcopal Church Center, 815 Second Ave., New York, NY 10017).

National, state, and local public policy also influences the level of violence and families' vulnerability to violence. Many religious groups have become involved in shaping this public policy through studying proposed legislation, raising pub-lic awareness of violence issues, and lobbying to support or oppose particular bills. The National Jewish Community Relations Advisory Council, for example, advo-cates full funding of the violence prevention programs included in the Omnibus Crime Bill of 1994 and opposes the death penalty. The United States Catholic Conference distributed statements on domestic violence (1992) and on substance abuse (1990) and has supported such legislation as a ban on assault weapons and the Brady Bill, which establishes a five-day waiting period before one can purchase a handgun. Local churches can contact their denominational headquarters to learn more about public policy issues related to violence. Religious groups hold diverse views about these issues, and even about which issues should be seen as relating to violence. The list could include gun control, prison reform, capital pun-ishment, juvenile justice, abortion, and violence on television, as well as the many broader ways in which government influences the strength of family and com-munity life (for example, in the areas of education, health care, and divorce law).

Supporting Victims of Violence

In addition to these efforts to prevent or reduce violence, religious groups sup-port victims of violence both in the immediate crisis intervention and in the long-term recovery process. Alongside police, health care workers, psychiatric service providers, family, and friends, many ministers assist victims in the aftermath of a violent attack such as a robbery or rape. It is important too that they continue to provide long-term emotional support, practical assistance, and spiritual guidance to violence victims and their families and friends. Victims' families need to work through their own feelings of powerlessness and failure to protect their loved ones. They often need guidance in their relationships with the victim. A woman who has been raped, for example, may withdraw from her partner. A man who has been assaulted may displace anger onto loved ones. Family members also may inadvertently impede the victim's recovery (for example, by implying that the victim is to blame). Ministers can help victims and their families by following their long-term progress and referring them to professional counseling when needed. Religious groups also should know about state victim assistance programs, which often compensate persons for medical expenses, lost income, counseling, funeral costs, and rehabilitation. Church members can accompany people through the difficult processes of the criminal justice system, including trial and sentencing. Moreover, religious communities should provide a safe place to explore the moral and spiritual questions raised by the victimization. Why did this happen to me? Where was God in this? What are the demands of forgiveness and of justice in this situation? Survivors of violence need to struggle with and eventually give some meaning to their experience.

Religious groups also may find important ministry in caring for those who have committed acts of violence and for their families, for example, through work in prisons, halfway houses, and juvenile detention centers. Some may hear a contemporary call in the biblical counsel: "Remember those who are in prison, as though you were in prison with them. . . ." (Heb. 13:3). Prison separates families, leaving children without parents and adults without partners. Ministry with those in detention facilities reminds persons that they remain part of a community, that they are cared for. It gives them too an opportunity for reflection, contrition, and reconciliation. The families of prisoners often also need spiritual guidance and material assistance. In caring for violent offenders and their families, many ministers demand accountability from the social institutions that help create conditions and cultural values that encourage violence. They seek new ways to help families "overcome destructive moral and economic pressures, discrimination, and dependency. . . . We need both to hold people accountable and offer them concrete help and hope for a better future" (United States Catholic Conference 1994).

Religious groups rightly are concerned about violence and its effects on families. Church members perform a valuable ministry in being present to victims, to those who commit acts of violence, and to the families of all. While violence is a complex problem, religious groups can help. In the face of the destruction of human life, churches have a responsibility to assert the sacredness of the human person. Every individual possesses a core value and dignity that is cherished by God. Whatever demeans or destroys that life is sinful. Churches also recognize the destructive effects of violence on human community. In seeking to reduce violence, they help to build up the body of Christ in the world, the unity of persons to which God calls us. Religious groups also can acknowledge that our failure to build strong and just communities promotes violence. They can witness to God's special concern for justice, for the protection of the poor and vulnerable. Finally, when faced with the pain of violence, churches and synagogues can offer hope that as individuals, as families, and as larger communities, we can be transformed and that the "God of peace" (Phil. 4:9) will be with us.

Bibliography

Adams, Carol J., and Marie M. Fortune, eds. *Violence Against Women and Children: A Christian Theological Sourcebook* (New York: Continuum, 1995).

American Psychological Association. *Violence and Youth: Psychology's Response. Volume 1: Summary Report of the American Psychological Association Commission on Violence and Youth* (Washington, D.C.: American Psychological Association, 1993).

Bard, Morton, and Dawn Sangrey. *The Crime Victim's Book* (New York: Brunner/Mazel, 1986).

Benson, Peter. *The Troubled Journey: A Portrait of 6th–12th Grade Youth* (Minneapolis: The Search Institute, 1993).

Dryfoos, Joy. *Adolescents at Risk: Prevalence and Prediction* (New York and Oxford: Oxford University Press, 1990).

Greven, Philip. *Spare the Child: The Religious Roots of Punishment and the Psychological Impact of Physical Abuse* (New York: Alfred A. Knopf, 1991).

Lester, David. "Religiosity and Personal Violence: A Regional Analysis of Suicide and Homicide Rates," *The Journal of Social Psychology* 127/6(1987): 685–86.

McGinnis, James. *Educating for Peace and Justice: Religious Dimensions,* vol. 3. (St. Louis: Institute for Peace and Justice, 1984).

United States Catholic Conference. *Confronting a Culture of Violence: A Catholic Framework for Action* (Washington, D.C.: United States Catholic Conference, 1994).

—CLAIRE WOLFTEICH

17

Families and Substance Abuse

The current understanding of addiction acknowledges that substance abuse affects both the user and others in her or his social matrix. Conservative projections estimate that at least four significant others in the family or social system suffer from a given person's substance abuse. *Substance abuse* is an umbrella term that encompasses all mood-altering chemicals: narcotics, depressants, stimulants, hallucinogens, cannabis, prescription or designer drugs, and our number one drug, beverage alcohol. Substance abuse is no respecter of race, creed, color, sexual orientation, gender, or social or economic status.

If the ministry of the church with families suffering from substance abuse is to be effective, at least three areas warrant specific attention: the church's attitude, awareness, and action.

Attitude

Attitudes shape behavior. Father Joseph Martin, a priest in Baltimore and a leader in alcoholism treatment, characterizes attitudes as "habits of the mind," which—like physical habits—are often tenacious. The prevailing social and ecclesiastical attitude toward substance abuse is at best ambivalent. Persons afflicted with substance abuse may be the subject of humiliating humor or of merciless moralism and condemnation.

Howard Clinebell, an early leader in the modern pastoral care movement, has delineated six attitudes the church takes toward alcoholism, ranging from seeing substance abuse as evidence of moral reprobation (sin) to seeing it as evidence of a reaction to oppressive societal pressures (sickness). But regardless of one's theological interpretation, a viable ministry needs to be conducted for the afflicted and the affected. The central biblical mandate to love thy neighbor disallows the luxury of selectivity. Though the behavior of substance abusers is often reprehensible, addicts are also people created, redeemed, and loved by God. They are in need of care rather than condemnation.

Family members and significant others who are adversely affected also meet ambivalent reactions. They may be pitied as martyrs or judged as moronic for their loyalty to the abuser. A viable ministry of healing requires that communities of faith resolve deep-seated ambivalent attitudes regarding the substance abuser and her or his significant others. The emotional antennae of the afflicted and the affected easily pick up the attitudes of would-be care givers. Intuitively they know whether a person is present out of pious pity, righteous condemnation, or moral superiority or is truly concerned, empathic, and accepting.

In reorienting its attitude, the church must acknowledge the universality of human brokenness as an antidote to moral superiority. Acknowledging the solidarity of shared humanness is a fundamental requirement for effectively counseling with addicts. The message of the church is often heard as conditional acceptance predicated on substantive change, but faith communities must move beyond righteous indignation, pious platitudes, and paternalistic pity to embrace their sisters and brothers ensnared in the web of this life-threatening condition. While some, such as Mark and Linda Sobels, have argued that addiction to substances can be treated as a behavioral disorder and others interpret it as a moral issue, studies consistently show that substance abuse is most effectively treated as an illness (Edwards 1985; Glatt 1995). This does not preclude the implementation of "tough love" for the afflicted and the affected. Accountability and responsibility are integral components for interrupting the addictive cycle and facilitating the recovery process for the whole family.

Awareness

The church cannot assist families struggling with substance abuse if it lacks awareness regarding this illness. Despite educational campaigns, knowledge about substance abuse is still woefully inadequate.

The first step in awareness is to acknowledge the existence of "denial." Social, ecclesiastical, familial, and personal denial flow from the shame that continues to plague those struggling with substance abuse. The conspiracy of silence and collusion of covering up results in the family's adjusting, readjusting, and finally maladjusting to the situation. Directly and nonjudgmentally naming the issue frees the family from using all of its energies in covering up.

Second, one must deal with the defense mechanisms that have developed throughout the period of addiction. Significant others who are protective of themselves and the substance abuser are quick to employ rationalization, minimization, and projection to cope with the situation. A careful dismantling of such defense mechanisms is a prerequisite for effective help.

Third, families may be helped if they become more aware of the damage being perpetrated on all members. Spouses or significant others of substance abusers succumb to devastating attacks upon their own self-worth and life goals. Children adopt or are assigned familial roles that have negative effects on their development. Sharon Wegscheider-Cruse, alcoholism specialist and family therapist, has described these roles as that of the family hero, scapegoat, forgotten child, or mascot. Care givers in communities of faith need to understand these roles so that an entree into the family system through the children can be made. Recent research has confirmed a strong correlation between substance abuse and familial violence. Those in ministry need to recognize all of the behaviors that can accompany substance abuse.

Joan Jackson, a pioneer researcher in substance abuse, suggests seven stages in a family's response to substance abuse:

Stage 1. Excessive use of mood-altering substances creates significant marital stress, but defense mechanisms allow both partners to avoid dealing directly with the issue.

Stage 2. The family engages in social isolation, which more intensely focuses the intrafamilial relationships and results in escalated marital difficulties, with deleterious effects upon the children.

Stage 3. Attempts at controlling use are abandoned, and coping mechanisms are devised to alleviate tension. The role of the substance abuser is relinquished in the family system. Hope that anything constructive will happen begins to wane.

Stage 4. The nonusing spouse takes control of the family system and often regards the substance abuser as a belligerent child who needs care and protection. The spouse, children, and significant others adapt to a pathological model of existence.

Stage 5. The pain in the family increases to the point that the spouse separates or divorces.

Stage 6. A complete reorganization of the family system occurs, leaving the substance abuser out of the picture.

Stage 7. If the spouse recovers, he or she is reincorporated into the family system with all of the concomitant readjustments that need to be made with his or her sober existence.

Even when the substance abuser recovers, the chances of reintegration with the family are limited if the family is not in recovery. Family members need to come to terms with the nature and impact of the illness and with their own feelings of anger, betrayal, disappointment, disillusionment, and skepticism. In general, the family that does not heal together does not stay together. Whether or not the family is reconstituted, the scarring that has occurred for spouse, children, and significant others can be long-lasting. The popularity of a twelve-step group called Adult Children of Alcoholics, for example, is evidence of the persistent impact in adult life of experiences encountered by the child who lives with a substance abuser.

Finally, the church also needs to be aware that there is both help and hope for the substance abuser and his or her family. Helplessness and hopelessness are intimate companions of family members who are struggling with substance abuse. When mobilized for action, the church can be pivotal in providing assistance.

Action

Ministry with families struggling with substance abuse usually takes place initially with those affected rather than with those afflicted. Spouses, children, extended family, employers, friends, or neighbors are more likely to seek out the ministry of the church if it is sought out at all. Pain can be God's greatest gift to those suffering because it prompts action. Most critical is to minister to the person who has sought out the help and to put her or him in touch with others who are struggling with the same pain. Alanon, Alateen, Alatot, Alafam, and Adult Children of Alcoholics are valuable twelve-step programs designed for family members and friends whose lives have been influenced by substance abuse.

The twelve-step programs provide education concerning the nature of substance abuse and its ramifications; consciousness raising concerning the complicity of family members in the enabling of the disease; a source of communal support to cope with a common malady and its concomitant dynamics; a way of life that can be healthy whether the substance abuser recovers or not; and a model of an alternate lifestyle that is not determined by substance abuse.

Communities of faith can be resources for support if they display both the proper attitude toward substance abuse and a greater awareness of its ramifications. Project ADEPT, launched by the Texas Conference of Churches in Austin, Texas, offers a good resource guide for addiction ministries. This is an educational, pastoral care approach to addiction that involves ordained as well as nonordained persons.

Communities of faith can also function as clearinghouses or coordinators for human services available in a given locale. The addresses of twelve-step programs, as well as treatment centers, phone numbers, cost, and philosophy of care can be made available to concerned persons. The training of congregational members could take place through something like the Stephen Ministry. Dwindling governmental and social support will make the role of the church and its ministry critical in the future.

Faith communities need to work cooperatively with each other and also with schools and other community agencies to address substance abuse. Religious leaders can exercise cooperative leadership in coordinating various initiatives with other community resources concerned with prevention, education, recovery, and the general health and well-being of all citizens.

In addition to these large-scale efforts, those afflicted and those affected need to see that the faith community is a "safe" place to air concerns. The church needs to present itself as a place where people will be heard, where people are believed, where assistance can be rendered, and where love of God and neighbor is the central guiding force. The covenantal love unilaterally offered by God to the community of faith should be offered to all suffering human beings. The church's mission is not only to those sitting under the sanctuary lights but also to those standing under the street lights.

The church's ministry of prevention must focus on children. For example, does the church's ministry intentionally communicate to its children that they are of ultimate worth and value as created children of God? Are the contacts that children have with the community of faith such that they feel included? Are children nourished in the faith and nurtured in relationships? Are they mentored by the faithful, accepted and loved for who they are? Many substance abusers have had a trying childhood, often marked by parental divorce, various kinds of abuse (including parental substance abuse), and other developmental traumas. A good children's ministry is no guarantee against substance abuse, but it is a significant preventive measure.

Is there a genetic link involved in substance abuse? If there is, it may in fact be triggered by an individual's experiences. For example, the high incidence of substance abuse among young African-American males may be connected in part to the effects of racism. Thus, in addition to ministering to individuals and families, the church needs to work prophetically for systemic change so that substance abuse no longer becomes the anesthetizing agent for the pain of social, racial, economic, and political injustice.

It has been said that we live in an addictive society, and indeed mortality caused by substance abuse ranks just below heart disease and cancer. As social services for those struggling with substance abuse continue to wane, the church should once again be assertive in exercising its ministry of healing.

The church's message and ministry is to the whole person: body, mind, and spirit. Addressing the needs of those affected by substance abuse as well as engaging in prevention requires a cooperative and concerted effort by the people of God. The community of faith is to function as a beacon of hope in the message it proclaims and as a bearer of help in the mission it claims. As the church lays claim to its source of hope and help in God and trusts in the guidance of God's Spirit, it can also be of inestimable help to families struggling with substance abuse.

Bibliography

Clinebell, Howard J. *Understanding and Counseling the Alcoholic* (Nashville: Abingdon Press, 1968).

Edwards, G. "A later follow-up of a classic case series: D.L. Davies' 1962 report and its significance for the present," *Journal of Studies on Alcohol* 46/3(1985): 181–90.

Glatt, M. M. "Controlled Drinking after a Third of a Century" *Addiction* 90/9(1995): 1157–60.

Jackson, Joan. "The Adjustment of the Family to the Crisis of Alcoholism," *Quarterly Journal of Alcohol Studies* 15/4 (1954): 562–86.

Johnson, Vernon. *I'll Quit Tomorrow* (San Francisco: Harper and Row, 1980).

Merrill, Trish. *Committed, Caring Communities* (Austin, Tex.: Project ADEPT, Texas Council of Churches, 1994).

Wegscheider-Cruse, Sharon. *Another Chance: Help and Hope for the Alcoholic Family* (Palo Alto, Calif.: Science and Behavior Books, 1981).

—ROBERT ALBERS

PART 3

Resources for Congregational Ministry with Families

18

Hebrew Scriptures and the Family

The Family Stories in Genesis
(Genesis 12–50)

The contemporary understanding of marriage as the fulfillment of romantic interests is just that—contemporary. Emphasis on affection and romantic love as the basis for marriage begins to appear in nineteenth-century family life. In contrast to this more recent perspective on marriage, the ancestral stories of Genesis 12–50 prescribe a paradigm of family as including parents and child. Cross-cultural data on kinship and marriage set the analysis of the family stories of Genesis 12–50 within the wider context of studies linking economics, production, and reproduction; that is, the family values of biblical Israel are centered around the survival of the family unit on a daily basis and from generation to generation. The ancestral narratives reveal a social system in which marriage is the appropriate status for both men and women, and the choice of a marriage partner has profound consequences for an individual's future: men must marry women from the line of Terah, father of Abraham (Gen. 11:27), if they are to be included within the Israelite lineage. As noted above, the purpose of marriage is to continue the lineage through procreation. The rationale for this emphasis on marriage and procreation relates to a larger societal interest in establishing the genealogy of early Israel, in determining who is a member of the community and who is not.

How does this understanding of the dynamics of the biblical family affect our appropriation of the texts of Genesis 12–50 as a resource for addressing challenges to the survival of family life at the end of the twentieth century? We can begin to answer this question by recognizing the emphasis in Genesis 12–50 on the importance of the birth of children, and on the fact that the failure of a couple to reproduce is understood as the fault of the wife: women are identified as barren (see, for example, Gen. 11:30 concerning Sarah), although sterility in men is never mentioned. This patrilineal definition of the role of women in the biblical text results in a social world in which a woman's identity comes through marriage and then motherhood. This insight helps us to understand better the conflict in Genesis between Sarah and Hagar (Genesis 16; 21). One woman, Sarah, may be married to the master, Abraham, but the other woman, Hagar, has borne him a child. Hagar is the woman who has fulfilled her biological destiny in the patrilineal family. This emphasis on motherhood pits the two women against each other; in the biblical texts, the patrilineal concern for perpetuation of the family forces women to compete against each other in the interest of securing their position in the household through a demonstration of their ability to continue the lineage (the same thing is true of the relationship between Leah and Rachel; Gen. 29:31–30:24).

The recognition of the relative infrequency of cooperation between women, and the regular occurrence of conflict between them, may appear startling to us as members of a society in which unity and sisterhood are emphasized, but the realization of this interpersonal dynamic provides us with evidence of a pattern of behavior disruptive to family life. Although women's domestic arguments are most often analyzed as a result of the conflicting loyalties between a woman as wife and a woman as mother—as wife a woman bears children for her husband's lineage, but as mother she sees these offspring bring family fission—this explanation of women's behavior portrays women as individuals who react to their circumstances and surroundings as victims of a system controlled by men. However, conflict-indicating behavior such as quarreling, jealousy, and anger can better be analyzed as a sign of women's attempts to control their situations and to exercise power over them.

It appears, then, that in Genesis 12–50 women's quarrels have as their context conflictual situations in which the interests of one woman are pitted against those of another. In such contexts, particular behaviors become a source of power; women exercise power through such behavior. Their actions are their acts of resistance. Women's conflict-indicating behavior can thus be viewed as an attempt to subvert power structures.

We are therefore dealing with a pattern of behavior that appears to have a common meaning. But we also need to recognize that women cooperate with each other when this behavior serves their purposes. Such circumstances appear less frequently in the biblical texts, though Lot's daughters (Gen. 19:30–38) and Naomi and Ruth (in the book of Ruth) provide examples of women working together. The conflict-indicating behavior of men appears less an act of resistance and more a man's attempt to displace his opponent from the scene. In other words, one man must deprive another man of something in order for the first man to succeed. Cain murders Abel (Gen. 4:8), Abraham expels Ishmael (Gen. 21:8–14), Jacob cheats Esau out of his birthright (Gen. 25:29–34) and tricks Isaac into giving him a blessing (Genesis 27), and Joseph's brothers sell him into slavery (Gen. 37:12–28). There are, of course, other examples of the same behavior between men found outside the book of Genesis. Striking because it is an exception to this expectation is the resolution of conflict between Abraham and Lot in Genesis 13. Rather than compete with each other, the two separate and go their own ways when they both become so wealthy that the land cannot support them (13:5–7).

Thus, in the family stories of Genesis it appears that women and men find themselves in conflict-laden situations in which they attempt to exercise self-interest. What distinguishes the two is that men attempt to gain power, whereas women appear to resist it. I believe we run a risk, however, if we argue that one form of power is superior to another. Ultimately the forms of conflict and power interconnect.

Let us return to where we began this essay. Given the fact that the Genesis texts prescribe that biology is destiny for women, how do we define motherhood today: biologically? legally? socially? How does the availability of expensive medical technology for treating infertile women factor into our discussion of this question? In this highly complex medical world in which many individuals seek professional intervention in parenting, biology is once again destiny. The availability of surrogate motherhood reinforces this biological definition of parenting because typically either the husband or the wife of the couple contributes biologically to the new life carried by a woman who is not party to the marriage. I intend these remarks as an argument not against motherhood but against motherhood as a strictly biological endeavor, a role forced on women as an identity marker. Moreover, we must bear in mind that such techniques for medical intervention in reproduction are tied to socioeconomic status. Only women of certain classes and ethnic groups are likely to be surrogate mothers, and only couples of particular classes and ethnic groups are likely to be able to afford such services.

In *From Margin to Center* bell hooks provides an Afrocentric feminist standpoint on motherhood. She comments on the relationship between biological mothers and what she calls "othermothers," other women who share the mothering responsibilities with the biological mother.

> This form of parenting is revolutionary in this society because it takes place in opposition to the ideas that parents, especially mothers, should be the only childrearers. . . . This kind of shared responsibility for child care can happen in small community settings where people know and trust one another. It cannot happen in those settings if parents regard children as their "property," their possession. (1984, 144)

Another issue relevant to family life can be recovered by means of the above interpretation. Through our efforts to recover the voice of Hagar, we hear the words of a single mother who is homeless and is struggling to keep her child alive in a system in which she has been exploited for her biological capabilities. She is defined by her son Ishmael and suffers for him after they are expelled from Abraham and Sarah's household (21:15–19). Of course, Hagar is also originally a surrogate mother for Abraham and his infertile wife Sarah. Thus the stories of Genesis address the socioeconomic problems of women whose bodies have been exploited because they have few, if any, other options for livelihood.

The above analysis of the biblical texts results in the privileging of a particular ideological position. It is an ideological position grounded in a vision of family life in which all family members can become equals; it is an ethics determined by certain values and principles that are nonnegotiable. This is an ethics of personal accountability for one's actions and a caring for the worth of all members of a family. It is an ethics we are all responsible for upholding.

Bibliography

hooks, bell. *From Margin to Center* (Boston: South End Press, 1984).

—NAOMI STEINBERG

The Creation Story
(Genesis 1:26–28)

> And God said, "Let us make humanity in our image, according to our likeness. And they shall rule over the fish of the sea and over the birds of the heavens, and over the beasts and over the entire earth, and over every creeping thing which creeps upon the earth."
>
> And God created humanity according to his image, in the image of God he created him, male and female he created them.
>
> And God blessed them and said to them, "Be fruitful and multiply and fill the earth and subdue it. And rule over the fish of the sea and the bird of the sky, and over all life which creeps upon the earth." (author's translation)

This famous excerpt from the first book of the Torah is the Bible's first reference to the creation of humankind. The context of this passage, the author's choice of language, and the commandments to the first human beings direct us to consider the partnership we share with God in creation and with each other as men and women who may bring children into the world.

The context of this quotation is God's creation of humanity on the sixth day of the week. The seven-day creation schema of Genesis 1:1–2:4a evidences a world created with order, pattern, and meaning. It is a creation over which God has no rival and is one that God judges to be good. All its objects, and all life, have been named by their Creator and given a purpose: to mark times and seasons, to receive God's blessing, to support life, and to contribute to God's future creation by reproducing. The outline of God's creative activity may be schematized as follows:

Day 1: light	Day 4: luminaries and stars
Day 2: firmament; Heaven	Day 5: sea creatures and birds
Day 3: earth, sea, vegetation	Day 6: animals, creeping things, beasts, humanity

Day 7: God abstains from work;
God sanctifies this day; the Sabbath (implied)

The literary pattern of this creation account mirrors its purpose, order, and goodness. Each column shows parallels in days 1, 2, and 3 with days 4, 5, and 6, respectively. The climax is the Sabbath, which has no parallel. Although the word *shabbat* is not used in the text, the context is clear. To abstain from work is the hallmark of Israel's institution of the Sabbath, the day of the week made holy by God. Humanity derives its value neither from men's and women's ability to work nor by being a means to an end. God's rest and Israel's imitation of that rest are a reminder of the intrinsic value of creation and especially of human beings. This idea is acknowledged when Israel is given the Ten Commandments, where it is written: "For in six days the Lord made heaven and earth, the sea, and all that is in them, and rested the seventh day; therefore the Lord blessed the sabbath day and hallowed it" (Exod. 20:11, RSV). The material world (days 1–6) comes from God's goodness; the spiritual world (day 7) reminds us that a spiritual dimension to the created order also exists.

It is into this schema, on day 6, that humanity is created. Like the other objects and creatures in the universe, humanity is created by an extraordinary act: God speaks. Unlike much of the literature of Israel's contemporaries, we do not read here of cosmic conflicts, unparalleled chaos and violence, or of petty or major disputes among deities. Only when creating humanity does God speak using the plural pronoun. This plural language inspired Jewish commentators in antiquity to speak of God's presence with the angels and Christian exegetes to speak of God's presence with the Trinity. Many modern commentators see vestiges of the Canaanite cosmogony of the divine council or of the plural form of the noun Elohim (God). It is also worth considering that only in the case of the creation of humanity does the text specify that male and female are created. Perhaps the plural language of the deity mirrors the ineffable quality of God that cannot be subsumed under one gender. The text does *not* say that man (males) image God and that woman does so derivatively. Rather, with neither discussion nor excuse, the text relates this extraordinary idea: Men and women image God. Human beings—whom we know experientially to be sometimes weak, cruel, violent, and destructive—image this good God who has created a world of goodness, harmony, and order. Humanity alone of all creatures shares in the divine essence. In the context of the ancient Near East, it is striking to note that only Israel spoke of all humanity imaging God. More frequent among Israel's neighbors was the belief that only the monarch imaged the gods.

The understanding that all men and women image God forms the foundation for Israel's respect for each individual's life. The great Jewish commentator Rambam (1135–1204) argued that it was our reason and our ability to search for correct moral action that allowed us to be compared to the very image of God. This philosophy is reflected in a famous talmudic passage which states, "Whoever destroys one soul is regarded by the Torah as if he had destroyed a whole world and whoever saves one soul is regarded as if he had saved a whole world" (*Sanhedrin* 37a). Although Israel had many gender-specific roles and laws for women and men, the fundamental worth and dignity of women is reflected in many passages throughout the Bible. Here is the first: a foundational statement concerning the equality of women made in God's image.

Humanity becomes partners with God in creation. Humanity has inherited a world created with careful classification, order, and design. It is God's choice that humanity is given all elements of the animal kingdom to supervise. The Creator so respects humanity that God speaks directly only to them, not to the animals. (Note that the blessings to the animals are in the passive voice.) With the increased concern for the environment that many theologians share today, it is striking to see that in this text the dominion and rule that humanity is to have over God's created world is not shown to be exploitative.

Humanity's role as partners in creation has a further element: continuation of the human race. Only in the context of having dominion over the creatures are they commanded to be parents. When God contemplates making humanity (v. 26), it is the role of humans as partners in creation that is paramount. When God speaks to them, his first words are to "be fruitful and multiply," but they are given only in the context of their participation in the protection and use of the earth and its creatures.

Just as God created the first human beings in a universe of order and harmony, so too should the human beings create a world of harmony for their offspring. This harmony comes from seeing the created world under the purpose of a divine will that created it in goodness. It is a world infused with inherent meaning. The world may have in it an inscrutable hierarchical arrangement, but in this text the hierarchy does not exist among the sexes. In this seven-day creation schema, there can be no debate as to who is more or less responsible for disobeying God, as occurs in Genesis 2–3. Both men and women image God. Both are commanded to have dominion over the animals. Both are blessed. Both hear God's command to have children. Both enter a world where people and animals are eating only herbs, plants, and fruits and are not destroying each other. And both enter a world where even God rests and makes a day holy.

It is this text that sets the tone for understanding the value of men and women in God's eyes. And it is this text that gives us a brief but powerful glimpse into the importance of both mother and father in the creation of new life. Stories of origins are accounts of what is most fundamental to a people. It is this equality of the role of father and mother that allows the author of Proverbs to say: "Hear, my child, the discipline of your father, and do not forsake the teaching of your mother" (Prov. 1:8, *Tanakh*).

This obedience to God's commandments, taught to Israel's successive generations by its mothers and fathers, brings about God's purpose for the world's design: a world that can be a dwelling place for God.

—SHARON PACE

The Grounding of Marriage
in the Order of Creation
(Genesis 2:18–24)

Genesis 2:18–24 recounts in a wonderful fashion the creation of woman as man's companion and the man's jubilant reaction to meeting her for the first time. The story is tinged with humor, for after God decides that it is not good for the man to be alone, he makes the animals who turn out to be unsatisfactory companions. The depiction of God as creating through a process of trial and error no doubt tickled the fancy of the original hearers.

A key term in the passage is the Hebrew *'ezer*, translated variously as "help-meet," "helpmate," "helper," and "partner." There are actually two Semitic roots that could be the underlying root of this Hebrew term. One means help in the sense of rescue or save. This is the root that most translators assume is the source of the term, even though translations involving the English word *help* hardly convey the full meaning. The other root means strength. The following Hebrew phrase, *kenegdo*, which is usually translated "fit for him" or the like occurs only here in the Bible. In later Mishnaic Hebrew, *neged* means "equal." Thus *'ezer kenegdo* may best be translated as "a power equal to him" (see Freedman 1983).

Whatever words are chosen to translate the Hebrew phrase, it is abundantly clear that the woman is not created as a subservient domestic servant. She is man's alter ego, his mirror image. She is not created simply for the purpose of procreation, nor simply to help the man till and keep the land. She is created as his equal partner and companion.

The popular saying that woman was created not from Adam's head to dominate him, not from his feet to be controlled by him, but from his rib to stand by his side is a postbiblical understanding, but it is consistent with the meaning of *'ezer kenegdo*. The rib possibly had its origins long before the Hebrew writer fashioned this story from more ancient material, in a wordplay in Sumerian between the word *rib* and the goddess of life, The Lady of the Rib.

When God brings the woman to Adam, he exclaims, "This at last is bone of my bones and flesh of my flesh" (2:23a). The "at last" indicates that after several false starts God has finally gotten it right. Finally, God has fashioned Adam's counterpart, the one who is like him, but unlike him all at the same time. By using Adam's rib as the basic building material, God has made a creature who is closely related to him. The phrase "bone of my bones and flesh of my flesh" is a formula of kinship (see Gen. 29:14; Judg. 9:2–3; 2 Sam. 5:1; 19:13). Phyllis Trible calls this first meeting of Adam and the as-yet-unnamed Eve the birth of eros, of sexual attraction (1983, 80). The joyful tone of 2:23 and the narrator's comments in 2:24 relating the preceding event to the union of male and female confirms that Adam's joy includes sexual attraction.

The wordplay in Genesis 2:23b, in which Adam says, "this one shall be called Woman, for out of Man this one was taken" is based on the similar sounds of man ('sh) and woman ('ishah), though the words may not be as related as they appear. Again, the main point is the kinship between Adam and Eve.

Although Adam's joy at meeting one who is like him but unlike him includes sexual attraction, it is not limited to sexual attraction any more than marriage is only about sex. The narrator's comment in 2:24 that "therefore a man leaves his father and his mother and clings to his wife, and they become one flesh," which is almost surely a later addition since Adam had no parents to leave, includes but goes beyond sexual union. The one flesh is not simply the physical union of sexual intercourse, nor simply the child that is the fruit of that union, but includes the spiritual and emotional intimacy that develops between partners over a lifetime of learning to live together in love.

Although the narrator's comment is framed androcentrically, focusing on the man's leaving his parents and joining his wife, it is equally true that women must psychologically leave father and mother and join their husbands. This leaving does not mean that husbands and wives divorce themselves completely from their original families. It does mean that their primary allegiance shifts as they create their own family.

Genesis 2:24 is sometimes interpreted to mean that monogamous marriage is the only form of partnership sanctioned by scripture. The Hebrew Bible is full of stories of other arrangements that are narrated with no explicit censure. Sarah gives Abraham Hagar as wife when she cannot conceive. Jacob marries the sisters Rachel and Leah and also their handmaids. David has several wives. Although there is rivalry between some of these co-wives, David's wives are not pictured as jealous of each other, though they do not have easy lives. Although polygamy seems strange to Westerners, in some parts of the world it is common and is accepted in some Christian communities, at least as an accommodation to preexisting conditions.

In recent debates over whether homosexual behavior is sinful, Genesis 2:24 has been cited as evidence that the only sexual pattern acceptable to God is heterosexual monogamous marriage. However, read in the context of the larger canon, whether the Jewish canon or any of the Christian canons, in which other patterns not only exist but are implicitly approved—especially the single life practiced by Jeremiah and Jesus—it is difficult to maintain that heterosexual monogamous marriage is the only pattern acceptable to God. Isaiah 56:4–5 welcomes eunuchs into the Israelite community. Jesus also allows for the possibility of eunuchs (Matt. 19:10–12).

Genesis 2:24 describes the most usual pattern. Most humans mate, but life can be full for individuals who remain single or who become single for various reasons after a period of marriage. The community that the phrase "one flesh" refers to can be achieved outside of a sexual relationship. In a similar way Jesus broadens the definition of family when he says, "whoever does the will of my Father in heaven is my brother and sister and mother" (Matt. 12:50).

Whether the interpretation of Genesis 2:24 as the usual pattern rather than the normative pattern leaves open the door for monogamous homosexual relationships is debated. Genesis 2:24 interpreted in canonical context does not clearly condemn homosexual partnerships; neither does it clearly approve of them.

Jesus specifically quotes Genesis 2:24 in answering a question about divorce (Matt. 19:3–9; Mark 10:2–9). He cites it as evidence that marriage is intended as a permanent arrangement. Human experience confirms that it takes a lifetime for deep intimacy to develop between mates. Divorce is sometimes necessary (though it is entered into too quickly in many cases), but it short-circuits the development of the one flesh that is the ultimate purpose and meaning of marriage.

Bibliography

Freedman, R. David. "Woman, a Power Equal to Man: Translation of Woman as a 'Fit Helpmate' for Man is Questioned," *Biblical Archaeology Review* 9/1 (Jan/Feb 1983): 56–58.

Trible, Phyllis. *God and the Rhetoric of Sexuality: Overtures to Biblical Theology* (Philadelphia: Fortress Press, 1983).

—ALICE OGDEN BELLIS

The Ten Commandments
(Exodus 20:2–17; Deuteronomy 5:6–21)

Each commandment must be understood within the context of the Deca-logue in its entirety. This article first considers the whole and then focuses on the commandment regarding parents and children.

The numbering of the commandments varies in the Jewish, Reformed, and Lutheran-Roman Catholic traditions. The Reformed numbering is followed here, with the prohibition of graven images constituting the Third Command-ment (Exod. 20:4; Deut. 5:8; it is elided with the Second in other enumera-tions), and a single coveting commandment (also characteristic of the Jewish numbering, which includes Exod. 20:2 as the first "word"). The number ten is fixed in the tradition (Exod. 34:28; Deut. 10:4).

The Hebrew Bible contains a number of Decalogue-like formulations like Exodus 34:17–26, but only Exodus 20:2–17 and Deuteronomy 5:6–21 are strictly so called. The Exodus version is probably the oldest, but the history of the transmission of the Decalogue remains obscure. The commandments were probably originally brief and negative (see Exod. 21:15, 17 and 35:3 for nega-tive formulations of the Fourth and Fifth Commandments). The differences be-tween Exodus and Deuteronomy (see below) suggests that over time they were expanded or adjusted in view of new community needs.

The hortatory character of the expansions (for example, Deut. 5:13–16) sug-gests that worship was the primary life setting for the commandments. Their collection in simple, direct, easy-to-remember form no doubt fostered a use be-yond the sanctuary and kept them alive in the community. That prophets like Jeremiah (7:9) and Hosea (4:2) cited them demonstrates their familiarity and importance. Their catechetical use may be postbiblical, yet the second-person-singular addressee and the redactional placement in both Exodus and Deuteronomy immediately prior to the two basic pentateuchal law collections suggests such an interest (see also the language in Exod. 24:12; Deut. 6:1–2, 7). This placement indicates that the Decalogue constituted a set of "core val-ues" that grounded the laws that follow and provided a base line for ongoing law development. That the Decalogue is presented as the unmediated speech of God reinforces its special place among the laws.

The two versions of the Decalogue are virtually identical, varying primarily in the motivations for the Sabbath commandment (compare Exod. 20:9–11 with Deut. 5:13–15). The inversion of "field" and "wife" in the Tenth Com-mandment in Deuteronomy (compare Exod. 20:17 and Deut. 5:21) is an im-portant change in that "wife" is removed from a list of property, suggesting a higher role for women. Such changes in the Decalogue, however minor, give an inner-biblical warrant for ongoing change in its formulation (as with other laws). The inclusion of the husband in the Tenth Commandment is an obvious example. A multitude of sins is often drawn into the interpretation of the commandments, but many threats to community like rape and child abuse were not mentioned explicitly and unfortunately may have been considered less important, perhaps shaping perspectives through the centuries.

The commandments are apodictic in form, straightforward declarations expressing core community concerns. No juridical consequences for disobedience are specified. Their being obligatory is not conditional upon their enforceability. As such, they are not motivated by negative reinforcement. These commands have a fundamental personal orientation, given by the "the LORD *your* God" (Exod. 20:2). The address to the individual "you" lifts up the importance of internal motivation rather than external coercion, as do the motivations that are attached to the Fourth and Fifth Commandments. The introductory reference to the exodus (Exod. 20:2) demonstrates that what follows is not a new form of slavery but continues the liberation theme.

Though the addressee is individual, the focus is less on private welfare than on protecting the life and health of the *community* (so the law generally, see Deut. 5:33). The link between Sabbath and creation (Exod. 20:11) suggests that the order of the entire creation is at stake; to obey the commandments is to be in tune with God's creational intentions. The issue is not simply order but life itself, salvation in the broad sense (see Exod. 20:2). That eight commandments are negatively formulated indicates that the focus is on the outer limits of conduct rather than specific behaviors. At the same time, that two commandments are positive implicitly commends the constructive side for each. The concern is not simply to protect and restrain but to promote the good, in much the same manner that Luther's Small Catechism asserts that the injunction against bearing false witness invites speaking well of the neighbor.

Exodus 34:1 speaks of two tables, but the division point is not made clear. It is common to divide the commandments between the Fourth and the Fifth. The first four focus on the relationship with God; the second six center on the neighbor.

In the first table, the First Commandment is considered the most important, especially in Deuteronomy, where it is reformulated positively in 6:5. The remaining commandments in the first table specify something of what it means to obey the First Commandment: exclusion of other gods, the divine name and the associated reputation of God in the world, and the setting aside of a specific time for remembering the work of God in both creation (Exodus) and redemption (Deuteronomy).

The second table of the law includes neighbors most close and those more distant. It lifts up the family first of all, especially the relationship between parents and children, and includes the faithfulness of husband and wife both in deed (adultery) and inner life (coveting). It is concerned about acts against the neighbor regarding life, spouse, and property (killing, adultery, stealing) as well as words (bearing false witness) and inner attitudes (coveting).

The primary placement of the Fifth Commandment in the second table of the law recognizes the foundational and universal character of the relationships involved. At no age do people cease to be children of parents. It is generally agreed, however, that the commandment is directed more toward adults than children. Perhaps especially in mind are cases where elderly parents are misused or abused when their physical and mental powers have receded. This dimension should be clearly evident in the teaching of this commandment to children, so as not to imply that they are the special object of its concern or that there will come a day when this obligation has been removed.

The inclusion of adults shows that obedience is not at the center of what it means to "honor." Honoring gathers up all dealings with parents, especially respect, esteem, care, affection, and appreciation. Physical and verbal abuse issues are lifted up in Exodus 21:15, 17. No one specific behavior is commanded; rather, this is an open-ended, never-ending invitation to respond in any way that honors parents. It is notable that father and mother are equally to be honored (see Lev. 19:3), and hence both are considered divine means for the life, health, and good order of the community. This is lifted up in the extension of the commandment, most fully in Deuteronomy 5:16.

In view of the "inner-biblical warrant" noted above, if this commandment were written today, it would take into account the grave problem of child abuse and promote parental responsibility toward children (see Luke 1:17; Eph. 6:2–4). It would also take into account that governmental authority at various levels has often been given responsibility for the commandment (as, for example, in nursing homes), and that in this case, adult children need to monitor how their governmental surrogates are handling honor. The extension of this commandment by the Reformers to include such authorities is legitimately based on such texts as Proverbs 24:21 and 1 Peter 2:13–17.

From a New Testament perspective, Christians have not been made exempt from these commandments. In fact, Matthew 5:17–48 (see Matt. 19:18–22, which cites only commandments from the second table, as in Rom. 13:9) states that they are to be pushed to their deepest level in the human spirit. The commandment to love (Matt. 22:37–40, where Jesus brings the two tables of the law together) does not set the commandments aside but incorporates them and extends them without limit as part of what it means to do what love requires.

Bibliography

Brueggemann, Walter. "Exodus," in *The New Interpreter's Bible* (Nashville: Abingdon Press, 1994), 839–53.

Fretheim, Terence E. *Exodus* (Louisville, Ky.: John Knox Press, 1991), 220–39.

Harrelson, Walter. *The Ten Commandments and Human Rights* (Philadelphia: Fortress Press, 1980).

Miller, Patrick D. *Deuteronomy* (Louisville, Ky.: John Knox Press, 1990), 71–97.

—TERENCE E. FRETHEIM

The Family in Community
(Leviticus 25)

Leviticus 25 continues the discussion of sacred and ritual times begun in Leviticus 23. It provides instructions for the observance of the sabbatical year (vv. 1–7). Every seventh year the land is to be given a rest, an extension of the rest associated with the Sabbath day (see Gen. 2:1–3; Lev. 23:3). The chapter also provides instructions for the observance of the year of jubilee (vv. 8–17). The Israelites are to count off "seven weeks of years," and in this year (whether the forty-ninth or the fiftieth is uncertain), land that has been rented out is returned to its original holders, and Israelites who have become indentured slaves are released. The chapter then addresses problems that might arise in the observance of jubilee (vv. 18–24) and in the redemption of indebted or indentured persons (vv. 25–55).

Theologically, these socioeconomic instructions are related to the ritualization of sacred times already anticipated in the initial process of creation (Gen. 1:14–15; 2:2–3) and concretized in the construction of the sacred year and its festivals (Lev. 23; 25). Narratively, the chapter constitutes part of the divine instructions for the construction of the sacred, covenant community ritually brought into being at Mt. Sinai (the larger narrative complex associated with Sinai is found in Exod. 19:1–Num. 10:10). Thus, the discussion of "family" in this text reflects multiple contexts: social and ritualized enactment, the theological construction of sacred times, creation theology, and the story of Israel's redemption and existence as a people in covenant with God. The economic status and well-being of the individual and the family are made to depend on the ongoing history of the community.

"The land" and "the Israelite" are the two thematic focal points of the chapter. Two primary statements provide the context for the discussion. First, the land belongs to Yahweh, and the Israelites dwell upon it as guests (vv. 23–24). Yahweh has assigned a piece of land to each family. Although the land itself may not be bought and sold, in a time of economic difficulty, the *use* of the land may be "sold." The original "owner," however, retains the right to redeem (that is, "buy back") the land. In the jubilee year the land reverts to "the primary holder." Second, Yahweh brought the Israelites out of Egypt, and they are the servants of Yahweh (v. 55). Because of this, no Israelite may become the permanent slave of another. Indentured or indebted Israelites must be "released" in the jubilee year. Thus, Yahweh's redemption of Israel from oppression and Yahweh's gracious gift of the land provide the foundations for the socioeconomic rulings in this text.

Verses 25–55 form the heart of this chapter's discussion of family. There are five basic units within this material: vv. 25–28, 29–34, 35–38, 39–46, and

47–55. Verses 25–28 provide the basic scenario. If a person encounters financial difficulty and rents out a piece of land to another person, the land may be "redeemed" in one of three ways. The closest relative, referred to as the *go'el* (v. 16), may, on behalf of the indebted relative, pay the debt on the land and thereby redeem it. The original holder, should circumstances allow, may do the same. Finally, if the land is not redeemed by the individual or a relative, it reverts to the original holder in the jubilee year (v. 28). The chapter clearly understands "redemption" to include economic status and well-being.

Following a discussion of houses and levitical property (vv. 29–34), the text addresses the status of an Israelite who becomes economically dependent on a relative (vv. 35–38). This person is to be treated as a resident non-Israelite (a *ger;* v. 35). Such a person may work for wages, may not be charged interest, and may not be used to make a profit (vv. 36–37). Here God's redemption of Israel from Egypt serves as a model for social relations within the Israelite community. Story and social practice are significantly related.

Verses 39–46 address the situation of Israelites who sell themselves to an Israelite who is not a family member (vv. 39–43) and the status of non-Israelite slaves (vv. 44–46). If an Israelite works for another in order to receive wages or pay a debt, he or she must be set free in the jubilee year (vv. 39–41). Such persons may not become permanent slaves, and they must not be treated harshly. Harsh treatment is also prohibited for non-Israelite slaves.

Finally, if a non-Israelite "buys" an Israelite (vv. 47–55), it is the responsibility of relatives to secure the release of the person. This situation parallels the "redemption" of the land, except in this case the concern is the economic "release" of a person. The individual may also secure his or her own release. If neither of these options becomes a reality, then release of the individual must come in the jubilee year. It is the responsibility of the Israelite community to make certain that the Israelite in this situation is not treated harshly. In this case, the whole community becomes an extended family and is charged to watch over the well-being and status of one of its own.

One central emphasis in these rulings is the "near-kin redeemer" (the *go'el*). Three primary groupings constituted the Israelite family structure: the tribe, the clan, and the household. The rulings in Leviticus 25 point to the clan (*mishpahah*) as the context for near-kin relations. The redeemer may be a brother, an uncle, a cousin, or a family member of one's own flesh (for "flesh" relations and efforts to construct "family" in terms of allowed and forbidden sexual partners, see Lev. 18 and 20). In addition to the redemption of land and indebted or indentured relatives, the near-kin redeemer was responsible to avenge the murder of a family member (Num. 35) and to produce and raise a male heir for a deceased male relative (Deut. 25:5–10). The extended family was responsible to watch over and protect the economic well-being, safety, and lives of its members.

The rulings in Leviticus 25 recognize that the community exists in the context of God's redemptive activity and grace. The life of the community must reflect the life of God. At the same time, the individual exists within a specific family within the larger Israelite community. The life of the extended family also must reflect the life of God. In this way, the individual, the family, and the community become a reflection of God's redemptive and gracious activity. In this text, redemption is understood in terms of economic realities. Land and the economic status of the individual Israelite are central concerns.

In Leviticus 25, socioeconomic concerns for the individual and extended family are extended to the larger creation story of the nation of Israel. The rulings on land and debt reflect theological constructs drawn from the nation's stories of creation and redemption. Yahweh has redeemed Israel, the family of God, and has placed the Israelites on the land as a gift and act of grace. Yahweh's creative and redemptive activities demand equitable and just treatment of all persons within the community. It is the responsibility of the extended family to watch over and protect the rights and economic stability of the family. At the same time, should the family be unable to help, Yahweh has established a means for the land to return to its original holder and for Israelites to gain their freedom in the ritualized observance of jubilee. Land returns to its original holder, and freedom from debt is granted to all Israelites. Redemption is understood as economic and personal freedom and is grounded in the gracious activity of Yahweh and the responsible and caring activity of the extended family.

Bibliography

Lemche, N. P. "The manumission of slaves—the fallow year—the sabbatical year—the jobel year," *Vetus Testamentum* 26 (1976): 38–59.

Ringe, S. H. *Jesus, Liberation and the Biblical Jubilee* (Philadelphia: Fortress Press, 1985).

Westbrook, R. *Property and the Family in Biblical Law* (Sheffield: JSOT Press, 1991), Supplement Series 113.

Wright, C.J.H. *God's People in God's Land: Family, Land, and Property in the Old Testament* (Grand Rapids: Wm. B. Eerdmans Publishing Co., 1990).

—FRANK H. GORMAN, JR.

A Prophetic Critique of Divorce
(Malachi 2:10–16)

The prophet Malachi is exceptional in the Hebrew Bible in adopting a critical attitude toward divorce. The relevant passage is found in Malachi 2:10–16. The standard translations of this passage conclude with the statement, "For I hate divorce, says the LORD, the God of Israel . . . ," and so render the passage as an unequivocal condemnation of divorce. Malachi, so understood, contrasts sharply with Deuteronomy 24:1–4, which assumes that a man can divorce his wife if "he finds something objectionable about her"; with Hosea 2, which speaks metaphorically of God divorcing Israel; and, in the Second Temple period, with Ezra, who required that Jews who had married foreign women divorce them. He is also in contrast with Jewish practice, as reflected in the Elephantine papyri from fifth-century Egypt and documents from the Dead Sea region that date from the Common Era and later in the Mishnah and Talmud.

The passage addresses two related but distinct transgressions (see v. 13: "this again [or: secondly] you do," author's translation). In the first instance, Judah is said to have married the daughter of a foreign god. Scholarship is sharply divided on the nature of this offense (for a summary of the debate see Hugenberger 1994, 27–47). One school of thought takes the daughter of a foreign god to mean a goddess. This interpretation is not required by the expression "daughter of a foreign god," but the phrase does carry implications of syncretism and idolatry. The more usual view is that the passage refers to marriage with foreign women, a phenomenon well known in the Persian period. Those who married foreign women were likely to give some acknowledgment to their cult and their gods. Yet the Jews who are guilty of this had not abandoned the cult of the Lord; otherwise they would not be concerned at the loss of one to bring an offering to the Lord of Hosts (2:12). The offense is syncretism rather than outright apostasy.

The second half of the passage (Mal. 2:13–16) deals more directly with problems of marriage and divorce. Here we are told that God refuses to accept the offerings of the Judeans "because the Lord was a witness between you and the wife of your youth, to whom you have been faithless, though she is your companion and your wife by covenant." Some scholars have denied that there is any reference to human marriage here, arguing that YHWH is the wife of youth, with whom Judah had a covenant (see Glazier-McDonald 1987, who concludes that the passage refers both to the divorced wife and to YHWH). Even if we accept the possibility that Malachi could reverse the usual gender roles by casting YHWH as wife, this line of interpretation would seem to be precluded by the statement that YHWH is witness "between you and the wife of your youth" (Mal. 2:14). There can be little doubt that the reference is to the breakup of actual marriages. Indeed, even if the passage were meant to refer metaphorically to the cult of YHWH, the metaphorical statement must still be intelligible on the primary, literal level.

Hosea's metaphor of marriage between God and Israel was conventional in its view of the adulterous wife. At the very least, Malachi is breaking with convention in denouncing the unfaithful husband. In contrast, the more typical biblical view is found in Proverbs 2:17, where it is the "strange woman" who "forsakes the partner of her youth and forgets her sacred covenant."

In view of the reference to the daughter of a foreign god in the preceding passage, it is commonly argued that the prophet was condemning his contemporaries for divorcing their Jewish wives in order to marry foreign women. There is no actual evidence, however, that this was the case. If it were, we might expect the prophet to mention it first, before the daughter of the foreign god, since such divorces would have paved the way for the idolatrous marriage. It is more likely that the problem of divorce is linked to the idolatrous marriage only as another instance of faithless behavior. It is noteworthy that the prophet does not call for the divorce of "the daughter of a foreign god" or give explicit sanction to divorce in any context.

The explicit mention of divorce in 2:16 is beset with textual difficulties, and the verse is possibly corrupt. The phrase usually rendered "For I hate divorce" reads *kî śānē' šallah* in the Masoretic text. The grammatical forms of *śānē'* and *šallah* are problematic. The verb *šallah,* "send," is usually taken as an infinitive, with the force of an abstract noun ("divorce"). The traditional interpretation appears to take *śānē'* as a verbal adjective used as a participle, with an implied first-person pronoun, so "I hate." But there is no first-person pronoun in the context. D. L. Petersen avoids this problem by translating "divorce is hateful" (1995, 194). Alternatively, the word *sane* can be construed as a third-person perfect, "he hated/hates," with an indefinite subject. By minor emendation, *šallah* can be repointed as a piel perfect, *šillah,* "he sent away." The problems of this phrase are already reflected in the ancient versions. Some Greek manuscripts read "But if you hate and send away . . . ," and others "But if you hate, send away!" (taking *šallah,* quite grammatically, as an imperative). The Scroll of the Minor Prophets from Qumran supports the latter Greek reading, thereby permitting, or even urging, divorce. In fact, this interpretation has broad support in the ancient versions (Vulgate, Targum) and in traditional Jewish interpretation (Talmud, Rashi, Kimchi, Maimonides). Nonetheless, it is difficult to reconcile with the remainder of the verse, which refers to covering one's garment with violence and ends with a warning against faithlessness. Malachi clearly intended to condemn divorce. The ancient Hebrew text in the Scroll of the Minor Prophets must be read as a correction of the text preserved by the Masoretes, attempting to clarify its sense and reconcile it with Jewish tradition.

The verb *śānē',* "hate," is commonly used in contexts of divorce, and indeed is often taken as a synonym for divorce in the Elephantine papyri. "To hate" in this context is simply a technical term for divorce, for whatever reason. In light of this observation, the NRSV translation, "I hate divorce," is almost certainly wrong. The expression in Malachi should be translated "for one repudiates, divorces . . . and covers his garment with violence." The subject is indefinite. The force of the statement is that one who "hates and divorces" is openly unjust.

This statement clarifies the "faithless action" against the wife of youth in Malachi 2:14. Malachi states no exceptions and makes no distinction between divorce that is justified and that which is not.

It is possible, of course, that Malachi assumed distinctions that he did not make explicit. Prophets are not lawyers and are not wont to make fine distinctions. Perhaps all we can safely infer from Malachi's enigmatic text is that he viewed the practice of divorce in his day as excessive and unjust. The concern of the prophet, however, is very different from that of the law codes and marriage contracts. He is not attempting to balance rights and obligations in a realistic and pragmatic way but to articulate an ideal and denounce its betrayal.

It is also possible that the statement "he repudiates, divorces . . ." is a secondary addition to the text of Malachi (see Petersen 1995, 204). This might explain the awkwardness of the sudden use of the third person. If this is so, Malachi may have been condemning the marital infidelity of husbands (a striking position in itself) rather than divorce. In this case, however, we would have to say that the glossator was more daringly original than the prophet, and this would be very unusual. It may be that the redactor was only making more explicit the abuses the prophet had in mind.

Malachi's understanding of marriage is obscured by the state of the text of 2:15, which ranks as one of the most difficult verses in the Hebrew Bible. The Hebrew literally reads, "and not one did, and had a remnant of spirit." The NRSV takes the "one" as a reference to God: "Did not one God make her?" The more usual interpretation, however, takes "one" as the object: "Did he (God) not make one?" On this interpretation there is an implied reference to Genesis 2:24, which says that man and wife become "one flesh." If this reading of the passage is accepted, then the word *še'ār*, "remnant," should most probably be repointed as *še'ār*, "flesh": "has He not made one, which has flesh and spirit." The text is too uncertain to warrant a confident conclusion, but many commentators see an allusion to Genesis here. The remainder of the verse, "and what does the one seek? godly offspring" (author's translation), can also be seen against a background in Genesis. In Genesis 1:28, the only injunction laid on the primal couple is to "increase and multiply and fill the earth" (author's translation), and this verse looms very large in the later Jewish understanding of marriage. On this interpretation, Malachi sees the goal of marriage in procreation. Extramarital relations are not constructive toward this goal. (See Prov. 5:16: "Should your springs be scattered abroad, streams of water in the streets?") Divorce is counterproductive. The tone of the prophet, however, is quite different from that of Proverbs. His outrage is primarily provoked by the injustice done to the divorced wife. While Malachi remains a solitary voice in the Hebrew Bible, his opposition to divorce was later taken up by the sectarians of the Dead Sea Scrolls (CD 4:20–5:2) and by Jesus of Nazareth.

Bibliography

Collins, J. J. "Marriage, Divorce, and Family in Second Temple Judaism," in *Families in Ancient Israel*, Leo Perdue, ed. (Louisville, Ky.: Westminster John Knox Press, 1997).

Glazier-McDonald, B. "Intermarriage, Divorce and the bat-'el nekar," *Journal of Biblical Literature* 106(1987): 603–11.

Hugenberger, G. P. *Marriage as a Covenant: A Study of Biblical Law and Ethics Governing Marriage, Developed from the Perspective of Malachi* (Leiden: Brill, 1994).

Petersen, D. L. *Zechariah 9–14 and Malachi* (Louisville, Ky.: Westminster John Knox Press, 1995).

—JOHN J. COLLINS

Naboth's Vineyard:
A Clash of Family Values
(1 Kings 21:1–16)

The story of Naboth's vineyard in 1 Kings 21 is told in rich narrative detail and has many salient themes. These include the abuse of royal power, the explanation for the eventual overthrow of Ahab's house, and the threat posed by a foreign queen to Israel's religious and social order. Within this story, however, we also see a fundamental clash of family values. To discover this and to highlight some implications this has for family and scripture, it is helpful to move through the story itself, noting its prominent features.

The story opens with a potential land deal (vv. 1–4). Naboth owns a vineyard. Ahab wants to procure it and so makes an offer. Naboth nixes the deal so that Ahab goes home depressed. Sounds routine. Yet within these simple actions one finds a significant theological framework indicating what the characters represent and why they act as they do. First Naboth: he is described as the Jezreelite who has a vineyard in Jezreel (v. 1). This is more than a mere geographical reference. It is a depiction of Naboth's identity. Who he is, where he lives, and the land that is his are all intertwined. This is borne out in his response to Ahab. Naboth refuses the deal not because of a concern about its fairness but because of his theology of land and family. He tells Ahab that the vineyard is his "ancestral inheritance" (v. 3). This means that he understands the vineyard to be a sacred gift from God given not just to him but to his family. Family is more than his immediate relatives. It includes his whole family that has gone before him and his family that will come after him. For Naboth this is a family affair, not a business affair. His family values recall Exodus 20:12; Leviticus 25:13–28; Numbers 27:1–11; 36:1–13 wherein the land given to the family by God is to be a perpetual gift for the family, wherein the landed inheritance marks a family's reality and identity as well as provides for its livelihood. To Naboth this vineyard is a familial reality and an identity marker spanning time. To exploit that for his own short-term advantage would be an act of profaning (of making common) the sacred gift that God gave to his family as its legacy. Hence his family values (which include God, land, the past, and the future) forbid him from selling the land to Ahab.

Ahab does not share the family values of Naboth. Samaria, his royal place of belonging, is not an ancestral inheritance given graciously by God. Rather it is a royal possession purchased just a generation ago by his father, Omri (1 Kings 16:24). Ahab also has a palace in Jezreel, and so to him land is something you get for a price to satisfy royal desires. Hence he makes a very fair offer so that he can use that vineyard for a royal vegetable garden. He offers Naboth a better vineyard or cash. It is Naboth's choice. But as we have noted, it is not Naboth's choice. Naboth does not so much refuse Ahab as he lives by his family values. When Ahab hears Naboth's response, he returns home so depressed that he goes to bed, turns to the wall, and refuses to eat (v. 4). He seems to know that he will never get his vegetable garden.

Jezebel now enters the drama as a good wife to Ahab. She comes to see what is ailing her husband (v. 5). In recounting the land deal gone sour, Ahab puts a selective spin on the details he chooses to give his royal spouse (v. 6). For example, he does not say how he came to Naboth, one of his subjects, as a polite equal. He does not tell her how he justified the deal to Naboth. He leaves out the offer of a "better" vineyard. He says absolutely nothing about God or ancestral inheritance, which was at the crux of the matter for Naboth. Though Naboth is a man devoted to God and family, Ahab presents him to Jezebel as an insubordinate subject who thumbs his nose at the king.

Jezebel's response to this selective report reveals her family values. Her comment, "Do you now exercise royal rule over Israel?" (v. 7a) could be rhetorical or sarcastic. Yet in either case her next steps show that in this matter she, not Ahab, exercises royal rule over Israel. She tells her husband to get up, eat up, and cheer up. Then she pronounces, "I myself will give to you the vineyard of Naboth the Jezreelite" (v. 7b). Here we start to see the clash of family values in the story. What Naboth cannot give to King Ahab because God has given it to his family as ancestral legacy, Jezebel claims she herself will give to her husband Ahab. Jezebel, too, has family values. She is daughter of one king and spouse of another king (1 Kings 16:31). She is as loyal to her values as was Naboth. What she values is the royal family's power to rule over its subjects as they see fit. To stand in the way of the royal family is blasphemy. Her job as the king's spouse is to support him in every way possible. To that end she hatches and carries out a plot so that she can give her husband the vineyard he desires.

Jezebel exercises royal power by writing letters in the king's name and sealing them with his seal (v. 8a). The letters are addressed to the family leaders in Naboth's own hometown. The plot is simple: declare a fast; seat Naboth in the prominent position of the gathering; put two sons of worthlessness at each side of him; have them accuse Naboth of blasphemy against God and the king; take Naboth out and stone him to death. Her plot reveals that Jezebel understands the cultural and theological means available to her to get the job done. As a woman in a patriarchal culture she is automatically in a subservient position. Consequently she knows that she must work through men. In this case, she will work through her husband's name and seal, the elders of Jezreel, and the sons of worthlessness. While she does not share the theology of Israel, she uses it to her full advantage. A fast was a solemn religious occasion in Israel. Here it seems related to a communal catastrophe, and through such a fast divine approval or relief would be sought. Jezebel uses it as a religious opportunity to uncover in public the culprit responsible for the communal catastrophe. She knows the requirement for two witnesses in capital cases (Deut. 17:6). She knows that stoning is an appropriate capital punishment (Deut. 17:7). Ironically, although her husband left theology out of the vineyard deal when he reported it to Jezebel, she uses theology to carry out her plot to procure the vineyard for her husband.

The family heads are loyal and obedient not to God, as was their neighbor Naboth, but to the royal house. And so they implement Jezebel's plot (21:11–13). Even though their instructions were in the king's name and bore the king's seal, they report back to the one who exercises royal power in Israel in this matter. They tell Jezebel, "Naboth has been stoned; he is dead" (21:14). Jezebel's family values of royal power seem to have won out. Upon hearing of Naboth's stoning and death, she delivers on her promise to give her husband the vineyard of Naboth the Jezreelite. Though she has heard that Naboth was stoned, she does not tell this detail to Ahab. Instead she just says that Naboth is dead (21:15). For his part, Ahab never asks how the vineyard he could not buy with money because of Naboth's family values is now available to him. Instead, he goes to possess the vineyard of Naboth the Jezreelite (21:16).

Ultimately, however, Ahab will not possess the vineyard. God sends the prophet Elijah to hold him accountable for this despicable act (21:17–19). In the end this accountability will mean the overthrowing of Ahab's family (21:20–22) including the death of Jezebel (21:23; 2 Kings 9:30–37) and the execution of Ahab's successor, his son Joram, at the site that Ahab wanted and which Jezebel thought she gave to her husband: the vineyard of Naboth the Jezreelite (2 Kings 9:21–26).

In what ways might this scripture relate to our understandings of family? It might be tempting to claim that Naboth had family values while someone like Jezebel could not. (Today, how often do we hear a group claim that they have family values while those they oppose lack family values?) Jezebel has family values. She is extremely loyal to her family values. But perhaps therein lies the problem. Her family values center almost exclusively on the royal family. To that end, her values lead to conduct that is exploitative, deceptive, and abusive to others beyond the family. She is not part of a larger community; she manipulates community for family goals. She deals in secrecy, which leads to death. Her horizons extend no further than issues concerning the family's power and what the family can attain for itself. She fails to consider the implications such family goals and actions have on the powerless or on community. Even religion is a tool to be used for her family's ends. God is never really taken account of, and accountability before God is never considered. The family is the be-all and end-all. Yet that which she does so successfully for family ultimately contributes to the demise of her family as is often the case when family becomes its own exclusive focus and motive.

Naboth, however, lives out of family values that have much wider perspectives. He does not function with regard to short-term advantage or immediate gain for his family. He focuses on what God has established for the healthy functioning of a family and its identity in the long run. He is fully aware of his family heritage from the past and knows that his actions have significant implications for the family that will come after him. His family lives in community, not isolation (though in the story that community betrays him). Ultimately, he sees God as the giver and sustainer of healthy, ongoing family functioning. Consequently, he is intentional in making decisions that not only have family implications but are faithful to God's perspectives.

Both Jezebel and Naboth have family values. But the family values of Naboth extend beyond the family itself to include the past and the future and, most important of all, to include God. In this story from scripture family is a penultimate value under the auspices of God's ultimate values.

Bibliography

Nelson, Richard. *First and Second Kings* (Atlanta: John Knox Press, 1987), interpretation.

Trible, Phyllis. "Exegesis for Storytellers and Other Strangers," *Journal of Biblical Literature* 114 (1995): 3–19.

Walsh, Jerome. *1 Kings.* (Collegeville, Minn.: Liturgical Press, 1996).

Zakovitch, Yair. "Addendum: The Tale of Naboth's Vineyard," in *The Bible from Within: The Method of Total Interpretation,* Meir Weiss (Jerusalem: Magnes Press, The Hebrew University, 1984), 379–405.

—RICHARD P. CARLSON

Family Relationships as Metaphor
(Hosea 1–3)

Hosea 1–3 sets forth three acts or scenes that explore family relationships as metaphors for the relationship of God and the people of northern Israel. Hosea prophesied in the midst of the politically and religiously turbulent eighth-century B.C.E., a time just before northern Israel's destruction and exile at the hands of the Assyrian empire.

Hosea 1 begins with God's command to the prophet Hosea to marry "a wife of whoredom," that is, a prostitute or at least a woman who engages in promiscuous sexual relations outside the bonds of marriage. This prophetic act reflected the religious adultery of the Israelites: "for the land commits great whoredom by forsaking the LORD" (Hos. 1:2). Promises of fertility and abundant crops to worshippers of the Canaanite god Baal tempted Hosea's audience of northern Israelites away from their exclusive commitment to Israel's God, Yahweh. Hosea complies with God's command and marries Gomer, daughter of Deblaim. They give birth to three children. God instructs Hosea to name the three children "Jezreel," "Not-Pitied," and "Not-My-People." The names signify the judgment that is about to come upon northern Israel and the dissolution of the relationship between Yahweh and the people of Israel.

These descriptions of Israel's future judgment suddenly shift into affirmations of hope and promise as we come to the end of Hosea 1. Israel will undergo judgment but will not ultimately be destroyed. God will keep the divine promises of innumerable descendants first made to Israel's ancestors, Abraham and Sarah, in Genesis 13, 15, and 17. The Israelites will be called once again "Children of the living God." Both northern Israel and southern Judah will one day be gathered together and restored to their land. Hosea's son "Not-My-People" will be renamed "My People," and Hosea's daughter "Not-Pitied" will be renamed "Pitied" (Hos. 1:10–2:1).

A similar movement from judgment to reconciliation occurs in Hosea 2. The scene opens with the husband's plea to the children, "Plead with your mother . . . that she put away her whoring." The punishment for not doing so is a terrifying one: "I will strip her naked and expose her as in the day she was born. . . . And turn her into a parched land, and kill her with thirst" (Hos. 2:2–3). Because the wife has "played the whore," saying, "I will go after my lovers," the husband (God) will imprison her with a hedge of thorns and a wall so that she cannot find her lovers. The wife (Israel) believes she has earned and owns what her lovers have given her: "my bread and my water, my wool and my flax, my oil and my drink" (Hos. 2:5). Of her vines and her fig trees, the wife says, "These are my pay, which my lovers have given me" (Hos. 2:12). The husband (God) responds, "She did not know that it was I who gave her the grain, the wine, and the oil." God will take back all of her crops and produce and destroy them because she "went after her lovers, and forgot me, says the LORD" (Hos. 2:8, 12–13).

In Hosea 2:14–23 the reader once again experiences a wrenching shift from fierce and disturbing judgment to promises of reconciliation and restoration. "Therefore, I will now allure her, and bring her into the wilderness, and speak tenderly to her." Israel, God's spouse, will no longer call God "My Baal" ("My Master") but "My husband." Moreover, God promises, "I will take you for my wife forever . . . in righteousness and in justice, in steadfast love, and in mercy."

Hosea 3 provides a third and final exploration of the relationship of God and Israel through the metaphor of Hosea's relationship to an adulterous woman. God commands Hosea to "love a woman who has a lover and is an adulteress, just as the LORD loves the people of Israel, though they turn to other gods" (3:1). Hosea responds to this command by buying the woman for the price of a slave (fifteen shekels of silver and a measure of barley). Hosea instructs the woman not to have sexual relations with anyone, including himself, for "many days" as a sign that Israel will flounder in exile without political or religious leadership for "many days." As in chapters 1 and 2, however, God's last word is a promise: "the Israelites shall return and seek the LORD their God . . . in the latter days."

What insights into family structure, relationships, conflicts, and reconciliations can we gain from these chapters of Hosea? First of all, there are obvious difficulties that need to be faced squarely in this text. In the history of biblical interpretation, many commentators have been troubled by God's command to Hosea to marry a prostitute or adulteress woman. More recently, feminist and other commentators have expressed outrage at the extremely negative images of the woman or "wife of whoredom" in Hosea, the inequality of the relationship of the husband (God/Hosea) and the wife (Israel/Gomer), the humiliation of publicly stripping the woman naked before her lovers, the violence of turning her (the land/the woman) into a parched land and killing her with thirst, the constraint of her freedom by building walls around her, the confiscation and destruction of her material belongings and produce, and the purchase of her as if she were a slave. Even the seemingly positive words of God in Hosea 2:14–15 about God's "alluring her" and speaking "tenderly to her" after the preceding violence and humiliation sound to some readers like the typical cycle of domestic abuse: acts of violence followed by the abuser's renewed assurances of love and affection.

The text of Hosea 1–3 uses an ancient, time-bound, and scandalous model of family relationships as a metaphor for the relationship of God and the people of God. As is often true of prophetic speech, Hosea's metaphor of husband and adulterous wife sought to shock an audience into the recognition of its rebellion against God and its ultimate hope in God's mercy and faithfulness to God's promises. The text's purpose is not to legislate or condone a particular model of human marital relationship, but the harsh offense of the text cannot be easily ignored.

The images of Hosea 1–3 are informed by a male-dominated culture. Yet Hosea elsewhere undercuts a strictly patriarchal perspective. For example, God in Hosea 4:14 pronounces guilt not on the women who are prostitutes or who commit adultery but on the men who participate in such actions. The male metaphor of God as husband is balanced by images of God feeding and caring for children in Hosea 11; such images are typically more female than male images in ancient Israel's culture. Moreover, the metaphor of God as husband and Israel as wayward wife is primarily designed to lead the readers, whether male or female, into identifying themselves as the adulterous worshippers of other gods and recipients of God's restoring love. The metaphor is an equal-opportunity indictment and promise.

Can anything good come out of Hosea 1–3? The text, despite its difficulties, affirms several important dimensions of family and marriage that other biblical traditions would support. Hosea 1–3 affirms fidelity and exclusivity as a positive goal in intimate marriage relationships and in the relationship between God and human worshippers. But the text also acknowledges the reality of human failures to live in accord with that goal. Such failures led even God to sever the relationship with Israel for a time. God instructed Hosea to name his child, "Not-My-People," "for you are not my people and I am not your God" (Hos. 1:9). If God must at some extreme times sever relationships with God's own people for a time, humans may need to do the same in human marriages that have failed. Despite such human failings, whether in matters of human marriage or faith in God, God promises to be faithful to God's promises. God's people who endure the pain and tragedy of broken families and marriages need to hear the ultimate word of God's grace, forgiveness, and hope as strongly today as in Hosea's ancient time. The ultimate will of God is for a relationship shaped by important prophetic notions of righteousness and justice and love. God proclaims to Israel, "I will take you for my wife forever . . . in righteousness and in justice, in steadfast love and in mercy" (2:20). These expressions of God's final will for Israel provide an alternative model of marriage and family relationships shaped not by inequality, shame, and violence but by justice and love.

Bibiography

Sherwood, Yvonne. *The Prostitute and the Prophet: Hosea's Marriage in Literary-Theoretical Perspective* (Sheffield: Sheffield Academic Press, 1996).

Weems, Renita J. *Battered Love: Marriage, Sex, and Violence in the Hebrew Prophets* (Minneapolis: Fortress Press, 1995).

Yee, Gale A. "Hosea," *The Women's Bible Commentary*, Carol Newsome and Sharon Ringe, eds. (Louisville, Ky.: Westminster/John Knox Press, 1992), 195–202.

—DENNIS T. OLSON

A Good Man's Code of Ethics
(Job 31)

The book of Job is a literary masterpiece, and chapter 31 reveals the basis for the deity's extraordinary assessment of its hero as blameless and upright, a religious man who avoided evil. Forced by circumstances to defend his innocence, the hero unveils his heart for public scrutiny of inner motive and resultant deed. His oath of innocence is directed beyond the ears of the three friends with whom he has contended for two rounds of debate, plus a partial third one. Convinced that he will receive a more favorable hearing from the deity, Job first ventures into the land of nostalgia while recounting happier days, then contrasts those times with his present misery, before at last bombarding heaven's gates with a declaration of integrity aimed at undermining any indictment against him, human or divine.

Whether viewed as oath or ordeal, the confession is intended to force the silent deity to respond. Instead, the youthful Elihu berates the friends and Job for six chapters before the Lord answers from a whirlwind, entirely ignoring Job's claims and focusing attention on the wonders of nature beyond the human domain. Unencumbered by the urgency of a human social order, the Creator views the world from the standpoint of eternity, which removes humankind from the central position. The speeches silence the hero, without giving enough information to enable readers to discern the real nature of his submission. The framing narrative in prose recreates the idyllic past, oblivious to the intervening skepticism that has undermined such a worldview.

Job's declaration takes the form of an oath: "I swear by El that if I have done X then let Y happen to me." Presumably, one who emerges unscathed after such a bold outcry cannot be guilty. Parallels for these imprecations exist in the Egyptian Book of the Dead (chap. 125) and the Code of Hammurabi. Normally, the result clause is omitted, possibly to increase the psychological dread by leaving the punishment unspecified. Job dares to defy tradition, stating four times the actual punishment envisioned (vv. 8, 10, 22, 40). The total number of offenses is unclear; the complete number fourteen (twice seven) may be intended. The entire confession, an ordered cacophony, teems with verbal links and rhetorical features, the most powerful of which is Job's defiant appeal for a divine weighing of his heart (against the feather representing justice) and the upheld defense, personally signed by a proud prince who is prepared to display an indictment on his shoulders. On two occasions Job's words carry barbs directed against the deity, who in contrast to Job has abused a loyal servant and has neglected to set a guard over divine eyes.

Job's code of ethics is grounded in a primal bond akin to that of an infant for its mother. It is relational, not an abstraction of principles. An "I" has acknowledged a kinship with another, a "Thou." This bond extends to all others regardless of social status, and it reaches within the mind where motives and thoughts reside long before they issue in deeds. When a valued relationship fails, this code moves an individual to risk death in an effort to restore the lost ardor. The bond links all humankind in a single family, assuring protection for marginalized citizens—the widow, the orphan, and the resident alien in the Bible—and even producing goodwill for enemies. Nevertheless, even Job's code of ethics suffers from the controls exercised by all worldviews in at least two respects. It presents a proud man whose view of women needs refinement ("If I have committed adultery, let my wife become someone else's sex object," v. 10, author's translation). It also indicts the deity when virtue is not rewarded.

However much this chapter rises above others of its day, both in literary power and religious sentiment, it still belongs to an ancient era. How can modern readers appropriate its insights and apply its teachings within the narrow confines of family life? The only legitimate means of doing so is by analogy, and the restraints of space in this volume prevent elaborate discussion. They do allow some suggestions that readers may carry to their logical conclusions.

A beginning point is the distinction between secret sins and those apparent to society at large. Naturally, sexual offenses span both areas, for even a secret rendezvous affects at least two persons. Job's insistence that he has not lusted implies that he has refused to view another person as an object of personal gratification. Similarly, his disavowal of adultery means that he recognizes the sacred bond of marriage and the sanctity of a family. The image of placing a guard over the eyes recalls that of securing the lips from unbecoming speech in Psalm 141:3. Both imply that the deity searches the mind and heart, so that nothing is hidden. The contemporary bombardment of the eyes with images chosen for maximal erotic appeal can be resisted by those who appreciate other persons' vulnerability and who value the family as the glue holding society together.

Other secret sins have social consequences as well. Deception, for example, in the form of fraudulent business practices, deprives others of good even though they do not know anything about the nefarious deeds. So, too, coveting. Greed leads to a consumerism characterized by slavery to "creature comforts" and the latest electronic gadget. This endless competition, already recognized by the observant author of Ecclesiastes, threatens the fabric of the community, resulting in disparity between the "haves" and the "have-nots." The natural capacity to deceive ourselves fuels this drive to obtain more. It can be overcome only by acknowledging the true owner of all things.

The social sins that Job disavows include a heartless abuse of power, an arrogance and unfeeling that denies the reality that all human beings constitute a single family, an inhospitable attitude that ignores suffering, and a vulnerability to peer pressure. Job views all people as creatures of one deity, and that includes the unfortunate of his day—slaves, widows, orphans. His compassion embraced them all, and he refused to bow to pressure from influential citizens. The modern reader can readily transfer God's concern for others to the contemporary scene with its vast array of citizens who have been marginalized on the basis of their race, religion, and income. One who takes seriously the link that unites us all in one big family will be compelled to feed the hungry, clothe the naked, and strive for a more just society. Like Job, this modern hero will become a parent to orphans, learn to extend goodwill to those who subscribe to dubious causes—the KKK, members of the free militias—while resisting their racism and paranoia to the end. Like Job, too, the modern individual who rises above the crowd will work to overcome the roots of poverty (and racism). Immigrants and migrant workers will be welcome in this person's society.

Two sins belonging to the secret category relate solely to the deity. Job denies having committed idolatry in either form, the worship of money or the adulation of nature. The issue is one of priority, the determining of ultimate concern. Job's inclusion of these two temptations stands as a constant reminder that the human creature, for whatever reason, tends to substitute perishable things for the eternal. The unknown author of the contest of Darius's Guards, recorded in 1 Esdras 3:1–4:41, relegates possessions and the sun to those things that eventually pass into oblivion, while the God of truth endures forever.

The declaration of innocence concludes on a surprising note, one that recalls the divine curse of the ground in Genesis 2–3. Job insists that he has honored the land, letting it lie fallow at appropriate seasons. The modern reader can certainly appreciate this ecological concern, and Job's counterpart will work at recycling, composting, preserving natural resources, saving endangered species, and the like. This will entail a lifestyle that attends to, among other things, the consumption of meat, use of water and other types of energy, the protection of the environment through every available means, planned parenthood, and the fair distribution of resources. The central role of the family in this concerted effort will move a step beyond Job 31, where the patriarch enjoys a position of honor above women and children. Happily, this concentration on the male hero, partly dictated by the plot, belongs to a bygone era. Not only has Job honored the land. He has not concealed his offense the way Adam (and Eve) did.

What does Job's confession of innocence contribute to contemporary ethical discussion as it pertains to family life? It goes beyond the external expression to inner motives; it pushes beyond legal requirements regarding slaves to the greater demands imposed by primal bonds; it defines ethical conduct comprehensively, embracing the whole body; it enlarges family ties to include the needy and even the hated; it acknowledges a single human family and only one creator. In short, Job answers Cain's question "Am I my brother's keeper?" with a resounding "yes." And my sister's keeper too.

—JAMES L. CRENSHAW

19

New Testament Scriptures and the Family

An Alternative Household Structure (Matthew 19–20)

Chapters 19–20 form a distinct section in the Gospel of Matthew as Jesus travels from Galilee (19:1) to Jerusalem (21:1). Scholars have struggled to identify how the chapters' subsections hold together. They have suggested that the journey to Jerusalem or instructions about discipleship unify them. But these claims lack specificity.

I suggest that the coherence of the two chapters is based in what the audience is assumed to know about household structures. Households were widely understood to comprise four standard features. Chapters 19–20 comprise subsections that utilize these four aspects. They employ characters that represent these dominant cultural understandings but show Jesus advocating a different structure. They depict the way of the cross (see 16:21–28) as a life that resists dominant values and structures.

Household Management and Structures

Discussion about what constitutes a household extends from Aristotle to the second century C.E. This tradition asserts that households are basic to a city or state's social order. Households consist of four elements: three relationships (husband-wife, father-children, master-slave) and a task (acquiring wealth). The household is androcentric, centered on the male. It is patriarchal and hierarchical because the husband/father/master rules over wife/children/slaves. The male manages the household. He also acquires and manages wealth outside the household and participates in a social network of obligations and duties. His wife is responsible for the private sphere inside the household. Discussions of household management focus, then, not just on a place but on societal ways of being, power, relationships, and the use of resources.

The material in Matthew 19–20 incorporates these four aspects of households.

19:3–12	Marriage and divorce
19:13–15	Children and the reign
19:16–30	Wealth and the household
20:1–16	The parable of the householder

20:17–28   Servants and ruling over
20:29–34   The healing of the blind men

The two chapters, though, do not endorse the hierarchical pattern of "ruling over." Rather, Jesus advocates that disciples live more egalitarian relationships. This alternative household structure embodies God's reign among disciples (4:17–25; 12:28).

19:3–12 Marriage and Divorce

In 19:3 the religious leaders question Jesus about divorce. Their question is androcentric, focusing on *a man's* actions. It assumes the patriarchal household structure of male power and reflects a debated question: Was the husband's power in divorce absolute ("for any cause" [19:3]) or restricted?

While the religious leaders want to talk divorce, Jesus claims authority to declare God's will for marriage (19:4–6), that male and female become "one flesh" (Gen. 2:24). This image does not maintain the differentiation of male and female that the household codes reinforced. Rather it offers unity, solidarity, mutuality, and equality.

The religious leaders cite Moses' practice (Deut. 24:1). Jesus asserts that this was not a command but an allowance for hard-heartedness. He permits divorce (but not remarriage) only in circumstances of *porneia* (19:9). The term *porneia* here probably indicates adultery, rather than marriages that appear incestuous after a person has converted to Christianity (Lev. 18). Jesus agrees with the disciples that such a marriage is demanding and restrictive for some men (19:10–11). Its alternative is not divorce but "one flesh" existence as "eunuchs for the sake of the kingdom of heaven" (19:12).

Jesus' resistance to unlimited male power reflects wider social resistance to the patriarchal pattern, blurring of male-female differences, and some changing roles for women through the first centuries. Eunuchs were considered marginal to households since their bodies did not reinforce male-female differentiation. Jesus offers an alternative and marginal existence to disciples.

19:13–15 Children and the Reign

In 19:13 the disciples rebuke people bringing children to Jesus. He counters them by welcoming and blessing the children (19:14–15). To such belongs the reign of the heavens (19:14).

Household traditions required children to be submissive and obedient to the father. Children were dependent and vulnerable, a threat to society (because of their lack of judgment, irrationality, evil nature, or ignorance). They had to be trained for their future social roles.

Yet there were some alternative and changing perceptions. Children were seen as gifts from God (Ps. 127:3–5). There are increased expressions of affection for children. Language for "small child" under the age of seven develops over the first centuries. We find increased references to "play" and the discovery of more toys. More lenient and appropriate educational approaches develop. The legal right to disobey a father is recognized in some situations.

In forbidding children to come to Jesus, the disciples reflect the prevalent attitude of the insignificance of children. But Jesus' response reflects a different valuing. In using the metaphor of children, Jesus affirms discipleship as an existence of permanent marginality and transition to God's reign. Disciples make up a new family without fathers (23:10), based not on birth but on their heavenly father (6:9), and live with their brothers and sisters, those who do the will of God (12:46–50).

19:16–30 Wealth and the Household

A rich man (19:22, 24), a man defined by his material wealth, seeks eternal life (19:16). To follow Jesus, he must divest his wealth by giving to the poor (19:21). His new identity will be defined not by his possessions but by his willingness to follow Jesus. In the process, he is helping to create a more egalitarian social structure. While acquiring sufficient wealth was part of usual household practices, a minority viewpoint protested the use of wealth to establish status. Jesus again resists dominant cultural values of the household codes, seeking a more just social order.

20:1–16 The Parable of the Householder

The alternative household order emerging in chapter 19 is interrupted by this parable. The parable does not demonstrate God's generosity as is often claimed. The use of "generosity" in some translations of verse 15 of chapter 20 is not accurate. And while the householder is generous to the last hired, he is not to the first hired. Rather, the parable concerns "the kingdom of heaven" (20:1), God's saving presence. It defines "whatever is right" (20:4) not as the upholding of hierarchy but as equal treatment (20:12).

The parable reinforces the basis for the alternative household order. Since a new "kingdom" or "reign" has come, new household structures are appropriate. God's reign transforms, upsetting conventional expectations and structures (20:10). The parable invites readers not to protest the different social order (20:11–12) but to recognize the householder's right to reverse patriarchal social patterns (20:14–15). It invites us to see the alternative, more egalitarian household pattern as "right" or "just" (20:4).

20:17–28 Servants and Ruling Over

This section concerns the fourth part of the household code, master-slave relationships. The subsection begins and ends with common material: Jesus' imminent death (20:17–19, 28), disciples (20:17–18, 20–28), and references to Gentiles (20:19, 25).

The mother of James and John requests places of honor for her sons (20:20–23). But Jesus connects her request to the Gentiles' ruling over others (20:25). The effect of that rule appears in verse 19's naming of the Gentiles as the agents of Jesus' death. Such rule does not belong in the households of disciples (20:26). By contrast, disciples are servants (v. 26) and slaves (v. 27), in imitation of Jesus who gives his life in service (a ransom, 20:28).

In the household codes and in social practice, slaves knew powerlessness, alienation, lack of self-determination, marginality, sexual exploitation, beatings, and insults. Many masters distrusted and feared slaves. While there was some legal protection for slaves, more often the law reflected property interests rather than humanitarian concerns. Yet some conditions were changing. Slaves received honor by associating with a respected master. Some concern for improved productivity meant better housing, food, and marriage possibilities. Reliance on the knowledge and skills of slaves for daily existence blurred distinctions with free people.

In naming disciples as servants and slaves, Jesus images an alternative existence of marginality, shame, service, and faithful obedience. It was also egalitarian in that among disciples there are no masters except one (23:10). There is also honor in the service of God, and in solidarity with Jesus who does God's will.

20:29–34 The Healing of the Blind Men

The two blind beggars, marginal characters beside the road, represent disciples. To "follow" Jesus on the way of the cross (20:34) is possible only if one cries out for God's mercy. To live this difficult, alternative household pattern is possible through God's mercy, as an expression of God's saving presence ("the reign of the heavens") manifested by Jesus (1:21–23; 4:17).

Conclusion

Various New Testament writers condone the cultural pattern of hierarchical households (Eph. 5:21–6:9; Col. 3:18–4:1; 1 Tim. 2:1–15; 5:1–2; 6:1–2; 1 Titus 2:1–10; 1 Pet. 2:18–3:7). But Matthew's Gospel takes a very different line. It urges disciples to live an alternative household pattern based on God's merciful saving presence, marked by more egalitarian relationships, and in contrast to the dominant hierarchical and patriarchal pattern.

Bibliography

Balch, David L. *Let Wives Be Submissive: The Domestic Code of 1 Peter* (SBLMS 26; Chico, Calif.: Scholars Press, 1983).

Barton, S. C. *Discipleship and Family Ties in Mark and Matthew* (SNTSMS 80; Cambridge: Cambridge University Press, 1994).

Carter, Warren. *Households and Discipleship: A Study of Matthew 19–20* (JSNTSSup 103; Sheffield: JSOT Press, 1994).

Crosby, M. *House of Disciples: Church, Economics and Justice in Matthew* (Maryknoll, N.Y.: Orbis Books, 1988).

—WARREN CARTER

Ascetic Widows in the Early Church
(Luke-Acts and 1 Timothy)

Asceticism strongly attracted women in the early church. The ideal of sexual continence is not a later development in the third and fourth centuries but seems to be rooted in New Testament teaching and ethos. It offered women an alternative to the conventions of marriage and motherhood and provided possibilities less available to them within the confinement of a patriarchal household. For most women in antiquity sexuality may primarily have been the bond that tied them to subordination under a husband, to domestic duties, to dangerous and frequent pregnancies, to submissive dependency in exchange for support and respectability. Renouncing sexuality meant a form of self-denial, but socially it offered a liberating alternative. It lessened some of the pain and risk of life, as ascetic women gained control over their bodies and were allowed an authority often otherwise denied them. They were subject to special restrictions, but these were different from the restrictions usually ruling women's lives. As far as our sources tell, ascetic women did not lament their renunciation.

An order of widows was established to provide for ascetic women (Acts 6:1; 9:39, 41; 1 Tim. 5:3–16). This made an ascetic life also possible for women with no means of their own. The church became the provider and made these "no-man's" women respectable—at least within the community itself. In the New Testament, widows are mentioned primarily in Luke-Acts and 1 Timothy. Soon after, Ignatius refers to virgins among the widows in Smyrna (*Smyrn.* 13:3). This reference, as well as a scrutiny of the passages in Luke and 1 Timothy, shows that the order of widows was not merely a means of providing care for the needy but a provision for ascetic women, be they widows or not.

Why were they called widows? Partly because the origin of the order reflects the Jewish concern and special care for widows. Furthermore, at this early stage most ascetic women in the Christian communities are likely to have been married. At the time women were given in marriage early, and these Christian women were not only first-generation Christians; many of them may also have been the first Christians in their families. In the first marriage a difference of age was common, which meant that women who survived their husbands became widows relatively young. At a time when women were a minority in the population, it was customary at least for young widows to remarry after a period of mourning. Augustus's legislation mandated remarriage for women who were of childbearing age with less than three children. In fact, it seems that most widows remarried also because they needed support. In the Christian communities, however, this problem was overcome, and widows were invited, even urged, to remain unmarried.

Family wealth and status or personal income through skill or trade made it possible for some women to support themselves and even keep "a house." A

widow of means could have considerable freedom, and well-off women sometimes accommodated a group of sister "widows." The story about the charitable Tabitha in Acts 9:36–43 refers to a group of widows in her house; and
1 Timothy 5:16 states that "if a believing woman has widows, she should take
care of them and not let the church be burdened" (my translation). This is different advice from the previous request that families take care of their own
(5:4). It refers to women who have received subsidies for taking widows into
their house. They are urged to care for the widows at their own expense. The
church should use its resources only for old widows who had no one on whom
they could fall back. The author calls them the real widows.

1 Timothy 5:3–16 does not initiate an order for widows but attempts to interfere with an existing one. Apparently it included young women as well as old
(v. 11); they were supported by the community (vv. 3, 8, 16) and had pledged
themselves to chastity (v. 12). They were active in works of charity, but their
main occupation seems to have been intercessory prayer.

The author of 1 Timothy insists that the community should enroll and support only the real widows. He wants to decimate the order by excluding any
woman under sixty years of age, any whose character he regards as question-
able, and any who could find support elsewhere. The younger widows are simply told to marry. Not only are these measures cost-saving; they also ensure that
a potential for unrest is brought under control. The author strongly opposes asceticism, suspecting that it leads to heresy. For women he advocates subordination in marriage and motherhood. He does not deny the ascetic ideal of the
widow but limits it to women too old for childbearing and well beyond the age
when remarriage was legally required. He domesticates the order; the real widows have previously fulfilled his ideals for womanhood, and this they should
teach the younger women.

The requirements of 1 Timothy may echo the original purpose of the order
of widows as the Christians adopted it from their Jewish roots. It was established to care for those in need. The Jewish provision for widows seems to have
been unequalled in antiquity. The Deuteronomic legislation states that God is
the helper of widows (and orphans), and God's people are obliged to care for
them. At the time of Jesus this was fulfilled through a system of organized care.
The "daily distribution" mentioned in Acts 6:1 reflects a similar, if not identical, provision in the earliest Christian community. The original intention was
to provide for the needy in the community through sharing and redistributing
resources. The order of widows seems to have developed as part of this, not
only to cover the specific need but also because of an idealization of the pious
and chaste widow.

In Jewish tradition Judith was an ideal figure in the pious imagination of the
Maccabean period. After the early death of her husband, she withstood all offers and temptations and led a life of chastity and fasting. Judith is a Jewish version of the Roman "univira," one man's woman, forever faithful to her one and
only husband. It is, however, interesting that much of the Roman material that
attests to factual cases consists of epitaphs raised by surviving husbands to

wives who died young. The early, prescriptive use of "univira" is related to ritual activities for women whose first husbands were still alive. As the term became detached from the cultic use and was used instead to express social approval, the Christians adopted it, applying it primarily to widows. It turned from being an elevation of the faithful, monogamous wife of higher social standing to becoming the ideal of the permanently chaste widow.

In Luke-Acts widows are mentioned more frequently than anywhere else in the New Testament. Luke reflects a background similar to the one presupposed by 1 Timothy. But he represents a position that defends the widows and embraces ascetic abandonment. The story about the widow's offering in Luke 21:1–4 and the saying about widows as victims of the scribes' greed in Luke 20:47 have Markan parallels. The rest is unique to Luke: the widow-prophet Anna (2:36–38); the widow at Zarephat (4:25f); the widow at Nain (7:11–17); the importunate widow (18:1–8). In Acts 6:1, complaints are issued on behalf of the widows of the Hellenists, and a group of widows is present at the raising of Tabitha (Acts 9:36–42). Some have suggested that Tabitha herself and most of the other women in Luke-Acts who appear independently of a man might have been widows: Peter's mother-in-law (Luke 4:38f); Martha (Luke 10:38–42); Lydia (Acts 16:14f); Mary, the mother of John (Acts 12:12). Luke never says that they are widows, but to many interpreters widowhood is the only possible explanation of these women's independence. Yet it is also maintained by the same interpreters that widows are utterly deprived women and that Luke's interest in widows shows his concern for the poor.

This contradiction of interpretation reflects the ambiguous position of a widow at the time. To become a widow was considered a misfortune, and often it was. The term *widow* reflects an exposed position. The Greek word, *chera,* means "she who is left without a man." The equivalent term in Hebrew, *almanah,* is derived from a root meaning "being mute." A widow was without voice in society since she had no man to speak for her. Yet a widow had greater freedom and right of self-determination than she could have had as a young girl or as a wife. For women of means the status of widow could well be preferable. The women in Luke assumed to be widows are all portrayed as patrons and benefactors. It is difficult and may not even be important to decide whether the patronae in Luke-Acts really are widows. Luke portrays them in any case as ascetic women since he seems to advocate ascetic discipleship both for women and men. As a disciple a woman no longer is blessed through marriage and motherhood but exclusively through hearing and keeping the word of God. Tabitha is called not widow but *mathetria,* the female form of *mathetes,* disciple (Acts 9:36). It may also be that Luke does not call these well-off women "widows" because the term itself continued primarily to convey social exposure and vulnerability.

In the Lukan stories widows are, with the exception of Anna, not individually named; they are identical with their role; their very appearance is a statement of need. The story in 7:11–17 illustrates Jesus' immediate perception and care for a woman who has lost her only son and sole support. But it does not move beyond the conventional image of a widow inviting compassion and charity. In Luke 21:1–4 Jesus watches a widow who places her whole livelihood in the temple's treasure chest. He seems to commend her act, and recent interpreters have found this praise offensive. In view of the lament from 20:47 they read the story as a complaint against religious leaders who have led widows astray by false pretensions of piety. They rescue Jesus by recasting the widow in the role of victim. But such a reading misses the focused contrast of the rich over against the poor widow. She transcends the role of passive recipient and victim. Her action should be judged not from our urge to pity her but from the radical requirements of discipleship elsewhere in the gospel (12:22–32; 14:25–34). By her deed she represents a critical and exemplary alternative over against the rich, as the disciples are contrasted to the rich ruler in Luke 18:18–30. A similar contrast is to the scribes in Luke 20:47. There is a strong note of irony in this verse: Not only does the widow's sacrifice contrast with the greed of the scribes; they are condemned for extorting from widows under the pretext of performing long prayers. Their victims are the true models of unceasing prayer.

The parable in Luke 18:1–8 plays on a well-known theme: a widow struggles to assert her rights against a corrupt legal system. Surprisingly she succeeds because of her wearisome importunity. The parable encourages the disciples to take the example of the widow and persist in prayer. Patristic sources attribute special effectiveness to the prayer of widows and regard it as a recompense for the support the widows receive. 1 Timothy 5:5 assigns the real widow to continuous prayer, and Anna (Luke 2:36–38) is said to pray night and day.

Anna is the exemplary ascetic widow. Apparently she fulfills the requirements of a real widow in 1 Timothy 5: she is very old, and she spends her life devoted to God, fasting and praying. But her case is far more complex. Anna is identified by her own family and tribe. No real interest is invested in the fact that she has once been married, nor are we informed whether she ever gave birth. The point about her marriage is its short duration, so that her life is marked by virginity ("having lived with a husband for seven years after her virginity" [my translation]), and then by widowhood. Even as a young widow she did not remarry. Most important, these credentials serve her function of public, prophetic proclamation. Anna is an ascetic prophet, as are the four virgin daughters of Philip who all prophesy (Acts 21:9).

Ascetic women played a significant role in the early church. An order of widows provided for them, and even if the practical requirements and arrangement may have varied, it made a life outside the constraints of a patriarchal household feasible and also respectable. It was a controversial provision since it threatened the conventional virtues for a woman's life such as marriage and motherhood. Neither were the ascetic widows easy to control for men wanting to affirm their authority. For many women the order of widows transformed vulnerability into opportunity.

—TURID KARLSEN SEIM

Jesus' Relationship to His Own Family

The Gospel writers are not very interested, as modern Westerners might be, in Jesus' family background and the psychology of his upbringing. Instead, Jesus' relationship to his family is portrayed primarily with a view to saying something about who Jesus was (and is) and what it means to become one of his followers. That is why the accounts are so selective. They are not concerned with biographical information for its own sake. They do not even tell us whether Jesus was married. What they are interested in is telling the story of Jesus in ways that show that in Jesus God is present in a new way for the salvation and judgment of humankind. What they say about Jesus and his own family tends therefore to be representative of what they want to say more generally about life in the new age that Jesus inaugurates.

In a way that is surprising to people today who identify Christianity automatically with strong family piety, Mark's Gospel portrays Jesus' relations with his family as fraught with misunderstanding. This is part of a larger theme in Mark about the hidden, subversive nature of divine revelation in Jesus. This theme is developed by means of irony, where those closest to Jesus repeatedly fail to discern that he is the Messiah, that the kingdom of God is present in him, and that the way of the kingdom is the way of losing one's life (even one's "family life") for his sake.

Significantly, neither Jesus' mother nor his father is given any role in salvation history, since Mark provides no genealogies or birth narratives or stories of Jesus' boyhood. Nor are they depicted as disciples, unlike the role accorded Joseph in Matthew and that accorded Mary in both Luke-Acts and John. Instead, Joseph is not mentioned at all, Mary is identified by name just once (Mark 6:3), and the family of Jesus disappears from the story early on. Indeed, it is remarkable how soon in Mark's narrative Jesus leaves his hometown of Nazareth (Mark 1:9); and that Capernaum becomes instead his base and the place where he has a house (Mark 2:1, 15; 3:20).

The two episodes in Mark where Jesus' relations with his kith and kin come to the fore are Mark 3:20–21, 31–35 and 6:1–6. The first follows hard upon Jesus' act of choosing twelve disciples (3:13–19). So it appears that, instead of choosing the company of his family, Jesus chooses the company of the twelve. Their task is to catch people (1:17; see also 3:14–15); family ties have to take second place (see 1:20; 10:28–30). However, when Jesus' people hear of the crowd at his home preventing Jesus and his associates from eating, they set out to take him into protective custody, in the belief that he is mad (3:20–21). When they arrive at the house, they stand outside the crowded house and send for him. But rather than heed their summons, Jesus looks at the crowd sitting around him and says, "Who are *my mother and my brothers? . . .* Here are *my mother and my brothers!* Whoever does the will of God is *my brother and sister and mother*" (3:33–35).

What is shocking about this is Jesus' apparent disregard for the demands of filial piety and family loyalty, made emphatic by the threefold repetition. Now Jesus' true kinsfolk are not those to whom he is related by blood but "whoever does the will of God." In a society where identity, role, and status are ascribed traditionally according to membership of an extended kinship group, what Jesus says is radical and subversive. Here the seeds of new patterns of sociability and a new kind of society are being sown (see 9:33–37; 10:13–16).

But, lest we conclude too easily that Jesus was antitradition and "against the family," we must reckon also with the fact that Jesus' position belongs within a tradition of its own, well recognized in biblical religion. It is the tradition, rooted in Israel's monotheistic faith and covenantal religion, that human identity comes first and foremost from God and therefore that allegiance to God takes priority over every other allegiance, even ties of blood and marriage (see Gen. 12:1–3; Exod. 32:25–29; 1 Kings 19:19–21). This tradition *goes together* with the tradition (grounded in the story of creation and the giving of the law) that honors natural ties and upholds family relations. So Jesus' response to the summons of his mother and brothers has to be heard as a rebuff to them only if they refuse to acknowledge his vocation as "Son of God," a vocation whose demands transcend the (otherwise legitimate) demands made on him as a son of Mary.

Nevertheless, the element of shock remains, and is intentional. It is Jesus' way of making a point and challenging the taken-for-granted. The shock is reinforced by the way Mark intertwines in the episode of Jesus' mother and brothers that of the scribes from Jerusalem who also come to the house, this time to accuse him of being demon-possessed (3:22–30; see v. 21)! Nor is it coincidental that the story goes straight on to tell of Jesus teaching the crowd by the sea the parable of the sower (4:1–20). For this raises for us the question: Is Jesus' family like the seed sown among thorns, where the "cares of the world" have come and choked Jesus' testimony among them, leaving them "unfruitful" (4:18–19, RSV)? Does the fact that Jesus' family remains "outside" the house (3:31) imply that they are among the ones "outside" for whom everything about Jesus and the kingdom is a riddle impossible to grasp (see 4:11–12)?

That this is indeed the case, at least during Jesus' lifetime, seems to be confirmed by the second episode concerning Jesus and his own family: his return to his hometown (6:1–6). This episode brings to a climax the theme of the misunderstanding of Jesus by his own kith and kin and anticipates Jesus' rejection by his people as a whole, culminating in the passion. The depiction of Jesus' mother and brothers as "outside," in 3:31–35, grows now to a depiction of the entire hometown of Jesus as one of open "unbelief" (6:6a). Strikingly, this is the only occasion in Mark where Jesus' power to heal is thwarted almost completely (6:5).

But how may we account for this crisis in Jesus' hometown? Why is it here that his authority as a wise teacher is challenged and that "he could do no mighty work," in stark contrast to the success of his miracle-working in the Decapolis and Galilee (4:35–5:43)? Especially significant is the exchange between the townsfolk and Jesus at the very heart of the episode (6:3–4). The "many" people present in the synagogue express their offense at Jesus by saying, "Is not this the carpenter, the son of Mary and brother of James and Joses and Judas and Simon, and are not his sisters here with us?" To this attempt to put him in his place, Jesus replies sharply: "A prophet is not without honor, except in his own country and among his own kin, and in his own house" (6:4, RSV).

This exchange invites two main observations. First, there is the element of conflict. Such conflicts occur frequently in Mark, often in a synagogue on the Sabbath (for example, 1:21–28; 2:23–28; 3:1–6). They show that the breaking in of the kingdom of God with the coming of Jesus is a challenge to conventional ways of seeing and doing things. Traditionally significant institutions like the synagogue (and the family) are seen in a new light and reinterpreted to make possible novel patterns of action and sociability. One such pattern is referred to explicitly at the beginning of our story: "He went away from there and came to his own country; *and his disciples followed him*" (6:1, RSV). It seems likely that the offense generated by Jesus' appearance in his hometown is related to the challenge that Jesus' itinerant lifestyle in the company of twelve chosen followers represented to a settled, peasant, household-based community. Noteworthy is the fact that after the rebuttal in Nazareth, Jesus resumes his itinerancy and even sends out the twelve in pairs as an extension of his own work (6:6b–13). It is as if the rebuttal in Nazareth consolidates not only the incomprehension of Jesus' kith and kin but also the alternative pattern of sociability developing around Jesus.

Second, the conflict focuses on the interrelated issues of identity and authority and the recognition of the same by the giving or withholding of "honor" and "faith." In traditional societies, personal identity is a matter not so much of "who am I?" but more of "to whom do I belong"; not so much of individual self-discovery as of what is given in group membership. The most significant group for defining identity in antiquity is the (extended) household. Precisely this conception lies behind the challenge to Jesus in the question put by the people in the synagogue (6:3). They see him in traditional terms where identity and authority are ascribed according to occupation ("the carpenter"), kinship group ("the son of Mary"), and accepted location ("and are not his sisters here *with us*?"). Over against this, the identity and authority of Jesus are conveyed in different terms: his appearance unannounced with a retinue of disciples (6:1); his adopting the role of teacher in the synagogue (6:2a); and his reputation for wisdom and miracle-working, which he seeks to confirm in the people's presence by his words and ritual action (6:2b, 5b).

Thus, at the heart of the conflict is a divergence between seeing Jesus in the traditional kinship and household terms of Galilean village life and seeing him with eyes of faith as the Spirit-inspired Son of God (1:1, 9–11, 12–13, and so on) bringing a new order (1:15) and a new "household" (3:35; 10:30) into being. A lot is at stake here: for on the former view, Jesus belongs to his kinsfolk and owes allegiance to them, while on the latter view, they owe allegiance to him, with all the implications for change that that must bring. The difference is stark and uncompromising. It is part of the larger theme of discipleship of

Jesus in the light of the gospel, summed up later by Jesus himself in the call for self-denial in 8:34–35.

Overall, then, Mark's portrayal of Jesus' relations with his kinfolk is negative. But, in terms of Mark's Gospel as a whole, this is what we might have expected. If Jesus' family fares badly, so do his disciples and the people of Jesus' native land as a whole. For Mark wants us to see that the truth about Jesus is hidden from those who lack faith—so much so that, ironically, those who are closest to Jesus seem in greatest danger of misunderstanding who he really is. Furthermore, Mark also wants us to see that what is true of Jesus is likely to be so for those who follow him. Having left behind their own households, they will belong to many new ones (10:28–30), but this will be at the heavy cost of the sometimes murderous enmity of the kinfolk they have left (10:30; 13:12–13).

There is no good reason to doubt that Mark's account reflects something of the historical reality. Given the prominence of members of Jesus' family in the post-Easter church, it is hard to imagine that such potentially damaging reminiscences would be invented—unless one accepts the suggestion that Mark, for his own "political" reasons, sharpens the hostility of the tradition towards Jesus' family in order to undermine the authority of James, the Lord's brother, in the Jerusalem church. Far more likely is the view that these reminiscences were preserved because they contribute theologically to Mark's profound exploration of the nature of revelation and faith, and also because of their relevance to the likely situation of Mark's readers confronting kinship-sponsored hostility and persecution themselves.

Certainly, Matthew takes over the Markan traditions with only minor modification (Matt. 12:46–50; 13:53–58), so he sees no reason to cast them aside as spurious and even adds others relevant to the theme (for example, Matt. 8:18–22; 10:34–39). The author of Luke-Acts gives a considerably more positive account of Jesus' relation with his family, not least in the prominence he gives to Jesus' mother Mary (Luke 1–2) and to Jesus' brothers, especially James (for example, Acts 1:14; 15:13). He also tones down the theme of misunderstanding that comes to him from Mark (see Luke 4:24; 8:19–21). Nevertheless, in the story of the boy Jesus in the temple (Luke 2:41–52), there are traces of the kind of misunderstanding between Jesus and his family that is more apparent in Mark and Matthew.

Interestingly, John, like Luke, gives prominence to Jesus' mother, though in a quite distinctive way. Two unique episodes are strategically placed at the beginning and end of Jesus' ministry. First, there is her rather uncomprehending exchange with Jesus at the Cana wedding (John 2:3–4). Then, poignantly, she reappears at the foot of the cross, where together with the beloved disciple she symbolizes the new family of faith brought into being by Jesus' life-giving word (John 19:26–27). For John, not Mary's biological relationship with her son is important but her faith relationship. So too, but conversely, with Jesus' brothers. Unlike Mary, they show no sign of faith (John 7:5), and there is no scene of final reconciliation at the cross.

For John, then, historical reminiscences depicting Jesus at odds with his kith and kin are allowed to speak at a more profound level, as in the other Gospels. They are allowed to convey the *theological* reality that Jesus is not known truly as the son of his mother and a sibling among siblings. He is known truly only by faith as the Son of God, belief in whom opens the way to eternal life in the eschatological family of the "children of God" (John 1:11–13).

Bibliography

Barton, S. C. *Discipleship and Family Ties in Mark and Matthew* (Cambridge: Cambridge University Press, 1994).

Barton, S. C., ed. *The Family in Theological Perspective* (Edinburgh: T. & T. Clark, 1996).

Brown, R. E., et al. *Mary in the New Testament* (Philadelphia: Fortress Press; New York: Paulist Press, 1978).

Ellis, I. "Jesus and the Subversive Family," *Scottish Journal of Theology* 38 (1985): 173–88.

Malina, B. J. *The New Testament World: Insights from Cultural Anthropology*, rev. ed. (Louisville, Ky.: Westminster/John Knox Press, 1993).

—STEPHEN C. BARTON

Lost: Two Rebellious Sons—Who Will Find? (Luke 15:11–32)

The parable in Luke 15:11–32 is a very familiar Bible story. It is a vignette of first-century family conflicts and their unexpected resolutions that still offers contemporary Christians patterns of restoring ruptured family and community relationships.

Like all Gospel parables, it begins with a familiar situation. What family does not know conflicting desires between parents and children and jealous rivalry among siblings? What community has not observed that some members faithfully labor for the good of the whole, while others go their merry way, only to end in ruin and in need of rescue?

In the first part of the Gospel story, the youngest son has decided to leave home to make his own way. In Jesus' day, such a thing was common enough; what was not usual, however, was for a son to demand his inheritance before his father's demise. This kind of request was tantamount to wishing his father dead and would have been heard as a shocking insult in the original telling. What is even more startling is that the father agrees! Equally disturbing is that the older son does not object or mediate in any way. He, too, seems to go along with the shameful arrangement.

So off goes the younger son, inheritance in hand, to a distant land. The parents' worst fears are realized, as he squanders it all on "dissolute living" (v. 13). He hits rock bottom, when, having spent all he had, a severe famine breaks out (v. 14). Having little recourse, he hires himself out to one of the citizens of that country, who sends him to his fields to feed the pigs (v. 15). To Jewish ears, this adds insult to injury, as the son not only has lost precious Jewish property but, worse yet, has lost it to Gentiles who keep unclean animals. And the son's plight worsens. As his hunger mounts, he would be happy even to fill up on the pigs' fodder. But no one offers him even this (v. 16).

Being a resourceful young man, he devises a plan to save himself (vv. 17–19). He remembers how well paid are his father's workers; they always have "bread enough and to spare" (v. 17). There is no need for him to die of hunger. He decides to go and ask his father to make him one of his hired hands (v. 19). There is no repentance on the part of this young man. His soliloquy, "Father, I have sinned against heaven and before you" (v. 18) is reminiscent of the words of Pharaoh to Moses, "I have sinned; the LORD is in the right, and I and my people are in the wrong. Pray to the LORD! Enough of God's thunder and hail! I will let you go" (Exod. 9:27–28). Though Pharaoh's words sound repentant, he is simply at his wit's end with the plagues. He has endured water turned to blood; infestations of frogs, gnats, and flies; diseased livestock; boils; and now thunder and hail. In desperation he mouths admission of sin; in truth he does not repent. Likewise, the young son in Luke 15:18

is rehearsing a strategy by which he may emerge alive from his dire plight and eat again.

The next scene in the parable has a startling twist that leaves the hearer quite puzzled. It shows the father watching and waiting for his errant son's return. In a first-century Mediterranean family, this is most unexpected behavior on the part of a patriarch who has been so grievously shamed by his son. A more expected reaction would have been for the father to rend his garments and declare the son disowned. Instead, he is longing for his return and at the first sight of his approach, he runs to meet him—a most undignified action for a patriarch. Putting his arms around the boy and kissing him (v. 20), the father shields him from any other repercussions from kin and neighbors who would be equally resentful of the shame his scandalous behavior has brought upon them.

As the son begins his rehearsed speech, the father silences him, not permitting him even to propose his plan to work for food (v. 21). Instead, the father calls for the best robe, a ring, and sandals to be put on him: all symbols of his freedom (v. 22). Not only that, the fatted calf is killed for a great feast (vv. 23–24).

There is more. From the start of the story, it is told that the man had two sons (v. 11). The dramatic reconciliation of the father with the younger son ends on a joyous note. But what of the elder son? He, too, is lost, but in an entirely different way. He has remained in the father's house but is no more at peace with him than was his younger brother. When he hears all the celebration over the return of his brother, he becomes enraged and refuses to go into the house (vv. 25–28). Again, the father does something most unusual for a first-century patriarch. He leaves the party and comes out to the elder son (who should have been helping him host the celebration) and pleads with him to join in (v. 28).

The jealousy and resentment that fester in this son are evident in his insulting explosion, "Listen! For all these years I have been working like a slave for you, and I have never disobeyed your command; yet you have never given me even a young goat so that I might celebrate with my friends. But when this son of yours came back, who has devoured your property with prostitutes, you killed the fatted calf for him!" (vv. 29–30). His outburst reveals that, not unlike his brother—who concocts a plan to become the father's hired hand—he, too, thinks of himself as a slave to his father. He dissociates himself from his brother by calling him "this son of yours." And he further interprets his brother's "dissolute living" (v. 13) as "devouring your property with prostitutes" (v. 30). This son is just as lost as the younger one in his inability to accept and celebrate his father's graciousness.

The father's reply, "You are always with me, and all that is mine is yours" (v. 31), leaves the hearer wondering: Will the elder son also be able to accept the costly love of the father? Will he be able to let go of his joyless resentment and slavish attitude that keep him from reconciled oneness with the other family members? As usual in Gospel parables, the story is open-ended. It is up to the listener to finish it.

In the context of Luke's Gospel, this is the third in a trilogy of parables that tell how God searches out the lost. The introductory verses of the chapter (15:1–2) make these parables a response to the complaint of Pharisees and scribes that Jesus welcomed sinners and ate with them. In the first parable Jesus asks these religious leaders to put themselves in the shoes of a shepherd who has lost one of the hundred sheep in his care (15:4). "Shepherd" was a familiar metaphor for God (Psalm 23), as well as for religious leaders who were to act on behalf of God (Ezekiel 34). The parable underscores both the importance of each sheep and the costly love that is required of a pastor to search out a lost one. The shepherd is responsible to the owner and must account for every sheep. He must expend great energy to find a stray sheep, searching over rough terrain and in rocky crags. Moreover, once he finds it, the sheep is in such a state of collapse that the shepherd must hoist it onto his shoulders and carry it back (15:5). This is no small task when a sheep weighs some sixty pounds! Yet the joy in finding it overshadows all the pain of bringing it back.

A second parable with identical contours uses a different image (15:8–10). Now it is a woman who searches for a precious coin of her daily earnings, indispensable for the subsistence of her family. Like the shepherd, she, too, expends great energy in searching out the lost. She lights a lamp, using up valuable oil, and sweeps out every nook and cranny until she finds the drachma. Just as a shepherd's diligent search for a sheep provided an apt image for how God seeks out the lost, so does the assiduous effort of a woman householder for a valuable coin. Both stories speak of the costly love on the part of God who is willing to expend any effort to bring back the precious lost one.

As the third parable in the series, Luke 15:11–32 makes the same point. God's boundless efforts to seek out the lost can also be likened to those of a father who pays a great price to get back his lost sons. He absorbs insult and shame from both his sons and yet goes out to each, offering them an unearned share in his riches. Reconciliation begins with the costly love offered by God, the shepherd, the woman householder, the father.

For anyone in authority, whether parent or pastoral leader, these parables offer a way to heal ruptured relationships that begins with the one who has been wronged taking the first step toward the one who is alienated. It asks a parent who has been deeply hurt by a child to relinquish his or her own pain and to extend an offer of forgiving love. For those who are lost, reconciliation means accepting unmerited love and entering into the ensuing celebration. The sheep, the coin, and the sons cannot make their own way back; the restoration of right relation depends on the godly person reaching out to such a one. Nor can children of a gracious God earn divine love by making themselves into slaves. Sons and daughters of God are always with God and always have access to all that is God's.

These parables do not, however, tell the rest of the story of what comes after the initial acceptance and celebratory welcome home. Other Gospel stories (for example, Matt. 18:23–35; 22:11–14; Luke 7:36–50) speak of a response in kind that is expected from one who accepts unmerited love. In families and in communities costly love is offered freely, but the price for those who accept it is to replicate such reconciling love in their own actions.

There is one glaring omission in the story of the father and the two sons: Is there no mother or daughter in this family? A story recounted by a minister to street children in Sao Paolo, Brazil, brings home the point. She tells of a time she introduced this parable to youngsters unfamiliar with Bible stories. When she got to the part where the younger son decided to return home, she stopped and asked the children if the boy would be able to go home. They debated about it, and finally, one of the boys asked, "Is there a mother in the house?" When she asked if that would make a difference, he said, "Yes, because if there is a mother, she will let him come home. She will pester the father, saying, 'You *will* let him in the house if he comes back, won't you? After all, he's our baby.'"

This young man, much like the first hearers of the gospel, lives in a patriarchal society, where the behavior of the father in Luke 15:11–32 is very feminine—not at all typical of a macho father who sees as an important part of his role the imposition of obedience and discipline so as to maintain his honor and that of his family. Yet "feminizing" the father does not put female figures into this parable. And herein lies a danger in this story. In a church that uses the term *Father* more than any other to address God, and that rarely, if ever, uses feminine images or terminology for God, patriarchy not only reigns on earth but also is divinized. When our foundational stories about God exclude female images, then believers are left with the message that being male is more God-like.

In a society and church where family structures and relationship patterns are changing, what is needed is not only a father figure with feminine qualities but female images that express equally well what the father image says of God. When the story of the diligent woman householder in Luke 15:8–10 is read in tandem with that of the father reaching out to his lost sons in Luke 15:11–32, we have such.

Bibliography

Bailey, Kenneth E. *Finding the Lost: Cultural Keys to Luke 15* (St. Louis: Concordia Publishing House, 1992).

Donahue, John R. *The Gospel in Parable* (Philadelphia: Fortress Press, 1988).

LaHurd, Carol Schersten. "Rediscovering the Lost Women in Luke 15," *Biblical Theology Bulletin* 24 (1994): 66–76.

Reid, Barbara. *Choosing the Better Part? Women in the Gospel of Luke* (Collegeville, Minn.: Liturgical Press, 1996).

—BARBARA E. REID, O.P.

Family in a Time of Social and Eschatological Crisis

Eschatological expectation was a source of hope to the first Christians. It was a vision of a different, recreated existence where suffering no longer had to be endured, where the gracious God alone reigned. But it was also a vision of their worst experiences and fears. For the new life to come, the old had to die. The period of transition was to be a time of crisis, marked by conflict, violent and dreadful. It was to be a time of trial and tribulation, of horror and hardship, of persecution and betrayal, of every evil force let loose in a last attempt at victory. It was to be a time when established structures collapse, when traditional values no longer apply, when this world is brought to its verge.

The Gospels render the eschatological expectations with an acute imminence: the social experience of the early Christians is depicted as belonging to the end-time events. Traumatic ordeals are converted into necessities of God's will and plan. Family relationships are seriously affected; the normal structures upon which one would depend for daily support and future security are no longer dependable. Values normally cherished become a threat; blessing turns to curse.

The eschatological imminence is evident in Mark 13. The disciples are warned to keep alert and not to be alarmed; to stay faithful and not to be led astray; to trust the guidance of the Holy Spirit. In times of persecution and trial brothers cannot be trusted, a father may betray his child, children will have their parents put to death (vv. 12f). This warning about treachery within the family may allude to scripture, perhaps to Micah 7:6. Matthew and Luke clearly quote this verse in material developed from Q (Matt. 10:35f; Luke 12:53). Micah 7:6 and Zechariah 13:3 may suggest that hostility in the family belonged to the standard inventory of the bitter strife and universal dissolution of the end time.

It has been more difficult to trace scriptural references for vv. 9–11 than for the rest of Mark 13. Most commentators therefore hold that beatings in synagogues and arrests by councils reflect the historical experience of the community. But they too sidestep the uncomfortable words about betrayal by family members in v. 12, attributing it to the influence of traditional prophetic-apocalyptic imagery and implying that it never really happened. 1 *Enoch* 100:1ff, *Jubilees* 23:19, and 4 Ezra 6:24 are often assumed to support this claim, but these passages do not indicate that disruption of family loyalties was a common sign of the collapse of social order in the end time. 4 Ezra 6:24 concerns friends; Jubilees 23:19 concerns generations—the universal strife includes "the youths with old men and old men with youths" —and 1 *Enoch* 100:1ff tells that in a horrendous show of violence, brother will slaughter brother, and a man his sons and son's sons. Mark 13:12, followed by Matthew 10:21, may develop the motif from Micah 7:6 in a manner similar to the intertestamentary literature. But the full quotation of Micah 7:6 in Matthew 10:35f and Luke 12:53 represents a rare focus on family conflict. This is most likely because of a particular historical situation and the experience of family disruption. The citation from scripture explains why certain members of a household are mentioned and others not, and means that bitter experience is qualified as part of God's will and plan.

The passage Mark 13:9–13 is not incorporated in the eschatological speech in Matthew 24–25; it is transposed to the great commission in Matthew 10. Here Matthew not only includes the Markan passage (10:16–23) but also introduces another word of Jesus, probably from Q, which reinforces the sense of family crisis (10:34–39 citing Micah 7:6). Jesus has come to bring a sword, setting the younger generation in a household against the elder, son against father, and daughter and daughter-in-law against the mother. This violates the commandment in the Decalogue to honor your father and mother and shows the degree of disregard for the traditional code of family values. Those who set family ties over commitment to Jesus are not worthy of him. The saying reverses the promise of the commandment for longevity: Life is lost, not found, by honoring parents. Following Jesus reverses conventional lifesaving structures and strategies; life is gained by being put to risk, as Jesus himself demonstrates.

The paradoxical words of Jesus in Matthew 10:39 acknowledge that respecting and maintaining family relations was the normal way to secure one's life. Outside a household one perished. Today when the emotional intimacy of family relations is idealized, we should not forget that households were the primary structure of sustenance and dependency both for the present and for the future through the procreation and care of children. Within the household, role divisions and power distribution expressed a patriarchal structure, as did the code of appropriate behavior. Well-ordered households were the core units of society and guaranteed its stability. Household management was as much a matter of public interest as of private, and a household falling apart would threaten to undermine the patriarchal order of society. To describe a dissolution of family ties was to describe a society going to pieces; to encourage such dissolution was subversive.

The shift from describing an eschatological family crisis to actually encouraging it is therefore crucial. This shift can be traced in the difference between Matthew 10:21 (Mark 13:12) and Matthew 10:34–39 (Q). The authoritative and intentional pronouncement, "I have come to," precludes understanding the agony of a family conflict as an unfortunate contingency. Nor does Jesus explain such conflict as an incidental result of controversial decisions and the demand for mobility. He simply states that he has not come to bring peace as might be expected. He brings a sword, severing those ties without which life was untenable. Painful family conflict is predicted not only as inevitable but as programmatic purpose.

This passage is remarkably devoid of eschatological language. It speaks of what the disciples can expect when they pursue God's mission. This is, however, eschatologically charged by the inclusion of Mark 13:9–13 earlier in the same speech. The disciples are sent on a journey that is marked by the eschatological reversal of social expectations. Matthew never reports the return of the disciples; the mission remains open-ended and constantly applicable. The eschatological requirements become normal accompaniments of discipleship. The eschatological crisis tearing families apart has become the cost of discipleship.

In antiquity it was commonly agreed that the higher calling of philosophy for the benefit of all, or God's calling to a person to study the Law, might take precedence over family affections and obligations. But the eschatological impetus in the synoptic passages is rare; in the words of Jesus, family obligations and discipleship are mutually exclusive.

It is often assumed that in the course of tradition the imminence of the eschaton is mitigated, and the church accommodates itself to live in this world, negotiating the compromises that proved necessary. Mark may urge the imminence, but in Luke the eschaton is suspended, and the book of Acts introduces the prolonged perspective of church history. The Jesus movement settles down, and well-managed households become part of the church-supporting structure. The eschatological family conflict subsides, and the radical ethos of abandonment is converted to an ethics of charity. The conventional family virtues are restored—even for Christians who are subordinate members of non-Christian households.

For Luke this is only partly true. His moral interest may color the eschatological teaching, transferring the attention from future to present. What matters is to be prepared through proleptic assimilation to the life of the resurrection, be it soon or late. Thereby a new morality compensates for the postponement of the eschaton, while the expectation is kept alive and credible. The present sign of the life to come is the praxis of those "who have been considered worthy of a place in that age and the resurrection from the dead": they refrain from matrimony (Luke 20:34–38). Here the eschatological disintegration of family is transformed into an ascetic ideal.

In Luke 14 the parable of the great banquet explains that those first invited did not come because they were acquiring property and marrying. When the next passage spells out the cost of discipleship (14:25–33), the reasons given in the parable for absence are reformulated as positive demands. The demand not to place family before Jesus is here replaced by even harsher words. Family—fully specified as father, mother, wife, children, brothers, and sisters—should be renounced. In Luke 18:28–30 the rich ruler cannot bring himself to abandon his wealth and security, while the disciples have left everything to follow Jesus. The inclusion of the wife in the lists involves an intensification toward asceticism. Family and even spouse have been abandoned—for the sake of the kingdom of God. Other reasons may not be good enough, but this is.

Luke does not promise that the old family will be replaced, as do Mark and Matthew. But the Gospels agree that family categories are transferred to the group of disciples. In conflict with his own family, Jesus claims as his family those who listen to and keep the word of God. Family is abolished but also extended. The community of followers is where support and survival should be sought.

In Mark 13:17 pregnant and nursing women are bewailed. The cruel emergencies of the end time make cherished blessings become curses. The wording plays on a well-known beatitude that is repeatedly reflected in Luke. When a woman exalts Jesus and his mother in traditional terms (11:27f), Jesus corrects her and replaces a mother's honor by the superior relationship to the word of God. In 23:28–30 Jesus tells the daughters of Jerusalem that in the days to come they will weep over themselves and their children while blessing those whom they would otherwise lament—the barren women. In a sharpened eschatological perspective the conventions reflected in the many stories about childless women whom God finally blesses with sons are invalid. Life is not secured by procreation.

The eschatological perspective may seem to render chronic liminality to discipleship. Jesus' followers are stripped of the characteristics of their former existence, and they live in contrast to values that are normally esteemed while awaiting the final bestowal of a new life. What may have had its beginning in need and apocalyptic prophecy emerged as ideals and virtues in the early church. The fear and anguish of domestic ostracism, of collapsing household support, of fatal family treachery is converted to an ethos of abandonment that is proclaimed to be the cost of discipleship. This develops ascetic features and is maintained by the church as a celibate option.

Of course, the crisis and critique of family obligations can be rendered harmless as apocalyptic imagery or as a state of emergency that was recalled long ago. But it remains a reminder, alive enough to give directions in similar costly situations and to help us avoid moral narrow-mindedness on behalf of "family values." What may seem the sign of a time of ultimate dissolution may be what the gospel demands. This is not the only voice in the New Testament on family matters, but its disquieting noise should continue to disturb us.

—TURID KARLSEN SEIM

Family Conflict Generated by Jesus' Proclamation of the Kingdom of God

There is an old adage: "Never discuss politics or religion at family gatherings." The saying captures well the experience that religion is very often the source of the most painful conflicts within families. In our contemporary settings such conflicts can be generated by family members who choose a different denomination or another faith altogether from the rest of their relatives. Some abandon any practice of religion, to the distress of observant kin. Disturbing, too, are divisions between family members that arise from contrasting theological perspectives within the same church. That religion is frequently a source of conflict among family members is our experience. But it is often the case that we expect the opposite: that religion ought to deepen unity and peace among kin.

The Gospel of Luke particularly emphasizes that the coming of Jesus brings peace. Zechariah sings of how John the Baptist's ministry prepares the way, guiding feet "into the path of peace" (1:79). At the birth of Jesus the angels proclaim peace on earth (2:14). And to those touched by his ministry of healing and reconciliation, Jesus says, "go in peace" (7:50; 8:48). In sending his disciples out on mission, Jesus gave the instructions, "Whatever house you enter, first say, 'Peace to this house!'" (10:5).

Other sayings, however, declare quite the opposite: "Do you think that I have come to bring peace to the earth? No, I tell you, but rather division!" (Luke 12:51; similarly Matt. 10:34). That Jesus declares his *purpose* is to bring division is startling. But a closer look shows that this, too, is a theme that runs throughout the Gospel. When the child Jesus is presented to Simeon in the temple, the prophet announces to his mother, "This child is destined for the falling and the rising of many in Israel, and to be a sign that will be opposed so that the inner thoughts of many will be revealed—and a sword will pierce your own soul too" (2:34–35). Simeon alludes here to Ezekiel 14:17, which describes a sword of discrimination separating those destined for destruction from those who will be saved. Simeon speaks of how some will be disposed to receive Jesus' message, while others will not be able to accept it. The difficulty in understanding Jesus and his mission extends even to his own mother and blood relations. Matthew uses the same image when he renders the saying, "I have not come to bring peace, but a sword" (10:34).

From the start, responses to Jesus and his mission are divided. According to Luke 4:22, when Jesus first proclaims his mission, "all spoke well of him and were amazed at the gracious words that came from his mouth." But when he intimates that his message is not only for Israel but for Gentiles as well, some are filled with fury and try to hurl him from the brow of the hill (4:28–29; similarly 5:21–26; 6:11; 7:16, 29–30; 8:4–8). Jesus brings good news of liberation

for the oppressed and downtrodden (4:18–19); but the same message is bad
news for the powerful and privileged (1:52–53).

The crux of the matter is that the peace that Jesus brings is not one that
smoothes over divisions by overlooking injustice or that avoids conflict (a common misunderstanding of "turn the other cheek" in Matt. 5:39; Luke 6:29).
Rather, Jesus' proclamation of God's reign and his ministry of reconciliation strike
at the very root of systems that perpetuate oppression. Jesus teaches his disciples
the blessedness of peacemaking (Matt. 5:9) by confronting injustice through nonviolent direct action that destabilizes an unjust situation and opens possibilities
for conversion (Matt. 5:38–48; Luke 6:27–36). Those who have a stake in maintaining the inequitable status quo do not react peacefully to such a mission.

Luke 12:52–53 describes how the conflict provoked by Jesus can strike even
at the heart of the family: "From now on five in one household will be divided,
three against two and two against three; they will be divided: father against son
and son against father, mother against daughter and daughter against mother,
mother-in-law against her daughter-in-law and daughter-in-law against
mother-in-law." This passage depicts a family that includes a father, a mother,
a son and his wife, and an unmarried daughter residing together. While Luke's
version portrays mutual hostility between the older and younger generations,
that of Matthew speaks only of the animosity of the son, daughter, and daughter-
in-law toward the father and mother (10:35). Making the allusion to Micah 7:6
more explicit, Matthew underscores, "and one's foes will be members of one's
own household" (10:36).

Whereas a modern family would tend to resolve this situation by having the
younger members move out on their own, such would not have been the case
in antiquity. A son's wife customarily moved into his parents' home and joined
his family. No unmarried daughter would live alone in her own apartment. In
the first-century Mediterranean world kinship and family ties were all-important
in providing identity, security, and protection. Ideally members of one household shared a religion (see, for example, Acts 10:44–48; 16:33 where all the
members of a household are baptized along with its head). When this is not the
case, a disciple is not left on his or her own but rather becomes part of a new
family of believers. Jesus redefines his kin as those who hear the word of God
and do it (Matt. 12:46–50; Mark 3:31–35). Luke 8:19–21 allows that Jesus'
blood relations may be among the family of believers. And in Acts 1:14 Jesus'
mother and siblings are named among the disciples gathered in the upper room
awaiting the coming of the Spirit. Whether or not a disciple remains connected
with blood relations, all members of the believing community are attached to
one another as "brother and sister."

Conflict in the family also arises from differing priorities. Preoccupation
with ordinary family concerns can leave one inattentive to signs of the end
times. Jesus advises his disciples, "For as the days of Noah were, so will be the
coming of the Son of Man. For as in those days before the flood they were eating and drinking, marrying and giving in marriage, until the day Noah entered
the ark, and they knew nothing until the flood came and swept them all away,

so too will be the coming of the Son of Man" (Matt. 24:37–39; similarly Luke 17:26–30).

Another saying of Jesus from the Q source speaks of the priority of commitment to Jesus: "Whoever comes to me and does not hate father and mother, wife and children, brothers and sisters, yes, and even life itself, cannot be my disciple" (Luke 14:26; similarly Matt. 10:37). The primary demand is that a disciple be wholly attached to Jesus and his mission, so that everything else is secondary, even family ties. Jesus is not advising disciples to despise their family. The sense of "hate" is as Matthew 10:37 renders it, "whoever loves father or mother more than me . . ." The saying in Luke 14:26 reflects the meaning of the Hebrew verb śānē, "to hate," which is "to leave aside." Jesus is naming family ties as one of the attachments that would make it hardest for a disciple to leave home to proclaim the gospel.

A disciple who does not love his or her own family members and who does not recognize God's love revealed in those closest at hand will not very well be able to share that divine love with outsiders. Many disciples are called to remain with their families and to proclaim God's love in that everyday context. Such a story is found in Luke 8:26–39, where a man healed of many demons wanted to accompany Jesus on his mission. Instead, Jesus directs him, "Return to your home and declare how much God has done for you" (8:39). Some disciples are called to leave behind their own world to become missionaries to peoples of other lands. Luke 14:26 advises all disciples, whatever their mode of spreading the gospel, that attachment to Jesus will sometimes take one away from beloved family members. But Jesus also assured his disciples, "There is no one who has left house or wife or brothers or parents or children, for the sake of the kingdom of God, who will not get back very much more in this age, and in the age to come eternal life" (Luke 18:29–30).

Christians should expect conflict, even in their own families. It can arise from differing expressions of faith commitments, differing interpretations of the gospel, and differing evaluations of the demands of discipleship. The Gospels attest that Jesus himself experienced, and even provoked, such conflict. Disciples find a new family within the community of believers. They attain a lasting peace (Luke 24:36) by faithfully continuing Jesus' mission of liberation for the oppressed and the practice of forgiving love (Luke 23:34).

Bibliography

Harrington, Daniel J. *The Gospel of Matthew* (Collegeville, Minn.: Liturgical Press, 1991).

Johnson, Luke T. *The Gospel of Luke* (Collegeville, Minn.: Liturgical Press, 1991).

Malina, Bruce J., and Richard L. Rohrbaugh. *Social-Science Commentary on the Synoptic Gospels* (Minneapolis: Fortress Press, 1992).

Osiek, Carolyn. "The Family in Early Christianity: 'Family Values' Revisited," *Catholic Biblical Quarterly* 58/1 (1996): 1–24.

Pilch, John J. *The Cultural World of Jesus* (Collegeville, Minn.: Liturgical Press, 1995, 1996).

—BARBARA E. REID, O.P.

Marital Relations
(1 Corinthians 7:1–11)

Historical and Literary Context

One of the key New Testament passages on marital relations is found in Paul's first letter to the Corinthians, which was written between 51 and 54 C.E. This letter responds to a situation of bitter and varied conflict within the Corinthian church. Paul writes from Ephesus in Asia Minor, where he has in hand a letter that some Corinthians had sent him (7:1), while simultaneously having his ear tugged by various oral reports that have reached him about individual and church behavior (see 1:11; 5:1; 11:18). Among the many sources of conflict were differences of opinion and practice in regard to marriage and sexual behavior. Indeed, within the first three decades of the early Christian movement these issues proved abundantly contentious (a fact that may give contemporary churches some consolation that they have not simply fallen away from an idyllic ancient period into purely "modern" controversies). In chapters 5 and 6 of this letter the apostle had given stern warnings against *porneia*, "sexual immorality." Chapter 7 continues with this concern, as Paul tries to steer a middle course on sexuality between the opposite poles of sexual libertinism on the one hand and mandatory celibacy on the other, positions that were likely represented in some forms within the Corinthian church. Many recent studies have argued that in particular the women at Corinth were motivated by ascetic ideals that led them to reject sexual relations and marriage. Paul's teachings to the Corinthian Christians on marriage and sexuality that are found in this passage are profoundly conditioned by two things: his overall concern for unifying this divided church, and the urgent apocalyptic outlook that pervades all of Paul's thought and counsel.

Because Paul's predominant concern in this letter is the reconciliation of the church, the section 7:1–11 has a certain evenhandedness, and even an invitation to discussion, as seen in the way he differentiates "concession" from "command" (7:6; compare 7:25) and his own counsel from Jesus' teaching (7:8, 10; compare 7:12, 25). While Paul's own preference for celibacy as the highest good is clear from v. 7 ("I wish that all were as I myself am"), he recognizes here as elsewhere in the letter the varied distribution of spiritual gifts and roles in the body of Christ. Verse 7b anticipates the themes to be developed at great length in chapter 12 of this letter on the body of Christ imagery for the church: "But each has a particular gift [*charisma*] from God, one having one kind and another a different kind" (compare 12:4–11). While *porneia* can never be tolerated, diversity in marital status is to be expected and honored, as Paul serially addresses the special situations of the married (7:2–7); the unmarried and widowed (7:8–9); those who have married but contemplate separation

(7:10–11); "the rest," that is, those who have married non-Christians (7:12–17); virgins (7:25–38); and widows (7:39–40). In this way Paul recognizes a divine plan and apportionment at work in the marital destinies of individuals (7:17), all of which he regards as incorporated into God's plan for all of creation, which is on the brink of catastrophic transformation (see 7:29 and 31: "For the present form of this world is passing away"). This apocalyptic view of history generates a characteristic Pauline paradox: it leads Paul on the one hand to minimize the importance of such immediate life issues as marrying or not marrying—given their precariously temporary nature—and on the other hand to raise the seriousness of sexual sins to a frighteningly immediate urgency—given his expectation that the coming end of the age will bring judgment on such things (the maxim "it is better to marry than to be burned up" is likely an intentional double entendre referring both to burning with passion and burning in the final judgment [compare 3:15]).

The Slogan of 1 Corinthians 7:1

The passage begins with Paul's introduction to the topics he will address next: "Now concerning the matters about which you wrote." After this introductory formula, Paul includes a simple, yet endlessly curious statement: "It is well for a man not to touch a woman" (7:1b). The meaning of the words themselves is not very difficult to discern: as stated, this is a flat condemnation of heterosexual intercourse ("touch" here is a well-recognized euphemism in Greek literature for the sexual act), written from an androcentric perspective. Though, significantly, the reason that such abstinence is "good" is not given, readers of the passage have inferred some possibilities from the larger context of chapter 7: for the sake of undivided concentration on religious matters, for spiritual enlightenment through disciplined self-mastery, or perhaps to maintain purity. If the latter view is in mind, then the statement is not only androcentric but in some sense misogynist, for it assumes that the woman is a source of contamination for the man (but not vice versa). But the rationale behind such proposed abstinence depends upon who uttered this statement.

Earlier translations, such as the RSV, regarded the statement as the apostle's own formulation and universal rule, which he intended as the umbrella under which the rest of the advice will fall. The difficulty with this view, however, is that much of what follows constitutes significant exceptions to this "rule." More recently many scholars have regarded the words as a quotation from the Corinthians themselves, as found in their letter. Thus the NRSV puts the words in quotation marks to signal this to the visual reader (but note that in oral proclamation this nuance would be lost). This is a common pattern in Paul's argumentation in this letter, to take up slogans from the Corinthians (likely from the different parties) and then reinterpret them in his own argumentation (see 1:12; 6:12; 8:1; 10:23). If we regard 7:1b as a slogan quoted from the Corinthians, what does Paul make of it?

1 Corinthians 7:2–7

Paul does not contest the viewpoint contained in 7:1b outright, and indeed 7:7a shows his support and personal exemplification of that dictum. Nonetheless 7:2–6 indicates that Paul does not consider sexual intercourse within marriage to be wrong, but rather he counsels mutual sexual congress of wives and husbands as is "their due" (*opheilec*), their "conjugal rights." While it may be "well" or "good" for a man to abstain from sexual intercourse, that does not mean, for Paul, that sexual intimacy in marriage is consequently wrong or evil. In fact, never in this chapter, or in any of Paul's letters, is sexual intercourse itself condemned. On the contrary, Paul issues imperatives: "let each man have his own wife and let each woman have her own husband" (my translation), thus affirming the positive value of sexual intercourse within the context of faithful monogamy. Ongoing sexual intimacy is to be the norm for such couples, which may be interrupted, by agreement, for short periods of concentrated prayer (this is the "concession" that v. 6 speaks about, not marriage itself). While celibacy may be "good," or "a higher good," sexual intercourse within the context of mutual marriage is to be the norm, and it is a charisma in its own right, a "particular gift" alongside the option of celibacy (7:7b).

Readers for many centuries, and particularly in our time, have correctly noted the balance and mutuality in Paul's advice for both partners in the marriage. In 7:2–4 he repeats each of three statements from both the male and female perspective (contrast 1 Thessalonians 4:4). This is particularly unusual in the ancient Greco-Roman context, which stressed the patriarchal household's insistence upon submission of lower orders to higher orders, women to husbands. In contrast, Paul argues that the obligations in the marital relationship are uniform for both partners, as are the benefits. In the Corinthian setting—where some apparently boasted, "I shall not be under anyone's authority!" (6:12b, my translation; the NRSV obscures the connection with the same verb, *exousiazein,* in our text)—it would likely come as a shock to hear Paul's strong countercultural declaration of mutual dominance in the marital relationship: "For the wife does not have authority over her own body, but the husband does; likewise the husband does not have authority over his own body, but the wife does" (7:4).

1 Corinthians 7:8–9

After addressing those already married, Paul turns to those who are not married. Consistent with the previous section, he first upholds celibacy, which he considers the highest good ("it is well" [7:8]), by appeal once more to his own example (see 7:7). But again he appreciates the powerful pull of sexual urges on people and commands that those who cannot "practice self-control" marry to carry out those urges in their only proper setting. Consistent with the rest of the chapter, in the light of the imminent end of the world, Paul counsels that they "remain" as they are, unmarried, for there is no time for change (see 7:20, 24). These verses do not give a positive rationale for human heterosexual marriage (note that even children are never mentioned!), but once again allow for it as the sole middle path between celibacy and sexual immorality for those who are not called to that first state. Perhaps in another context Paul could have extolled the virtues of the married life (perhaps he himself was previously married—we do not know), but here his major concern is prophylactic: protecting the church from what he considered the demonic power of sexual immorality.

1 Corinthians 7:10–11

Next in his series of addresses Paul turns to those who are married but have separated or are contemplating separation. This is one of the rare places in his letters where Paul cites a teaching of the historical Jesus. Because of its attestation here and in the synoptic sources Mark and Q (Matt. 5:31–33; 19:3–12; Mark 10:2–12; Luke 16:18), it is clear that some form of a saying forbidding divorce was genuine to Jesus, though its exact phrasing and justification are disputed. In Paul's argument here it is first the woman who is told not to seek the dissolution of the marriage through separation. It appears that in the church at Corinth some women in the church were separating from their husbands, some perhaps in the pursuit of celibacy. Despite the blanket prohibition of divorce, Paul makes a qualification in practice by offering two alternatives to the woman who does separate: either "remain" unmarried or else become reconciled to her husband (though given an ancient woman's dependence upon marriage for material support for herself and her children, we may wonder if this afforded a real alternative). Once again we note the mutuality in expression, for Paul gives two forms of the injunction against dissolution of marriage, one regarding a woman's initiation and one a man's (whereas the synoptic divorce sayings deal only with a man's right of divorce). Also consistent with the previous arguments in 1 Corinthians 7, here no positive rationale for maintaining a marriage is given, such as either of the appeals to Genesis 1:27 and 2:24 found on the lips of Jesus in Mark 10:6–8, for that was not Paul's purpose. Here Paul seeks to promote the dual values of celibacy preferred and reconciliation pursued in family and church relationships.

Contemporary Reactions

Modern readers of 1 Corinthians 7:1–11 will of course vary in their appreciation of what Paul is trying to do in this passage. Many contemporary Christians accept divorce without question in certain circumstances. Certainly Paul's ultimatum to the separated woman in 7:11—remain unmarried or return to your husband—has found many critics today, especially in the case of those women who leave abusive relationships. Contemporary churches that wish to be guided by this text should be aware of two ways in which it rests upon time-conditioned assumptions. First, Paul's whole argument here is rooted in his apocalyptic sensibility, which is quite foreign to many (though by no means all) contemporary Christians. Second, the purpose of this passage is not to reflect upon Christian marriage, per se, but rather to defend the Christian community against *porneia* in the interim period before the Lord returns (a perspective also at a remove from many modern-day Christians). But the text also shows that Paul did not think that there was a single answer for all persons (hence his treatment of persons of different status one after another) and that he saw the need for compromise and pastoral concessions in the life of faith. His insistence upon the dangerous effects of sexual immorality, not only for individuals but for the whole community, might deserve renewed hearing, as a basis for Christian community sexual ethics that could combat current, overly individualized and privatized ethical norms. While contemporary Christians may be disappointed that Paul does not here sufficiently extol marriage's positive virtues, he does assume that it remains the expected pattern of human sexual relationships. But most of all we may take away from this passage Paul's surprising insistence upon the mutuality between the woman and the man that should exist in the marriage relationship, in direct contrast to the prevailing ethos of his, and much of our, day.

Bibliography

Deming, Will. *Paul on Marriage and Celibacy: The Hellenistic Background of 1 Corinthians 7* (Cambridge: Cambridge University Press, 1995).

Fee, Gordon D. *The First Epistle to the Corinthians* (Grand Rapids: Wm. B. Eerdmans Publishing Co., 1987).

MacDonald, Margaret Y. "Women Holy in Body and Spirit: The Social Setting of 1 Corinthians 7," *New Testament Studies* 36 (1990): 161–81.

Wire, Antoinette Clark. *The Corinthian Women Prophets: A Reconstruction through Paul's Rhetoric* (Minneapolis: Fortress Press, 1990).

Yarbrough, O. Larry. *Not Like the Gentiles: Marriage Rules in the Letters of Paul,* Society of Biblical Literature Dissertation Series 80 (Atlanta: Scholars Press, 1985).

—MARGARET M. MITCHELL

Healed Women as
Models of Servant Leadership
(Luke 4:38–39; 8:1–3)

In the Gospels, is family life identified as the model for relations among the community of believers? One might conclude this from John's Gospel where the brother-sister relations of Martha, Mary, and Lazarus, all unmarried, incarnate the close bond that unites the followers of Jesus. Enjoying equal status and power, the followers are simultaneously siblings, friends, servants to each other, and members of the family of Jesus, since all call upon the same Father as their own.

From a converse perspective, is the ideal relationship for family members understood in the Gospels as a dissolution of the traditional power structure? Is discipleship, permeated by the ideal of humble service, a better model for family, undoing and replacing the convention of patriarchal dominance with an alternative experience of social equality in which the "first shall be last and the last shall be first"? Is a discipleship among equals an alternative to the family structured as a hierarchy of power relations, extending from the patriarchal head down through the zones of decreasing power, from governmental ruler to fathers and husbands, brothers, and sons, and ending with women, children, aliens, and slaves?

Some passages in the Gospels test the authenticity of radical commitment to Jesus by pitting loyalty to Jesus against a disciple's identification with the nuclear family. "Whoever loves father or mother more than me is not worthy of me" (Matt. 10:37) and "Let the dead bury their own dead; but as for you, go and proclaim the kingdom of God" (Luke 9:60). However, this tension needs to be qualified by references to family members who benefit in some way when their relatives become disciples. The healing of Simon Peter's mother-in-law is one such case (Matt. 8:14–15; Mark 1:29–31; Luke 4:38–39).

Each Synoptic Gospel nuances the relation between Peter's discipleship and the woman's healing somewhat differently. For Mark, the brothers Simon and Andrew, as well as the brothers James and John, answer the summons of Jesus to follow him (Mark 1:16–20) before Jesus heals Simon's mother-in-law (1:29–31) in the presence of the four new disciples; the ones who appeal to Jesus for her healing could be the four themselves or other members of the household. The sequence suggests that the two pairs of brothers, newly committed as disciples of Jesus, invite him to bring his healing power into the precincts of the nuclear family, dissolving the hard line that separates disciples from their relatives by blood or marriage.

In correlative acts of compassion, Jesus exorcises an unclean spirit from a man in the synagogue (Mark 1:21–28), and he takes a woman's hand, helps her up, causing a fever to leave her. She then serves (*diekonei autois*) her two sons, their two friends, and Jesus, implying that she sets about the household tasks of hospitality and meal preparation. Women readers may wonder if the release from the fever was such a great favor to the mother-in-law, now faced with a house full of famished guests returned home from Sabbath services in the synagogue where a dramatic healing had just taken place!

From a theological perspective the sequence of events proposes a logic about healing: It authenticates the good effects that result when Jesus teaches in the religious institution and demonstrates his power over the forces of dehumanization. The restorative power released by Jesus and his new followers into Simon's house overflows and benefits an older woman. Her physical restoration at the hand of Jesus summons her from bed, drives out the fever, and ends the isolation she has suffered inside her son-in-law's house. Instead of enduring the helplessness of being talked about and interceded for while she was sick, she now regains her power to speak for herself as presumably she did before the attack of fever.

Luke, by contrast, precedes the call of Peter, James, and John (5:9–11) with a series of healings, including that of Simon's mother-in-law (4:38–39) and mentions the fever's severity (*pureto megalo*), which he rebukes and drives away like a demonic force. Instead of having the call to discipleship come first, Luke describes the healing of a demoniac (4:31–37) and other healings from demonic possession (4:40–41) as pedagogical preparation for the call of Peter after the miraculous catch of fish. The assent of Peter, James, and John is followed by more healings, the cleansing of a leper (5:12–14), and the forgiveness-healing of the paralytic let down through the roof (5:17–26). For Luke, healing acts as pedagogical preparation for a call to discipleship, confirms for the disciple that the response is leading in a benevolent direction, and demonstrates that compassionate acts of healing are a constant feature of the service done by Jesus in company with his followers. In fact, the entire ministry of Jesus may be understood as a work of healing, according to the metaphor by which Jesus describes his work: "Those who are well have no need of a physician, but those who are sick" (Luke 5:31).

While the reader may good-humoredly ask whether the mother-in-law's burden of kitchen duties should be considered reward or punishment for having regained her health, she does immediately exercise her autonomy and power to serve them (*autois*). Luke and Mark note that she serves the family and its guests, including Jesus, appropriating her status as hostess, elder, and matriarch in the family. Matthew emphasizes the direct ministerial relation between the woman and Jesus, and her hands now serve him (*auto*) in reciprocity for his hand having healed her.

Admittedly, the passage can be read as dismissive of women's service; the only ministry that is really "theirs" is welcoming guests, serving meals to famished men, and acting as maid. On the other hand, the role of matriarch of the house— serving her guests—links this table service to authority within the house-church as a gathering place for liturgy and center for hospitality to missionaries. A variety of services exercised through the role of matriarch-hostess-leader is implied by the mention of the mother of John Mark (Acts 12:12), Lydia (Acts 16:15, 40), Chloe (1 Cor. 1:11), and Phoebe (Rom. 16:1–2).

A similar vocabulary of service within the household, redolent with dual references to women's ministerial role before kitchen table and liturgical altar, occurs in Luke 10:38–42 where Martha welcomes Jesus into her house and serves him. The passage may be considered not as a historical event but as a parable about disciples who are sisters in the household of the faith. The conversation between Martha and Jesus raises the many questions debated by Luke's community: Do women have direct access to Jesus or only through the mediation of men? Should women's service be confined to housework and meal preparation within the home, or is women's household service a viable metaphor for understanding the role of presider at the liturgical table? Does women's interpretation of Jesus' teaching come only through male disciples, or do women within their own circle of female relationships enjoy the immediacy of ongoing conversation and debate with Jesus about his instruction? Is the ambiguous answer Jesus gives Martha about the choice portion a confirmation of Mary's liturgical role in claiming her share of the sacrificial offerings once reserved for priests? The parable raises issues about the liturgical expression of women's ministry in house and church and implies an alliance between Mary and the male disciples who dedicate themselves to the ministry of the word (Acts 6:4).

Luke alone of the evangelists notes that Galilean women accompanied the Twelve and Jesus on missions and served them (*diekonoun autois*) by supporting them out of their own resources (Luke 8:1–3). One notable difference between female and male disciples in Luke is the fact that these women "qualified" as disciples because they had been healed of evil spirits and infirmities. While some might read this distinction as a proof of their earlier weakness—they had been restored to wholeness, much as sinful women received forgiveness from Jesus—another interpretation is called for. In contrast to the twelve male disciples, whose illnesses are never mentioned, the women's status as followers is especially credible. The women's personal experience provides constant and personal testimony to new audiences about the compassionate and benevolent character of Jesus. Telling their own story of transformative healing, they authenticate the integrity of Jesus' message. In particular, they can speak familiarly to other women as a sisterhood, inspiring hope and confidence that God's compassion observes no hierarchy. If the male disciples want an immediate proof of Jesus' power, they point not to their male companions but to Mary Magdalene, Joanna, Susanna, and many other women. The women's service to the mission of Jesus includes the testimony of their own transformation in body and spirit, as healing available to others, grounding the claims of the Twelve.

To correct the disciples' preoccupation with social status, Jesus intervenes in their debates over who is greatest by pointing to a child, "Whoever receives this child in my name receives me. . . . For the one who is least among all of you is the one who is the greatest" (Luke 9:46–48, author's translation). The honor accorded women as those who serve Jesus contrasts with their conventional social status, for women and children are "least" in the power pyramid of the patriarchal family. In terms of Jesus' teaching, the service of the "least," the women, is counted as the highest expression of discipleship.

A similar dispute over status arises among the disciples at the Last Supper, and Jesus responds, "Let the greatest among you be as the youngest, and the leader as the servant" (Luke 22:27, author's translation). For Luke, the dispute must be addressed as the meaning of service relations within the community of believers. His redaction is significant, because the response of Jesus in Mark contradicts the request of the siblings James and John, who presume "brotherhood" with Jesus means the most honored places at the family table (Mark 10:35–45). Matthew also refers to a nuclear family context and has Jesus correct not only James and John but their mother who has requested that they sit on the right and left of Jesus (Matt. 20:20–27). From reading Mark and Matthew, we might conclude that the struggle for status instead of service is specific to a patriarchal family structure. In Matthew, the focus on the nuclear family is highlighted by a mother's initiative; ambitious to sustain male privilege (and through theirs, her own), the mother of Zebedee's sons presses their cause to Jesus.

It is Luke who acknowledges that the community itself, however inspired by egalitarian ideals, has members who must hear the corrective to arguments about status. The humble and generous service of women is exemplary and powerful because they testify, as the Twelve do not, to an experience of personal healing. Women's servanthood is dignified by Jesus. The service of Simon Peter's mother-in-law, along with that of Mary Magdalene, Joanna, and Susanna, overturns a competitive model of relations both in the patriarchal family and within the community of disciples. To pay attention to what healed women do is to learn what servanthood, leadership, and ministry mean for all followers of Jesus, whether they are related through blood or through shared faith.

Bibliography

Ricci, Carla. *Mary Magdalene and Many Others: Women Who Followed Jesus.* Translated by Paul Burns. (Minneapolis: Fortress Press, 1994).

Ryan, Rosalie. "The Women from Galilee and Discipleship in Luke," *Biblical Theology Bulletin* 15 (1985): 56–69.

Seim, Turid Karlsen. *The Double Message: Patterns of Gender in Luke and Acts* (Edinburgh: T. & T. Clark; Nashville: Abingdon Press, 1994).

—MARIE-ELOISE ROSENBLATT

20

Families and Worship

The family is widely acknowledged as a central context for religious life and worship in all the great world religions. We discuss the theme of worship and the family here, however, from within the Christian tradition because it is the tradition we know from the inside. It is our prayer that our observations and suggestions will have significant transfer value for families from other religious communities as well.

We explore the family and worship from two perspectives: first, the ways that contemporary and diverse families can be included dynamically in the corporate worship of the congregation (the *ecclesia,* the gathered assembly of the body of Christ), and second, the ways that worship may be created and sustained within the family setting (the *ecclesiola,* the small, intimate body of Christ in the home).

Before we turn to these concerns, it is important to consider some basic assumptions that we bring to this enterprise.

First, life is sacred. All persons and all of nature are gifts to us from God. God's grace is built into the very fabric of life. Worship does not bring God's presence into life otherwise devoid of God's grace. Worship celebrates and calls our attention to the reality of God's ever-present spirit. As theologian Karl Rahner puts it: "The world is constantly and ceaselessly possessed by grace from its innermost roots. . . . It is constantly and ceaselessly sustained and moved by God's self-bestowal" (1976, 166).

If we assume God's loving and righteous presence within all of nature and persons, our lives will be profoundly different. We will see God's spirit, alive and vibrant, in each person we meet and in the animal and plant world we use to sustain our families. Martin Buber, the Jewish thinker, said it well in his classic *I and Thou* (1955). He proposed a seemingly revolutionary idea: Each one of us is sacred. If we act on this assumption we will treat all other persons as *Thous.* When we treat others as sacred *Thous* we become *I-Thou* in our inner lives. When we treat others in our family or in the human family as things to be used for our selfish purposes, as *its,* we become *it*-like ourselves. We are never merely an *I;* we are always an *I-Thou* or an *I-it.* If we want to discover the eternal, living God, the eternal *Thou* in our midst, we will do so by treating others as persons in whom God's spirit is alive. Buber also maintained that once we have treated another person as a *Thou,* the experience has a certain *I-it* quality when it is past. *I-Thou* relationships must constantly be reenacted, made new, and celebrated. This fact is a central reason that worship rituals in the family must be repeated and renewed.

Second, ritual in the family and in life in general is inevitable. The issue is whether our family rituals are life-affirming and God-centered or life-denying, wooden, and dead. Erik Erikson, in *Toys and Reason* (1977), his seminal study of the power of ritual and the normal stages of ritualization in human experience, concludes that the human family communicates its various visions of reality, its beliefs, values, and worldviews via the rituals we employ. Such rituals (related to eating, washing, dressing, naming, working, and so on) reveal the way we "look at" or see life. Rituals that affirm life as sacred and essentially valuable have great restorative power. In this environment a spiritual and mysterious quality can be found that permeates the family's consciousness and blesses the parents and children in their quest for personal identity and a sense of eternal meaning. Rituals that become compulsive or legalistic can become hurtful and dehumanizing. Such rituals he calls *ritualism*.

The reason rituals can become wooden, legalistic, or dead is that they have been made into idols. This happens when a sense of playfulness, of leap, or leeway is absent from the ritual. Erikson made this discovery by studying the rituals found in the play of children. He found that when a ritual became unproductive for children, they were free enough to innovate in a playful way, to develop a new ritual that was life-giving rather than life-denying. He believes adults can also view rituals playfully. Rituals in our families or in society that cease to carry a humanizing vision can and should be changed. Erikson sees the possibility of the renewal of society's vision through children who create a stability in basic re-ritualizations, through young people who either confirm the vision or reform it by dissent or revolt, and through adults who recognize that when rituals fall into *ritualism* people can be sufficiently playful to innovate, re-ritualize, and create new rituals relevant to the ever-changing challenges our families must face in a "future shock" society (1977, 173).

This way of thinking is similar to that of Orthodox theologian Alexander Schmemann, who sees that our natural human nature is to adore God, to receive the gifts of the natural world as a priest who utters prayers of thanksgiving, blesses the gifts, and distributes them justly to all of God's family. This is an image of the "universal priesthood" and a natural foundation for a "priesthood of parenthood," where parents are natural priests to their children as they celebrate the gifts of God and treat these gifts as a Eucharist, "breaking bread and pouring wine" for their children but also for all of God's human family (1973, 14).

Ernest Boyer reinforces the importance of such a "priesthood of parenthood" when he affirms the spiritual power of a rich ritual life within the family. He says, "The spirituality of the family . . . is one of the most rigorous and most difficult, but it is also among the most rewarding and transforming of all the great spiritual disciplines. . . . what it reveals is the love and the holiness at the very core of all that is. It does this by asking that a person dedicate himself or herself to live the daily expression of two sacraments, the sacrament of the care for others and the sacrament of the routine. These are both hard sacraments to live, but within the first, love is revealed, and within the second [is revealed] the sacredness of the ordinary activity. To live both together is to find in the truest manner possible the presence of God" (1984, 57).

Third, rituals of meaning have to be sensitive to certain important rhythms. These are the unique rhythms of each family in relation to the rhythms of current life in our highly mobile and pluralistic society, in relation to the rhythms of the great celebration of the Christian year, in relation to the rhythm involved in moving from stage to stage in the life cycle. Sensitivity is needed to discern the best times to pause to celebrate God's ever-present reality. It is also critical to determine the length of the celebration; the repetition of certain meaningful prayers, stories, and dramatic or artistic elements; the rhythm of established rituals; and the playful and innovative re-ritualizations needed to keep family worship alive. An appropriate rhythm and relation needs to be established between the family's participation in the corporate worship experience of the faith community and the family's unique celebration of God's ongoing creation and redemptive presence in the home setting. The latter involves decisions that the family makes about the possibilities of worship moments in the morning, in the evening, at mealtimes, and at special times within the family's history, such as anniversaries, and birthdays, baptismal anniversaries, and dates commemorating ancient and contemporary saints and heroes (see the section on family liturgies in Sloyan and Huck 1970, 27–39).

Finally, the family is understood as a "reflection" and extension of the larger family in Christ that is the church. These families—the *ecclesiola*, the household of faith, and the *ecclesia*, the bonding of many households of faith, in the church—exist together in an intimate relation where the *ecclesiola* is naturally an image and expression of the *ecclesia*.

These assumptions undergird the following discussion of the family's full participation in the worship of the gathered body of Christ and the family's more intimate expressions of worship within the small body of Christ in the home.

The Family's Participation in the Worshipping Community of Faith

In many congregations there are hurdles to overcome in order to include whole families in the worship life of the faith community. A denominational leader of workshops on the family and worship told us recently, "I don't find too many churches that really 'get it,' when it comes to including children and parents together in worship." Not a few churches structure their schedules so that children are in church school while adults are worshipping. This pattern separates the family and prevents children and youth from owning and experiencing the central celebration of the faith community.

With varying degrees of success, many churches have kept the family together in worship through a children's sermon, after which children leave for classes. A few churches have developed a shorter family service as an option on Sunday morning, seeking to integrate worship and study for all family members in an hour-and-forty-five-minute period. A current movement is to offer an alternate service on Saturday evening that is much more participatory and that includes the whole family. Another trend is to integrate church education and worship with study and worship in the home following the lectionary readings from scripture and the various seasons of the church year. A variation on this pattern is to prepare young children (ages three to seven) to experience and respond creatively and existentially (through play) to worship in a special educational program, built on the major elements in worship, with the eucharistic celebration as a model and the Montessori approach to learning as the methodology (see Berryman 1991). Still another option has been the development of family clusters with several families meeting in homes on a regular basis with family fun, meals, study, and worship (see Sawin 1979).

These explorations are moving churches to think of corporate worship experiences not as adult oriented only but as church family oriented, where individual families participate creatively and meaningfully with equal regard for the contributions of parents and children of all ages. Such an image emerged articulately in the late 1970s and early 1980s in the work of David Ng and Virginia Thomas. They maintained that all who are baptized are to be seen as full members of the church. Baptized children and youth as well as adults are to be included not only by invitation but by active participation, in the roles and functions of the worship experience and present in the minds of those who design corporate worship. The presence and participation of children, youth, parents, and persons at all the stages of life greatly enrich the worship and reveal the integrity of the Christian claim that "God's kingdom is for all, and that God's love draws all together. . . . children and adults worshiping together make the statement of faith" (Ng and Thomas 1981, 20–29, 124).

Carolyn Hardin Engelhardt, director of the Paul Vieth Resource Center of Yale Divinity School, makes a strong case for integrating religious education and worship. This means to her that parents and congregational members alike will "identify the congregation's worship as the most important experience for all ages to participate in weekly." Engelhardt continues to confront the church when she says, "There is no inner consistency in our faith life when we let children experience a single hymn and a prayer of confession and then ask them to leave the service of worship. There is no sense to what we are doing when children experience only confession of our sins and no offering. There is a broken picture when children are asked to see the bread but never know what is done with it and never eat it themselves but instead must look and leave. (Is it like being asked to a party only to be told to go home after greeting the guests?)" (1990, 6, 7).

Pastors and worship committees in increasing numbers of churches are taking seriously such admonitions and are seeking to include the total church family in worship. This means designing liturgies that involve participation by people of all ages and also including people of various ages in the planning and leading of corporate worship. We see this happen when husbands, wives, and children from different families lead in the Advent candle-lighting ceremonies;

or when children's, youth, and bell choirs take part with joy and abandon; or when children, youth, and parents are greeters, ushers, acolytes, or participants in eucharistic celebrations; or when church school classes sponsor infants for baptism and bring in the water for the font and surround the parents and godparents with their presence and care; or where confirmands and their parents participate in the sprinkling of the congregation during celebrations of baptismal renewal. Children in fifth or sixth grades and older can be trained to read scripture well, to create prayers and litanies that the entire congregation may use. The younger children can make drawings or paintings of themes for various celebrations in the church year. These drawings or paintings may be used on the cover of worship bulletins. A gallery of children's art can be established. Banners and stoles made by children or youth or by families can be used in worship. Families can create worship centers. There are many ways to include the whole family, if there is a decision to do so. (See Morris 1988 for many other suggestions.)

One possibility is for congregations to open the communion table fully, especially to baptized children. There is probably no more profound experience for a child to have than to go to the Table with his or her parents and with the whole faith community—to go and be fed, not just go as an observer. Such participation is controversial among some Christians, but in research conducted recently we saw a major trend to include children with their families at the Table. (See Browning and Reed 1995 for a study of seven denominations and major trends.)

Pastors can be more sensitive to the whole congregation in their sermons and prayers. This means that pastors will have children and youth as well as adults in their minds as they prepare and deliver sermons. It does not mean that pastors talk down to younger members of the family. Issues dealt with in sermons can be challenging and can stimulate internal dialogue as well as dialogue within the family setting without being overly ponderous. Elizabeth Achtemeier reminds pastors that the Christian faith is, at base, about human relationships. She says, "In the biblical faith, every family relationship affects the relationship with God, just as, vice versa, God is at work in every area and relationship of family life" (1987, 31). She underscores that Christian marriage and family life, when authentic and growing, are genuinely revolutionary in our society. She concludes that preaching about the family of faith should be aimed at transformation rather than conformation.

A children's sermon provides another way for churches to include children and keep the family together in corporate worship. Although this pattern is increasingly being questioned, it is well established in many churches. The danger is that it will become a "cute time" in which children are used to entertain the adult congregation. Alan Smith offers fine counsel when he says that "children need to be intentionally included in the total life of the local manifestation of the body of Christ" and that the children's sermon should give expression to such inclusion (1984, 22). Likewise, other members of the church family need to be included during the children's sermon. This means that the children and the pastor (or Christian educator or layperson in such a role) should be well located in the chancel area with good sound equipment to catch the quieter voices of children. Some resources are available that involve parents and others in the congregation actively in the conversations built into the children's moments. One pastor tells of bringing a large sheet of newsprint with the heading "Thank you, God, for . . . ." He asks the children to tell why they are thankful and records each response. When members of the total congregation share their feelings of thanksgiving to God, their contributions are also recorded. At other times he creates a prayer of intercession with children and the congregation, asking them to complete the sentence: "God, please watch over and take care of . . . ." Then the children and the congregation recite the prayer they have written together (Wetherwax 1990, 9). Several books offer suggestions for involving the children and the congregation in active, experiential learning and worship through the children's sermon (see, for example, Baker 1995).

Sonja Stewart and Jerome Berryman have developed an approach to educate children from ages three to seven to participate fully in worship through the use of "godly play." They have designed a rich range of experiences built around the basic elements of worship; they employ the Montessori method, with the eucharistic celebration as the model. While Berryman and Stewart believe that children should be included in Sunday worship, they recognize the unique way that children learn and express themselves through play. They agree with Soren Kierkegaard (1941, 532) that "it is the rape of children, be it ever so well meant—to force the child's existence into decisive Christian categories." Rather, children should be able to play with holy things. In order to enhance this playful engagement with the experience of the genuine worship of God, they take young children "apart from the worshiping congregation so they become able to worship meaningfully with the congregation [later]" (Stewart and Berryman 1989, 13). Children in groups of twelve go apart with two leaders to a specially equipped room. The children gather around a focal shelf with a candle and figures of the Holy Family and the Good Shepherd. Around the walls are shelves of Bibles and books on the parables of the church, the saints, and the story of how we got the Bible. In addition, there are art supplies and painting trays, a rug box, clay, books, kneeling tables, and a place for "work in progress" to be kept from one week to the next. The objective is for children to assemble in God's name; hear the proclamation of God's word through simply told stories and to explore its meaning through the use of figures, clay, drawing, and painting; give thanks to God in the eucharistic feast (the children prepare the tables and eat fruit, cheese, bread, and juice and talk about the feasts Jesus gave); and go forth in God's name (the children sing and receive a good word about a gift for ministry each has delivered—for example, "The story you made for Jimmy in the hospital is great"). This pattern follows the fourfold nature of the corporate worship in which the children will participate with their parents and the whole congregation later (Stewart and Berryman 1989, 17).

Jerome Berryman, a priest and canon for religious education at the Episcopal Cathedral in Houston, Texas, has conducted research in relation to this design and has written with great sensitivity and awareness of the deeply spiritual nature of children and their ability to respond to God at an existential level over time. Each child is encouraged to have "work in progress" that reveals through art or other expressions what is going on in his or her inner life. Berryman has found that children work on deeper existential issues than we often expect—the major ones being "death, the threat of freedom, aloneness, and the need for meaning" (1991, 57; see also Berryman 1995; Rosner 1990).

Berryman deepens our understanding of the meaning of worship for all of us. He dialogues with Soren Kierkegaard's description of worship in his classic *Purity of Heart Is to Will One Thing.* Kierkegaard said that most people see worship in the following way: the audience is the congregation, the prompter is God, and the players are the religious leaders—priests, ministers, and rabbis. In Kierkegaard's view the audience is God, the prompter is the religious leader, and the players are the congregation (the people are the worshippers). According to Berryman, we are all players: God, the congregation, the religious leaders, and the building space. In the language game that takes place, the religious leader should function as "an experienced player-coach" who is in and out of the game, aware of the use of space, time, the resources of the great faith stories, and the consciousness of the worshipper concerning these existential issues (Berryman 1991, 10).

Worship and education in church can be integrated with worship and study at home when families follow the lectionary readings in scripture and the seasons of the church year. In this way the family unit (whatever its form) is brought together both in corporate worship and in the home setting around the same rich biblical themes of the faith. A movement emphasizing the interrelationship of education and liturgy emerged in the 1970s and 1980s. Built around the views of John Westerhoff and others, Joseph P. Russell (1979) developed an early design. The United Church of Christ then published in 1994 *The Inviting Word: A Worship-Centered, Lectionary-Based Curriculum for Congregations.* This beautifully designed curriculum is enhanced by a journal, *In Seasons,* which provides many rich suggestions for the integration of worship and education in the congregation and in the home. The journal has ideas for the celebration of the great festivals of the church year, leadership training outlines, sermon seeds, and an overview of creative ways to work with families and persons of each age level. In addition, *Imaging the Word* (1994), a guide for home worship, follows the seasons of the church year, offering a rich selection of art, poetry, stories, and music. It is an exceptional resource.

The pastor of one church that has been using these resources summarizes her experience by saying, "The lectionary provides a way for our worship committee, our education program, our missions group—all of our committees—to work together. Reflection on common Scripture and prayer becomes central to all our work."

A very unusual and creative variation of Berryman's "godly play" approach is one designed by Gretchen Wolff Pritchard in *Offering the Gospel to Children* (1992). She employs drama and art to illuminate biblical stories and also myths and legends from secular literature that have captured the essentials of the gospel. She trusts that the messages of love, reconciliation, and overcoming fears lead children to faithful and hopeful lives. Stories such as "The Flower of Life," a Mexican fairy tale, or William Steig's "Sylvester and the Magic Pebble" are illustrations. She also adapts Berryman's approach in a Good Shepherd program where children join their parents in the corporate worship service after the passing of the peace in the liturgy and go to the eucharistic table with their parents.

Pritchard affirms "pew art" for children who are worshipping with their families. She believes in involving children actively in celebrating the great festivals. She describes in detail how she touches their imaginations when celebrating events such as Palm Sunday prayer walk, the Community of Saints, the Feast of Corpus Christi, the Celestial City, and Three Kings' Saturday. She records the responses of children to master faith stories such as the Cain and Abel story. She has discovered that "confronting the Cain and Abel myth allowed children to see their own angers and jealousies side by side with the world's potential fury and aggression. One boy, whose relationship with his little brother was particularly rocky, worked over the story again and again with his parents during the week with obvious fascination and relief at the discovery that he was not the first to harbor murderous fantasies toward a younger brother" (Pritchard 1992, 29–30).

The Family Cluster Model, created by Margaret Sawin, is another example of a program that brings families together in worship, study, and close, supportive relationships. In this design several families cluster together in various homes to strengthen one another in family fun, discussion of stories or parables of the faith, fellowship around eating, and sometimes celebrating the Eucharist together. Sawin has written sound resources to guide the formation of such cluster groups and to nurture high-quality learning and worship experiences (see Sawin 1982). Persons from all types of family patterns can feel welcome and supported in such family clusters, which in turn are related with integrity to the total worshipping and serving community and to each home setting.

Finally, our own work concerning a sacramental approach to education and liturgy places a strong emphasis on the role of parents as members of the *ecclesia* in mutual ministry to one another and as priests to their children. The faith community needs to experience a paradigm shift, from seeing the ministers or priests as the primary persons supporting families to seeing the entire congregation as ministering persons with each emerging family. Such a concept can be fostered by the support of young couples prior to the participation of their first child in the liturgical and educational life of the congregation. Some possibilities are prebirth and prebaptismal nurture of the couple; prayers of thanksgiving in the liturgy concerning the birth; the surrounding of the parents with sponsors who may be peers, younger persons, or seniors; education and sharing about the meaning of baptism in advance of the baptismal celebration. Such practices require follow-up support and nurture of the family, including encouraging the new family to be present in the total life of the church. Our recommendation is for the baptism celebration to include baptism in water and

Spirit, blessing by the laying on of hands of parents, grandparents, and sponsors, and participation in the first Eucharist for the child. The Communion of an infant can be accomplished with the use of a small spoon. This ancient pattern of initiation is finding increasing use in the churches. This is the classic unified initiation that was used in the early church and is still used in the Eastern Orthodox church. The Spirit blessing of confirmation or of baptismal affirmation, then, can and should be repeated at the various stages in life when the person grows in her or his self-understanding and commitment to the ministry of the body of Christ. Similar experiences can surround parents in churches that dedicate infants or elect them into the catechumenate with baptism to follow later. Following the recognized stages of human and faith development, we have suggested educational and liturgical designs throughout life for families and for the church family. These are grouped around the classic sacraments of marriage (and family life education from birth on), reconciliation (dealing with the healing of relationships in the family and society that become strained and broken), unction (the continuing need for healing and wholeness in all phases of life and death), ordination (of clergy and the consecration of laity for their participation in the general ministry of all believers in family, work, community, and world), the central place of the eucharistic celebration, and the renewal of commitment through baptismal affirmation at different times in life (see Browning and Reed 1985, 1995).

Several of the above suggestions for the inclusion of the family in the worshipping community of faith also call for cooperation and authentic forms of worship within the home. The *ecclesia* and the *ecclesiola* are not separate spheres of faith and worship. We bring one to the other and vice versa. The wholeness of our experience, both blessing and bane, is what we take to corporate worship. Resources of God's blessing and purpose we take from the gathered church to our homes. It is not uncommon for children to "play church" at home. In the largest sense, that is what family worship in the home truly is.

We turn now to a consideration of some of the specific possibilities of worship in the home, recognizing that in the discussion of the family in the liturgy we have already opened up possibilities for the home. We enter this subject also aware that there is great variety in the shapes, sizes, and dynamics of families.

Worshipping in the Family Setting

Well-known author Charlie Shedd tells about his pilgrimage toward humility in respect to any wisdom about bringing authentic faith alive in families. As a young pastor before he had children, he was confident in speaking to fathers and mothers about raising their children in faith. The title of his first message was "Some Suggestions for Parents." Then he and his wife had their own children, and his title changed to "Feeble Hints to Fellow Strugglers." After his children grew up and left the nest, he started his conversation with parents with "Does anyone here have a few words of wisdom?" (see Erickson 1994).

Up front, it is important to acknowledge how necessary but also how complicated—even difficult—it can be to create moments of worship and celebration in the home setting. There is no need to list all of the conflicting forces evident in the often fast-paced lives of most contemporary families. Some of the best suggestions could come from families that have incorporated periods of family communication, sharing, reflection, fun, and worship and celebration. Such families do exist, and many of the following suggestions come from reports of their lives at various stages in the family life cycle.

Flexibility seems to be required. The diversity of family portraits prevents us from suggesting any family worship form that may not have to be adjusted or recreated.

In *A Book of Family Prayers* (1979), Gabe Huck indicates that one way to deal with the diversity of families is to address prayer to households. Besides mother, father, and children, "household can mean single-parent families, older couples, young couples without children, single persons, or even a person alone. It is in all such basic units that the Christian life needs expression in prayer" (Huck 1979, 2). Huck's fine book reminds parents that "children learn to pray from parents and others who live in God's presence and who respond with prayer. They learn to pray, not because parents feel that they ought to pray for the child's sake, but because parents have a love of praying and a habit of praying for their own sake" (1979, 3). Huck wrote prayers and meditations for households for the liturgical year from Advent to Pentecost, and for what is called "ordinary time." He includes a rich range of scripture, prayer, litanies, and blessings for various times during the day (morning, evening, mealtime) and for special occasions such as marriage, birth, departing, returning, illness, and death. Two other excellent resources are *Welcome Home: Scriptures, Prayers, and Blessings for the Household* (Torvend, ed., 1995) and Edward Hays's *Prayers for the Domestic Church* (1995).

It is important for household members to make some agreements or covenants with one another regarding family worship. Some suggestions follow (many of them taken or adapted from Held 1987, 23–24):

1. Agree on regularly scheduled times for conversation and communication about what persons are experiencing, culminating in sharing of scripture, personal faith stories, activities, questions or issues, and prayer. These times may be daily or weekly. The time or times should be mutually acceptable, experimental, recognizing that everyone can give feedback about the feasibility of the agreement, including the need for a change to a more workable time.
2. Agree on the length of time the worship will take. High-quality but brief periods seem best if the worship is to be regular, inspiring, and not seen as burdensome.
3. Agree on where the worship will take place. Possibly designate a certain place as a worship center in the home. This center can be prepared with signs and symbols made

by participants representing the different seasons of the year or different concerns in the world or in the family.

4. Possibly use family meetings as a time to involve everyone in planning the worship experiences. At such time different members can agree to prepare for and lead the worship periods, including young children with help. It is especially important for both the mother and father to share leadership roles and thereby to model mutual ministry.

5. Develop a bank of worship resources aimed at your particular family or household situation. Have these resources available for all to use in their preparation and leadership. Keep adding new resources. Invite contributions from all members. Most denominations have published resource materials for home use.

6. Seek to create an atmosphere of joy and freedom of expression, characterized by good listening and dialogue about where God's creative presence is experienced in the lives of those present.

7. Be informal, natural, flexible, and open to change.

8. Seek to relate the worship, reflection, and action of the family/household *ecclesiola* to the worship, education, and actions of the faith community, the *ecclesia*. Each reinforces and supports, but also critiques the other.

It is important for families to make adjustments according to the realities present in the family life cycle. For instance, young couples, prior to having children, can enhance the quality of their relationships and the depth of their communication if they can make agreements about their spiritual growth just as they make other agreements about work, leisure, and community involvement. With both persons working, it is very easy for couples to rush through their early life together without pausing for moments of discussion about ways to give expression to the commitment made at their wedding. Sometimes it is helpful to join other young couples for discussion of issues of faith and everyday values and goals in life. They can search the scriptures, pray for and support one another, be strengthened by the joy that can surround meals and outings. There is considerable interest on the part of young people in developing spiritual disciplines along with their interest in physical conditioning. There are many guides available to enhance the spiritual growth of young couples (see, for example, Clinebell 1992; Baldwin 1991; Wright 1989; Fox 1991). If couples, prior to having their first child, have already discovered the joy and meaning of playful but serious effort to grow spiritually, they will have established some rituals that can be refined when they have children.

The same is true for couples or single parents at the time of the "empty nest" stage in midlife or at the older adult period. Having already established a basic pattern of worship in the home, they can be more comfortable with any adjustments or re-ritualization needed to keep the spiritual dimension of life vibrant and alive. (See Duvall 1977 for a discussion of the key life issues for families in the eight stages in the family life cycle. Family worship will focus on different life tasks for families at each stage, to some degree.)

Families with Young Children

When parents are planning worship moments with young children, they should be ready for surprises and for more intuitive spiritual awareness than sometimes expected. Oxford University researcher Edward Robinson in *The Original Vision* (1977) identified a number of adults who reported that they had in some way been "affected by some power beyond themselves" as children. JoAnne Taylor has followed up on Robinson's study with interviews and drawings from children, ages four to twelve, regarding their spiritual experiences. She found that children sometimes live more naturally with a sense of God's presence in their lives than do adults. Taylor discovered that one of the ways parents and teachers can engender religious faith is to *listen* to children as they share their perceptions through words or art. Her book, *Innocent Wisdom: Children as Spiritual Guides* (1989), is a good model for parents to follow as they plan creative ways to involve their children in family worship experiences.

Gertrude Mueller Nelson (1986, 3) illustrates the spiritual sensitivity of young children by telling about her daughter, Annika, almost four years old. Nelson had been sewing and had left scraps of fabric in a wastebasket. Later, she found Annika in the back yard affixing the long bright strips of fabric to a long pole with tape. Annika explained, "I'm making a banner for a procession. I need a procession so that God will come down and dance with us." With that she lifted her banner and began to dance. Nelson reflects on the fact that she had witnessed a "holy moment" and that she had learned anew how real is the sense of wonder of children, "how innate and easy their way with the sacred."

Parents of young children often find mealtimes and bedtimes to be natural moments for worship. Many of the resources for family devotions have prayers and activities built around meals. The most effective prayers for young children may be prayers they express concerning the ways they are thankful to God, illustrated by drawings or other activities. Debbie Grafton O'Neal (1994, 5–8) offers many options, including singing and spoken prayers.

Bedtime conversations and prayers can be especially natural and warm. "Read me a story" is an expected request. A beautifully illustrated story book is Susan Swanson Swartz's *Families of God* (1994). The book is racially and ethnically inclusive. The text and the illustrations set an open and affirming frame of reference for subsequent growth. Jeanne S. Fogle's *Seasons of God's Love: The Church Year* (1988) is especially good for families with children five to seven years of age. It is a single story about nature's seasons and the seasons of the Christian year. Another beautifully written and illustrated book for bedtime reading is by a Jewish writer, Sandy Eisenberg Sasso (1994). *In God's Name* is about the names we give to God, depending upon our experience. Eventually, all images come together, and we see that each name is somehow true and still "God is One."

Families with Elementary-Age Children and Teens

Families with elementary-age children and teens are at the point where parents and children can make the agreements outlined earlier and can share responsibility for leadership of the family's worship life. It is crucial that everyone gets "on board" and sees the worship moments as relevant to the life issues the family is facing.

Family worship times can be opportunities for honest conversations about what each person really believes about God, Jesus, the Bible, prayers, the church, and what these beliefs mean for everyday life. Delia Halverson's *How Do Our Children Grow* (1993) is designed to stimulate such honest dialogue in the family setting. She is sensitive to the different levels of discussion appropriate for preschool children through teens, but her reflections on the nature of God, Jesus, the Bible, and prayer are thoughtful and probing. Using a story format, Eldon Weisheit has designed *Family Time Story Devotions* (1994) in a way that helps family members identify with certain life experiences. Some of the story themes reveal the point: "They say I'm stupid," "He's a pest," "I didn't do it," "You won't let me have any fun," "I'm all alone."

Explore inside the Bible (1994), by Fiora Walton, offers many creative activities especially for families with elementary-age children. The activities focus on how the Bible came to be, its makeup, and its key stories.

The idea of taking a playful but serious approach to family devotional times has been pursued with imagination by Mike and Amy Nappa in *52 Fun Family Devotions* (1994). They center their sessions on a biblical story with an application to a contemporary life issue such as sibling rivalry, peer pressure, forgiveness, or the use of money. There is always an action-oriented, fun element in the devotional time. For instance, if kids are picking at each other often, "try placing an unfrosted cake on your dinner table and pick it apart during a meal, leaving a large pile of crumbs. (Just smile when your family questions your behavior!) After dinner, ask someone to read Galatians 5:15 and relate how words can destroy people like picking at a cake destroys dessert. Then sprinkle the crumbs over some ice cream and spend some time building each other up while enjoying a treat." The final two phases are the discussion of the interrelationship of the scripture and the action, and a prayer time.

The United Church of Christ's *Word Among Us* curriculum has many suggestions for home discussion and worship for all ages. In addition, three volumes of very engaging resources have been especially designed to enrich family discussions and worship, titled *Imaging the Word* (Laurence et al. 1994; Blair et al. 1995).

Because of the effectiveness of the lectionary-centered church-year pattern, many other resources are emerging. Several help families celebrate the great festivals of the year. This is especially true for Advent, Christmas, Easter, and Pentecost. An illustration of such resources is Jeanne Heiberg's *Advent Arts and Christmas Crafts* (1995). With fine attention to family rituals, prayer, and blessings, the author goes well beyond the making of Advent wreaths to help families create tree decorations, Christmas creches, Epiphany chains, star mobiles, crowns, and many other items that involve children and parents and enrich family worship experiences.

The seasons present the faithful with a rich treasury of music. For many families this presents opportunities of transfer from gathered *ecclesia* to *ecclesiola*. Having a hymnal or hymnals at home is an easy asset for intimate enjoyment in worship for some families. A talented member of the family who plays a musical instrument can provide leadership. Some families genuinely gifted in music can sing together in parts praising God and blessing one another in the fun and joy that music making can create. A good place to start is with the collection *Canons, Songs, and Blessings,* by Helen and John Kemp (1990).

One of the most difficult challenges for parents is to keep the interest and participation of the teenage members of the family. The fact that teenagers are significantly influenced by such involvement is well established. The Search Institute's study of youth attitudes found that "family religiousness" ranked highest in its impact on the maturity of faith among youth. "This included families where the parents talked about faith and God with their children, practiced family devotions, and worked together on projects that helped others" (Halverson 1993, 11).

Ways to keep teenagers engaged in family communication and celebration include inviting teenagers to take leadership roles, reinforcing the agreement to save at least one time during the week for family communication and worship, and employing videos, E-mail, and the World Wide Web as resources for the family (see Clapp 1984). E-mail messages to and from grandparents or older brothers and sisters in college or at work can greatly enrich the quality of family life. The use of the Internet can help the family be in communication with others working on important social issues of our day. Soon many churches will have their own Home Page on the World Wide Web. This will make possible the creating of liturgical and educational resources for families on a parishwide basis. Young people can bring their expertise to such a project, not only with their confidence and facility with the media but also in writing and designing Home Page resources that are "on target" concerning the real issues in their lives. It is also important to encourage teen members of the family to develop the habit of personal prayer and reflection. One example of a devotional resource for youth is William L. Coleman's *Teen Stress: Stories to Guide You* (1994). The meditations address life issues such as peer pressure, cheating, stress regarding dress, and sexual pressures. Newbery Honor author Gary Paulsen's *The Tent: A Parable in One Setting* (1995) and *The Rifle* (1995) are beautifully written stories aimed at teens. Another resource is *The Book of Virtues: A Treasury of Great Moral Stories,* edited by William J. Bennett. Bennett recognizes the richness of the moral guidance that can come from other world religions but focuses mostly on those coming out of literature and Christian tradition.

Videos can be used to stimulate conversation for family times. Commercial movies like *A Mother's Courage: The Mary Thomas Story* (about the mother of Isaiah Thomas), *Born Free, Charley,* and *The Adventures of Tom Sawyer* raise deep issues. Many children's video series are now available, including *Fairie Tale Theater* and *Rabbit Ears Productions* (see Schultze and Schultze 1995). Also, most denominational centers have extensive audio and video libraries. One series to help parents get started with family worship is *Praying with Children* by LeAnn Ciampa (1991). Six ten-minute videotapes address ways to pray with children: prayers of thanksgiving; prayers for self, family, and others; prayers for the world; prayers in times of crisis; and creative prayers with children. A video especially appropriate for parents and teenagers is *Ekklesia,* a twenty-eight-minute video produced by Mennonite Media Ministry (1995) concerning what it means to love and forgive one's enemies, especially those who could threaten homes and lives. It stresses peacemaking.

Finally, whether the family is at worship in the *ecclesia,* the gathered body of Christ, or in the *ecclesiola,* the small body of Christ in mutual ministry in the home, it is important to remember that these rituals must be life-giving rather than perfunctory and wooden. When they become perfunctory, we are called to find fresh forms for our worship in which all family members feel ownership. Any re-ritualization brings us to the question of the real purpose of our worship together. Paul reminds us that each of us is "holy and beloved" and that the purpose of our worship is to create an environment where we "clothe" ourselves "with compassion, kindness, humility, meekness, and patience," a quality of life where we will "be with one another and if anyone has a complaint against another, forgive each other." Above all we should "clothe" ourselves "with love, which binds everything together in perfect harmony. And let the peace of Christ rule in your hearts, to which indeed you were called in the one body. And be thankful. Let the word of Christ dwell in you richly; teach and admonish one another in all wisdom; and with gratitude in your hearts sing psalms, hymns, and spiritual songs to God" (Colossians 3:12–16). In this inspiring vision of worship, each person is seen as holy and sacred; each is treated with love and compassion as a *Thou;* each is strengthened to bring peace and harmony within a family and beyond. With Paul, we can respond with heartfelt thanksgiving to God and intercession for others and all God's creation in and through the unique forms of the authentic worship we create.

Bibliography

Achtemeier, Elizabeth. *Preaching about Family Relationships* (Philadelphia: Westminster Press, 1987.)

Baker, Brant D. *Welcoming Children: Experiential Children's Sermons* (Minneapolis: Augsburg, 1995.)

Baldwin, Christina. *Life's Companion: Toward Writing as a Spiritual Quest.* Illustrations by Susan Bowlet (New York: Bantam Books, 1991.)

Berryman, Jerome. *Godly Play: A Way of Religious Education* (San Francisco: Harper-San Francisco, 1991.)

————. *Teaching Godly Play: The Sunday Morning Handbook* (Nashville: Abingdon Press, 1995).

Blair, Susan A., Sharon I. Gouivens, Catherine O'Callaghan, and Grant Spradling, eds. *Imaging the Word*, vol. 2. (Cleveland: United Church Press, 1995). (See also Laurence et al. 1994; vol. 3 is in process.)

Boyer, Ernest, Jr. *A Way in the World: Family Life as Spiritual* (New York: Harper & Row, 1984.)

Browning, Robert L., and Roy A. Reed. *The Sacraments in Religious Education and Liturgy: An Ecumenical Model* (Birmingham, Ala.: Religious Education Press, 1985.)

————. *Models of Confirmation and Baptismal Affirmation: Liturgical and Educational Issues and Designs* (Birmingham, Ala.: Religious Education Press, 1995).

Buber, Martin. *Between Man and Man* (Boston: Beacon Press, 1995).

————. *I and Thou* (New York: Charles Scribner's Sons, 1958).

Ciampa, LeAnn. *Praying with Children* (Nashville: Abingdon Press, 1991).

Clapp, Steve. *The Third Wave and the Family* (Champaign, Ill.: C-4 Resources, 1984).

Clinebell, Howard. *Well-Being: A Personal Plan for Exploring and Enriching the Seven Dimensions of Life: Mind, Body, Spirit, Love, Work, Play, the Earth* (San Francisco: Harper-San Francisco, 1992).

Coleman, William L. *Teen Stress: Stories to Guide You* (Minneapolis: Augsburg, 1994).

Duvall, Evelyn M. *Marriage and Family Development* (New York: Harper & Row, 1977).

Engelhardt, Carolyn Hardin. "No Substitution: Worship and Education," *Reach*, Sept. 1990.

Erickson, Kenneth A. *Helping Your Children Feel Good about Themselves: A Guide to Building Self-Esteem in the Christian Family* (Minneapolis: Augsburg, 1994).

Erikson, Erik. *Toys and Reason: Stages in the Ritualization of Experience* (New York: W. W. Norton, 1977).

Fogle, Jeanne S. *Seasons of God's Love: The Church Year* (Philadelphia: Genera Press, 1988).

Fox, Matthew. *Creation Spirituality: Liberating Gifts for the People of the Earth* (San Francisco: Harper-San Francisco, 1991).

Halverson, Delia. *How Do Our Children Grow? Introducing Children to God, Jesus, the Bible, Prayer, the Church* (Nashville: Abingdon Press, 1993).

Hays, Edward. *Prayers for the Domestic Church* (Leavenworth, Kan.: Forest of Peace 1995).

Heiberg, Jeanne. *Advent Arts and Christmas Crafts: With Prayers and Rituals for Family, School and Church* (New York: Paulist Press, 1995).

Held, Ann Reed. *Keeping Faith in Families* (Belleville, Ill.: National Presbyterian Mariners, 1987).

Huck, Gabe. *A Book of Family Prayers* (New York: Seabury Press, 1979).

Kemp, Helen, and John Kemp. *Canons, Songs, and Blessings* (Garland, Texas: Choristers Guild, 1990).

Kierkegaard, Soren. *Concluding Unscientific Postscript.* Translated by David Swenson and Walter Lowrie (Princeton, N.J.: Princeton University Press, 1941).

Laurence, Kenneth T., Jann Cather Weaver, and Roger Wedell, eds. *Imaging the Word*, vol. 1 (Cleveland: United Church Press, 1994). (See also Blair et al. 1995; vol. 3 is in process.)

Morris, Maggie. *Helping Children Feel at Home in Church* (Nashville: Discipleship Resources, 1988).

Nappa, Mike, and Amy Nappa. *52 Fun Family Devotions: Exploring and Discovering God's Word* (Minneapolis: Augsburg, 1994).

Nelson, Gertrude Mueller. *To Dance with God: Family Ritual and Community Celebration* (New York: Paulist Press, 1986).

Ng, David, and Virginia Thomas. *Children in the Worshipping Community* (Atlanta: John Knox Press, 1981).

O'Neal, Debbie Grafton. *Thank You for This Food: Action Prayers, Songs, and Blessings for Mealtime.* Illustrations by Nancy Munger (Minneapolis: Augsburg, 1994).

Paulsen, Gary. *The Rifle* (New York: Harcourt Brace Jovanovich, 1995).

———. *The Tent: A Parable in One Setting* (New York: Harcourt Brace Jovanovich, 1995).

Pritchard, Gretchen Wolff. *Offering the Gospel to Children* (Cambridge-Boston: Cowley Publications, 1992).

Rahner, Karl. *Theological Investigations XIV* (London: Darton, Longman & Todd, 1976).

Robinson, Edward. *The Original Vision* (Oxford: Religious Experiences Research Unit, 1977).

Rosner, Patricia L. *Consider the Children: Planning for Young Children during Worship* (St. Louis: Christian Board of Publications, 1990).

Russell, Joseph P. *Sharing Our Biblical Story: A Guide to Using Liturgical Readings as the Core of Church and Family Education* (Minneapolis: Winston Press, 1979).

Sasso, Sandy Eisenberg. *In God's Name.* Illustrated by Phoebe Stone (Woodstock, Vt.: Jewish Lights Publishing, 1994).

Sawin, Margaret M. *Family Enrichment with Family Clusters* (Valley Forge, Pa.: Judson Press, 1979).

———. *Hope for Families* (New York: Sadlier, 1982).

Schmemann, Alexander. *For the Life of the World* (Crestwood, N.Y.: St. Vladimir's Seminary Press, 1973).

Schultze, Quentin, and Barbara Schultze. *The Best Family Videos,* 2d ed. (Minneapolis: Augsburg, 1995).

Sloyan, Virginia, and Gabe Huck. *Children's Liturgies* (Washington, D.C.: Liturgical Conference, 1970).

Smith, W. Alan. *Children Belong in Worship: A Guide to the Children's Sermon* (St. Louis: CBP Press, 1984).

Stewart, Sonja M., and Jerome W. Berryman. *Young Children and Worship* (Louisville, Ky.: Westminster/John Knox Press, 1989).

Swartz, Susan Swanson. *Families of God,* Illustrated by Deborah A. Kirkeeide. (Minneapolis: Augsburg, 1994).

Taylor, JoAnne. *Innocent Wisdom* (New York: Pilgrim Press, 1989).

Torvend, Samuel, ed. *Welcome Home: Scriptures, Prayers, and Blessings for the Household* (Minneapolis: Augsburg, 1995).

Walton, Fiora. *Explore inside the Bible* (Minneapolis: Augsburg, 1994).

Weisheit, Eldon. *Family Time Story Devotions* (Minneapolis: Augsburg, 1994).

Wetherwax, John. *A Special Time for Special People: Children's Moments in Worship* (Brea, Calif.: Educational Ministries, 1990).

Wright, Wendy M. *Sacred Dwelling: A Spirituality of Family Life* (New York: Crossroad, 1989).

—ROBERT L. BROWNING
ROY A. REED

PART 4

Families in History

21

Families in Ancient Israel

The Hebrew Bible has a very clear-eyed view of family. It presents the family as the basic institution of society, and yet at the same time it understands the problematics of this very difficult institution. The stories of the Bible highlight issues and questions that continue to concern us today.

Male and Female
God Created Them

The biblical stories of humanity's creation see the nuclear family as part of the very definition of humanity. In the first chapter of Genesis, when God creates humanity, "male and female [God] created them" (Gen. 1:27). The essential, almost ontological nature of the male-female pair-bond is emphasized even more in the story of humanity in Genesis 2. Adam, the earthling, is created a single being from the clay of the earth. When God decides to create a companion for Adam, God creates additional creatures from the earth's clay. But none of these turns out to be a suitable companion, and so God "splits the Adam," building a new creature not from the clay but from the earthling itself. When God brings her to Adam, Adam acknowledges her immediately as part of his very flesh. The narrator interrupts with an aside to the audience, to hammer home the message: "therefore a man leaves his father and his mother and cleaves to his wife, and they become one flesh" (Gen. 2:24, RSV). There is no true human life, says the story, without family.

Ancient Near Eastern stories cast light on the meaning of "suitable companion." In the Gilgamesh epic, when the gods decide that Gilgamesh needs a suitable companion, they make a new superior being, Enkidu, another male. In the lesser-known Agushaya hymn, when Ea realizes that Ishtar needs a suitable companion, he creates another "virile" goddess, Saltu. The appropriate companion for a male is another male, for a female, another female. In contrast, the Bible (which does not consider the genders radically different from each other) creates a model of cross-gender companionship. This is very attractive to contemporary thinking, but in its eagerness to eliminate barriers between the genders and encourage companionship between marital partners, the Bible also seems to have assumed that *all* pair-bonding is male-female. What does such an assumption do today? Do we say that the verse was unconsciously heterosexist, and extend our own view of the pair-bond? Or do we say that the verse offered conscious and purposeful prescription, and use it as a prescriptive and restrictive definition of family?

"He Will Rule over You"

The nature of this "one flesh" pair-bond becomes clear in the next chapter. When the humans acquire knowledge, they have to leave the incubator-garden and enter the real world as we know it. This is the world of civilization, and it carries a price: toil and pain, and, for the woman, hierarchy and control: "Your desire is for your husband [or: your husband's desire is for you] and he will rule over you" (Gen. 3:16, author's translation). The pair-bond has a head, and the head is male.

The male-headed family was the norm of the ancient world, and ancient Israel would not have known anything but classic ancient patriarchy. The story builds this patriarchy into civilization as we know it. Once again, the modern reader has a choice in reading: Is the passage descriptive of marriage at that time, or is it prescriptive even for us today? And does asserting a more equal marriage contradict a divine dictum, or does it work for a more perfect humanity and head us back toward a peaceful Eden? The way we read stories may influence the way we see the world; the way we see the world certainly influences the way we read the text.

Control and Its Limits

The male head of household "rules" in his house, and his wife and children are his, almost extensions of himself. He has the right to control them and to determine their destiny. The Bible doesn't deny these rights, standard in the ancient world and in our own not-too-distant past, but nevertheless sees problems in these patriarchal rights and ultimately curtails them. Genesis and Judges present a time when families reigned supreme, where the father of the extended family had unrestricted rights of control over his children. Abraham can give his wife away, can send his son away, can bind his son for slaughter; Lot can give his daughters to the mob; Abraham, Isaac, and Jacob can decide who will be their heirs; Judah can contract marriage for his sons and order his daughter-in-law to be killed. The stresses of the Genesis family are so clear that contemporary readers often label it "dysfunctional." But these stresses are not unique to the family of Abraham. They are structural, normal consequences of the ordinary exercise of the rights of the heads of extended patriarchal families. These stress points bring the Genesis family to the brink of disaster over and over again, and it survives only because it is rescued at the last minute, usually by divine intervention. The same rights and the same stresses appear in the families of the book of Judges. Caleb gives his daughter away in a battle oath; Jephthah apparently kills his daughter after *his* battle oath; the Levite sends his concubine out to the mob. But the families in Judges are not as lucky as the Genesis family. God no longer intervenes in the life of individuals. And the result is death and disaster, and ultimately civil war.

The Davidic monarchy curtailed the rights of the heads of household in the establishment of a centralized state. The state interposed the local council, a central judgeship, and the king as public levels of authority that could monitor family behavior. Deuteronomy reflects this growth of public authority. Fathers cannot choose who will be the chief heir; the firstborn must be the heir. Fathers do not kill their recalcitrant children; they bring them to the council of elders, who then sentence them. The diminution of paternal authority should not be exaggerated. Fathers still maintain much real power even when legal authority resides in the council. Once the parents of a recalcitrant son denounce him, for example, the council condemns him. Nothing is said about investigating the case, but the authority to pass sentence rests with the council, and the whole people execute by stoning. The case of the accused bride is similar. If her husband claims that she is not a virgin, her father takes possession of the marital sheet and shows it to the council. In real terms, he has the opportunity and power to bloody it or not. If he presents an unbloodied sheet, the girl is stoned for being faithless to her father's house. The state does not take all power from the fathers, but it does claim its interest. Limits are set on the power of parents over children and of husbands over wives. The Bible's genuine desire to strengthen and protect marriage yields to its commitment to social justice and to the prevention of the abuse of the vulnerable in the moral and political chaos depicted at the end of the book of Judges.

Male-Dominated Marriage

The hierarchies of dominance do not disappear, only their excesses. Parents have control over their children, and husbands over wives. The dominance of husband over wife is embedded in the semantics of biblical Hebrew. A wife not exclusively faithful to her husband is said to be faithless (in Hebrew, *zanah,* often translated as "whored"), a term never used for a husband's actions. The husband's reaction to such faithlessness is a jealousy tinged with righteous indignation (Hebrew *qana'*), an emotion belonging to one who can command fidelity. He is "head of household," his wife is *his.* She may not offer her allegiance to any others, and they are not to poach on the husband's preserve.

The right of a husband to the exclusive fidelity of his wife gives him the prerogative of "righteously indignant jealousy." Numbers 5:11–21 provides a procedure in which a suspicious husband takes his wife to the temple and she drinks a potion of the words of Torah dissolved in a solution of holy water and dust from the floor of the sanctuary. The priest adjures her that if she is guilty, "her belly will swell and her womb fall"; if she is innocent, nothing will happen. But even if she later gets pregnant—proof positive that she was innocent—her husband will not be punished for false accusation. It is the prerogative of husbands—and may even be their duty—to monitor their wives' behavior.

The Rhetoric of Faithlessness

The rights of fathers to judge and punish children and of husbands to judge and punish their wives are so axiomatic to ancient listeners that they give rise to biblical Israel's understanding of the relationship of Israel to God as son to father or wife to husband. These metaphors express the intimacy and sense of kinship that Israel feels for God. At the same time, they express Israel's acknowledged obligation of exclusive fidelity to God. Like a wife, Israel can "be faithless" (*zanah*); like a husband, God will be righteously jealous (*qana'*). The prophets Hosea, Jeremiah, and Ezekiel use the metaphor of marriage to indict Israel as the wayward wife and depict God as the punishing husband. The cultural belief that husbands and fathers reward and punish enables Hosea and his listeners to understand the disasters they are suffering through his analogy of God and Israel as husband and wife. *Just as husbands expect exclusive fidelity from their wives,* God expects exclusive fidelity from Israel. *Just as husbands punish their wayward wives,* so God is punishing Israel for her failure to show this exclusive fidelity. In the real life of the listeners, husbands and fathers judge and punish; in the same way, the people of ancient Israel see their own difficulties and disasters as the punishments and chastisements of God the father or God the husband.

Our contemporary ideas of family relations have recently undergone considerable change, though not to everyone's happiness. The one-sided nature of adultery has given way to a demand (a theoretical demand) that married men also engage in sexual behavior exclusively with their marital partners. Our model of marriage is not as hierarchical as the ancient model, and the issue of control and monitoring is a very real one. What is the definition of adultery, who judges whether faith has been broken, and what should be done about it are all issues of considerable ethical discussion and generally private decision making.

The behaviors of dominance are also increasingly being rejected. As a society, we no longer allow husbands to beat their wives. Even though in reality we do not do enough to stop it, we label the behavior abusive and consider the woman a battered wife. And we no longer want to allow parents to abuse their children. There is considerable debate about the degree to which the state should operate to restrict it, and the term *family values* is often used as a code for leaving families to their own devices, which in reality means leaving them to the control of the most powerful party. The understanding of the stories of Judges and the laws of Deuteronomy that you need a state to intervene to stop family abuse presents a discussion that continues today in our political arena.

The issues of hierarchy and control lie at the base of many contemporary disputes. Our political life is predicated on an egalitarian ideology, though political rights for women and African Americans are quite recent, and economic rights are still far from equal. Nevertheless, our governing idea is that all people *should* have equal rights, equal access to the law, and equal obligations. The biblical system, on the other hand, is not at all egalitarian. In its carefully constructed hierarchy every person had a niche, and niches are decidedly not equal. Parents ruled their children, husbands ruled their wives. The tension between the ideals of orderly hierarchy and egalitarianism fuels our current debates. The old worry that the absence of hierarchy is chaos is echoed today in the desire of many to strengthen the position of fathers so that *they* can control their sons.

Despite these disputes, even the advocates of a minimalist state do not believe that men should be able to batter their wives and children. Our contemporary sensitivity to domestic violence and abuse makes our theological metaphors of God as the chastising father or husband highly problematic. Using these paradigms of chastisement risks reinscribing a belief that superior hierarchical status and power justify the use of force against those who are below. Even if we consciously deny the right to humans and leave it only to God, we nevertheless convey the message that power can use force against the weak. Our metaphors for the divine human relationship should reflect our new consciousness that fathers and husbands cannot be allowed to beat their sons and wives. In the same way, we should no longer grant God the right to beat us into submission.

The denial of God's right to abuse us is not really a restriction on God's power. It is a limitation on our own imagination and analogical thinking. To say that God does not have the right to beat us means that we will no longer understand the disasters that befall as occasions when God-the-father is beating his son or when God-the-husband is battering his wife. Disasters cannot be seen as chastisements without at the same time legitimating the right of the powerful to use their power to injure those less strong. As our notions of family become less tied to rights of dominance, so too our understanding of our close family relationship with God must reflect the mutuality, tolerance, and benevolence that we expect among members of human families.

—TIKVA FRYMER-KENSKY

22

Families in the Greco-Roman World

The questions that are being raised in our own culture about the definition of *family* make especially pertinent an inquiry into how family was conceived and practiced in Greco-Roman culture, since that ancient culture has influenced our own in so many ways. Scholars have begun to see that it may be impossible to define *the* Greek or Roman family, for varying social contexts and personal circumstances resulted in a wide variety of actual family arrangements. Nevertheless, certain characteristics of the Roman family may be regarded as basic.

What Is a Family?

First, it is important to define *familia* and *domus,* from which our words *family* and *domicile* or *domestic* are derived. In the *Oxford Latin Dictionary* the term *familia* is defined first as "all persons subject to the control of one man, whether relations, freedmen or slaves, a household," second as "the slaves of a household," third as "a group of servants domiciled in one place," and fourth as "a body of persons closely related by blood or affinity." According to the first definition, those in the power (*potestas*) of the *paterfamilias* include the *materfamilias,* sons and their children, daughters, and adopted children, of whom all were equally heirs except for a wife who had entered the marriage under terms (*sine manu*) by which she remained a member (and heir) in her father's *familia.* Because of this potential ambiguity in a wife's legal relationship to her husband's *familia,* the Romans inclined to use the term *domus* to indicate the actual living unit, the household, including the wife, the children, the grandchildren, and the domestic slaves. The Greek term *oikos* also covered both the place of dwelling and those who lived there. In humble households who could not afford slaves, the *domus* might include only the nuclear family.

In common usage, *familia* included all those who were related by blood through males (agnatic kin). Thus children were in the same *familia* as their father's brother and his children, as well as their father's sister. But they were not related to their aunt's children nor to their mother's siblings or their children. Nor were the children of a daughter regarded as part of her father's *familia.* On the other hand, *domus* could refer to all blood kin, including all ancestors and descendants.

Second, the Romans regarded the family as based on biology but not determined by it. That is, while the biological reproduction by married women and men created the beginnings of kinship bonds and of society in general, the shape and future of any particular family were subject both to the ease of divorce and remarriage for both men and women and to the common practice of extending the family unit through adoption, usually of adult males rather than small children.

Third, a Roman household usually included a number of domestic slaves, to perform not simply menial tasks but those requiring great skill and a considerable sense of responsibility. In sharp contrast to the slavery later practiced in the "New World," many Greek and Roman slaves were highly educated and functioned as managers and physicians as well as teachers and personal secretaries. Nonetheless, before the law they were socially and legally "dead" until they were set free (manumission was a normal and not infrequent household practice). At that point the former slave, if owned by a Roman citizen, was now a freedman or freedwoman and also a Roman citizen, a fact that amazed even their Greek contemporaries.

Fourth, the Roman household had a sacred aura. As Cicero wrote: "What is more sacred, what is more protected by all religion than the house of each and every citizen?" The *Lares* (spirits of the ancestors) and *Penates* (guardians of the family larder) were the focus of the private cult in each household.

Fifth, the honor of the *paterfamilias* depended largely on his ability to protect his *domus,* and conversely the virtue of the members of the household embellished his prestige. The father and master had a general responsibility to care for all in his *domus,* including the responsibility of providing a decent burial for each one. Grave inscriptions announce the warm bonds between husbands and wives and between parents and children.

Because any family will include human beings with varying needs as well as diverse mental and physical capacities and developments, the relationships among the members are bound to be asymmetrical to a degree. Greek and Roman family life was certainly organized more asymmetrically, hierarchically, and patrilineally than in contemporary Europe and the United States, in accord with the sense that slavery was an inevitable institution and that males, particularly the patriarchs, bore sole responsibility for public life.

Family Values and Gender Roles

Both Greek and Roman philosophers and rhetoricians nurtured a sharp distinction between the private sphere of the household and the public sphere of the city. All males and most females in these cultures regarded the public realm as superior to the household and linked public life with civilization, freedom, mobility, and acquired honor. Boys were raised to find their primary identity in this realm, learning early that they symbolized the honor of their households and that their personal honor needed to be defended daily from the challenges of other males. Not to do so would bring shame on themselves and their households. Likewise, girls were raised to find their identity within the household, which was regarded as inferior to the city and which was linked with nature and limited movement. Females symbolized the virtue of shame; they could bring honor to themselves and the males of their household by their shy and restrained behavior, by their purity, and by their sexual exclusiveness. Not to do so was regarded as acting shamelessly, that is, as contributing to social chaos.

The male householder, then, functioned both as the representative of his *domus/oikos* in the eyes of his fellow citizens and as the agent of his household's subordination to the loftier goals of the city. In these roles, men were to demonstrate self-mastery, wisdom, and courage. In contrast, women, with interior household business as their domain, were to demonstrate obedience, chastity, and silence (which Aristotle had claimed was *the* distinctly female virtue).

Patriarchy and Property

In antiquity, patriarchal family organization was strongly encouraged by the process of developing iron technology for use in both agriculture and warfare, forcing the men increasingly to group together for protection. And in Roman society, all families gained their basic sustenance from agriculture, with the result that the property passed along within a family determined a Roman's social status more than any other factor. Responsible heirs, then, were essential to a family's honor.

Often, beginning with ancient Greek commentators, the power and authority of the oldest male in a Roman family (*patria potestas*) have been presented as the archetypical examples of unrestrained patriarchy. The Roman jurist Gaius noted that "there are hardly any other men who have over their children a power such as we have." Yet the resulting image of the severe figure who indeed possessed the legal right to kill his children has been projected from a narrow reading of Roman law rather than from evidence of how fathers generally acted in their families.

Indeed, fathers who acted cruelly to their children were condemned, and to kill a son was almost always regarded as a sacrilege. There is no evidence that Roman children lived in daily fear of their father's wrath. In contrast, paternal moderation, even toward serious filial misbehavior, was praised as a virtue. Furthermore, the husband's need for the cooperation of a wife who had her own property (and who could initiate divorce) must have tempered his treatment of their children.

Yet as long as his father was alive, a son was not able to will property to his potential heirs. And the father not only had considerable influence over the marriage of his children but also had the right, until the mid-second century C.E., to break off a marriage. To be sure, the fathers of about one-third of all Roman children had died before the children reached age fifteen, when girls from elite families were beginning to marry. By age twenty-five, when most sons were entering marriage, the fathers of less than half were still alive. And by age forty, only about one-tenth had living fathers. Thus in contrast to a popular misconception, there were few old patriarchs dominating large extended households.

Family Piety, Loyalty, and Betrayal

For readers in our culture perhaps the most striking aspect of family life among the Greeks and Romans is the profound emphasis they placed on loyalty among siblings. While it is widely assumed in modern Western kinship practice that the individual will experience her or his deepest sense of emotional bonding in marriage, in sharp contrast the tightest unity of loyalty and affection in the world of the early Christians was found among siblings. The emotional bonding that we assume will be the mark of a healthy wife-husband relationship was in the ancient world the mark of brother-brother, brother-sister, sister-sister relationships (and also of mother-son relationships).

Since it is the case that in Western kinship systems persons conventionally find their strongest affective bonds in marriage, it is hardly surprising that interpersonal treachery is epitomized in stories of spousal betrayal, adultery, and divorce, which seem to have unending power to captivate the American public. In sharp contrast, in Greco-Roman culture treachery in its most extreme, despised, and engrossing form was felt in strife and betrayal among blood brothers. For example, in Hellenized Judea the writer of 2 Maccabees observes that Jason attacked his kinsman Menelaus in an attempt to regain the priesthood, "not realizing that success at the cost of one's kin is the greatest misfortune." And in his *Metamorphoses* the Roman poet Ovid illustrates his view of the extreme breakdown of social relations during the late Republic by pointing out that "friend was not safe from friend . . . and even between brothers affection was rare" (1.127–151). The readers of Mark's Gospel could grasp immediately the seriousness of the warning that as God's judgment approached, social relations would become so strained that "brother will hand brother over to death" (13:12).

Thus in ancient Mediterranean cultures it was not adultery and marital divorce but the breakdown in sibling solidarity that was viewed as the most telling evidence of the deterioration of the family and of society. While a treacherous brother was regarded as the worst social evil, sibling loyalty and solidarity constituted the apex of positive human relationships.

Between parents and their children the virtue of *pietas* (dutiful respect) formed the core of the Romans' ideal of family relations. While many historians have stressed the obligation of sons and daughters of any age to defer to their father's will, it was also the case that a father could display *pietas* to a son, indicating that this virtue included compassion as well as duty. The term was also used to describe the devotion between brothers or the behavior of husbands who accepted death in place of their wives.

In Roman culture a clear distinction was made between a father's power over his children, a relationship in which a sense of mutual obligation and concern was the rule, and an owner's power to exploit his or her slaves as they wished, including whipping.

The Importance of Children

The high infant mortality rate among Greeks and Romans is a central aspect of the sharp differences between our sense of the cycles of birth and death and theirs. The children who lived were praised for acting like adults who might soon enough be called on to provide their parents with support or a proper burial and commemoration. The very poor were commonly forced by their circumstances to "expose" (throw away) their infants. Those whom they were able to raise represented a critical investment in the future, and their labor from an early age would benefit the family economy. In contrast to our culture, adoption was quite often of nephews and grandsons, and usually of adults rather than of children.

The Family in Society and Culture

The earliest surviving Latin literature presents family relationships as affectionate and pleasurable. Cato, the father of Latin prose, wrote that he was more honored to be praised for being a good husband than to be judged a great senator (*Cato maior* 20.2). The household and family was no mere private refuge but a powerful focus of relationships thriving at the heart of public life. In the Roman empire the conjugal family household was the fundamental focus of human loyalties. The cult of the ancestors gave a family a distinct sense of its own past and future hope.

Roman society was characterized by the great distance between the top and bottom of the social scale and the fundamental distinction between the honorable citizen and the rightless slave. Among the citizens themselves fine distinctions of rank and status made the unending quest for honor and influence a major preoccupation of males in both the public and private spheres.

Conclusion

The many differences between our concepts of family and those of the Greco-Roman *oikos/familia* should alert us to the dangers of serious misunderstanding that occur when we project our individualist views into the ancient texts. An appropriate grasp of these texts can be achieved only through contextualizing these households in both their public functions and their private relations. And these relations must be analyzed in the context of typical, comparatively short, life spans in antiquity. Moreover, in contrast to our culture's emphasis on individual achievement and personal guilt, the ancients' profound concern for acquiring honor and avoiding shame for the *familia* should critically inform our reading of all Greco-Roman texts, especially those that deal with interpersonal relationships.

Bibliography

Bradley, K. R. *Discovering the Roman Family* (New York: Oxford University Press, 1991).

Casey, James. *The History of the Family* (Oxford: Basil Blackwell, 1989).

Dixon, Suzanne. *The Roman Family* (Baltimore: Johns Hopkins University Press, 1992).

Rawson, Beryl, ed. *The Family in Ancient Rome: New Perspectives* (Ithaca, N.Y.: Cornell University Press, 1986).

Saller, Richard P. *Patriarchy, Property, and Death in the Roman Family* (Cambridge: Cambridge University Press, 1994).

—S. SCOTT BARTCHY

23

Families in Early Christianity

The lasting contributions of early Christianity to the Western Christian tradition of family have been significant and wide-reaching. A current understanding of family would conclude that not all of them have been helpful. It does not take great knowledge of the Bible to think of biblical passages that cause more problems than they solve. Yet the Bible and the legacy of early Christianity have provided the framework upon which the Western Christian ideals of family have been constructed. The lasting contributions can be summarized in five points: relativization of the demands of family of origin with regard to the demands of the gospel; encouragement to harmony within the family through relationships of submission; justification of the patriarchal ideal of family structure by the fatherhood of God; imaging of family relationships after the analogy of theological relationships, thus enhancing the dignity of the family; and display of the variety and flexibility of family structures.

First, one strong image of family that arises from the New Testament, in particular from the Synoptic Gospels, is that the family of origin cannot be trusted to support one's call to discipleship, and in some cases can be a definite obstacle. This attitude takes its cue from the attitude of Jesus himself in these Gospels, more strongly in Mark than in the others. Early in Mark, members of Jesus' family come to the place where he is preaching to take him home because they think he is out of his mind (Mark 3:20). Three chapters later, when they try again, Jesus' answer rejects the exclusive claims of blood ties in favor of a widened understanding of family based on discipleship: "Whoever does the will of God is my brother and sister and mother" (Mark 3:31–35; Matt. 12:46–50; Luke 8:19–21, though the remark is toned down some in Luke). Later sayings of Jesus about family include a rejection of candidates for discipleship who do not love Jesus more than family members (Matt. 10:37) and the promise of reward to those who have left house and family in order to receive the rewards of discipleship (Matt. 19:27–29; Mark 10:28–30; Luke 18:28–30). Disciples are also warned that in time of persecution, siblings, parents, and children will betray each other (Matt. 10:21; Mark 13:12). Jesus even declares that an inevitable result of his call to discipleship will be the pitting of family members against each other (Matt. 10:34–36; Luke 12:51–53).

The picture does not look promising for the family life of disciples. Such sayings must have been comforting and supportive, however, to early Christians who were indeed facing betrayal by family members because of their faith, and may well originate in memories of trouble between Jesus and his own family of origin. Even Jesus' mother, revered in later centuries as the first disciple, does not play that role in Matthew and Mark. In Luke, she is messianic prophet before his birth (Luke 1:46–55) but lacks understanding of her son's precocious awareness of his destiny when he loses his parents in the temple (Luke 2:48–50); yet she is with the disciples after his death (Acts 1:14). Only in John is the unnamed mother of Jesus the launcher of his public ministry at Cana (John 2:5), a member of his group of disciples (John 2:12), and witness at the cross (John 19:25–27). These are the images of her that have been nourished by later tradition.

It is not so much that the Synoptic Jesus rejects or despises family life, for many of his miracles restore family members to each other. But there is the solemn warning that all social ties, even the most intimate ones, must be relativized in light of the demands of the gospel. A process begins here that will continue through the early tradition in different ways: family images and terms are reapplied to the community of believers, so that the family of origin, though very important, takes second place to the family of the church. Family bonds are not abolished, but they are reshaped and widened.

A somewhat different picture is presented by some other New Testament literature, and this is the second lasting contribution. The so-called "household codes" of Colossians, Ephesians, and 1 Peter encourage the kind of subordinate relationships that were a common feature of Greco-Roman and Jewish family ideals: wives to husbands, (adult) children to parents, and slaves to masters. The patriarchal male husband, master, and father is idealized as a source of earthly authority in the name of God, just as he is representative of the power of the state in the conservative social philosophy of the time, in spite of ample evidence of women heads of households, women slave owners, and adult children operating independently of their fathers. In these biblical texts, the demands of discipleship do not stand in tension with those of family; rather, they are *fulfilled* in the carrying out of family responsibilities. The passages are not intended only for all-Christian families. A passage in 1 Peter 2:18–3:7 makes clear that wives and slaves of unbelieving husbands and masters fulfill their faith and mission by the same kind of submission. While the theme of submission is problematic for us, we often pass over Ephesians 5:21, which attempts to set the tone for all that is to follow: "Submit to one another out of reverence for Christ." Thus all household relationships are to mirror the reverence that Christians should have for Christ himself.

What is seldom realized by readers of those texts today is that in their own context, they also take a significant progressive step forward. Instead of addressing only the male authority figure as do other discussions of household management, the New Testament household codes address both sides of the relationship, and the subordinate member first: wives, then husbands; children, then parents; slaves, then masters (Eph. 5:22–6:9; Col. 3:18–4:1). In doing so, they acknowledge both the personhood of the subordinate member and the responsibility of both sides to uphold the quality of family life. While we can no longer agree with what they take for granted—the subordinate nature of the relationship—we would do well to take to heart these other lessons learned from them.

The third contribution, one that is also being critically assessed today, is the pervasive symbolization of social control under the image of fatherhood. Not only the New Testament household codes but the entire theological structure of Christian revelation casts the fatherhood of God as source of Trinity, creation, and our understanding of the role of Jesus. Especially the Gospel of John—with its strong casting of the God-Jesus relationship as Father-Son—and the later trinitarian formulas based on it have made it next to impossible for Christian piety to imagine God any other way.

This fixing of normative God-images has had its effect on the family. Matthew 23:9 ("Call no one on earth father because you have one Father in heaven") has been forgotten in favor of Ephesians 3:14–15 ("I bend my knees before the Father after whom all family [Greek, *patria*, patriarchal lineage] in heaven and on earth is named") (author's translations). The relativity of earthly patriarchal social structures intended by Matthew was soon displaced—or perhaps never taken seriously in the first place—by a reinforcement of patriarchal authority in the name of the fatherhood of God. Consciously or unconsciously, men in family relationships are able to think of themselves as images of a male God in a way that women are not. From benevolent fatherly figures to formal patriarchal titles for religious leaders, from "father knows best" to battered wives and incest, the patterning of male authority after that of God has resulted in, and even encouraged, abuse of power over others. Yet the fatherhood of God has been a source of spiritual strength and consolation for multitudes, and the role of fathers in families has so eroded in some cultures that fathers have been called an "endangered species." In this age of heightened awareness of the dignity and freedom of all persons, the crucial role of fathers in families must be encouraged and nurtured. Yet, while affirming the legitimate rights and authority of fathers, we must cast a critical eye on the human-divine analogy as it is used in this context as well as on the temptation to abuse power in God's name.

A fourth contribution is closely related to the previous one. While we were discussing above a less helpful result of human-divine imaging, we must here also acknowledge the helpful aspect of this kind of theological reflection. The imaging of family life and relationships after heavenly realities has also in many ways helped to enhance the dignity of family life and the dignity of human persons. The imaging of the fatherhood of God has served as a sobering reminder to human fathers of their solemn responsibility to mirror divine qualities. Trinitarian theology locates family life—albeit an exclusively masculine family in the dominant tradition—within the Godhead itself (early Christian and medieval imagery of the feminine aspects of Christ and the Holy Spirit were never allowed to become mainstream). The frequent casting of believers as children of God fosters not so much an unhealthy dependency as a loving trust and another reminder that the family is the domestic church, the microcosm and mirror of the whole church.

The author of Ephesians is responsible for applying an established biblical metaphor of the marriage of God and Israel to Christ and the church in a passage that has molded not only thinking on marriage but ecclesiology as well (Eph. 5:22–33). As Christ loves the church and gave himself up for her, so husbands are to love their wives, and wives are to submit to their husbands as the church does to Christ. The attractiveness of this passage has enabled Christian marriage to assume an extraordinary dignity, for it is the very reflection of the mystery at the heart of our faith. At the same time, it has in the judgment of many locked theological reflection on marriage into a pattern of subordination. If marriage is the image of Christ and the church, who would dare tamper with it? Such thinking is unable or refuses to see that the metaphor only works *because* of the prior social assumption of marriage as an unequal relationship. With a change of conviction about social equality in marriage, the metaphor needs adjustment. Nevertheless, without metaphors such as these, the sacramental or theologically symbolic nature of marriage could never have been developed.

Finally, early Christianity witnesses to the many forms that family can take. While our popular image is the nuclear family, the ancient Christian family more often included a much larger group of people. "Family" normally meant not the nuclear blood family, though they may have lived together as a unit, but the extended intergenerational network of relationships, as well as all those who shared one roof, whether related by blood or legal ties, as in the case of slaves, freedmen, and freedwomen. In other words, *family* was a fluid concept that embraced all kinds of living arrangements in many different kinds of households. Soon in Christian thinking, because of some of the factors discussed above, *family* also took on a new meaning: the church assembly. The patterns of loving relationships and of submission were subsumed into ideals of church; for example, in the writings immediately following the New Testament, submission of wives does not appear, but the obligation of submission has been diverted to church leaders, to whom all others are to submit. (Later, the submission theme returns in discussions of marriage, based on New Testament passages.)

Thus early Christianity shows us the many ways in which family was understood and lived. It teaches that the forms and concepts often considered essential by one age are really historically relative and that the family will continue to evolve into new forms as our awareness of human needs and abilities develops.

—CAROLYN OSIEK, R.S.C.J.

24

Families in Medieval Christianity and the Reformation

The Roman Catholic Church of the twelfth through sixteenth centuries treated marriage and the family as a natural, sacramental, and contractual unit. First, the Church taught, marriage was instituted at creation to enable man and woman to "be fruitful and multiply" and to raise children in the service and love of God. Since the fall into sin, marriage also became a remedy for lust, a channel to direct one's natural passion to the service of the community and the church. Yet marriage was subordinate to celibacy; propagation was less virtuous than contemplation. Clerics and monastics were to forgo marriage as a condition for ecclesiastical service. Those who could not do so were not worthy of holy orders or offices. Second, the Church taught, marriage, when properly contracted and consummated, rose to the dignity of a sacrament. The temporal union of body, soul, and mind within the marital estate symbolized the eternal union between Christ and his Church and conferred sanctifying grace upon the couple and the community. Couples could perform this sacrament in private, provided they were capable of marriage and complied with rules for marriage formation. Third, marriage was a contractual unit that prescribed a relation of love, service, and devotion and proscribed unwarranted breach or relaxation of one's connubial and parental duties.

The Church built upon this conceptual foundation a comprehensive canon law of sexuality, marriage, and family life that was enforced by church courts throughout Christendom. Consistent with the naturalist perspective, the canon law punished contraception, abortion, infanticide, and child abuse as violations of the created marital functions of propagation and child rearing. It proscribed unnatural relations (such as homosexuality, incest, and polygamy) and unnatural acts (such as bestiality, masturbation, and oral sex). Consistent with the sacramental perspective, the Church protected the sanctity and sanctifying purpose of marriage by declaring valid marital bonds to be indissoluble and by dissolving invalid unions between Christians and non-Christians or between parties related by various legal, spiritual, blood, or familial ties. It supported celibacy by dissolving unconsummated vows to marriage if one party made a vow to chastity and by punishing clerics or monastics who contracted marriage. Consistent with the contractual perspective, the canon law ensured voluntary unions by dissolving marriages entered into by mistake or under duress, fraud, or coercion. It granted to man and woman alike the rights to enforce conjugal debts that had been voluntarily assumed, and emphasized the importance of mutual love among the couple and their children.

The Protestant reformers of the sixteenth century replaced the Catholic sacramental model of marriage and the family with a social model. Like Catholics, Protestants retained the naturalist perspective of the family as an association created for procreation and mutual protection. They largely retained the contractual perspective of marriage as a voluntary association formed by the mutual consent of the couple.

Unlike Catholics, however, Protestants rejected the subordination of marriage to celibacy and the celebration of marriage as a sacrament. According to common Protestant lore, the person was too tempted by sinful passion to forgo God's remedy of marriage. The celibate life had no superior virtue and was no prerequisite for ecclesiastical service. It led too easily to concubinage, homosexuality, and other sins and too often impeded the ministerial office. It was thus a common symbolic act of the early Reformation for monks and nuns to renounce their vows to chastity, to marry, and to join the Protestant leadership. Moreover, according to Protestants, marriage was not a sacrament of the heavenly kingdom but one of the three created estates of the earthly kingdom, alongside the visible church and the state. Participation in the family required no prerequisite faith or purity and conferred no sanctifying grace, as did true sacraments. Rather, the family had distinctive secular uses for life in the earthly kingdom. It revealed to persons their sin and their need for God's marital gift. It restricted prostitution, promiscuity, pornography, and other public vices. It taught love, restraint, care, nurture, and other public virtues. Any fit man and woman were free and encouraged to enter such a union, with minimal conditions or controls.

As an estate of the earthly kingdom, the family was subject to civil law, not canon law. To be sure, church officials should continue to communicate divine and moral principles respecting sexuality and parenthood. Church consistories and councils could serve as state agents to register and consecrate marriages and to discipline infidelity or abuse of spouse and child. All church members, as priests, should counsel those who seek marriage and divorce and should cultivate the moral and material welfare of all baptized children. But principal legal authority over marriage and the family lay with the state, not the church.

Despite the bitter invectives against the canon law by early Protestant theologians, Protestant rulers and jurists appropriated a good deal of the traditional canon law of marriage and the family. Theologically offensive and obsolete provisions were naturally discarded, but what remained was put to ready use. Thus traditional canon law prohibitions against unnatural sexual relations and acts and against infringements of marital and procreative functions remained in effect. Canon law procedures treating wife and child abuse, paternal delinquency, child custody, and the like continued uninterrupted. Canon law impediments that protected free consent, that implemented biblical prohibitions against marriage of relatives, and that governed the relations of husband and wife and parent and child within the household were largely retained.

The new Protestant theology of marriage and the family, however, also yielded critical changes in this new civil law. Because the reformers rejected the subordination of marriage to celibacy, they rejected laws that forbade clerical and monastic marriage and that permitted vows of chastity to annul vows of marriage. Because they rejected the sacramental concept of marriage as an eternal enduring bond, the reformers introduced divorce in the modern sense, on grounds of adultery, desertion, cruelty, or frigidity, with a subsequent right to remarry at least for the innocent party. Because persons by their lustful nature were in need of God's soothing remedy of marriage, the reformers rejected numerous canon law impediments to marriage not countenanced by scripture. Because of their emphasis on the pedagogical role of the church and the family, and the priestly calling of all believers, the reformers insisted that both marriage and divorce be public, communal acts in order to be legitimate. Promises of marriage required parental consent, two witnesses, church consecration and registration, priestly instruction, and open disclosure in the community. Actions for divorce had to be announced publicly in the church and community and adjudicated in painfully open and full hearings.

After the sixteenth century, these two theological models of marriage and the family lay at the heart of Western family law. The medieval Catholic model, confirmed and elaborated by the Council of Trent in 1563, flourished in southern Europe, Iberia, and France, and their colonies in Latin America, Quebec, Louisiana, and other outposts. A Protestant social model rooted in the Lutheran two-kingdoms theory dominated portions of Germany, Austria, Switzerland, and Scandinavia, together with their colonies. A Protestant social model rooted in a parallel Calvinist covenant theology came to strong expression in Calvinist Geneva and in portions of Huguenot France, the Pietist Netherlands, Presbyterian Scotland, and Puritan England, and was eventually transmitted to Puritan New England and portions of the middle American colonies. Something of a hybrid between these two models prevailed in Anglican England and its many colonies.

Until well into the twentieth century, these time-tested Catholic and Protestant models of marriage and the family were commonplace in America. At the turn of this century, leading American jurists still spoke of marriage as a "state of existence ordained by the Creator," "a consummation of the Divine command 'to multiply and replenish the earth,'" and "the only stable substructure of social, civil, and religious institutions." The United States Supreme Court spoke regularly of the family as "a sacred obligation," "a holy estate," and "a divine office." Until the 1950s, American law countenanced only monogamous unions between a man and a woman and punished polygamy, incest, and homosexuality. It required that betrothals be formal and that marriages be contracted with parental consent and witnesses. It required marriage licenses and registration and solemnization before civil or ecclesiastical authorities. It prohibited marriages between couples related by various blood or family ties. It discouraged marriage where one party was impotent, deranged, or had a contagious disease. Couples who sought to divorce had to publicize their intentions, to petition a court, to show adequate cause or fault, and to make provision for their children.

It is only in the past three decades that this Christian lore and law of the family has been systematically spurned. Today, a private contractual perspective of marriage and the family dominates American public life and law—unbuffered by complementary sacramental or social perspectives and unreceptive to a constructive familial role for the church, state, or broader community. Marriage is viewed at large and at law as a simple contract to be formed, maintained, and dissolved as the parties see fit. Antenuptial contracts that allow marital parties to define their own rights and duties have gained increasing acceptance. Requirements of parental consent and witnesses to marriage have disappeared in many jurisdictions. No-fault divorce statutes have reduced the divorce proceeding to a formality. Traditional laws against fornication, sodomy, bestiality, and other offenses are largely dead letters. The functional distinctions between the rights of the married and the unmarried couple, the heterosexual and the homosexual partnership, the single-parent and the dual-parent household, the legitimate and the illegitimate child have been considerably narrowed by an array of new statutes and constitutional cases.

Many of these recent changes have helped to bring greater liberty and equality within the American family and to purge it of some of the excessive paternalism and patriarchy of the past. But these massive changes to the traditional theology and law of the family have come too easily and hastily, with too little attention to their catastrophic psychological and social costs, and too little reflection and resistance from Christian theologians and jurists.

To bring to light medieval Catholic and Reformation Protestant traditions is neither to wax nostalgic about a golden age of the Western family nor to offer an exportable system of theory and law to govern this institution. It is, instead, to point to a pastoral and prophetic resource that is too little known and too little used today. Too much of the contemporary church seems to have lost sight of its rich theological traditions on marriage and the family, of the ability of our forebears to translate their enduring and evolving perspectives on marriage and family life into legal forms—both canonical and civil. There is a great deal more in those dusty old tomes and canons than idle antiquaria. These ancient sources ultimately hold the theological genetic code that has defined the contemporary family for what it is—and what it can be.

Bibliography

Brundage, James A. *Law, Sex, and Christian Society in Medieval Europe* (Chicago: University of Chicago Press, 1987).

Noonan, John T. *Contraception: A History of Its Treatment by the Catholic Theologians and Canonists* (Cambridge, Mass.: Harvard University Press, 1965).

Ozment, Steven E. *When Fathers Ruled: Family Life in Reformation Europe* (Cambridge, Mass.: Harvard University Press, 1983).

Witte, John, Jr. *From Sacrament to Contract: Marriage, Religion, and Law in the Western Tradition* (Louisville, Ky.: Westminster John Knox Press, 1997).

—JOHN WITTE, JR.

25

Families in the Nineteenth and Twentieth Centuries

The family patterns of any society are deeply rooted in its history. Judaism, Greek and Roman culture, early Christianity, medieval Catholic canon law, and the legal and religious transformations of the Protestant Reformation—in its Lutheran, Calvinist, and Anglican strands—have all influenced the shape of American family life. Reformation influences, especially in their Calvinist patterns, influenced the family life of the early New England colonies and set the tone for family patterns in many other parts of the country. Anglican patterns helped shape the mid-Atlantic and southeastern states. Catholicism influenced family patterns and family law in Florida, California, and the Southwest. More distinctively Lutheran patterns permeated the upper midwestern states. As our other historical chapters have demonstrated, these Protestant and Catholic patterns were themselves influenced by Hebrew, Greek, and Roman family models. In short, the rich tapestry of family patterns in the United States is woven of the threads of a number of historical and cultural sources.

Both conservative and progressive voices in the contemporary American debate over the family have lineages in American history. Both the Puritan or Calvinist family of the Northeast and the Anglican-influenced family of the mid-Atlantic and southern states were undergoing transformations by the time of the Revolutionary War. Armed conflict with England, the beginnings of urban industrialization, the rise of revivalism, and the influence of the English and Scottish Enlightenment unleashed progressive cultural forces in American thinking about families. As historian Linda Kerber has shown, this new liberalism functioned to curtail the authority of fathers and increase the freedoms of women and children.

The more conservative cultural transformations that created the classic image of the American middle-class family occurred during the early and middle decades of the nineteenth century. Industrialization took men away from farm and craft and into the wage economy of towns and cities, especially in the Northeast. But the new concerns with efficiency, productivity, and profit did not stand alone in shaping the life of families; the revivalism of the Second Great Awakening also played a role. Methodist-style preaching, conversion, and spirituality interacted with the forces of the new industrial economy to stabilize and sanction the classic modern American family built around the wage-earning husband and the domestic, economically dependent wife and mother.

Methodist and Presbyterian revivalism used the household codes of Ephesians 5:21–33, Colossians 3:18–4:1, and 1 Peter 3:1–7 (which emphasized the authority of husband over wife, children, and slaves) to endow the model of male headship in the industrial family with the aura of New Testament authority. New Testament scholar David Balch has shown how these household codes stemmed from the writings of the Greek philosopher Aristotle (*Nicomachean Ethics*, bk. 8, chaps. 9–12) but also shaped the family theory of most Mediterranean urban centers during the period of Roman Hellenism. These codes enshrined ideals about families that some New Testament authors assumed, even though they also amended them to make them gentler and more egalitarian. Practical theologian Pamela Couture in *From Culture Wars to Common Ground* (Browning et al. 1997) has shown that mid-nineteenth-century southern families, urban black families, westward-migrating pioneer families, and immigrating ethnic Catholic families all tried to imitate this model, even though the unique aspects retained from their local family traditions made for many variations (and there were some exceptions).

This nineteenth-century family was stable in contrast to late-twentieth-century families. Divorce was rare, although many children were deprived of parental support because of the early deaths of their parents. The nineteenth-century middle-class family—often called the "Victorian" family by historians—was more companionate and child-centered than earlier Puritan families of the Northeast or the slave-owning families of the mid-Atlantic or Southeast. Although the Victorian family isolated women from political and economic power, it also freed them for volunteer activity in church and society and for the education of their children and themselves.

But the nineteenth-century middle-class ideal of the family led to increased economic dependency of wives on wage-earning fathers, decreased the economic contributions of women to family well-being, split the public world of paid work and politics from the private world of home and child care, and maintained the patriarchal control of husbands and fathers, although it was now expressed more affectionately. For example, among many nineteenth-century Christians, the intimacy of the religious conversion experience became a model for the intimacy of a shared life between husband and wife.

In the latter part of the nineteenth century, this family form became hardened by the emerging fundamentalism of portions of evangelical Protestantism. Fundamentalist men began to reassert control of church life after a long drift toward what historian Ann Douglas has called the "feminization of American Christianity." Fundamentalist churches worked to bolster the patriarchy and separate spheres of the nineteenth-century family as a way of protecting male authority in churches from the tendency of markets to pull fathers away from home and church.

These trends put in place the conservative party of the contemporary American debate over the family. When Republicans came to power in national politics in the 1980s, they built on elements of American culture that had their origins in the nineteenth century. They helped build a grand coalition of conservative political and religious forces in American public life. This coalition was dedicated to the defense and preservation of the nineteenth-century middle-class family pattern. The nineteenth-century family patterns they idealized were also defended by other religiopolitical organizations such as Focus on the Family, the Moral Majority, the Christian Coalition, the Family Research Council, and the Traditional Values Coalition. These groups influence the voting patterns of approximately one-third of American adults.

These conservative pro-family groups have tried to preserve the nineteenth-century response to the destructive consequences of market rationalization, but other groups in American life have taken a very different approach to these same forces. Linked historically to the Enlightenment, rights-oriented, and antipatriarchal strands of American history, these groups—the liberal and progressive wings of the Democratic party, liberal political scientists, liberal and progressive feminists, and the liberal wings of mainline Protestant churches—have taken a positive attitude toward the changes in the postmodern or postindustrial family that have accompanied the new market forces in the twentieth century. They have supported the move of wives and mothers into the wage market and the consequent increase in the economic independence of women. They have been more willing to accept the disruption that market employment and market-driven consumption have visited on families as trade-offs for the increased freedom and autonomy of both men and women.

Social scientists from 1960 to 1985 were for the most part positive about family change and believed that increased divorce, later marriages, more single parenthood, more stepfamilies, and other family experiments were not harmful. Rather, as sociologist Jessie Bernard contended in *The Future of Marriage* (1977), these changes were thought to contribute to the increased freedom, choice, and self-actualization of both women and men, and especially women.

From 1960 to the 1980s, progressive political and religious voices joined with liberal social scientists to proclaim a new theory of family equality. They drew inspiration from the equal-rights movement of the 1960s and claimed that all family forms were equally good for children, mothers, and men if society could only learn to accept them. In light of the prominence in the 1970s of this progressive wing in the American family debate, the reassertion of conservative religiopolitical forces in the 1980s should be understood in part as an antithesis to a prior culturally powerful liberal thesis. Conservatives used the phrase "secular humanism" to refer to these progressive movements and felt that they were permeating government, the courts, public education, the professions, and the mass media.

The conflict between progressive and conservative forces in the struggle over the American family was so intense that in 1991 sociologist James Davison Hunter published a book with the revealing title *Culture Wars: The Struggle to Define America.* This war is still with us and is limiting the capacity of both religious institutions and the state to deal effectively with the crisis confronting families in North America. When this conflict is placed in historical context, neither conservatives nor progressives appear to be on solid ground. The nineteenth-century middle-class family, regardless of its strengths, cannot be identified with the Christian family, nor does evidence support the proposition that all family forms are equally good for children, mothers, and fathers.

Classic Protestant perspectives have invoked the idea of "orders" or "estates" of creation thought to be implied in Genesis 2:24 ("Therefore a man leaves his father and mother and clings to his wife, and they become one flesh") and reaffirmed by Jesus in Matthew 19:4–6. These scriptures were held to proclaim the centrality of a lifetime commitment of the conjugal couple to each other and to their children. Catholicism has supplemented biblical supports for the integrity of the conjugal couple with appeals to nature or natural law.

To celebrate the integrity of the conjugal couple does not, however, necessitate uncritical support for the work patterns—wage-earning father and domestic mother—of the nineteenth-century industrial family. Nor does it mean that we should affirm the patriarchy of this nineteenth-century family pattern, even in its softer forms. Finally, affirming the centrality of the conjugal couple should not imply an uncritical affirmation of the modern nuclear family in its isolation from extended family and wider community. On the other hand, we should not demonize the nineteenth-century modern or industrial family or blind ourselves to its strengths in its time and place. In exposing its patriarchy, its artificial division between public and private, its isolation of men from the domestic sphere, and its barring of women from the public world, we should not become cavalier about the importance of family stability, fidelity between husband and wife, and the value of the residential presence of both fathers and mothers for the well-being of children. Hence, neither strong conservative nor hardened progressive responses to the family crisis are adequate.

Rather, a middle path should be chosen. This middle perspective, which we call *critical familism,* promotes preparation for and support of the stable, egalitarian husband-wife partnership in which both partners have equal access to the privileges and responsibilities of the public and the private-domestic world. A critical familism would incorporate the following additional elements: a powerful retrieval and reconstruction of the marriage traditions of our religious institutions; strong support by the value-creating institutions of civil society, the media, the market, and the government for the egalitarian marital partnership described above—this could be called a *critical marriage culture;* appropriate government welfare and tax provisions to make the formation of such families affordable; much more attention by churches, schools, and local governments to education in communication skills, conflict management, mentoring, and other continuing supports needed to make such unions possible and sustainable; and practical help from churches, civil society, and government for all families with children, regardless of form or pattern.

Bibliography

Balch, David. *Let Wives Be Submissive: Domestic Code of 1 Peter.* (Atlanta: Scholars Press, 1983).

Bendroth, Margaret. *Fundamentalism and Gender: 1875 to the Present* (New Haven, Conn.: Yale University Press, 1994).

Bernard, Jessie. *The Future of Marriage* (New York: World Publishing, 1972).

Browning, Don, Bonnie Miller-McLemore, Pam Couture, Bernie Lyon, and Robert Franklin. *From Culture Wars to Common Ground: Religion and the American Family Debate* (Louisville, Ky.: Westminster John Knox Press, 1997).

Douglas, Ann. *The Feminization of American Culture* (New York: Alfred A. Knopf, 1977).

Hunter, James Davison. *Culture Wars: The Struggle to Define America* (New York: Basic Books, 1990).

—DON BROWNING

PART 5

General Resources
for Family Ministry

A Directory of Resources for Families

During the past twenty years scholarship in theological schools and the secular academy has paid slight attention to the family. The greatest creative ferment in this area has been in individual congregations and in voluntary associations dedicated to specific problems. Here there are many resources and many issues on which a practical theological dialogue is needed. In this section we provide a directory of major religious and secular organizations that serve or do advocacy with families.

The following is a national directory intended for use by professional ministers, lay leaders, and others seeking resources for families. The number of resources and services for families has increased dramatically in recent years, making it virtually impossible to provide a complete and fully up-to-date guide. This is particularly true of resources on the Internet, about which more will be said below. The information in this directory was correct as of March 1998.

The new resources are also provided by institutions and organizations with various interests. For-profit, private sector service providers such as hospitals and clinics advertise and charge fees much as does any other business. Medical and mental health professionals associated with these organizations may charge more for their services than some people are able or willing to pay. Advertisements should not necessarily be taken as indications of the quality of these providers. Advertisements for specialty services may simply be designed to attract patients to the more general services that the organization provides.

Moreover, association with a church should not necessarily be taken as an indication of the religious character of the services provided. Many service providers actively seek such associations in order to get clients. Association of a mental health professional with a church does not, for example, mean that a mental health professional offers faith-based counseling or treatment.

The new resources are also highly specialized. This specialization benefits families by permitting them to choose among providers and to obtain services tailored to their needs. It also requires families in need and those who minister to them to sift through the array of resources for those that are most appropriate.

We encourage those seeking family resources to be both assertive and selective. People should not hesitate to ask questions of various social service providers to get a sense of their organizations and whether their services fit particular needs. Many services provided by religious and denominational organizations are open to those outside their particular faith traditions. Some services may be geared toward evangelization or conducted from a faith perspective not suited to the needs of particular individuals and families. Asking appropriate questions can ensure that families find and choose the best services for their needs.

Users of this directory will want to be aware that family resources are available at several levels. First, there are congregational and denominational resources, often the first source of information for church members. Individual congregations and denominations may also provide services for people outside their denominations. Second, there are local resources serving particular municipalities or regions. While we have generally not included local services unless they are large and serve extensive areas, readers should be aware that many of the national organizations listed in this directory can refer them to local chapters and agencies. Finding local resources in rural areas may pose the greatest challenge. Though rural resources are fewer and less well known than urban and suburban services, they do exist, and we have been particularly vigilant in seeking out these resources for rural families. Finally, there is the national level, which is the focus of this directory. With the advent of the Internet, these national agencies have been able to reach out to people across the nation to a greater extent than at any time in the past.

In compiling this directory, we have interviewed pastors, librarians, social service directors, and others involved in the "helping professions" to obtain their suggestions on finding and evaluating local services. Another resource that was valuable for us and would be useful for readers to consult is the "Tip Sheet" available from the Family Resource Coalition of America, 20 North Wacker Dr., Suite 1100, Chicago, IL 60606; phone (312) 338-0900; fax (312) 338-1522; http://chtop.com/frc.htm. In light of the proliferation of resources, we urge users of this directory to be imaginative in their search for family resources that may not be included. Our investigation leads us to urge that several sites not be overlooked by people seeking resources beyond those listed in this directory.

Congregations. Many congregations compile their own directories of local social services. In some communities interdenominational groups of local religious leaders have worked together to compile a list of helpful organizations in the area. Pastors can also refer individuals to psychologists, psychotherapists, and other counselors.

Mental Health Services. For specific information, consult the Yellow Pages in your area. Listings in the Yellow Pages may vary from one locale to the next, but mental health resources are often listed under the categories "Marriage, Family, Child, and Individual Counselors," "Mental Health Services," "Psychologists," "Psychiatric Social Workers," and the "Psychiatry" listing of physicians by specialty.

Hospitals and Health Services. Medical centers are increasingly providing and advertising a number of specialty services that may be valuable resources for families. In addition to providing individuals with referrals to physicians for specific health problems, medical facilities are increasingly taking a more holistic approach by providing services that can educate and assist the individual's family as well. Examples of such services in general hospitals include drug and alchohol addiction treatment that may include aftercare; treatment of psychological and emotional disorders that may include 24-hour crisis hotlines and specialized programs for those who have been physically abused; specialized services for children, adolescents, and seniors; home health care and specialized programs for those with terminal or degenerative illness, including hospice, pain management, and Alzheimer's programs; and, most important, family-centered practice and social work divisions. One local hospital even had a program specifically directed at "Families in Crisis."

Psychiatric hospitals also offer specialized programs to deal with sexual trauma, work pressures, relationship issues, and suicide. One Chicago psychiatric hospital advertises an adult day care service. Many of the medical centers listed in the Yellow Pages under "Hospitals" provide extensive lists of these and other services, but where hospitals do not advertise the services described above, this list can serve as a guide for users of this directory who may want to inquire about the availability of particular services at hospitals near them.

Social Service Agencies. The social service sector has been the site of the greatest development of family-oriented services. These agencies may provide direct assistance or referrals to other services. Those interested in finding out more about such agencies can check the Yellow Pages under "Social Service Organizations" and "Human Services Organizations," particularly for organizations that specifically address families and children. Many of these listings cover the usual social services. Searches of the local Yellow Pages have turned up not only such specific services as a Parental Stress Service Hotline, a Sudden Infant Death Syndrome Alliance, and a Bi-Racial Family Network, but also organizations such as Gamblers Anonymous and Debtors Anonymous, which may provide information helpful to families dealing with these social problems.

Universities. Those who live near a university may find that universities are a valuable resource for the entire community. Some universities have departments or projects concentrating on the family or childhood. These departments can be sources of speakers and other information.

Libraries. Local libraries may contain published directories and indexes of organizations and associations that can be helpful resources. The libraries may themselves also sponsor programs and events of interest to families.

United Way. The United Way is a fund-raising organization for nonprofit agencies, charitable organizations, and volunteer associations. The United Way keeps a directory of all the organizations that it supports and can direct inquirers to local services. For information on family services near you, or inquiries concerning funding for starting up such services, contact the United Way of America, 701 North Fairfax Street, Alexandria, VA 22314-2045; phone (703) 836-7100; www.unitedway.org.

Newspapers. Local newspapers often list times and locations of various meetings, events, and programs of interest to families. In some metropolitan areas, newspapers on parenting provide a good source for announcements about parent support activities and are distributed at no charge. Parenting newspapers can be found in shopping areas and other public places where free publications are distributed, as well as in community centers.

A final note on Internet resources. The on-line resources included in this directory are numerous, but they certainly do not exhaust the possibilities. Only organizational web sites and the larger on-line networks have been included. The landscape on the World Wide Web is constantly in flux, with sites being added, removed, and constantly updated. The sites in this directory have been selected for relevance and permanence. The information superhighway does, however, contain many other paths worth exploring—so be resourceful!

Contents

Adoption 308
African-American Families 310
Children 311
Conflict Resolution 313
Death and Grieving 314
Denominational Resources 315
Disability and Chronic Illness 318
Divorce 319
Domestic Violence 320
Education and Parental Involvement 321
Elder Care 322
Family Organizations 324
Family Professionals 325
Fathers 326
Finances 328
HIV/AIDS 329
Homelessness 330
Home Schooling 331
Homosexuality 332
Latino Families 333
Marriage 333
Mental Illness 335
Mothers 335
Parents 337
Pregnancy 338
Publications 339
Rural Families 340
Sex Education 341
Single Parents 341
Stepfamilies 343
Substance Abuse 343
Youth 344

ADOPTION

Adoptive Families of America   **Phone:** (612) 535-4829
2309 Como Ave.   **Toll Free:** (800) 372-3300
St. Paul, MN 55108   **Fax:** (612) 645-0055
                                     Net: www.AdoptiveFam.org

This organization promotes adoption and supports adoptive families by providing information on adoption and the dynamics of adoptive families, as well
as assistance to adoptive family support groups and those wishing to start them.
It also publishes a magazine for members, holds an annual conference, and
maintains a free help line available to the general public.

Bethany Christian Services   **Phone:** (616) 459-6273
901 Eastern Avenue, NE   **Toll Free:** (800) 239-7573
Grand Rapids, MI 49503   **Fax:** (616) 224-7611
                                    Net: www.bethany.org

This agency provides pregnancy counseling, foster care, and adoption service
from a Christian and pro-life perspective. Pregnancy counseling is provided to
all women, regardless of faith commitment, but potential adoptive parents must
be Christian. The agency screens adoptive parents and provides educational
programs, support services, and counseling for adoptive children and families
created by adoption.

Committee for Single Adoptive Parents
P.O. Box 15084
Chevy Chase, MD 20815

This organization provides information on agencies that accept applications
from single people. It also provides the name of state and local groups of single adoptive parents, names of prospective and actual single parents, and book
recommendations. It also publishes the *Handbook for Single Adoptive Parents.*

Evangelical Child
  and Family Agency   **Phone:** (630) 653-6400
1530 North Main Street   **Fax:** (630) 653-6490
Wheaton, IL 60187   **Net:** www.awebpresence.com
                                       /wheaton/ecfa.htm

This agency provides pregnancy counseling, adoption services, and foster care
from a Christian and pro-life perspective. Prospective adoptive parents are required to be Christian. Adoption services are also limited to prospective parents
from Illinois and Wisconsin. While the pregnancy counseling services are free,
the organization does charge fees for adoption and other counseling services.

International Concerns for Children   **Phone:** (303) 494-8333
911 Cyprus Drive   **Fax:** (303) 494-8333
Boulder, CO 80303-2821   **Net:** fortnet.org/ICC

This organization provides annual reports updating regulations on adoption in countries around the world. It is helpful to those considering international adoption.

Latter Day Saints Social Services   **Phone:** (801) 240-3339
10 East South Temple Street,   **Fax:** (801) 240-4632
   Suite 1200
Salt Lake City, UT 84133

This Mormon social service organization provides a variety of services to women facing unplanned or crisis pregnancies. While most services are provided to members of the Mormon Church, the crisis pregnancy services are open to people of all faiths.

National Adoption Center   **Phone:** (215) 735-9988
1500 Walnut Street, Suite 701   **Fax:** (215) 735-9410
Philadelphia, PA 19102   **Net:** www.adopt.org

This organization works to expand adoption opportunities for children with special needs or from minority cultures. It works with social workers and other adoption professionals to bring children and families together. It also offers information and referral services.

The National Adoption
   Information Clearinghouse   **Phone:** (703) 352-3488
P.O. Box 1182   **Toll Free:** (888) 251-0075
Washington, DC 20013-1182   **Fax:** (703) 385-3206
                                      Net: www.calib.com/naic

This organization maintains a computerized information database containing titles and abstracts of adoption documents. It fills information requests on topics related to adoption and provides computer printouts of relevant articles. It also provides referrals to adoption agencies, support groups, and experts.

North American Council
   on Adoptable Children   **Phone:** (612) 644-3036
970 Raymond Avenue, Suite 106   **Fax:** (612) 644-9848
St. Paul, MN 55114-1149   **Net:** cyfc.umn.edu/Adoptinfo/
                                           nacac.html

This coalition of support and advocacy groups for adoptive parents is committed to assisting the adoption of special-needs children in this country and abroad. It provides referrals to local resources for parents wishing to adopt these children.

AFRICAN-AMERICAN FAMILIES

See also Family Resource Coalition under "Family Organizations" and Ecumenical AIDS Resource Center under "HIV/AIDS."

Association of Black Psychologists   **Phone:** (202) 722-0808
821 Kennedy Street, NW   **Fax:** (202) 722-5941
Washington, DC 20040   **Net:** www.abpsi.org

This organization of African Americans in the mental heath professions seeks to enhance the well-being of black people in America, to promote the constructive understanding of black people through positive research approaches, and to develop psychology that is consistent with the experience of black people. It sponsors an annual convention, publishes six periodicals, and has chapters in most major metropolitan areas. Committees include the Black Family Task Force.

Inroads, Inc.   **Phone:** (314) 241-7488
10 South Broadway, Suite 700   **Fax:** (314) 241-9325
St. Louis, MO 63102   **Net:** www.inroadsinc.org

This organization prepares talented minority youth for corporate and community leadership by placing them in high school internships with sponsoring organizations in business and industry. Internships are awarded on the basis of African-American, Hispanic, or Native American status, as well as demonstrated academic achievement, interest in careers in business and industry, and a desire to improve self, family, and community.

National Black Child
   Development Institute   **Phone:** (202) 387-1281
1023 15th Street, NW   **Toll Free:** (800) 556-2234
Suite 600   **Fax:** (202) 234-1738
Washington, DC 20005   **Net:** www.nbcdi.org

This organization is dedicated to improving the quality of life for black children and families through services and advocacy. It provides members information on child care, education, child welfare, and health in its newsletter and periodic updates and sponsors an annual conference.

National Black Women's
Health Project   **Phone:** (202) 835-0117
1211 Connecticut Ave., NW,   **Fax:** (202) 833-8790
   Suite 310   **E-mail:** nbwhpdc@aol.com
Washington, DC 20036

This advocacy organization is committed to improving the health of African-American women. The core of its program is its nationwide network of self-help groups, but it also supports a research center, an international information and advocacy service, and various programs to encourage exercise, nutrition, and health education for black women. It also publishes a news magazine and produces educational films.

CHILDREN

Big Brother/Big Sisters of America   **Phone:** (215) 567-7000
230 North 13th Street   **Fax:** (215) 567-0394
Philadelphia, PA 19107   **Net:** www.bbbsa.org

This organization matches children up with adult men and women who serve as role models, especially for children from single-parent homes. The organization is nondenominational but may have information on organizations like Jewish Big Brothers and Catholic Big Brothers in the area. It usually matches children with adults of the same sex but sometimes provides cross-gender parings.

Children's Defense Fund   **Phone:** (202) 628-8787
25 E Street, NW   **Fax:** (202) 662-3540
Washington, DC 20001   **Net:** www.childrensdefense.org

This organization is dedicated to providing a voice for American children, particularly those burdened with poverty, disability, or minority status; to educating the nation about the needs of children; and to encouraging preventive investment in children. Projects include the Black Community Crusade for Children and promoting the observance Children's Sabbaths as a way to raise consciousness of the problems of children in religious communities. Religious groups can obtain Children's Sabbath packet by contacting the organization.

Childserv   **Phone:** (773) 693-0300
8675 West Higgins Road, Suite 450   **Fax:** (773) 693-0322
Chicago, IL 606312   **Net:** www.childserv.org

This organization is dedicated to serving children and families through prevention, early intervention, child advocacy programs, and out-of-home placement for children who cannot remain with their family of origin. Direct services are provided to people in the Chicago metropolitan area.

Ecumenical Child Care Network   **Phone:** (773) 693-4040
8675 West Higgins Road, Suite 405   **Fax:** (773) 693-4042
Chicago, IL 60631   **Email:** eccn@juno.com

This organization provides information, advocacy, and consulting on child care issues. It supports federal initiatives that promote high-quality, affordable care and education for young children, including universal childhood immunization, Head Start expansion, equitable food stamp programs, family and medical leave, and services for family preservation and support. It publishes a newsletter and other publications.

*National Child Care
  Information Center*   **Phone:** (800) 616-2242
301 Maple Ave. West, Suite 602 **Fax:** (800) 716-2242
Vienna, VA 22180   **Net:** ericps.ed.uius.edu/
                                nccic/nccichome.html

This web site is maintained by the United States Department of Health and Human Services and related agencies serving children and families. In addition to an Internet guide with links to other child care resources, the site offers information on publications and bulletins, organizations and related professions, forums and conferences, research and resources, federal programs, how to find child care, and tribal resources for Native American Families.

National Children's Coalition   **Phone:** (500) 675-KIDS or
267 Lester Ave., Suite 104   (510) 286-7916
Oakland, CA 94606   **Net:** www.slip.net/~scmetro/ncc.htm

This web site contains, in addition to information and entertainment for children, a Youth and Children's Resource Net with resources on children of interest to parents, churches, and others interested in children's issues.

Urban Family Institute   **Phone:** (202) 234-5437
1400 16th Street, NW, Suite 101   **Fax:** (202) 232-3299
Washington, DC 20036-2266

This organization works to improve the lives of urban children through information, advocacy, and direct service. Direct services include after-school activity sites with adult supervision, residential houses for homeless children, and neighborhood institutions in churches, clinics, and schools to provide safe environments for children and their families.

CONFLICT RESOLUTION

See also Academy of Family Mediators under "Family Professionals."

Association of Family
*   and Conciliation Courts*   **Phone:** (608) 251-4001
329 West Wilson Street   **Fax:** (608) 251-2231
Madison, WI 53703-3612   **E-mail:** afcc@afccnet.org

This organization advocates and provides information on court-connected mediation and educational programs for parents and children going through separation and divorce.

Mennonite Conciliation Service   **Phone:** (717) 859-3889
21 South 12th Street   **Fax:** (717) 859-3875
P.O. Box 500   **Net:** mennonitecc.ca/mcc/
Akron, PA 17501-0500   **E-mail:** mcs@mccus.org

This organization, affiliated with the Mennonite Church, provides resource bibliographies for conflict management in home, school, and congregation to people of all faiths. It also publishes a quarterly newsletter and provides information on justice issues through a variety of audiovisual and print materials.

National Institute for
*   Dispute Resolution*   **Phone:** (202) 466-4764
1726 M Street, NW, Suite 500   **Fax:** (202) 466-4769
Washington, DC 20036-4502

This professional organization is dedicated to promoting fair, effective, and efficient conflict resolution processes and programs, to fostering the use of conflict resolution in new arenas, and to stimulating innovative approaches to productive resolution of future conflicts. It maintains a research service and publishes a newsletter and a journal.

Parenting for Peace and Justice   **Phone:** (314) 533-4445
The Institute for Peace and Justice **Fax:** (314) 533-1017
4144 Lindell Boulevard, Room 408   **Net:** members.aol.com/ppjn
St. Louis, MO 63108

This ecumenical Christian organization provides resources on peace to the general public, particularly through its newsletter and leadership training in churches. Parenting for Peace and Justice is a special division focusing on family issues.

DEATH AND GRIEVING

Abundant Resources, Inc.   **Phone:** (612) 557-0272
15655 40th Ave. North   **Fax:** (612) 557-6334
Plymouth, MN 55446   **E-mail:** zalaz002@tc.umn.edu

This organization publishes materials on death and loss, including a bibliography and an educational curriculum suitable for use in schools, funeral homes, churches, support groups, and hospices. It also provides teacher training workshops, presentations, and consultations.

The Compassionate Friends   **Phone:** (630) 990-0010
P.O. Box 3696   **Fax:** (630) 990-0246
Oak Brook, IL 60522-3696   **Net:** longhorn.jjt.com/~tcf_national

This mutual assistance, self-help organization offers friendship and understanding to parents and siblings who have suffered the death of a child. It does not address situations involving the loss of a parent, spouse, or adult child or sibling. It also provides information on printed materials and its local support groups. The phone lines are staffed by volunteers who can provide support and further information.

Continental Association of Funeral
*   and Memorial Services*   **Phone:** (920) 868-3136
6900 Lost Lake Road   **Toll Free:** (800) 765-0107
Egg Harbor, WI 54209-9231

This umbrella organization for local and regional memorial societies provides literature on affordable funeral options. These societies have arrangements with local undertakers who provide inexpensive services for a predetermined cost and serve as advocacy groups for members with complaints. The organization provides books, pamphlets, and forms with answers to questions about funeral planning.

Funeral and Memorial Societies
*   of America*   **Phone:** (802) 482-3437
P.O. Box 10   **Net:** www.funerals.org/famsa
Hinesburg, VT 05461

This organization provides many of same services as the Continental Association listed above, but it also has a web site for quick access to information.

Rainbows
1111 Tower Road
Schaumburg, IL 60173-4305

Phone: (847) 310-1880
Toll Free: (800) 266-3206
Fax: (847) 310-0120
Net: www.rainbows.org

This organization offers training, curricula, personnel support, and follow-up for those establishing peer support groups of children and adults affected by death, divorce, or other painful family transitions.

DENOMINATIONAL RESOURCES

(CHRISTIAN—ECUMENICAL)

**Commission on Family Ministries
and Human Sexuality**
National Council of the Churches
of Christ
475 Riverside Drive
New York, NY 10115-0050

Phone: (212) 870-2673
Fax: (212) 870-2030
Net: www.ncccusa.org/nmu/
mce/fandaministr.html

This division of the interdenominational National Council of the Churches of Christ provides information on resources for family ministries, sex education, and rituals for recognizing family events.

(CONSERVATIVE JEWISH)

**United Synagogue
of Conservative Judaism**
Department of Education
155 Fifth Avenue
New York, NY 10010

Phone: (212) 533-7800
Fax: (212) 353-9439
Net: www.jtsa.edu/uscj

This denomination maintains the On-Line Family Education Pages with ideas for nurturing and celebrating Jewish family life.

(EVANGELICAL LUTHERAN CHURCH IN AMERICA)

Lutheran Social Services
8765 West Higgins Road
Chicago, IL 60631

Phone: (773) 380-2684

This organization oversees a large number of community service organizations, including hospitals, counseling centers, children's services, retirement homes, social service agencies, immigration and refugee services, and services for the developmentally disabled. Many are specifically family-oriented and they are open to people of all faiths. Information on local services can be obtained by calling local ELCA churches.

(JEWISH)

Jewish Community Center
**   Association of North America**   **Phone:** (212) 532-4949
15 E. 26th Street   **Fax:** (212) 481-4174
New York, NY 10010

This organization publishes the *Directory of Jewish Community Centers,* which lists locations of these centers across the country.

(LUTHERAN CHURCH—MISSOURI SYNOD)

Lutheran Family Association
**   Family Connection**   **Phone:** (314) 268-1180
3558 South Jefferson Avenue   **Toll Free:** (800) 351-1001
St. Louis, MO 63118   **Net:** www.lcms.org/lfa/FCRes.html

This hotline service operates seven days a week during the daytime hours for those seeking direction in their family lives. Volunteers pray with callers, direct them to Christian resources, and mail them free family information. The organization also publishes a quarterly newsletter.

(PRESBYTERIAN CHURCH, U.S.A.)

Presbyterian Mariners   **Phone:** (303) 425-5033
11555 W. 78th Drive   **Fax:** (303) 425-0899
Arvada, CO 80005-3427   **Net:** www.feist.com/~pmariners

This organization's primary emphasis is the support and nurture of marriage and families. It provides an annual program book containing topics, outlines, and additional resources for local meetings, a quarterly newspaper, and audiovisual and printed materials on family ministry. The organization charters groups in congregations across the country, has an annual conference, and provides opportunities for families to serve in Mission Work camps.

(ROMAN CATHOLIC)

Archdiocese of Chicago
155 E. Superior
Chicago, IL 60611

Phone: (312) 751-8351
Fax: (312) 787-1554
Fax: www.archdiocese-chgo.org

The Archdiocese of Chicago is representative of resources at diocesan centers across the country. These centers seek to lift up the vocation of marriage and family. It offers marriage preparation for engaged couples, marriage enrichment retreats and seminars, and instruction in natural family planning and parenting. There are also father/son and mother/daughter programs and programs for single parents. Many programs are in Spanish as well as English.

Catholic Charities U.S.A.
1731 King Street #200
Alexandria, VA 22314

Phone: (703) 549-1390
Fax: (703) 549-1656
Net: www.catholiccharities
usa.org

This national office supports local Catholic Charities agencies throughout the country. These agencies provide crisis pregnancy hotlines and counseling, pregnancy assistance, adoption services, and parenting programs for adolescents. They also provide services for the elderly and residential care, foster care, and group home care for children.

(UNITARIAN UNIVERSALIST)

Unitarian Universalist Association
of Congregations
25 Beacon Street
Boston, MA 02108

Phone: (617) 742-2100
UUSC: (800) 388-3920
Fax: (617) 367-3237
Net: www.uua.org/bookstore/
family.html

The Unitarian Universalists affirm a "free and responsible search for truth and meaning" and are open to the religious wisdom of all faiths. They operate a bookstore and mail-order catalogue with sections on families and parenting, including curricula for parents as "resident theologians" in their families and resources on social justice and being a Unitarian Universalist parent. The denomination's service committee (UUSC) is involved in a range of domestic and international social justice concerns including family issues.

(UNITED CHURCH OF CHRIST)

United Church Board for
  Homeland Ministries   **Phone:** (216) 736-3800
700 Prospect Avenue   **Fax:** (216) 736-3803
Cleveland, OH 44115-1100   **Net:** www.ucc.org/educate
                                      /family.htm

The United Church of Christ (UCC) is an ecumenically oriented Protestant denomination that affirms people of all races, ethnicities, genders, abilities, economic classes, and sexual orientations. It offers many services to families. The
denomination publishes a national directory of member organizations, as well
as curricula for Bible study, Sunday school, adult education, multicultural education, and classes on sexual abuse and ministering to people with AIDS. The
UCC also offers an educational program on human sexuality and celebrates a
"Festival of the Christian Home."

DISABILITY AND CHRONIC ILLNESS

See also Alzheimer's Disease and Related Disorders Association and National
Federation of Interfaith Volunteer Caregivers, Inc. under "Elderly."

Family Caregiver Alliance   **Phone:** (415) 434-3388
425 Bush Street, Suite 500   **Net:** www.caregiver.org
San Francisco, CA 94108

This organization assists family caregivers of adults suffering memory loss from
chronic or progressive brain disorders such as stroke, traumatic brain injury,
brain tumors, AIDS dementia, and Alzheimer's, Huntington's, and Parkinson's.
It provides education, research, services, advocacy, publications, newsletters,
and general information.

Internet Resources for
  Special Children   **Net:** www.irsc.org

This web site provides information relating to the needs of disabled children
on a global basis. This includes information for parents, family members,
caregivers, friends, educators, and medical professionals who interact with
disabled children. The focus is on the abilities that such children do possess,
as well as improving the environment for these children, creating positive
changes, and enhancing public awareness and knowledge of children with
disabilities.

National Information Center
  for Children and Youth
    with Disabilities   **Phone:** (202) 884-8200
P.O. Box 1492   **Toll Free:** (800) 695-0285
Washington, DC 20013-1492   **Fax:** (202) 884-8441
                                       Net: www.nichcy.org

This clearinghouse provides information on disabilities involving children and young adults. It provides personal responses to questions on disability issues, referrals to other organizations, information searches of its databases and library, free publications, and assistance to parents and professional groups. The standard packet for information requests is large and includes a publications list, state resource sheet, national toll free numbers, a list of national resources, and several back issues of their newsletter.

DIVORCE

See also Rainbows under "Death and Grieving."

The Divorce Page   **Net:** www.divorcesupport.com

This web site addresses a wide range of issues pertaining to divorce, including a section on religious and spiritual issues.

North American Conference
  for Separated and
    Divorced Catholics   **Phone:** (541) 893-6089
NACSDC Central Office   **Fax:** (541) 893-6089*51
P.O. Box 360   **Net:** www.eoni.com/~nacsdc
Richland, OR 97870

This organization seeks out Catholics who have left the Church because of separation, divorce, or remarriage and works toward their reconciliation with the Church. It promotes local support groups and peer ministry, as well as providing programs and resources to ministers. It is open to non-Catholics and works with similar groups in other religious denominations.

Ministry for Separated
  and Divorced Catholics   **Phone:** (312) 751-8353
Department of Family Ministries   **Fax:** (312) 787-1554
Archdiocese of Chicago   **Net:** www.archdiocese-chgo.org
155 E. Superior Street
Chicago, IL 60611-2931

This organization is open to widowed, separated, and divorced people of all faiths. The program involves a beginning weekend, a six-week program of presentations and discussions on coping, and support groups. Financial assistance is available for those who cannot afford the cost of the programs.

DOMESTIC VIOLENCE

Center for the Prevention of Sexual
  and Domestic Violence   **Phone:** (206) 634-1903
936 North 34th Street, Suite 200   **Fax:** (206) 634-0115
Seattle, WA 98103   **Net:** www.cpsdv.org

This interreligious agency provides educational materials on the nature and prevention of domestic violence; child abuse of an emotional, physical, or sexual nature; and how to educate congregation members about these problems. It also publishes a newsletter and offers training workshops for clergy, seminarians, and religious educators.

Child Abuse Prevention Network   **Phone:** (607) 255-7794
Family Life Development Center   **Fax:** (607) 255-8562
G20 Van Rensselaer   **Net:** child.cornell.edu
Cornell University
Ithaca, NY 14853

This organization provides the latest statistics and information on child abuse and programs for prevention and intervention.

National Committee to Prevent
  Child Abuse   **Phone:** (312) 663-3520
332 S. Michigan Ave., Suite 1600   **Fax:** (312) 939-8962
Chicago, IL 60604-4357   **Net:** www.childabuse.org

This organization provides information, advocacy, assistance, and support for child abuse prevention and treatment to professionals, volunteers, and laypeople. It conducts nationwide awareness campaigns, publishes materials, sponsors events, provides training, acts as an information clearinghouse, develops model prevention programs, and provides parental education and other services to families. Information about specific programs and local chapters is available from the national committee. Its web site provides helpful parenting tips.

National Coalition Against
  Domestic Violence   **Phone:** (303) 839-1852
P.O. Box 18749   **Fax:** (303) 831-9251
Denver, CO 80218-0749   **Net:** webmerchants.com/ncadv

This organization works toward the empowerment of battered women and children and the elimination of violence toward them by providing information, advocacy, assistance, and support. It works with individuals and organizations at the local, state, and national levels to support community-based, nonviolent alternatives, such as safe house and shelter programs, and to eradicate social conditions that contribute to violence against women and children. The organization is not a crisis hotline, but it can refer callers to local women's shelters. It can also provide information on starting a battered women's shelter.

Parents Anonymous	**Phone:** (909) 621-6184
675 W. Foothill Blvd., Suite 220	**Toll Free:** (800) 421-0353
Claremont, CA 91711	**Net:** www.parentsanonymous-natl.org

This organization is committed to helping parents who want to improve their relationships with their children by supporting parents in day-to-day challenges and averting crisis situations that can lead to abuse and neglect. It is based on a self-help model and is led by parents with the support of professional resource people. Members share phone numbers and have access to crisis intervention and twenty-four-hour-a-day support by people who understand what they are experiencing. State and regional agencies refer individuals to local chapters.

Rainbow House/Arco Iris	**Phone:** (773) 521-5501
2313 South Millard	**Fax:** (773) 521-4866
Chicago, IL 60623	**E-mail:** rainbow@lgc.org

This Chicago organization assists women and children experiencing family violence. It offers a free residential shelter program providing individual and group counseling, weekly peer support groups, skill development workshops, advocacy and assistance for legal protection and child custody, and assistance with housing, finances, health, and job placement. It also has nonresidential counseling and support programs, engages in community education, and maintains a twenty-four-hour crisis and referral hotline. It has become a model for domestic violence shelters across the country.

EDUCATION AND PARENTAL INVOLVEMENT

Alliance for Parental Involvement	
in Education	**Phone:** (518) 392-6900
P.O. Box 59	**Fax:** (518) 392-6900*51
East Chatham, NY 12060-0059	**Net:** www.croton.com/allpie

This organization assists people in getting involved in their children's education, whether that education takes place in public school, private school, or at home. It has pamphlets with information and resource lists, a catalogue of books and resources, a mail-order lending library, assertiveness training seminars, and newsletters. It also provides referrals to parents, professionals, and organizations with expertise in education and families.

National Coalition of
  Education Activists
P.O. Box 679
Rhinebeck, NY 12572-0679

Phone: (914) 876-4580
Fax: (914) 876-4661
Net: members.aol.com/nceaweb

This organization is composed of parents, teachers, union and community activists, child advocates, and others working for changes in local school districts. It encourages and assists activists in their efforts to develop, promote, and implement progressive school reforms. It creates networks of families, local schools, churches, and other public institutions. It provides a newsletter, annual conferences, access to parent and teacher organizations, skills workshops for parents and teachers, and an information bank of materials, speakers, training, model schools, and other resources.

Parent Line   **Net:** www.parentline.com

This parent information system provides information to involve parents in their child's education by providing a link between parents, teachers, and students. Participating teachers and school provide telephone access to homework and course information, school announcements, upcoming events, and other information that can be accessed by parents. Outbound calling allows direct communication between parents and teachers. For technical information on how to set up this system, see the web site above.

United States Department
  of Education
Publications for Parents
600 Independence Ave., SW
Washington, DC 20202

Phone: (800) USA-LEARN
Fax: (202) 401-0689
Net: www.ed.gov/pubs/parents.html

This government web site lists information of interest to parents.

ELDER CARE

Alzheimer's Disease and Related
  Disorders Association
919 N. Michigan Avenue, Suite 1000
Chicago, IL 60611-1676

Phone: (312) 335-8700
Toll Free: (800) 272-3900
Fax: (312) 335-1110
Net: www.alz.org

This organization is dedicated to improving the quality of life for Alzheimer's sufferers and their families through support, education, advocacy, and research. Specific services include support groups for families, educational groups for children, day care for patients, respite services and financial aid, educational materials and programs, a speakers bureau, and a newsletter. The organization has many local chapters.

**American Association
of Retired Persons**
601 E Street, NW
Washington, DC 20049

Phone: (202) 434-2277
Toll Free: (800) 424-3410
GIC: (202) 434-2296
Net: www.aarp.org

This organization for people over the age of fifty provides information, education, and legislative and consumer advocacy from its national headquarters and regional offices. Among the range of services provided are such family-oriented programs as the Grandparent Information Center (GIC), which provides information on programs, support groups, service interventions, research activities, and resources available to help grandparents cope with surrogate parent roles.

American Society on Aging
833 Market Street, Suite 511
San Francisco, CA 94103-1824

Phone: (415) 974-9600
Fax: (415) 974-0300
Net: www.asaging.org

This organization of professionals in issues concerning aging promotes the well-being of aging people and their families and enhances the abilities and commitment of those who work with them. It provides professionals with information and research grants and advocates public policy changes for the benefit of aging. It also publishes several periodicals on aging, maintains a library, and sponsors annual national conferences, week-long summer series, and forums on issues such as "Religion, Spirituality, and Aging."

Children of Aging Parents
1609 Woodbourne Road, Suite 302-A
Levittown, PA 19057-1511

Phone: (215) 345-5104
Toll Free: (800) 227-7294
Fax: (215) 945-8720

This information and referral organization for caregivers of the elderly produces and distributes literature and a newsletter, offers individual peer counseling in person and by telephone, provides employee assistance programs, and assists in developing national caregiver support groups.

National Association for Home Care
228 Seventh Street, SE
Washington, DC 20003

Phone: (202) 547-7424
Fax: (202) 547-3540
Net: www.nahc.org

This information and advocacy organization represents the interests of Americans who need home care and the caregivers who provide them with in-home health and supportive services. It offers legal assistance; research, clinic, and policy information; insurance benefits; discounts on registration at its meetings; educational, training, and public relations materials; a magazine, newsletter, and other publications; and, if requested, a consumer's guide to choosing a home health care agency.

National Council on Aging
409 Third Street, SW
Suite 200
Washington, DC 20024

Phone: (202) 479-1200
Fax: (202) 479-0735
Net: www.ncoa.org

This organization provides information and networking services to those involved with the care of the elderly in senior centers, adult day care centers, hospitals, religious groups, and other institutions. It publishes three periodicals, maintains an electronic bulletin board, and holds conventions.

National Federation of Interfaith
  Volunteer Caregivers
368 Broadway, Suite 103
Kingston, NY 12401

Phone: (914) 331-1358
Toll Free: (800) 350-7438
Fax: (914) 331-4177
Net: www.nfivc.org

This interfaith organization assists congregations of all faiths in providing effective care to the elderly, the disabled, and their families. The national federation provides direct assistance to Interfaith Volunteer Caregiver Projects, which are grassroots organizations of faith congregations in communities that provide services like shopping, visiting, personal care, light housekeeping, chores, and respite care to those in need. It also offers networking opportunities, information, an annual conference, and a newsletter.

FAMILY ORGANIZATIONS

Family Resource Online   **Net:** www.familyresource.org

This web site contains numerous links to family resources in various categories. An excellent on-line resource!

Family Resource Center   **Net:** www.familyvillage.
                                                wisc.edu/center.htm

This on-line organization lists a variety of family resources.

Family Resource Coalition
  of America
20 North Wacker Dr., Suite 1100
Chicago, IL 60606

Phone: (312) 341-0900
Fax: (312) 338-1522
Net: www.chtop.com/frc.htm

This organization builds and supports resources within communities that strengthen and empower families through advocacy, information distribution, assistance, and consultation. It maintains the nation's largest database on family support programs and has a large catalogue of publications, including a quarterly report, a bimonthly networking newsletter, and an occasional newsletter on policy. It sponsors national conferences on family issues and has Latino and African-American caucuses serving the special needs of those communities.

Focus on the Family
Colorado Springs, CO 80995

Phone: (719) 531-3400
Toll Free: (800) A-FAMILY
Fax: (719) 531-3424
Net: www.family.org

This influential, evangelical Christian organization is dedicated to the preservation of the home and to biblical concepts of morality, fidelity, and parental leadership. Under the leadership of Dr. James Dobson, it produces radio broadcasts and audiovisual materials and publishes books, a monthly newsletter, and magazines targeting a variety of concerns and age groups—all available for mail-order and subscription for the price of a suggested donation. The organization provides personal contact through its staff of chaplains through phone counseling and written correspondence. It also provides seminars for care providers and maintains crisis pregnancy centers and basketball camps for urban youth.

FAMILY PROFESSIONALS

Academy of Family Mediators
Militia Drive
Lexington, MA 02173

Phone: (781) 674-2663
Fax: (781) 674-2690
Net: www.igc.apc.org/afm

This organization provides mediation services to families facing separation and divorce and a variety of other conflicts and issues. It offers referrals to local mediators and information on mediation training for people in a variety of professions. It also holds conferences and has a wide selection of educational materials, books, video and audio tapes, and professional publications.

American Association of Marriage
   and Family Therapists
1133 15th Street, NW, Suite 300
Washington, DC 20005

Phone: (202) 452-0109
Fax: (202) 223-2329
Net: www.aamft.org

This professional organization for those in the field of marriage and family therapy is involved in research, education, accreditation, credentialing, and advocacy of family issues in federal, state, and local governments. It develops curricula on marriage and family therapy, holds conferences and training institutes, and publishes two periodicals.

American Association of
  Pastoral Counselors   **Phone:** (703) 385-6967
9504A Lee Highway   **Fax:** (703) 352-7725
Fairfax, VA 22031-2303   **Net:** www.metanoia.org/aapc

This interfaith and interdenominational organization seeks to set professional standards for pastoral counseling, to provide certification for pastoral counselors and accreditation for pastoral counseling centers and training programs, to promote counseling with a theological perspective, and to establish relations with ecclesiastical and professional groups. It provides individual counseling in churches, synagogues, hospitals, seminaries, and community mental health centers and offers consultation with congregations and secular organizations. It also publishes the *Journal of Pastoral Care,* a newsletter, and a membership directory.

National Christian Counselors
  Association   **Net:** www.ncca.org

This professional organization provides academic and clinical training, as well as certification and licensing to Christians of all denominations. It specializes in curricula for educational facilities and Christian colleges and universities.

National Council on Family Relations **Phone:** (612) 781-9331
3989 Central Avenue, NE, Suite 550   **Fax:** (612) 781-9348
Minneapolis, MN 55421-3921   **Net:** www.ncfr.com

This organization provides a forum for family professionals to share knowledge and information about family issues. It has state and regional affiliate councils and maintains a database of experts in different family fields and can provide callers with referrals. It holds an annual conference and publishes two journals and a newsletter.

FATHERS

Center for Fathers and Families   **Phone:** (916) 424-3237
8636 Elk Way   **Fax:** (916) 421-8752
Elk Grove, CA 95624-1546

This community resource center provides family enrichment to equip fathers and families to respect and care for one another. It offers a couples communication course and a father/daughter seminar and trains leaders for father support groups in the state of California.

Dad's Den   **Net:** www2.portage.net
                                        /~rborellidads.html

This web page, started by a new father intended primarily for new fathers, provides hints, support, and advice on parenting. It contains links to other sites on the net.

Fathering Magazine   Net: www.fathermag.com

This on-line magazine for men with families maintains a homepage with links to the magazine and other resources for fathers.

FATHERNET
Children, Youth, and Family
   Consortium
201 Coffey Hall
1420 Eckles Ave
University of Minnesota
St. Paul, MN 55108

Phone: (612) 626-1212
Fax: (612) 626-1210
Net: www.cyfc.umn.edu/Fathernet

This on-line service provides information, research, opinion, and policy documents related to the involvement of men in the lives of their children.

Fathers' Forum   Net: www.parentsplace.com/
readroom/fathers/index.html

This web page for new and expectant fathers is maintained by a marriage and family therapist who researches men's development as fathers. It has a page of resources for men and fathers with links to other resources for fathers on the Internet.

Fathers' Resource Center
430 Oak Grove Street, Suite B3
Minneapolis, MN 55403

Phone: (612) 874-1509
Fax: (612) 874-1014
Net: frc@winternet.com

This family service agency professes to take a "moderate stance which is pro-father, but not at the expense of women." Its on-line publications include the *Father Times Newsletter* and an extensive resource list for fathers with many links to other sites.

National Center for Fathing
10200 W. 75th Street, Suite 267
Shawnee Mission, KS 66204

Phone: (913) 384-4661
Toll Free: (800) 593-DADS
Fax: (913) 384-4665
Net: www.fathers.com

This evangelical Christian organization promotes fathering through research and education. It conducts conferences, workshops, and small group meetings to help men assess and improve their fathering skills. It initiates research projects, develops programs to equip fathers in multicultural settings, and has special fathering groups for divorced fathers, stepfathers, and fathers who are incarcerated or in the military. It also has a daily radio broadcast and publishes books and the bimonthly newsletter *Today's Father.*

Promise Keepers	**Phone:** (303) 964-7861
P.O. Box 103001	**Toll Free:** (800) 888-7595
Denver, CO 80250-3001	**Fax:** (303) 964-7759
	Net: www.promisekeepers.org

This influential and predominantly evangelical Christian ministry is dedicated to uniting men to live godly lives in their families and other personal relations. It has weekend conferences in stadiums across the country and fosters the growth of men's groups in local congregations. It also produces a number of publications. Conference dates and other information is available on-line.

FINANCES

See also Single Parent Ministry under "Single Parents."

American Council on Consumer	
Interests	**Phone:** (573) 882-3817
240 Stanley Hall	**Fax:** (573) 884-6571
University of Missouri	**Net:** riker.ps.missouri.edu/DH/ACCI
Columbia, MO 65211	

This organization provides a forum for the exchange of ideas and information among individuals and organizations committed to improving the well-being of individuals and families as consumers. It maintains an on-line research network, provides networking opportunities, keeps an employment opportunity listing, holds an annual conference, and publishes three journals, a newsletter, and a membership directory.

American Consumer Credit	
Counseling	**Phone:** (781) 647-3377
24 Crescent Street	**Fax:** (781) 893-7649
Waltham, MA 02154	**Net:** www.consumercredit.com

This organization provides information and counseling for individuals in financial difficulty.

Christian Financial Concepts
P.O. Box 2377
Gainesville, GA 30503-2377

Phone: (800) 722-1976
Net: www.cfcministry.org

This evangelical Christian financial and career training ministry promotes biblical stewardship principles in personal and family finances. They offer financial information for families and even have a ministry for single parents.

Gamblers Anonymous
International Service Office
P.O. Box 17173
Los Angeles, CA 90017

Phone: (213) 386-8789
Fax: (213) 386-0030
Net: www.gamblersanonymous.org

This twelve-step support group helps people control the compulsion to gamble and avoid the resulting financial problems that can harm individuals and their families. It includes a Gam-Anon division for family and friends affected by someone else's gambling habit.

HIV/AIDS

See also National Federation of Interfaith Volunteer Caregivers and National Association for Home Care under "Elder Care," as both of these organizations provide services needed by AIDS patients.

AIDS Pastoral Care Network
4753 North Broadway
Chicago, IL 60640

Phone: (312) 334-5333
Fax: (312) 334-3293
Net: www.mcs.com/kinsella/apcn

This organization serves people directly or indirectly affected by HIV/AIDS in the Chicago metropolitan area. It conducts workshops on pastoral issues related to AIDS and the training of volunteers, and provides crisis counseling, public interfaith services, consultation on legislative issues, a monthly newsletter, and support groups and bereavement groups for family, friends, and partners.

Ecumenical Information AIDS
  Resource Center
642 North Broad St., Suite A2
Philadelphia, PA 19130

Phone: (215) 236-8081/8050
Fax: (215) 236-6763
Net: www.critpath.org/eiarc/eiarc.htm

This organization provides resources for faith communities, especially African-American churches, that are infected with or affected by HIV/AIDS.

Gay Men's Health Crisis
119 West 24th St.
New York, NY 10011

Phone: (212) 807-6664
Hotline: (212) 807-6655
TTY: (212) 645-7470
Net: www.gmhc.org

This was one of the first agencies to deal with the AIDS crisis in America and has comprehensive services, including referrals to doctors and hospice services, legal and financial counseling, a "buddy system" for AIDS patients and trained support people, and support groups for people with AIDS and their family and friends. Free food and services are available for those with full-blown AIDS in the New York area. The organization also engages in public advocacy for gay rights and AIDS research funding and maintains a catalogue of educational resources on AIDS.

AIDS National Interfaith Network
1400 Eye St., NW, Room 1220
Washington, DC 20005

Phone: (202) 842-0010
Toll Free: (800) 288-9619
Fax: (202) 842-3323
Net: www.thebody.com/anin/
aninpage.html

This interfaith organization represents nearly two thousand organized AIDS ministries across the country. It provides faith-centered programs for networking, collaboration, and public policy advocacy on issues dealing with AIDS. While it does not provide direct support for HIV/AIDS sufferers, it is open for membership to AIDS ministries and organizations and provides book lists, conferences, and a newsletter.

National Pediatric HIV
    Resource Center
30 Bergen St., ADMC#4
Newark, NJ 07107

Toll Free: (800) 362-0071
Fax: (973) 972-0399
Net: www.pedhivaids.org

This organization provides training for people who care for children infected with HIV/AIDS and provides information about the disease and caring for it, as well as advice for families with infected children.

HOMELESSNESS

National Interfaith Hospitality
    Networks
120 Morris Avenue
Summit, NJ 07901

Phone: (908) 273-0030
Net: www.nihn.org

This is a national association of local networks of church and synagogue congregations providing shelter, job counseling, child care, and parent education

to homeless families. These networks also engage in public education and advocacy on issues of homelessness.

HOME SCHOOLING

*Latter Day Saints Home
    Educators Association*   **Phone:** (801) 723-5355
2770 South 1000 West
Perry, UT 84302

This organization, affiliated with the Mormon Church, was founded by home-
schooling mother Joyce Kinmont and is open to people of all faiths. Kinmont
has written several books on home schooling, which are available to order,
along with recommended curriculum materials.

*Clonlara School Home Based
    Education Program*   **Phone:** (313) 769-4511
1289 Jewett Street   **Fax:** (313) 769-9629
Ann Arbor, MI 48104   **Net:** www.clonlara.org

This organization provides guidance and counseling to home educators. The
tuition fee includes the Clonlara curriculum, the support of a teacher who corresponds with the schooling family, mediation between the family and education officials, standardized testing, assistance in acquiring textbooks, letters of
recommendation for students, a parent guidebook, help in applying for public
assistance, and advocacy on issues pertaining to children's education in divorce
or child custody hearings. The organization also publishes a bimonthly
newsletter and holds an annual national conference.

*The Drinking Gourd: Multicultural
    Home-Education Magazine*   **Phone:** (425) 836-0336
P.O. Box 2557   **Fax:** (425) 868-1371
Redmond, WA 98073

This magazine is one of the few home-schooling resources to address multi-
culturalism. Its bimonthly publication is filled with home-schooling resources
and ideas, including articles on home schooling, letters from home schoolers,
educational trend information, pen pals, book reviews, and a directory. It also
has a bookstore with curricula and textbooks for mail-order.

Family Learning Exchange   **Phone:** (360) 491-5193
P.O. Box 5629   **Net:** www.flexonline.org
Lacey, WA 95509-5629

This organization publishes monthly newsletters for home schoolers. In the past, it has published *Family Learning Exchange,* a journal of natural learning, family learning, and home schooling; *Jewish Home Educator's Network,* offering support and resource information to Jewish home schoolers, regardless of affiliation or level of observance; and *Bo Nilmod,* another publication for Jewish home schoolers. The on-line newsletters include articles on home schooling, letters from home schoolers, and reviews of resources.

National Homeschool Association   **Phone:** (513) 772-9580
P.O. Box 290   **Net:** www.alumni.caltech.edu/
Hartland, MI 48353-0290   ~casner/nha

This organization advocates individual choice and freedom in education by serving families who home school and informing the general public about home schooling. It produces a quarterly journal, holds an annual conference, provides a networking and referral service for home schoolers, monitors legislation that could affect home schooling, and informs its members of changes in the law.

HOMOSEXUALITY

Gay and Lesbian Parents
   Coalition International   **Phone:** (202) 583-8029
P.O. Box 50360   **Fax:** (201) 783-6204
Washington, DC 20091   **Net:** abacus.oxy.edu/QRD/www/
                                         orgs/glpci/home.htm

This organization provides support, advocacy, and referrals to local resources for parents and children of lesbians and gays.

Parents, Families and Friends
   of Lesbians and Gays (P-FLAG)   **Phone:** (202) 638-4200
1101 14th St., N.W., Suite 1030   **Fax:** (202) 638-0243
Washington, DC 20005   **Net:** www.pflag.org

This organization promotes the health and well-being of gay, lesbian, and bisexual persons and their families and friends through support in coping with an adverse society, education to enlighten the public, and advocacy to end discrimination and secure equal civil rights. Its local chapters provide opportunities for dialogue about sexual orientation and act to create a society that is healthy and respectful of human diversity.

LATINO FAMILIES

See also Archdiocese of Chicago under "Denominational Resources," Family Resource Coalition under "Family Organizations," Facilitating Open Couple Communication, Understanding, and Study under "Marriage," and Twin Services under "Pregnancy."

Avance Family Support and
Education Program   **Phone:** (210) 270-4630
301 South Frio, Suite 388   **Fax:** (210) 270-4612
San Antonio, TX 78207

This organization has received attention in recent years for strengthening and supporting disadvantaged Hispanic families by keeping the children in school and educating the parents for employment. It provides programs on parent-child education, child development, fatherhood, couples, adult literacy and higher education, child abuse and neglect intervention, and youth development and delinquency prevention. The national office provides training and materials on starting local chapters.

Latin American Parents'
Association   **Phone:** (718) 236-8689
P.O. Box 339
Brooklyn, NY 11234

This organization is a national support group that helps parents of all ethnicities with the adoption of children from Latin America.

MARRIAGE

Association for Couples in
Marriage Enrichment   **Phone:** (910) 724-1526
P.O. Box 10596   **Toll Free:** (800) 634-8325
Winston-Salem, NC 27108   **Net:** home.swbell.net/tgall/acme.
                                       htm

This organization provides opportunities and resources to strengthen couple relationships and enhance personal growth, mutual fulfillment, and family wellness. It provides leadership training, organizes support groups, local chapters and retreats, and has a newsletter and bookshop. The programs are intended more for enrichment than for dealing with serious conflict.

Interpersonal Communication
     Programs, Inc.   **Phone:** (303) 794-1764
7201 South Broadway, Suite 210   **Toll Free:** (800) 328-5099
Littleton, CO 80122   **Fax:** (303) 798-3392
                                    E-mail: icp@comskills.com

This organization is of particular value to religious leaders who want to sharpen their marriage counseling skills. It provides materials, training, and certification for professionals to administer its programs and help individuals, couples, families, and teams communicate skillfully and resolve conflicts collaboratively. The program "Couple Communication" is particularly useful. A catalogue of programs and information on certification workshops is available.

Facilitating Open Couple
     Communication,
     Understanding, and Study   **Phone:** (402) 551-9003
Family Life Office   **Fax:** (402) 551-3050
Archdiocese of Omaha, Nebraska   **E-mail:** flo@omahoflo.creighton.edu
3214 North 60th Street
Omaha, NE 68104-3495

This program developed by the Roman Catholic Church concentrates on attitudes and concerns that individual couples consider important for discussion and decision-making before marriage. It is used by the couple under the supervision of a marriage counselor or member of the clergy, and it gives couples information about themselves and their partner, including needs and requirements, and similarities and differences, in personal relationships and marriage. Materials include an instruction manual, the evaluative tests, and computer scoring diskettes, and they are available in Spanish, Braille, cassette, and nondenominational editions.

Prepare/Enrich, Inc.   **Toll Free:** (800) 331-1661
P.O. Box 190
Minneapolis, MN 55440-0190

This organization provides diagnostic tools for clergy to help couples identify strengths and weaknesses in their relationships. Prospective clergy and counselors are required to attend a one-day workshop on administering, interpreting, and counseling on results of the program's evaluation of the couple's compatibility.

Worldwide Marriage Encounter   **Phone:** (909) 863-9963
2210 E. Highland Ave., Suite 106   **Toll Free:** (800) 795-LOVE
San Bernadino, CA 92404-4666   **Fax:** (909) 863-9886
                                    Net: www.wwme.org

Marriage Encounter began as a Catholic marriage enrichment program, but it is now an interfaith organization with several denominationally specific "expressions." It consists mainly of weekend retreats at which a team of trained couples and religious leaders work with couples on communication skills and after which couples become members of local support communities that are like extended families. The organization also sponsors Engaged Encounter and Family Encounter weekends. International Marriage Encounter is the ecumenical expression of the program and can be reached at (800) 828–3351. United Marriage Encounter, the Protestant expression, can be reached at (800) 634–8325. The Episcopal and United Methodist programs have their own web pages.

MENTAL ILLNESS

The Minirth Meir New Life Clinics   **Phone:** (972) 669-1733
2100 N. Collins Blvd., Suite 200   **Toll Free:** (800) 229-3000
Richardson, TX 75080

These clinics provide inpatient and outpatient counseling from an evangelical Christian perspective in all areas of mental health. They also have a catalogue of Christian self-help books, audiotapes, and videotapes. Facilities are located worldwide.

National Alliance for the
   Mentally Ill (NAMI)   **Phone:** (703) 524-7600
200 N. Glebe Road, Suite 1015   **Helpline:** (800) 950-6264
Arlington, VA 22203-3754   **Fax:** (703) 524-9094
                                  Net: www.nami.org

This grassroots organization is committed to helping the mentally ill and their families. It provides through its Helpline a listing of local self-help groups for people with a variety of concerns related to mental illness. It also provides educational materials, an extensive list of publications, research funding, and advocacy at the local, state, and federal levels.

MOTHERS

FEMALE (Formerly Employed
   Mothers at the Leading Edge)   **Phone:** (630) 941-3553
P.O. Box 31   **Net:** members.aol.com/femaleofc/
Elmhurst, IL 60126   home.htm

This organization is for women who have left the paid workforce to raise their children at home, but does not oppose mothers who work outside the home.

It has a monthly newsletter and local chapters, which organize support groups, playgroups, babysitting cooperatives, membership directories, community resource guides, and "mom's-night-out" activities.

Moms Online   **Net:** www.momsonline.com

This web site contains the magazine *Moms Online* and a Resource Center with listings of off-line resources, bibliographies, and links to other web sites. There are separate lists of national and state resources. The national list contains a list of religious organizations.

Mother & Child Online   **Net:** www.earthnet-ltd.com/
                                   motherchild/toc.htm

This on-line magazine contains information on parenting and information for mothers and fathers as well. It contains all the back issues and links to other parenting sites.

Mothers at Home   **Phone:** (703) 827-5903
8310A Old Courthouse Road   **Toll Free:** (800) 783-4MOM
Vienna, VA 22182   **Fax:** (703) 790-8587
                                   Net: www.netrail.net/~mah

This organization supports mothers who choose to stay at home with their children and provides to the general public education and advocacy on issues related to mothering. It publishes a magazine called *Welcome Home* and provides listings of local support groups.

Mothers Without Custody
  (MWOC)
P.O. Box 36   **E-mail:** jisham@aol.com
Woodstock, IL 60098

This organization strengthens the role of noncustodial parents through sharing information and experiences. It publishes a bimonthly newsletter containing practical advice to parents on caring for their children and their rights as noncustodial parents, as well as a series of pamphlets on parent-ing issues. It also provides support groups for women who do not have custody of their children, and its local chapters may provide legal referrals. Lists of local chapters are available from the national headquarters above.

PARENTS

Active Parenting Publishers
810 Franklin Court, Suite B
Marietta, GA 30067

Toll Free: (800) 825-0060
Fax: (770) 429-0334
Net: www.activeparenting.com

This secular organization produces video-based parent-training programs and offers workshops to train instructors. They have also copublished a religious periodical called *Active Christian Parenting*.

MELD (Formerly: Minnesota Early Learning Design)
123 North Third Street
Minneapolis, MN 55401

Phone: (612) 332-7563
E-mail: meldctrl@aol.com

This organization is a source of information, self-help, and support for parents. Parents are organized into groups of parents with children the same age. The groups are led by peer facilitators and last for two years. The program builds on parents' strengths with an emphasis on problem-solving and decision-making, and the organization offers training and assistance to those wishing to start parent support programs.

National Parent Information Network
ERIC Clearinghouse on Elementary
    and Early Childhood Education
University of Illinois at
    Urbana–Champaign
Children's Research Center
51 Gerty Drive
Champaign, IL 61820-7469

Phone: (800) 583-4135
Net: ericps.ed.uiuc.edu/npin/
    abtnpin.html

This organization provides information to parents and those who work with parents and fosters the exchange of parenting materials reviewed for reliability and usefulness. Its resources are open to all parents and parent educators.

Parenting for Peace and Justice Network
The Institute for Peace and Justice
4144 Lindell Blvd., Room 408
St. Louis, MO 63108

Phone: (314) 533-4445
Fax: (314) 553-1017
Net: members.aol.com/ppjn

This interfaith, transracial, and transnational association of families seeks well-being, wholeness, peace, and justice in their own families and the wider community. The organization produces a bimonthly newsletter and other publications, as well as mailings on presentations, programs, family camps and retreats, congregational workshops, and information on local family support groups.

Parent News   Net: parent.net

This weekly on-line parent magazine offers links to parenting resources, movie reviews, a library of past issues, advice forums, and its bookstore.

Parent Soup   Net: www.parentsoup.com

This large on-line network is the site of a number of organizational web pages and other resources for parents.

ParentsPlace.com   Net: www.parentsplace.com

This is another large on-line network organized in various reading rooms encompassing organizational web sites and other constantly updated parenting resources.

Positive Parenting   Net: www.positiveparenting.com

This on-line magazine provides resources and information for parents, including articles, organizations, lists of local and on-line parenting instructors, a bookstore, and information on training to become a parenting instructor.

PREGNANCY

La Leche League International   **Phone:** (847) 519-7730
1400 N. Meacham Road   **Toll Free:** (800) LALECHE
Schaumburg, IL 60173-4048   **Fax:** (847) 519-0035
                                    Net: www.lalecheleague.org

This organization encourages mothers to breast-feed their children by providing information, education, and mother-to-mother support. It promotes a better understanding of breast-feeding as an important element in the healthy development of the baby and the mother. Information is available on local chapters, which provide further information and support from mothers who volunteer. It has a catalogue of books, videotapes, and other products.

RESOLVE   **Phone:** (617) 623-1156
1310 Broadway   **Helpline:** (617) 623-0744
Somerville, MA 02144-0744   **Fax:** (617) 623-0252
                                     Net: www.resolve.org

This is a national organization for those struggling with infertility. It provides publications, information on fertility drugs and procedures, and referrals to local chapters, many of which have support groups on fertility problems and whether to adopt.

Twin Services   **Phone:** (510) 524-0863
P.O. Box 10066   **Fax:** (510) 524-0894
Berkeley, CA 94709   **Net:** www.parentsplace.com/
                                          readroom/twins

This organization gives families with twins information, advice, and moral support to help them raise healthy and happy children. It offers publications on caring for twins and triplets, provides referrals to other national resources on multiple births, schedules speakers on the topic of multiple births, and offers telephone consults in English and Spanish.

PUBLICATIONS

Cook Communications Ministries   **Phone:** (719) 536-0100
Colorado Springs, CO 80918   **Toll Free:** (800) 533-2201
                                     Net: www.cookministries.com

This evangelical Christian organization publishes education and ministry-oriented resources. The family ministry resources include resources for divorced people and single parents. These and other materials are available for purchase.

Christianity Today, Inc.   **Phone:** (630) 260-6200
465 Gundersen Drive   **Fax:** (630) 260-0014
Carol Stream, IL 60188   **Net:** www.christianity.net

In addition to the magazine, *Christianity Today,* this company publishes a number of family magazines. *Campus Life* is addressed to students and gives biblical answers to questions on dating, friendship, peer pressure, and relationships with family. Three yearly supplements provide practical information on college and financial aid. *Marriage Partnership* supports traditional relationships between the sexes through interviews with Christian couples, real-life stories, and columns on managing family finances, parenting, and strengthening marriages. *Today's Christian Woman* is written for women concerned with living their faith and offers regular articles and columns on women in the workplace, love and marriage, parenting, and friendship.

Good Family Magazines   **Phone:** (719) 531-7776
P.O. Box 36630   **Fax:** (719) 535-0172
Colorado Springs, CO 80936-3663

This division of the evangelical Christian Cook Communications Ministries publishes three family magazines. *Christian Parenting Today* combines traditional moral values with insights from family professionals and biblical directives giving parents practical advice on how to raise children. *Parents of Teenagers* focuses on topics such as communication, behavior, and values that equip parents with the foundation that they need to raise teenagers. *Virtue* supports women in the traditional roles of wife and mother.

RURAL FAMILIES

Cooperative State Research,
    Education, and Extension Service **Phone:** (202) 720-3029
United States Department of
    Agriculture   **Fax:** (202) 690-0289
Washington, DC 20250-0900   **Net:** www.esusda.gov

This organization promotes healthier, more respectable, and more productive individuals, families, and communities in rural areas. It has programs to promote resiliency, development, and resource management in families, as well as model programs on child care and education for children, youth, and families at risk. It also oversees the well-known 4-H program for youth.

National Family Farm Coalition   **Phone:** (202) 543-5675
110 Maryland Avenue, NE, Suite 307 **Fax:** (202) 543-0978
Washington, DC 20002

This mission of this organization is to bring together farmers and others, not only on issues of agricultural policy, but also to create and support viable family farms and rural communities. It is engaged primarily in the distribution of information through its newsletter and by directing farm families to bankruptcy services, rural ministry services, food stamps, and hotlines for hardship cases.

National Rural Families Conference
Division of Continuing Education   **Fax:** (913) 532-5637
Kansas State University   **Net:** www.dce.ksu.edu
College Court Building
Manhattan, KS 66506-6006

This annual conference is aimed at those who work with and research the special needs of rural families. Participants include educators, health workers, church leaders, legal personnel, county extension agents, mental health professionals, social service workers, and ministers. It provides information and the latest research on resources for rural families.

SEX EDUCATION

See also Commission on Family Ministries and Human Sexuality and Unitarian Universalist Association of Congregations under "Denominational Resources."

Wait Trainer   **Net:** members.aol.com/WaitTrain

This on-line site lists resources on abstinence-based sex education programs for schools, teens, young adults, single adults, parents, and churches. It also lists reasons for and posts research and statistics on postponing sexual involvement until marriage.

SINGLE PARENTS

See also Committee for Single Adoptive Parents under "Adoption" and Big Brothers/Big Sisters of America under "Children."

National Organization of
*   Single Mothers*   **Infoline:** (704) 888-KIDS
P.O. Box 68   **Fax:** (704) 888-1752
Midland, NC 28107   **Net:** www.parentsplace.com/
                                  readroom/nosm

This organization is committed to helping single mothers meet the challenges of daily life with wisdom, dignity, courage, and a sense of humor. It seeks to empower these families and unite them with others in a network of mutual support and action. It has a bimonthly newsletter and establishes nationwide self help and support groups.

Parents Without Partners, Inc.   **Phone:** (312) 644-6610
401 North Michigan Avenue   **Toll Free:** (800) 637-7974
Chicago, IL 60611   **Net:** www.parentswithoutpartners.org

This organization provides self-help, support, and socialization for divorced, widowed, and never-married single parents and makes referrals to local groups and organizations.

Single Magazine **Net:** www.singleagain.com

This on-line magazine is published specifically for divorced, separated, or widowed single parents. It provides information on dealing with these changes and experiences, including articles on health, finances, counseling, relationships, and spirituality.

Single Parent Resource Center **Phone:** (212) 951-7030
31 East 28th Street **Fax:** (212) 951-7037
New York, NY 10016

This organization provides a variety of direct services to single-parent families in the city of New York, as well as information, consultation, and referrals to those living in other parts of the country. The New York services focus on homeless families, women returning to the family from prison, substance-abusing parents, and low-income working parents, especially through summer camps and other respite opportunities for parents. It offers publications, products, and training to start support groups. Its Single Parent Training Institute offers assistance and training to organizations serving single parents.

Single Mothers by Choice **Phone:** (212) 988-0993
P.O. Box 1642 **Net:** www.parentsplace.com/
Gracie Square Station   readroom/smc/index.html
New York, NY 10028

This organization provides a quarterly newsletter, a member directory, information on sperm banks and adoption agencies, and also provides "Thinkers Workshops" for single women considering motherhood. It provides primarily emotional support and does not provide financial assistance or shelter for single mothers.

Single Parents Ministry **Phone:** (800) 722-1976
Christian Financial Concepts **Net:** www.cfcministry.org/ministry/
P.O. Box 2377   ministry.htm
Gainesville, GA 30503-2377

This organization provides advice and information from an evangelical Christian perspective on the financial problems faced by single parents. It publishes the books *What Every Widow Needs to Know* and *The Financial Guide for the Single Parent* with an accompanying budget workbook. It is also developing a resource list of ministries for single parents.

Sole Mothers International   **Net:** home.navisoft.com/solemom
c/o Diane Chambers
P.O. Box 450246
Atlanta, GA 31145-0246

This on-line organization exists for the benefit and encouragement of single parents and provides information and resources to ease the burden of parenting alone. It includes articles and resources, child support information, self-help legal resources, member networks, a department for single fathers, advice from professionals, and information on careers, finances, safety, parenting, domestic violence, and reading lists.

STEPFAMILIES

Stepfamily Association of America   **Phone:** (402) 477-STEP
650 J St., Suite 205   **Toll Free:** (800) 735-0329
Lincoln, NE 68508   **Net:** www.stepfam.org

This network seeks to educate society and change attitudes toward stepfamilies through research and media coverage. Although it does not provide therapeutic advice directly, it does provide a catalogue of stepfamily resources and a list of local chapters and support groups throughout the country. It also provides advocacy for stepfamilies at the national level, holds an annual conference, and publishes the quarterly *Stepfamily,* the book *Stepping Ahead,* and a catalogue of publications and resources.

SUBSTANCE ABUSE

Al-Anon Family Group
Headquarters, Inc.   **Phone:** (757) 563-1600
1600 Corporate Landing Parkway   **Infopak:** (800) 356-9996
Virginia Beach, VA 23454-5617   **Meetings:** (800) 344-2666
Net: www.al-anon.alateen.org

Al-Anon is a twelve-step, self-help group that helps families and friends of current and recovering alcoholics. It has an international directory of group information and a clearinghouse of recovery literature. Alateen is a program for teenagers who have been affected by someone else's drinking. While it cooperates with Alcoholics Anonymous, it is not affiliated with it and serves those affected by alcoholics rather than the alcoholics themselves.

Narcotics Anonymous World
Service Office   **Phone:** (818) 773-9999
P.O. Box 9999   **Fax:** (818) 700-0700
Van Nuys, CA 91409   **Net:** www.wsonic.com/index.htm

This companion program to Narcotics Anonymous is a twelve-step program for the family and friends of people who abuse drugs. Like Al-Anon Family Group, it is for those affected by the drug abuse of others, not the drug abusers themselves.

National Institute on Alcohol Abuse
 and Alcoholism   **Phone:** (301) 443-3860
6000 Executive Boulevard—   **Net:** www.niaaa.nih.gov
 Willco Building
Bethesda, MD 20892-7003

This division of the United States Department of Health and Human Services is the lead federal agency for research on the causes, consequences, treatment, and prevention of alcohol-related problems. It conducts and supports biomedical and behavioral research into the effects of alcohol on the human mind and body, prevention and treatment research, and epidemiological studies. It provides the latest information on alcoholism.

YOUTH

Jewish Council for Youth Services   **Phone:** (312) 726-8891
25 East Washington Street   **Fax:** (312) 726-8923
Chicago, IL 60602-1805   **Net:** www.jcys.com

This local organization is loosely associated with the National Jewish Federation and provides services to Jews and non-Jews alike.

National Conference of
 Synagogue Youth   **Phone:** (248) 557-6279
NSCY Regional Office   **Net:** www.judaica.com/ncsy
15919 W. Ten Mile Rd., Suite 100
Southfield, MI 48075

This is the world's largest orthodox youth organization and is affiliated with the Orthodox Union. It seeks to reverse trends toward intermarriage and assimilation. It also allows Jewish teens and pre-teens to form friendships and explore the meaning of their Judaism together. The web site contains an extensive directory of local contacts.

North American Federation
 of Temple Youth   **Phone:** (914) 987-6300
UAHC Department of Youth Activities   **Fax:** (914) 986-7185
P.O. Box 443, Bowen Road   **Net:** www.rj.org/nfty
Warwick, NY 10990

This youth arm of the Union of American Hebrew Congregations provides Reform Jewish teenagers with a variety of programs and services through its 450 Temple Youth Groups throughout the United States and Canada.

United Synagogue Youth
USY Central Office
Rapaport House
155 Fifth Ave.
New York, NY 10010-6802

Phone: (212) 533-7800
Fax: (212) 353-9439
Net: www.uscj.org

This high-school-age affiliate of the United Synagogue of Conservative Judaism maintains a web site describing the wide range of activities that it offers to its 15,000-person membership.

Young Life
420 North Cascade Ave.
Colorado Springs, CO 80903

Phone: (719) 473-4262
Net: falcon.cc.ukans.edu/~bvolk

This interdenominational organization promotes evangelical Christianity among young people. It conducts weekly informal meetings, weekend and week-long retreats, and small Bible study groups at local churches. It offers fun and fellowship for young people and produces the publication *Relationships*.

Youth for Christ
P.O. Box 228822
Denver, CO 80222

Phone: (303) 843-9000
Fax: (303) 843-9002
Net: www.gospelcom.net/yfc

This evangelical Christian organization sponsored by Rev. Billy Graham conducts evangelizing activities in schools, neighborhoods, and correctional institutions and organizes conferences, retreats, concerts, and rallies.

Youth Info

Net: youth.os.dhhs.gov

This web site developed by the United States Department of Health and Human Services provides the latest information on America's adolescents. Among its offerings are information for parents of teens and links to other youth-related web sites maintained by the Department.

compiled by
M. CHRISTIAN GREEN
TODD YONKMANN